THE PRINCIPLES OF VEGETABLE-GARDENING

THE PRINCIPLES OF VEGETABLE-GARDENING

By

L. H. BAILEY

Twelfth Edition

GYAN

Published by

GYAN

Gyan Publishing House
5, Ansari Road
Daryaganj, New Delhi-110002
Phone: 011-47034999, 9811692060
E-mail: books@gyanbooks.com

Distribution Network
gyanbooks.com
India, USA, Canada, UK, Australia, France

ISBN : 978-81-212-6569-0 (PB)
First Published, 1912

2nd Impression 2022

Printed at: Gyan Press, Delhi.

THE PRINCIPLES OF VEGETABLE-GARDENING
Author: L. H. BAILEY

THE PRINCIPLES OF VEGETABLE-GARDENING

BY

L. H. BAILEY

TWELFTH EDITION

1912

CONTENTS

PART I

GENERAL VIEW

CHAPTER I

CHAPTER II

CHAPTER III

CHAPTER IV

CHAPTER V

CHAPTER VI

CHAPTER VII

PART II

VEGETABLE-GARDENING CROPS

CHAPTER VIII

CHAPTER IX

CHAPTER X

CHAPTER XI

CHAPTER XII

CHAPTER XIII

CHAPTER XIV

CHAPTER XV

CHAPTER XVI

CHAPTER XVII

CHAPTER XVIII

CHAPTER XIX

CHAPTER XX

THE PRINCIPLES OF VEGETABLE-GARDENING

PART I—GENERAL VIEW

CHAPTER I

THE LAY-OUT OF THE PLANTATION

VEGETABLE-GARDENING, or olericulture, is the art and business of raising kitchen-garden vegetables, and the applications of the various sciences thereto. The term kitchen-garden vegetable, or "vegetable" in the gardener's sense, is impossible of definition. It is approximately true to say that the term applies to the edible part of an annual or at least an herbaceous plant. Vegetables are not often used in the dessert, and therefore belong more properly to the kitchen than do the fruits. There is exception to this in the melon; and it is significant that this is often included with the fruits by European writers. The only complete idea of the use of the term is to be obtained from a detailed catalogue of the products which are called vegetables, and this inventory will be found on a later page; in the meantime, it may be well to say that leading vegetables are potatoes, cabbages, onions, tomatoes, asparagus, peas, beans, cucumbers, squashes, celery, lettuce.

Market-gardening is the growing of vegetables for sale. The American term truck-gardening is really synonymous, although it is sometimes used in connection with the larger market-gardening enterprises. An arbitrary distinction between market-gardening and truck-gardening was made by J. H. Hale in the work for the Eleventh Census. In Bulletin 41 of the Census Bureau, truck-gardening is understood as the business "carried on in favored localities at a distance from market, water and rail transportation being necessary," while market-gardening is "conducted near local markets, the grower of vegetables using his own team for transporting his products direct to either the retailer or consumer." This distinction is not a fundamental one, and is not the general understanding of the terms; but it seemed to be necessary, for statistical reasons, to make the separation.

By common consent, the whole subject of vegetable-gardening is considered to belong to that part of husbandry known as horticulture. In its smaller and intenser applications, it is unquestionably horticulture, for it is gardening; but in its larger and looser applications, as in the field culture of squashes and tomatoes, it is quite as properly agriculture. The sweet potato is generally considered to be a horticultural crop, particularly in the North, but the Irish or round potato is generally regarded as a farm crop. Sweet corn is a horticultural crop, whereas other corn is not. These examples show that the demarcation between agriculture and horticulture is an arbitrary line. The boundary is determined almost wholly by custom. It is scarcely worth while to attempt to trace it.

1. THE IDEALS IN VEGETABLE-GARDENING

The success of any business depends largely on the clearness with which its promoter conceives of the aims and purposes which he is to attain. Many persons grow crops because their fathers grew them, because they know how to grow them, or because the land and locality are adapted to them. This is well; but it is better if the grower can also picture to himself the destination of the crops which he is to raise. That is, he should grow a crop for a distinct purpose. Good farming, like any other business, is primarily a matter of ideals.

There are two great types of vegetable-growing,—growing for home use, and growing for market or commercial profit. Leaving aside for the instant the special subject of home-gardening, we may observe that market-gardening is itself of two categories,—that which grows products for the common and general markets, and that which grows them for particular or special markets. In the former, the products compete with other like products in the open market; they take their chances. In the latter, the products are taken to some special customer, and are thereby removed from general competition. In the former business,—which is generally known as market-gardening proper,—by far the greater effort is devoted to the growing of the crops and in securing them at such seasons that they contend with the least competition. The chief skill required is that of the vegetable-grower; for the business of marketing is delegated. In the latter business, much effort must be given to the hunting out of special customers and markets: here the skill of the marketman is nearly as important as the skill of the vegetable-grower.

The growing of vegetables for home use requires different abilities than the growing for market. Here quality and a uniform and constant supply are the desiderata; in the market growing, quantity and attractiveness, and a bountiful supply at stated times or seasons, are the desiderata. The home-use garden should receive the more minute and skilful care to develop the utmost excellence in the product. The more discriminating the home, the greater is the skill required of the gardener. There is as much skill required in securing a well-grown melon or cauliflower as in raising a violet or chrysanthemum.

Vegetable-gardening for money is not an easy business. In fact, nothing is easy if it is worth the having. The competition is great. The margin of profit is small. There are risks incident to season, diseases, insects, glut in markets. Many of the products are quickly perishable. Quality generally counts for less in vegetables than in fruits. Most vegetables are culinary subjects, not luxuries; and the prices are therefore not high. Nearly every person who has a bit of ground grows a few vegetables. In most cases, earliness of crop is a prime requisite; and to secure the crop very early requires the closest attention to all the details of the plant-growing. One must often find a personal customer; and this customer rarely takes pains to wait for the produce of one grower or to search for it in the market, for the supply of vegetables is usually great: consequently, the small grower may have to peddle his vegetables. In most cases, the market-gardener must keep long hours and must work hard. He must not expect great reward the first year or two on a new place. He must learn his soil, market and climate. If he is a good plant-grower and a good business man, he will succeed. If he is only a plant-grower, he will probably be a slave to the marketman.

There are many market-gardeners who make great profits from given pieces of land, but they are usually old hands at the business, and they do not make equal profits every year or on every acre. They know the markets thoroughly. In particular cases, when competition is not severe, ample rewards may come easily to the novice; but these are the exceptions. A special crop well grown, or produced much ahead of the normal season or much behind it, may turn a handsome profit. Glass-grown products often bring fancy prices; but the risks are also great. Some of the best locations for small market-gardens are in the neighborhood of small cities, where competition is likely to be less severe than in the great markets, and where the grower may deal directly with the consumer. The man who has a large area, and sufficient capital to run it effectively, can dictate to the market, and can grow sufficient stuff to bring a fair reward even at very close margins. Prices are less than they were a few years ago, and there is no prospect of any important permanent increase.

The person who likes the business, and who goes into it with a full appreciation of all the difficulties and discouragements, will almost surely succeed. To such person, it is a most attractive business, for the returns are quick; and it is inexpressible delight to bring forth a satisfactory product at the exact time when it is wanted. A good vegetable-garden is a perennial satisfaction.

2. THE GEOGRAPHY OF VEGETABLE-GARDENING

There is a market-gardening center or area in proximity to every large city. The market determines the location of the business.

There are certain regions, however, which are so well adapted by nature for the business of vegetable-growing, that they have become market-garden centers despite great distance from market; but they all have easy access to market, either by rail or water. They are in proximity to trunk lines of railroad or steamship ports. There are two natural factors which determine the location of these gardening centers,—climate and soil. These centers are in climates which are milder than those in which the chief markets are located. They are able to grow early crops; for earliness is usually essential to success in market-gardening. These centers are in sandy or light-soil areas. Such lands are early, easy to work, and respond quickly to fertilizers, tillage and other treatment.

Fig. 1. Showing the trucking centers of Georgia. By Professor Starnes. Shaded areas are devoted to general trucking; dotted areas to watermelons.

Compared with the total cultivable area, the acreage of the vegetable-gardening districts is small, and it is usually scattered. Even the extensive vegetable-growing of the South, which the northern grower often fears so much, looks small when it is platted on a map. The accompanying maps illustrate these statements, and suggest that there is almost unlimited opportunity for geographical expansion of the business. Fig. 1 shows the parts of Georgia in which vegetable-gardening centers have been developed. The areas of oblique line shading (seen near the coast, at Augusta on the Savannah river, and in the extreme northwestern part) represent the general trucking centers growing produce for the northern markets. The dotted areas show the melon regions. Fig. 2 shows the regions in Florida from which the vegetables are shipped (in the months specified) to the northern markets. In Alabama, the only important trucking region is tributary to Mobile, although there are developing points along some of the lines of railroad.

Vegetable-gardening areas to supply the central and northern markets of the Mississippi valley are indicated for me as follows, by P. M. Kiely, St. Louis: "The largest shipping point in the South for vegetables is Crystal Springs, Miss. Solid trains daily out of there are no unusual sight during the shipping season, largely tomatoes, however. On the same road (I. C. R. R.), and not far from there, are Terry, Gallman, Hazelhurst; further down, in Louisiana, devoted mainly to strawberries, are Independence, Amite City, Hammond, Tickfaw, etc. However, New Orleans in spring, and, in

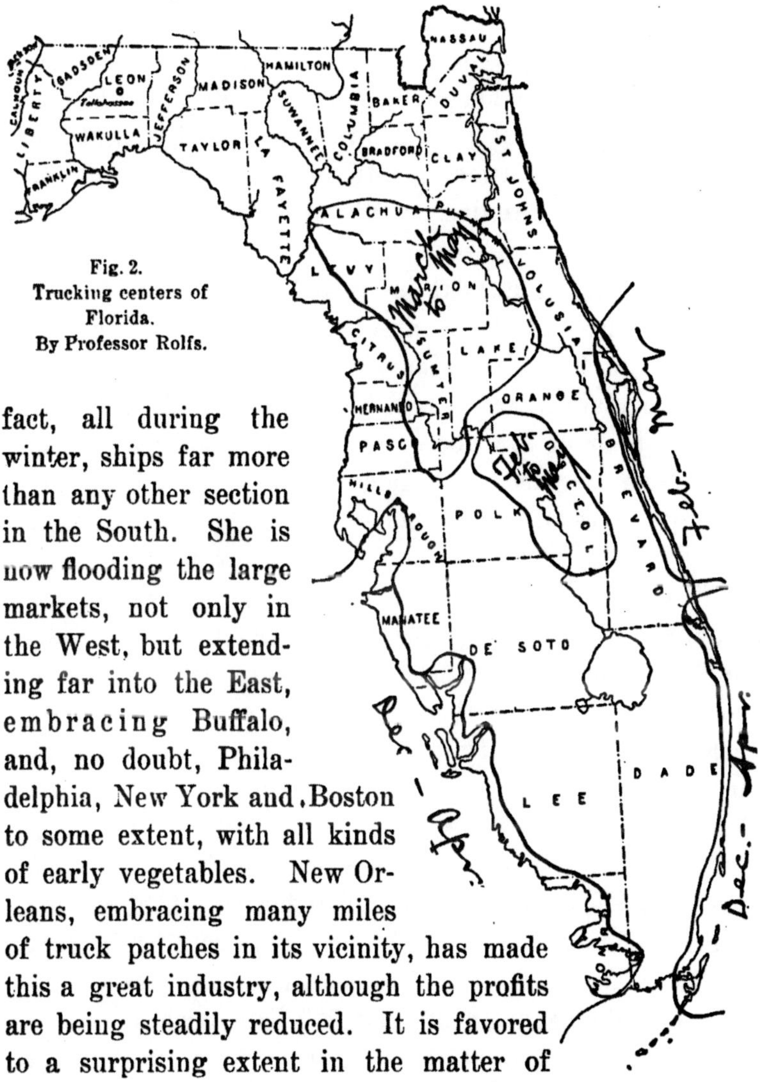

Fig. 2.
Trucking centers of Florida.
By Professor Rolfs.

fact, all during the winter, ships far more than any other section in the South. She is now flooding the large markets, not only in the West, but extending far into the East, embracing Buffalo, and, no doubt, Philadelphia, New York and Boston to some extent, with all kinds of early vegetables. New Orleans, embracing many miles of truck patches in its vicinity, has made this a great industry, although the profits are being steadily reduced. It is favored to a surprising extent in the matter of express rates to all the principal markets, nearly all such goods going out by express. Most of the goods are packed in sugar barrels and iced, and the express charges are so small that they do not cut away a large portion of the proceeds, as is usually the case when shipping long distances by express. Mobile, Ala., is doing a good deal in this way, to which might be added fifteen or twenty stations along the Mobile & Ohio railroad running northward in Alabama and Mississippi.

"Our market is next interested in Texas territory. Jacksonville and Tyler are perhaps the two leading points, and have been for years, although more fruits than vegetables are raised there. Alvin, Texas, has become a great strawberry section, and some area has also been devoted to vegetables in that and nearby shipping points. Vegetable-growing has also come to the front in a very prominent way far down on the Gulf coast, at Corpus Christi and Rockport, and a number of intervening points between there and Galveston. The territory between Houston and Galveston also discloses a great many pear orchards, vegetable fields and strawberry patches. In fact, the industry in those parts is growing very rapidly. Western Arkansas, with Van Buren as a center, will control, ship and distribute this coming season (1899) through one man, who will manage the distribution of crops for some twelve or fifteen different organizations in that section. Over 400 car loads strawberries, nearly 500 cars cantaloupes, and at least 500 cars Irish potatoes, together with several hundred cars of miscellaneous stuff, at least 1,500 cars in all, will be shipped from this section. Jacksonville, Texas, is the leading distributing and growing point in that section of the state, and will do similar work for the different associations in that line. It will probably ship over 500 cars tomatoes and at least 500 cars cantaloupes and melons, also 500 to 600 cars Irish potatoes."

The foregoing figures and geographical data are given only as illustrations of how widely scattered, far removed and relatively small are the truck-gardening centers which supply many of the great markets. It is no part of the purpose to show all the centers, nor necessarily even the most important ones. A complete survey of the subject from that point of view would require a volume.

To facilitate statistical study, the Eleventh Census divided the United States into twelve great sections or districts:

1. New England district: The field crops supplying Boston and other New England cities, and the greenhouse products supplying all the large cities of the east.

2. New York and Philadelphia district: New York state, Long Island, New Jersey, and Pennsylvania, which contributes largely to the New York and Philadelphia markets.

3. Peninsular district: Delaware and the eastern shore counties of Maryland and Virginia, which supplies all the northern and some of the central west markets.

4. Norfolk district: Eight southeastern counties of Virginia and eight northeastern counties of North Carolina, which largely supplies northeastern and central western markets.

5. Baltimore district: Western Maryland, West Virginia and that part of Virginia not in the peninsular and Norfolk districts, largely tributary to Baltimore, Washington and northern cities, as well as local canning factories.

6. South Atlantic district: North Carolina, South Carolina, Georgia and Florida, supplying northern markets, east and west.

7. Mississippi Valley district: Alabama, Mississippi, Louisi-

ana, Tennessee and Kentucky, tributary to north central and northwestern cities.

8. Southwest district: Texas, Arkansas, Missouri and Kansas, largely tributary to St. Louis and Kansas City.

9. Central district: Ohio, Indiana, Illinois, Michigan, Wisconsin, Iowa and Nebraska.

10. Northwest district: Minnesota, North Dakota and South Dakota.

11. Mountain district: Idaho, Wyoming, Utah, Nevada, Colorado, New Mexico and Arizona.

12. Pacific Coast district: California, Oregon and Washington.

3. THE EXTENT OF VEGETABLE-GARDENING

There are no detailed figures of the extent of our vegetable-gardening industry. The best are those made ten years ago by the Eleventh Census and published in Bulletin 41 (March 19, 1891), by J. H. Hale. These figures show that upwards of $100,000,000 were invested in truck-farming, and the product for 1890, after paying freights and commissions, amounted to $76,517,155. Five hundred and thirty-four thousand four hundred and forty acres of land were devoted to the industry, and this required the labor of 216,765 men, 9,254 women, 14,874 children, and 75,866 horses and mules. The value of the implements employed was $8,971,206. Yet, great as this industry was, the greater part of it had developed within the last thirty years.

It is to be expected that the Twelfth Census will show large gains over these figures. The acreage of truck crops was distributed as follows, according to the Census of 1890:

	Acres
Watermelon	114,381
Cabbage	77,094
Pea	56,162
Asparagus	37,970
Sweet potato	28,621
Melon	28,477
Potato	28,046
Tomato	22,802
Spinach	20,195
Celery	15,381
Bean (string or snap)	12,607
Cucumber	4,721
Kale	2,962
Beet	2,420
Miscellaneous	82,601
	534,440

The distribution of these crops, by acres, was as follows:

Districts	Asparagus	Beets	Snap or string beans	Celery	Cabbage	Cucumbers	Kale	Watermelons	Other melons
1 New England	242	83	65	443	1,586	272	.....	210	645
2 New York and Philadelphia	6,592	864	2,710	4,058	41,054	870	110	7,320	7,223
3 Peninsular	2,640	67	615	97	3,275	313	590	2,469	1,160
4 Norfolk	1,973	116	1,098	130	9,790	285	878	2,974	1,784
5 Baltimore	2,270	134	585	198	4,165	360	261	620	475
6 South Atlantic	14,090	766	3,465	......	3,309	1,265	690	55,726	1,102
7 Mississippi Valley	2,323	144	1,376	46	2,816	354	240	6,069	1,343
8 Southwest	1,719	60	1,875	313	2,730	894	170	8,098	2,238
9 Central	5,864	186	818	9,812	6,103	108	23	28,771	12,210
10 Northwest	135	.....	......	150	400	......	.....	......	......
11 Mountain	12	.....	......	18	496	......	.....	390	18
12 Pacific Coast	119	.....	......	116	1,370	......	.....	1,734	279

Districts	Peas	Irish potatoes	Sweet potatoes	Spinach	Tomatoes	Miscellaneous	Aggregate
1 New England......	1,476	427	....	310	305	774	6,838
2 New York and Philadelphia......	9,446	2,361	4,660	3,262	6,990	10,615	108,135
3 Peninsular	3,224	1,295	4,860	2,128	416	2,565	25,714
4 Norfolk............	5,858	3,305	3,187	5,965	525	7,507	45,375
5 Baltimore	5,170	2,860	3,150	1,980	3,780	11,173	37,181
6 South Atlantic.....	12,899	5,850	3,133	1,838	2,986	4,322	111,441
7 Mississippi Valley .	5,879	4,071	1,160	1,590	3,170	5,599	36,180
8 Southwest.........	3,281	3,602	3,725	1,378	2,918	3,888	36,889
9 Central............	7,555	2,845	4,556	1,744	1,362	25,457	107,414
10 Northwest.........	60	....	....	....	60	278	1,083
11 Mountain..........	90	840	....	....	....	1,969	3,833
12 Pacific Coast	1,224	590	190	....	290	8,454	14,357

It is to be noticed that these figures do not cover the entire commercial vegetable-gardening of the country, but only that which was officially designated as truck-gardening (page 2).

"Taken in its entirety, this comparatively new industry is found to be in a healthy, prosperous condition. New sections are being developed from year to year that to a certain extent affect the prosperity of some of the older ones, and there is likely to be more or less shifting of trucking centers every few years, all upon advancing lines, however. New and better methods of culture, with the further invention of labor-saving machinery, must of necessity reduce the cost of production. Better transportation facilities will place the products of these farms in cities and towns more promptly, in better condition and at less cost; while the ever-increasing population and wealth of the cities and towns insure a greatly increased consumption at satisfactory prices for first-class productions."

A special enumeration of the seed-farms of the United States was made by J. H. Hale, under the auspices of the Eleventh Census bureau (Bull. 111, Sept. 4, 1891). Starting with the establishment of Landreth's seed-farm, at Philadelphia in 1784, the industry had enlarged to 596 farms, with a total of 169,851 acres devoted exclusively to the business. The ten years which have elapsed since the Census was taken have seen large developments in the seed-growing business. The acreage of the different seed-crops was as follows:

	Acres		Acres
Field Corn	16,322	Sweet Corn	15,004
Bean	12,905	Cucumber	10,219
Pea	7,971	Muskmelon	5,149
Squash	4,663	Tomato	4,356
Potato	4,102	Watermelon	3,978
Onion	3,560	Asparagus	1,437
Cabbage	1,268	Beet	919
Turnip	885	Radish	662
Carrot	569	Lettuce	486½
Parsnip	374	Pepper	365
Onion sets	352	Eggplant	252
Spinach	150	Kale	105
Pumpkin	105	Flower Seeds	81
Parsley	75	Celery	71
Dandelion	39¾	Salsify	26
Rhubarb	25	Kohlrabi	19
Endive	16	Leek	13½
Collards	13	Okra	13
Cauliflower	11	Nasturtium	2
Corn-salad	1½	Cress	1½
Celeriac	½		

More than one-half the farms were established since 1870, and this is an indication that the business, as a whole, is prospering. "So far as reported, there were but two seed-farms in the country previous to 1800 (one of these was established in Philadelphia in 1784, and the other at Enfield, New Hampshire, in 1795), only 3 in 1820, 6 in 1830, 19 in 1840, 34 in 1850, 53 in 1860, 100 in 1870, 207 in 1880, and 200 more were established between 1880 and 1890, leaving 189 unaccounted for as to date of establishment. But, as the proprietors of the older seed-farms take great pride in this matter, it is safe to assume that 90 per cent of the unreported farms have come into existence within the last twenty years." "Of the 596 seed-farms in the United States, 258, or nearly one-half, are in the North Atlantic division, the original center of seed production. These farms have an acreage of 47,813, or an average of 185 acres per farm, while in the North Central division there are 157 farms, with an acreage of 87,096, or an average of 555 acres per farm. The seed-farms of Massachusetts and Connecticut average 142 acres per farm, while those of Iowa and Nebraska are 695 acres in extent, and are producing seeds on a scale of equal magnitude to the other products of that section of the country. Several of these seed-producing farms embrace nearly 3,000 acres each."

"From general information obtained from the seed-farmers, and a study of the figures in this bulletin, it appears that this branch of agriculture has kept fully apace with the general march of national progress.

Prior to 1850 all the seed-farms of the country were in the few northeastern states of the Union, Connecticut and New York, for more than half a century producing more seeds than all other states combined; and while each has at present more seed-farms than any other state, the general westward tendency of all that pertains to agriculture has stimulated seed-growing on a very extensive scale in the central west and on the Pacific coast."

The publications of the United States Treasury Department show that our imports of vegetables are very important, as compared with the exports. The following summary figures for four years show the fluctuations and the footings:

1896	Imports	Exports
Jan. . .	$130,575	$135,295
Feb. . .	122,983	112,195
March .	170,953	98,480
April . .	210,909	102,168
May. . .	249,998	105,258
June . .	231,700	131,695
July . .	121,976	123,881
Aug. . .	157,561	163,734
Sept. . .	148,345	185,347
Oct. . .	214,076	258,415
Nov. . .	193,098	262,338
Dec. . .	166,340	241,156
Total .	$2,118,514	$1,919,962
Correc'd total.	$2,118,603	
Excess of imports. .		$198,641

1897	Imports	Exports
Jan. . .	$119,403	$180,112
Feb. . .	129,293	156,698
March .	192,200	172,237
April . .	465,293	171,020
May . .	437,120	185,105
June . .	227,241	237,881
July . .	146,522	229,886
Aug. . .	57,921	242,474
Sept. . .	89,994	267,360
Oct.. . .	155,138	278,826
Nov. . .	152,184	209,429
Dec. . .	150,675	180,935
Total .	$2,322,984	$2,511,963
Correc'd total.	$2,322,986	
Excess of exports. .		$188,977

1898	Imports	Exports
Jan.	$125,801	$163,978
Feb.	128,476	202,493
March	169,699	193,089
April	283,533	156,097
May	425,681	117,633
June	148,810	139,588
July	142,906	142,714
Aug.	119,958	261,163
Sept.	160,433	376,523
Oct.	153,998	310,912
Nov.	169,408	307,095
Dec.	136,423	275,473
Total	$2,165,126	$2,646,758
Excess of exports		$481,632

1899	Imports	Exports
Jan.	$90,967	$184,254
Feb.	126,502	153,199
March	211,007	219,936
April	368,785	165,043
May	342,918	168,025
June	155,329	234,254
July	112,818	293,754
Aug.	145,639	258,001
Sept.	155,756	362,180
Oct.	179,910	335,983
Nov.	199,220	300,109
Dec.	238,808	250,919
Total	$2,327,659	$2,925,657
Correc'd total to March, 1900	$2,336,131	$2,926,458
Excess of Exports		$590,327

The greatest import months are April, May and June. Following is a list of dutiable vegetables for the largest month in 1896–9 (May, 1898):

	Bushels	Value
Beans and dried peas	8,957	$5,714
Onions	229,264	213,924
Potatoes	298,944	135,261
Pickles and sauces		37,951
All others in their natural state		8,879
Prepared or preserved		23,952
Total		$425,681

The heaviest export months are August to November. During the four years the greatest export month was September, 1898:

	Bushels	Value
Beans and peas	83,677	$130,469
Onions	52,298	38,103
Potatoes	105,452	80,160
Vegetables, canned		99,464
All others, including pickles and sauces		28,327
Total		$376,523

4. EQUIPMENT AND CAPITAL

The estimates for the equipment of a vegetable garden range from $25 to several hundred dollars an acre. This range represents the great variety of conditions in which market-gardening is undertaken. The amount of capital required to stock and to run a market-garden is determined primarily by four considerations: (1) the general type of business, whether intensive or extensive, near to market or far away; (2) the kinds of crops to be grown, whether requiring highly enriched land, much glass, or high-priced labor; (3) the general condition of the farm, whether it is in good tillage or run down, drained or undrained, heavy or light soil; (4) the man.

The best known estimate is Peter Henderson's,—$300 per acre. This amount is astonishingly large to the general farmer; but market-gardening, when at its best, is an intensive business, and to half do it is to fail. As a rule, farmers do not put sufficient capital into their business to make it pay. They are afraid to risk anything. They work short-handed and at a disadvantage. A business man will buy a farm which will scarcely pay the taxes, put more money into it than it is worth, and make it pay. Some of our most successful farmers are men who were not raised on the farm.

"The small amount of capital required to begin farming operations creates great misconception of what is necessary for commercial gardening," writes Peter Henderson,* "for, judging from the small number of acres wanted for commencing a garden, many suppose that a few hundred dollars is all sufficient for a market-gardener. For want of information on this subject, hundreds have failed, after years of toil and privation. At present prices (1886) no one would be safe to start the business of vegetable market-gardening, in the manner it is carried on in the neighborhood of New York, with a capital of less than $300 per acre, for anything less than ten acres; if on a larger scale, it might not require quite so much. The first season rarely pays more than current expenses, and the capital of $300 per acre is all absorbed in horses, wagons, glass, manures, etc."

Rawson treats the question as follows: † "Among gardeners, opinions vary as to the area that an individual may wisely include in his plans. Many have an idea that five acres of land will be enough; others put it at ten; while it is known that some cultivate a hundred acres or more at a profit. The amount of capital required varies, to some extent, with the amount of land cultivated, but not in proportion. While it might require about $3,000, with the labor of three men

*Gardening for Profit, new ed. 17.

†Success in Market-Gardening, 68.

and two horses, to properly handle two acres, I estimate that there would be needed about $5,000, six men and three horses for ten acres, and that $20,000, forty men and twenty horses would be sufficient for one hundred acres."

These estimates of Henderson and Rawson apply to the most intensive market-gardening near the large cities. Hotbeds and manures are very large items. Farther away from the cities, on cheaper land and in the growing of general-purpose and general-season crops, much less capital is required. Even in the neighborhood of large cities, one may often start on a much more modest scale if he is content to work up slowly. Quinn remarks* that he knows "personally a large number of well-to-do market-gardeners—men now worth from ten to forty thousand dollars each—none of whom had five hundred dollars to begin with. Industrious, hard-working men, these, who at first turned every available dollar into manure and reliable seeds." Greiner writes† that "much can be done on a very few acres of land. If land is plentiful and cheap, he may have a sufficiency to support horse and cow. Otherwise five acres would be enough for a start. The capital should be sufficient to pay for the place and the implements and equipment needed. Among the latter is a small forcing-pit, or greenhouse, and a number of hotbed sashes. Outside the place and horse, $400 or $500 might answer for a small beginning. There is no need of going beyond the reach of one's available capital.

*Money in the Garden, 21.

†The Young Market-Gardener, 9.

If the business does not prove profitable, the less money invested the better. If it turns out as anticipated, the profits from it will soon put the right man in the situation to extend his operations. In a few years' time much can be done from even a very modest start."

If one has insufficient capital to enable him to make the most from his place, it will be better for him to concentrate his energies on a part of it. The remainder of the place can be seeded to clover or put into other green-manure crops to fit it for subsequent use; or it may be used for the growing of forage for the horses or mules. Market-gardening is an intensive business.

Burnet Landreth, who has made a study of this subject,* makes two classes of market-gardeners—those who are "satisfied to live on inexpensive land far removed from market, and to use what others would term an incomplete line of implements, and be satisfied with what nature develops in the ordinary routine of their business," and those who, "more progressive, locate in the outskirts of great cities, consequently upon high-priced land, and have everything new in the way of labor-saving appliances."

"The first class of gardeners," he explains, "may be termed experimental farmers, men tired of the humdrum rotation of farm processes and small profits, men looking for a paying diversification of their agricultural interests. Their expenses for appliances are not great, as they have already on hand the usual stock of farm tools, requiring only one or two seed drills, a small addition to their cultivating implements, and

---

*Market-Gardening and Farm Notes, 5.

a few tons of fertilizers. Their laborers and teams are always on hand for the working of moderate areas. In addition to their usual expenses of the farm, they would not need to have a cash capital of beyond $20 to $25 dollars per acre for the area in truck. Other men, in ordinary farming districts, purchasing or renting land, especially for market-gardening, taking only improved land of suitable aspect, soil and situation, and counting in cost of building, appliances and labor, would require a cash capital of $80 to $100 per acre. For example, a beginner in market-gardening in South Jersey, on a five-acre patch, would need $500 to set up the business and run it until his shipments began to return him money. With the purpose of securing information on this interesting point, the writer asked for estimates from market-gardeners in different localities, and the result has been that from Florida the reports of the necessary capital per acre in land or its rental (not of labor), fertilizers, tools, implements, seed and all the appliances, average $95, from Texas $45, from Illinois $70, from the Norfolk district of Virginia the reports vary from $75 to $125, according to location, and from Long Island, New York, the average of estimates at the east end are $75, and at the west end, $150.

" Market-gardeners, living ten miles out of Philadelphia, on tracts of twenty and thirty acres, devoting all their land and energies to growing vegetables, sometimes paying $40 per acre for rent, estimate that the necessary capital averages from $200 to $300 per acre. according to the amount of truck grown in hotbeds. These same men calculate the profits to be from $150 to $250 per acre.

"Very different is the case on the immediate outskirts of Philadelphia, and other large cities, with the five- and ten-acre gardeners, employing several men to the acre, sometimes a larger force, where high rents, high wages, intense manuring and expensive forcing-houses combine to swell the expenses to an astonishing degree, often over $600 or $700 per acre being absorbed the first year, and without which ready capital at command the suburban cultivator would be driven to the wall before the close of the first season, as he works under heavy expenses, and he must have ready cash to meet them, especially if the first season be an unprofitable one. Of course, the $600 or $700 per acre which may be expended the first year by a gardener having forcing-houses, with all the entailed expenses, need not be repeated the second, not more than one-half of it, and, indeed, it is absolutely necessary to reduce expenses, as the profit in trucking would not warrant such an annual cash outlay."

Following is a detailed estimate for buildings and appliances to operate a ten-acre farm for general gardening near one of the eastern cities, by E. J. Hollister, a market-gardener who has had much experience in the middle states and West (prices of 1898-9):

EQUIPMENT

Dwelling house	$600 00
Barn, sheds for tools, and shelter in which to prepare vegetables for market	300 00
Horses and horse tools—	
2 work horses	200 00
1 set double harness	35 00

1 lumber wagon	$50 00
1 light market-wagon	75 00
1 2-horse plow	20 00
1 1-horse plow	8 00
1 harrow	12 00
1 roller	20 00
1 5-tooth Planet cultivator	7 00
1 11-tooth Planet cultivator	8 00
1 Planet Jr. seed drill, No. 5	12 00
1 celery hiller	8 00
Hand implements—	
1 hand cultivator, single wheel	5 00
6 garden rakes	3 00
6 hoes	3 00
6 planting trowels	1 50
200 feet of line and reel	1 50
1 wheelbarrow	5 00
1 spade	1 00
1 short-handled square shovel	1 00
1 long-handled round-pointed shovel	1 25
2 long-handled manure forks	1 50
Carpenter's tools—	
1 hand saw	2 00
1 square	75
1 plane	1 00
1 set brace and bits	2 00
1 hammer	1 00
1 hand ax	75
Frames—	
30 3 x 6 hotbed sash	75 00
600 feet pine lumber for hotbed frames	12 00
30 wooden shutters or mats for hotbed protection	15 00
1 force pump	10 00
50 feet of hose for watering hotbeds	6 00
Well near hotbeds	25 00
	$1,529 20

ESTIMATED WORKING CAPITAL

Seeds	50 00
Fertilizer for 5 acres	150 00
Man to help for 7 months	200 00
Grand total	$1,929 20

The following estimate is made by Irving C. Smith, of J. M. Smith's Sons, Green Bay, Wis., well known high-class market-gardeners. The estimate supposes that the area is ten acres of land in a fair state of cultivation, and that the party desires to make a first-class market-garden to supply the varying needs of the market (prices of 1898-9):

House for proprietor, with cellar full size	$900 00
Stable 16 x 24, with buggy shed attached	200 00
Packing house 22 x 44, 16 feet studding, stone wall, brick-lined cellar, making two stories and cellar	600 00
Cooler 14 x 16 feet	150 00
Ice house 16 x 20 feet, 16 feet studding	110 00
Onion shed 16 x 20	85 00
Hay shed for berry covering	50 00
Tool and wagon shed	75 00
Buildings	$2,170 00

Water plant, including piping	$800 00
200 feet $1\frac{1}{4}$-inch rubber hose	75 00
100 hotbed sash 32 x 72 inches	185 00
Frames for hotbeds	60 00
31 blankets for winter protection, 7 x 9 feet, $2.25	70 00
Water plant and hotbeds	$1,190 00

1 team draft horses, 3,200 lbs.	$250 00
1 horse, roadster, 1,200 lbs.	125 00
1 heavy double harness	30 00
1 heavy single, $17; one buggy harness, $18	35 00
1 heavy wagon, 3-inch tire	45 00
1 one-cord box for same, top section to lift off	20 00

1 low wheel truck with plank top	$25 00
1 one-horse medium weight wagon	30 00
Box, flat, and bolster springs for same	17 00
1 buggy	50 00
1 one-horse spring delivery wagon	85 00
1 pair heavy work sheds	35 00
1 pair light delivery sheds, $25; box, $8	33 00
1 hay rack, $6; one dump box, $2	8 00
Horses and vehicles	$788 00

1 steel plow, $15; one cutaway harrow, $25	$40 00
1 Meeker smoothing harrow, $20; a tooth harrow, $7	27 00
1 plank leveler, home-made	3 00
1 5-tooth cultivator, $6; one 14-tooth cultivator, $3	9 00
1 one-horse weeder, $10; one steel scraper, $5	15 00
Horse tools	$94 00

1 New Model seeder, $6; one hand weeder, $7	$13 00
2 Planet Jr. straddle cultivators (6-inch hoes)	6 00
1 Gem cultivator, $4; one Mathew cultivator, $3	7 00
1 Fire-fly plow, $2; one onion puller, $3	5 00
1 corn planter, $1; one berry box machine, $25	26 00
1 knapsack sprayer, $12; one dry powder gun, $7	19 00
1 kraut cutter, $3; one grindstone, $3	6 00
3 long-handled shovels, and 1 short-handled shovel	3 00
3 6-tine forks for general use; one barley fork for berry covering; one hay fork; one 4-tine fork	4 00
2 14-tooth steel rakes and three wooden rakes	2 00
6 hoes, $2; two dozen large and small knives, $3	5 00
1 hammer, 1 hatchet, 1 saw, 1 square for daily use	3 00
1 large wheelbarrow, $7; one dump wheelbarrow, $3	10 00
Scales, capacity 900 lbs.	17 00
Water cans and pails, $4; garden line, $1	5 00
Repair tools, consisting of carpenter tools, punches, coldchisels, wrenches, etc.	25 00
Miscellaneous garden tools	20 00
Hand tools, etc.	$176 00

Hay for berry covering	$30 00
800 melon boxes and glass 8 x 10	50 00
5,000 feet common lumber for onion sheds, celery pits, etc., $50; cedar posts for celery pits, $15	65 00
100 cords of stable manure	150 00
Seeds, $75; three months' expense for labor, $300	375 00
Cash for sundry expenses	300 00
Cash and sundries	$970 00

Summary

Buildings	$2,170 00
Water plant and hotbeds	1,190 00
Horses and vehicles	788 00
Horse tools	94 00
Hand tools	176 00
Cash and sundries	970 00
Total	$5,388 00

"In the foregoing estimates I have endeavored to mention only those things which are necessary and will be used frequently on the place, saying nothing of house furniture. Many other things will be needed, which will be made on the place or bought as occasion requires. Some will object to the item of water plant and hose; but if one expects to secure the best, or indeed, any very desirable results, it is necessary. The cost would vary greatly, of course, in different localities. Glass houses are not necessary to grow plants for spring setting, but more properly come under the head of winter gardening: so they are not included. Before the garden has run two years, there will be required at least another $50 in boxes, screens, home-made tools, etc. It is presumed that by July 1 enough goods can be sold to pay running expenses."

T. Greiner, a well known market-gardener and author, of western New York, gives me the following estimate of cash required to start a market-garden of ten acres near one of the eastern cities:

"It is useless to make an estimate of cost of place including dwelling house and barn, as this may be anywhere between $1,000 and $5,000, according to location. In case of scarcity of working capital, it might be advisable or necessary to rent rather than buy a place. Buying is preferable, as the owner has the benefit of the permanent improvements of a place. But rather than be short otherwise, I would be a renter. A forcing-pit or greenhouse seems to me one of the first necessities, in fact, indispensable for best success. There should be a shed for preparing and washing vegetables. It must contain tank, pump or other water supply, etc. Another necessity is a full equipment of best tools, including garden drill, hand wheel-hoe, Meeker harrow, etc. My estimate of working capital, outside of the place and buildings, would be something like this:

Greenhouse, with heater and pipes	$250 00
2 horses	150 00
Wagons and harnesses	150 00
Plows, harrows, cultivators, small tools	100 00
Hotbed sash, lumber, etc.	60 00
Force pump, hose, well or other water privileges	40 00
Seeds	50 00
Manures	150 00
Total	$950 00

"If growing winter vegetables is to be added, or to be made a prominent feature of the business, the estimate of cost will have to be materially modified."

The style of vegetable-gardening differs so much in different parts of the country that estimates should be secured in one's own locality before embarking in the business. Some of these differences are evident in the contrasts of the inventories here presented.

The following estimate for the neighborhood of Boston is made for me by W. W. Rawson. He thinks it "a very moderate sum with which to stock a market-garden in New England:"

Estimate for buildings, tools and equipments to operate a market-garden of ten acres near a large city in New England

Dwelling house	$1,000 00
Barn and outbuildings	1,000 00
Three horses	200 00
Harnesses	100 00
Wagons and cart	400 00
Tools, machines, etc.	300 00
200 hotbed sashes	220 00
Lumber for fences, frames, shutters, etc.	300 00
200 feet of hose	25 00
	$3,545 00

Running Expenses

Seeds	$100 00	
Manures and fertilizers	500 00	
Help, 3 men 8 months	800 00	
Incidentals	200 00	
		$1,600 00
		$5,145 00

A. Jefferies, Norfolk, Va., makes the following estimates of the necessary capital to purchase and work a ten-acre truck farm:

"Ten acres within say about four miles of Norfolk cannot be counted at less than $1,000. In fact, ten acres with a comfortable house can not be had for less than $1,600. The cost of one good horse (two would be better) and spring wagon, cart, plows, cultivators and harrows, $200; seeds, fertilizer and manure (all would have to be bought the first year), say $250; a cow, two pigs, and fifty hens, $60. From the ten acres one should sell the first year, $1,000 worth of farm products. The second year he should sell at least $2,000. The years following, this sum could be increased by intensive farming, such as should go with 'ten acres enough,' up to $500 per acre, in case the brain was used to fertilize with—as there is no fertilizer equal to brains. We have cases in which $2,000 has been received from sales in one year from one acre, and many cases in which at least $1,000 worth of produce has been sold from an acre. The proper manipulation of good soil here by a 'ten-acre-enough' brain, will show astonishing results. Our truckers are covering too much ground. They are not thorough enough.

"A man can start here with very limited capital, provided he is made of the right material and is willing to go slow at start and work his way in, instead of paying his way in. In fact, the men who have begun with small means and good heads have made a better success than those who had more money. A man can grow forage enough on one acre to keep two cows one year."

5. THE HOME GARDEN

The things to be considered in the home garden are: (1) a sufficient product to supply the family; (2) continuous succession of crops; (3) ease and cheapness of cultivation; (4) maintenance of the productivity of the land year after year.

The amount of product to be grown depends on the size of the family and its fondness for vegetables. An area 100 x 150 feet is generally sufficient to supply a family of five persons, not considering the winter supply of potatoes; but the area must be well tilled and handled. Consult Fig. 3.

The ease and efficiency of cultivation are much enhanced if all the crops are in long rows, to allow of wheel-tool tillage, either by horse or wheel-hoe. The old practice of growing vegetables in beds usually entails more labor and expense than the crop is worth; and it has had the effect of driving more than one boy from the farm. These beds always need weeding on Saturdays, holidays, circus days, and the Fourth of

July. Even if the available area is only twenty feet wide, the rows should run lengthwise the plot and be far enough apart (from one to two feet for small stuff) to allow of the use of the hand wheel-hoes, many of which are very efficient. If land is available for horse-tillage, none of the rows should be less than thirty inches apart, and for large-growing things, as late cabbage, four feet is better. If the rows are long, it may be necessary to grow two or three kinds of vegetables in the same row; and in this case it is important that vegetables requiring the same general treatment and similar length of season be grown together. For example, a row containing parsnips and salsify, or parsnips, salsify and late carrots, would afford an ideal combination; but a row containing parsnips, cabbages and lettuce would be a very faulty combination. One part of the area should be set aside for all similar crops. For example, all root-crops might be grown on one side of the plantation, all cabbage crops in the adjoining space, all tomato and eggplant crops in the center, all corn and other tall things on the opposite side. Perennial crops, as asparagus and rhubarb, and gardening structures, as hotbeds and frames, should be on the border, where they will not interfere with the plowing and tilling.

The best results in maintaining the productiveness of the land are to be secured when it is possible to practice rotation of crops, manures and tillage. Even in a small area, this rotation can be practiced to a considerable extent. The area which is devoted to root-crops this year may be given to corn or melons next

EAST.

Crops				Width
Asparagus.	Rhubarb.	Artichoke.		6 ft.
Parsnip.	Salsify.	Cucumbers, followed by Fall Spinach.		6 ft.
Peas				4 ft
Early Potatoes or Peas, followed by Celery.				4 ft.
Early Cabbage and Cauliflower.				3 ft.
Beets.	Turnips.			3 ft.
Lettuce, early and late.	Winter Radish.	Endive.	Parsley.	2½ ft.
Onions, with early Radish sown in row.				2½ ft.
Bush Beans.				2½ ft.
Late Cabbage.				4 ft.
Early Corn and Summer Squash.				4 ft.
Late Corn.				4 ft.
Tomatoes and Pole Beans.				4 ft.
Musk and Watermelon.				6 ft.
Winter Squash.				8 ft.
				8 ft.

WEST.

Fig. 3. Tracy's plan for a home garden. The length of rows will be determined by the amount desired.

C

year. It is particularly important to rotate if diseases and insects become serious on any one crop; and in this case, the greatest care should be taken to select those crops, for the rotation, on which the parasites cannot thrive. For example, the club-root of the cabbage and cauliflower will work on turnips. Insects and diseases should be starved out in the rotation. There are some insects which cannot be starved out in a small area, and it is then necessary to stop growing the crop for a year or two. The cabbage maggot is an example. If this pest obtains a good foothold in the home garden, cabbages and cauliflowers may be discontinued until the insect disappears; and this is often a cheaper solution of the difficulty than to attempt to destroy the insect with the bisulfide of carbon treatment. If one lives on a farm, the cabbage patch may be placed on the farther part of the estate for a year or two. When the maggot has quit the area, the cabbage patch may be made again on the old ground.

In a family garden of 100 x 150 feet, the rows running the long way of the area, eight or ten feet may be reserved on the borders for asparagus, rhubarb, sweet herbs, flowers, and possibly a few berry bushes. A strip twenty feet wide may be reserved for vines, as melons, cucumbers and squashes. There remains a strip seventy feet wide, or space for twenty rows three and one-half feet apart. This area is large enough to allow of appreciable results in rotation; and if it is judiciously managed, it should maintain high productiveness for a lifetime.

Of the home vegetable-garden, Hunn writes as follows in the "Garden-Book:"

"Make the vegetable-garden ample, but economize labor. Plant the things in rows, not in beds. Then they can be tilled easily, either by horse- or hand-tools. Wheel-hoes will accomplish most of the labor of tillage in a small garden. Have the rows long, to avoid waste of time in turning and to economize the land. One row can be devoted to one vegetable; or two or more vegetables of like requirements (as parsnips and salsify) may comprise a row. Have the permanent vegetables, as rhubarb and asparagus, at one side, where they will not interfere with the plowing or tilling. The annual vegetables should be grown on different parts of the area in succeeding years, thus practicing something like a rotation of crops. If radish or cabbage maggots or club-root become thoroughly established in the plantation, omit for a year or more the vegetables on which they live.

"Make the soil deep, mellow and rich before the seeds are sown. Time and labor will be saved. Rake the surface frequently to keep down weeds and to prevent the soil from baking. Radish seeds sown with celery or other slow-germinating seeds will come up quickly, breaking the crust and marking the rows. About the borders of the vegetable-garden is a good place for flowers to be grown for the decoration of the house and to give to friends. Along one side of the area rows of bush-fruits may be planted.

"A home vegetable-garden for a family of six would require, exclusive of potatoes, a space not over 100 by 150 feet. Beginning at one side of the garden and running the rows the short way (having each row 100 feet long), sowings may be made, as soon as the ground is in condition to work, of the following:

Fifty feet each of parsnips and salsify.

One hundred feet of onions, 25 feet of which may be potato or set onions, the balance black-seed for summer and fall use.

Fifty feet of early beets, 50 feet of lettuce, with which radish may be sown to break the soil and be harvested before the lettuce needs the room.

One hundred feet of early cabbage, the plants for which should be from a frame or purchased. Set the plants 18 inches to 2 feet apart.

One hundred feet of early cauliflower ; culture same as for cabbage.

Four hundred and fifty feet of peas, sown as follows :

100 feet of extra early.
100 feet of intermediate.
100 feet of late.
100 feet of extra early, sown late.
50 feet of dwarf varieties.

If trellis or brush is to be avoided, frequent sowings of the dwarfs will maintain a supply.

After the soil has become warm and all danger of frost has passed, the tender vegetables may be planted, as follows:

Corn in five rows 3 feet apart, three rows to be early and intermediate, and two rows late.

Tomatoes, one row, plants 4 to 5 feet apart.

One hundred feet of string beans, early to late varieties.

Vines as follows :

10 hills of cucumbers, 6 x 6 feet.
20 hills of muskmelon, 6 x 6 feet.
6 hills of early squash, 6 x 6 feet.
10 hills of Hubbard squash, 6 x 6 feet.

One hundred feet of okra.

Twenty eggplants.

Six large clumps of rhubarb.

An asparagus bed 25 feet long and 3 feet wide.

Late cabbage, cauliflower and celery are to occupy the space made vacant by removing early crops of early and intermediate peas and string beans.

A border on one side or end will hold all herbs, such as parsley, thyme, sage, hyssop, mints."

The "American Agriculturist" for February 17, 1900, prints the following sketch of a "City Man's Garden :"

"The plot of ground upon which is the garden was bought

fifteen years ago at a cost of ten cents per square foot. It is located upon a commanding site in one of the fashionable suburbs of Boston. The garden is divided in two parts (Figs. 4 and 5), separated by a street. On the terrace (Fig. 4) are planted twelve varieties of grapes, which are being trained over an arbor. Scattered about the place are apple, pear, plum, peach,

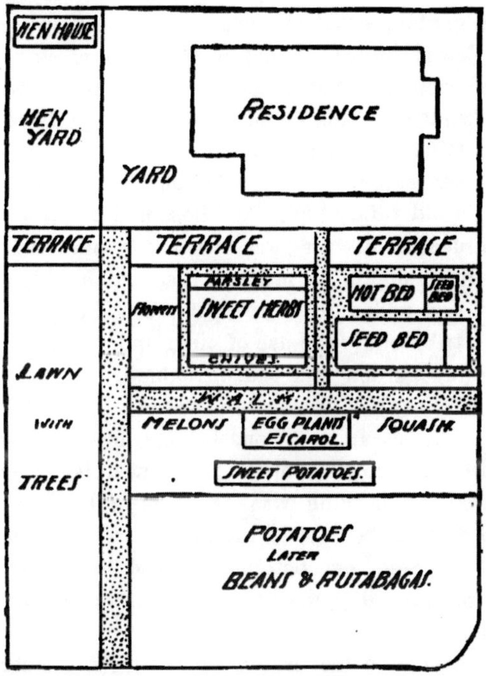

Fig. 4. A city man's home garden.

apricot, cherry, chestnut and mulberry trees, which are just coming into bearing and have great promise.

"The lower garden (Fig. 5) comprises 4,650 square feet, most of which has been cultivated by Mr. Hauck for thirteen years, who says: 'It is still my hobby, my pride. It is situated on a gentle, sunny slope, gaining all the moisture from the hill above. The soil is dark, mellow and rich, with a clay bottom, and through years of cultivation almost free from stones and noxious weeds.' The tools used comprised a lot of miscellaneous garden implements, and a Planet Jr. seed drill and a combined wheel-hoe and cultivator. I believe in raising as many different varieties of vegetables as my limited space permits. * * * It has been customary with me for several years to use barnyard manure and Bowker's fertilizers alternately, so in November (1898), after clearing the garden, a good layer of manure and an application of lime were plowed under. Every inch of ground is utilized. As soon as one crop disappears another one makes its appearance and takes its place. This enables me to always have something new for the table and plenty of it.

"Water was supplied for irrigation during dry weather by rigging up an old rotary pump and hose and connecting with the cistern. Bordeaux mixture was used for spraying tomatoes, beans and other plants to prevent rust and blight, and a little Paris green was added to it for potatoes. Freedom from cutworms was attributed to the use of lime and plowing in the fall, as an adjoining garden was badly troubled. A row of old bean vines was left as bait for green worms, and cabbage plants planted near by escaped. Squash vine borers were removed with a knife by cutting open the vines, lengthwise, where they appeared. The vine was then carefully bandaged with a wet rag and a fair yield obtained. The Bordeaux-Paris green mixture used on potatoes proved fatal to eggplants, but hellebore proved quite satisfactory for keeping off the potato bugs.

"One hotbed 3 x 6 feet was used in which to start the seeds of early vegetables. Plantings were made in the open ground as soon as the weather permitted, and were continued at intervals throughout the season whenever there was a vacant spot in the garden. The following varieties of vegetables, mostly in five- and ten-cent packets, were planted: Pole and wax beans, beets, borecole, kale, cabbage, carrots, cauliflower, celery, celeriac, corn, cucumber, corn salad, endive, eggplant, kohlrabi, lettuce, muskmelon, onions, peppers, peas, salsify, radish, spinach, squash, tomato, turnip, rutabagas, escarole, chives, shallot,

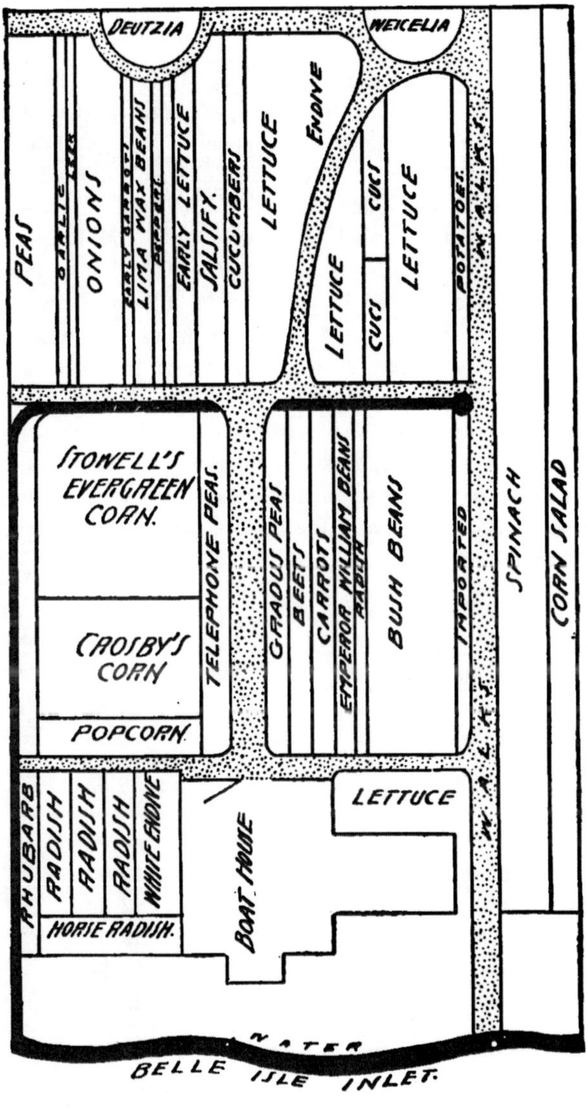

Fig. 5. How the city garden is arranged and planted.

parsley, sweet and Irish potatoes, and nearly a dozen different kinds of sweet herbs.

"The garden was planted as shown by the cuts. In the larger garden (Fig. 5) tomatoes followed peas, turnips the wax beans, early lettuce for fall use took the place of Refugee beans. Corn salad succeeded lettuce. The spinach was followed by cabbage, while turnips, beets, carrots, celery and spinach gave a second crop in the plot occupied by Gradus peas and Emperor William beans. Winter radishes came after Telephone peas, Paris Golden celery was planted in between the hills of Stowell's Evergreen corn, and gave a good crop for home use without blanching. The plot of early corn was sown to turnips. The hotbed was used during the late fall and winter to store some of the hardy vegetables, and the latter part of October there were placed in it some endive, escarole, celeriac, and the remaining space was filled up by transplanting leeks, chives and parsley.

"The value of the garden and the cost of the same are shown in the following table:

Products for home use	$54 24
Products sold	65 75
Products given away	11 36
Plants sold	3 75
Plants given away	3 45
Total	$138 55

Expenses

Plowing and harrowing	$3 00
Manure	2 00
Seeds	10 00
Insecticides	1 20
Labor	42 00
Total	$58 20
Profit	$80 35"

Probably the general farmer, more than any other person, needs to be urged to have a good vegetable-garden. Professor

Roberts gives the following advice for the "Farm Garden" in his "Farmstead":

"The farm garden should be ample and contain not only enough vegetables and small fruits for the use of the family, but a surplus to sell or to give away. The farmer used to large areas is reluctant to undertake anything so small as he imagines the garden to be; hence, too often he plows it and leaves the planting and cultivation of it to the 'women folks.' If he knew how to manage a garden he would find that the half-acre of land devoted to small fruits and vegetables could be made the most profitable and pleasurable part of the farm. Higher remuneration is received for the time spent in harvesting the products of a large, well

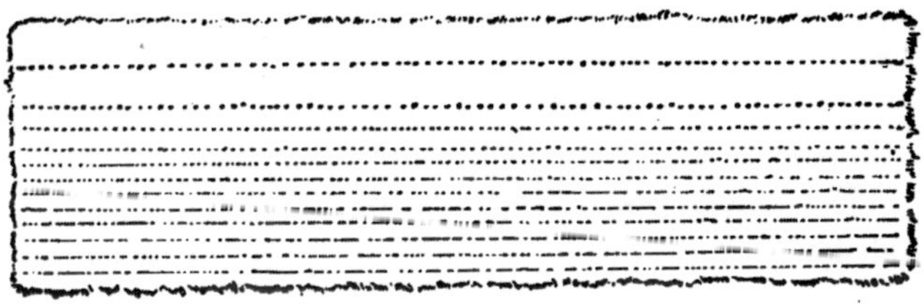

Fig. 6. Plan of a farm home garden.

kept garden, than in harvesting the cereals or milking the cows. It must be said, however, that there are good reasons for the farmer's distaste for gardening, for the gardens, as usually laid out, necessitate the maximum of hand-culture and the minimum of horse-culture. The result of such gardens is a minimum of products secured by maximum of effort, and a resultant surplus of weeds.

"The garden should be about four times as long as it is broad, unfenced when possible, near to the house, and should be, in miniature, a farm with the cereals, grasses and large fruits left out (Fig. 6). The side farthest from the dwelling should be devoted to the perennial plants, such as grapes, currants and other bush-fruits. Everything should be planted in straight rows, with spaces sufficiently wide between the rows to admit of horse-hoe culture. The grapes and blackberries might occupy one row, the raspberries and currants a second row, rhubarb, asparagus and like plants a third row. The spaces between these various fruits should be eight feet, as it is poor economy to so crowd vines and bushes as to force them to struggle the year through for plant-food and moisture. A rod or two of land, more or less, virtually amounts to nothing on the farm. Crowding the plants is only admissible in the city or village; here the plants may receive unusual care, and often may be irrigated at fruiting time from the city hydrant. The rows of ordinary vegetables may be thirty inches apart, except in case of such plants as onions, lettuce and early beets. These small, slow-growing esculents should be planted in double rows. Starting from the last row of potatoes, a thirty-inch space is measured off, a row of lettuce planted, and then one foot from this a row of beets or onions; then leave a space thirty inches wide and again plant double rows, if more of the small esculents are wanted. The larger spaces may be cultivated by horse-hoe and the smaller spaces by hand-hoe. The entire garden which is to be planted in the spring should be kept fertile and plowed early in the spring, leaving that part of it which is not designed for immediate planting unharrowed. It may be necessary to replow. It certainly will be necessary to cultivate several times that part of the garden which is used for late-growing crops, such as cabbage and celery. As a rule, the farmer cannot afford to attempt to raise two crops on the same land the same year, since labor is everything and the use of land nothing; therefore, better prepare the ground by two or three plowings for the late crops than to attempt to raise them on land which has parted with much of its readily available plant-food in producing the early crop. Then, too, land which has produced one crop is likely to be deficient in moisture, while land that has been plowed two or three times during the summer and kept well harrowed will be moist and contain an abundance of readily available plant-food. Early in the spring, when the land is cold and often too moist, it is best to leave the soil rough for a time if it is not to be planted immediately, that it may become somewhat dry and warm. As a rule, the garden should not be fenced, but the chickens should be restrained by fences a part of the time; at other times they may have free access to the garden, where they are often very beneficial in reducing the insect enemies."

Professor Thomas Shaw writes* of a plat of ordinary ground in Minnesota comprising the nineteenth part of an acre, which for four years kept a family of six matured persons abundantly supplied with vegetables all the year, with the exception of potatoes, celery and cabbage. "In addition, much was given away, more especially of the early varieties, and in many instances much was thrown away. In other words, the produce that could thus be obtained from an acre of land similarly situated would abundantly supply, with nearly all the vegetables named, nineteen families, comprising, in all, 114 individuals."

---

*"Minnesota Horticulturist," 1900, p. 102.

CHAPTER II

GLASS

In order to protect and to forward plants, various glass covers are used; and these covers, of every kind and description, are usually spoken of as "glass." They comprise all the range of forcing-hills, cold-frames, hotbeds and glasshouses.

Every vegetable-gardener, however small his area, needs glass. Thereby he is enabled to secure a crop in advance of its normal season. He becomes, in a measure, independent of season or even of climate. The vegetable-gardener is less subject to loss from vagaries of frost than the fruit-grower is. He can cover his plants. The plants are also more amenable to treatment: he can sometimes harden them off, so that they withstand frost. He can grow them at such times as to escape the dangerous season: the fruit-grower's plants must stand and take it.

The end and aim of all glass is to forward plants beyond their season. This result is obtained by protecting the plants from unpropitious weather or by actually forcing them. An example of the former object is the protection during winter of hardy plants which are started in the fall. The plants are kept alive in the cold weather by means of the covering, but they do not grow. There are two general types of the forcing* of plants: they may be started under glass, and then transplanted into the open; they may be grown to maturity under glass.

1. QUANTITY AND COST OF GLASS REQUIRED

How much glass the vegetable-gardener needs depends (1) on how intensified his operations are, (2) in what season he wants the major part of his crops, (3) the region in which he is, (4) the kinds of crops he grows. These factors are largely determined, in their turn, by the man's location with reference to market, and the price of labor and land. Very small areas sometimes have sufficient glass to cover them.

Glasshouses are increasing in number and popularity. They are driving out hotbeds for the forcing of winter stuff. But for general vegetable-gardening, the coldframe and hotbed will remain, although their relative importance is likely to diminish. These humble structures are desirable because they are cheap, because they allow the person quickly to change or modify his business (a great advantage on rented land), and because they can be removed when the spring forcing

*The author should say that the word *forcing* is used in many senses. He uses it as a generic term to express the idea of making plants grow and bear at other times than their usual or wonted season in the given place or locality. Most greenhouse plants are not forced: they grow and bear in their normal season, and we afford them the climate to enable them to do so. Thus begonias are not forced, merely because they bloom in March: carnations and tomatoes are. The term forcing is often used in a very special sense by florists to designate the rapid driving-out of bloom from bulbs and tubers, as with lilies-of-the-valley and tulips.

is done, allowing the land to be used for other purposes. See Figs. 7 and 8. In this book, it is not intended to discuss permanent glass buildings, as forcing-houses. The growing of winter vegetables in the North is a special business, and demands a volume to itself.*

Vegetable-gardening glass is usually computed in sashes. A normal sash is 3 x 6 feet in surface area. Sashes are combined into frames. A frame is a box covered by four sash,—that is, an area 6 x 12 feet. For general and mixed vegetable-gardening, about twenty-five sash are sufficient for an acre of garden, considering that the plants are to be transplanted to the field, not matured under the sash. If one is growing particular crops, as tomatoes, fifteen sash may be sufficient. For the best kind of home gardening, when it is desired to mature spring lettuce and radishes under glass as well as to transplant stuff into the open, from thirty-five to fifty sash may be needed to the acre.

In growing plants for transplanting, a sash may be estimated to accommodate four hundred to five hundred cabbage and cauliflower plants, three hundred to four hundred tomatoes and eggplants, six hundred to eight hundred lettuces. When the plants are transplanted in the frames, only one-third to two-thirds these numbers can be accommodated. If the plants are started very late and are not transplanted, as many as

---

*There are three American books devoted exclusively to vegetable-growing under glass: Winkler's "Vegetable Forcing," 1896; Dreer's "Vegetables Under Glass," 1896; Bailey's "Forcing-Book," 1897.

Fig. 7. The use of hotbeds on rented land in the suburbs of New York city.

Fig. 8. A German suburban market-garden on rented land, showing temporary structures.

eight hundred tomato or cabbage plants can be grown under one sash. In general, one may expect to gain one month on the crop of hardy things like cabbages, and two to three weeks on tomatoes. In order to gain two weeks on the crop, however, it is necessary to gain three or four weeks on the sowing. In extra-good hotbeds, greater gain can be secured; but it is not common.

In figuring on the amount of glass required, the gardener must consider that many of his plants may fail after they are set in the field. There are risks of frost, cold rains, droughts, worms. He may lose plants while they are still in the frames. The grower should start at least half more plants than he expects to raise. The surplus may be left in the frames until the transplanted subjects are thoroughly established.

The general estimate of cost per sash is $4, this amount including the cost of one-fourth of the frame and the covers. A well-made mortised plank frame, costs $4 to $5. A sash, unglazed, costs from $1 to $1.25. Glazing costs 75 cents. Mats and shutters cost from 50 cents to $1 per sash, depending upon the material used.

The following sample estimate, by a gardener, illustrates the method of casting up one's outlay for the season's glass. It is an estimate for a market-garden of one acre, in which it is desired to grow a general line of vegetables. It supposes that half of the acre is to be set with plants from hotbeds.

One-eighth acre to early cauliflower and cabbage, about 2,000 plants; if transplanted would require two 6 x 12 frames, from

200 to 250 plants being grown under each sash, or 1,000 plants from each frame.

These frames may be used again for tomato plants for the same area, using about 450 plants. This will allow a sash for every fifty-five plants. Plants for this area may be grown in one frame, but would be crowded and not as stocky as if given more room.

One frame should be in use at the same time for eggplants and peppers, two sash of each, growing fifty transplanted plants under each sash.

Two frames will be required for cucumbers, melons and early squashes.

If one wishes to grow extra-early lettuce, an estimate of sixty to seventy heads should be made to a sash.

It is assumed that celery and late cabbages are to be started in seed-beds in the open.

If spinach is grown in frames, the sash used for one of the late crops above may be used through the following winter.

This makes a total of five frames, the cost, depending on make and material, from $1 to $5 ; twenty sash and covers, at $2.75, $55 ; manure at market price, calculating at least three or four loads per frame. This is a liberal estimate of space, and should allow for all ordinary loss of plants, and for discarding the weak and inferior ones. It supposes that most or all of the plants are to be transplanted once or more in the frames. Many gardeners have less equipment of glass.

2. THE MAKING OF FRAMES

In the planning of a coldframe or hotbed, the builder must have in mind the following objects to be attained: (1) a sufficient and uniform supply of heat; (2) ample protection from cold; (3) facility for ventilation; (4) facilities for obtaining water; (5) plants to be near the glass, and yet to have head-room for growth of tall kinds; (6) ease and convenience of manipulation; (7) cheapness and durability.

Location and exposure.—Ideally, the land on which frames are set should slope gently to the south or southeast. The area should be well protected from the cold and prevailing winds. A wind-break is necessary. This may be a pronounced rise of land to the north or west, a building, a wall, or a hedge. If none of these shelters exists, a temporary one may be made. A board fence 5 to 8 feet high is the common resort. A screen of cornstalks (Fig. 9), evergreen boughs, or other material, may serve the purpose. Rawson recommends a board fence, and says that, "for convenience, the fence or wind-break should slant back a little from the bottom,—about one foot; it will then form a better support for mats and shutters when leaned against it, and will be much more convenient in working around the beds."

The frames should be near the residence and easy of access. They will need frequent attention, particularly in changeable weather. Frames which are far from the house, or which are cut off by snowdrifts or mud, are likely to suffer in critical times. Water supply should be at hand. If pipe-water cannot be had, a good well or cistern, with force-pump, should be provided. Some provision should also be made for warming the water in cold weather, for very cold water chills and delays the plants and wastes the heat of the bed.

If land is sufficient and the garden area remains year by year in approximately the same place, it is advisable to have a permanent frameyard. The wind-

Fig. 9. Hotbeds protected by a screen of cornstalks. Some of the sash are covered with short hay at night, and some with matting.

breaks, water supply and other accessories can then be well provided. Pits can be dug for the hotbeds and the sides stoned or bricked. These pits retain heat better than surface-built beds, are less exposed to winds, and are permanent; but they are more expensive in the beginning. The pits can also be filled in the fall with manure or litter, and if this is pitched out at any time in winter or spring, an unfrozen area is at once ready for the making of the hotbed. Pits should be tile-drained, unless the soil is very loose and the bottom is below the frost line of the surrounding unpro-

Fig. 10. A frame. It accommodates four sash, and measures 6x12 ft.

tected land. If many frames are employed, they should extend in parallel rows, six or seven feet apart, so that a man walking between can water or tend two runs.

Building the frame.—The common type of frame is shown in Fig. 10. It is a little over 12 feet long, is 6 feet wide, and is covered with four 3x6 sash. It is sometimes made of ordinary lumber loosely nailed together. If one expects to use coldframes or hotbeds every year, however, it is advisable to make the frames of 2-inch stuff, well painted, and to join the parts by bolts or tenons, so that they may be taken apart and stored until needed for the next year's work. Figs. 11 and 12 suggest methods of making the frames so that they may be taken apart. The pieces for the sash to slide on are made of stuff three inches wide mortised into the frame. These pieces have a strip or mounting nailed along their middle to hold the sash to its place. The frames are sometimes held together merely by stakes driven into the ground. This does very well for use late in the season and for temporary frames.

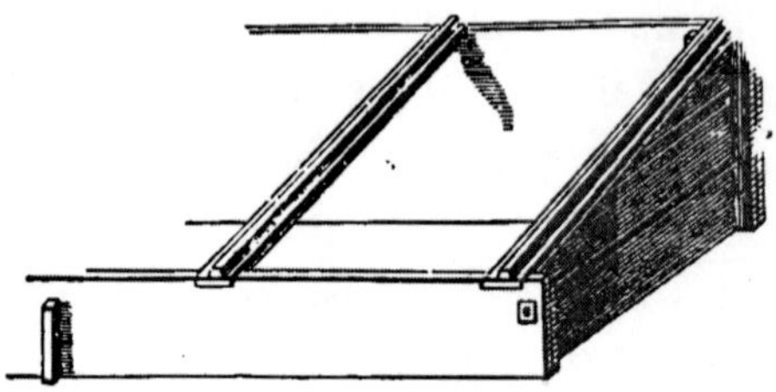

Fig. 11. A method of making a frame.

The depth of the frame must be governed largely by the plants which it is desired to grow, and by the length of time they are to remain in the bed. Have the plants as near the glass as possible and yet give them room in which to grow. If the frame sets on top of the manure, the back side may be 12 to 15 inches high, and the front side 8 to 10 inches.

3. HOTBEDS

A hotbed has artificial bottom heat. This heat is ordinarily supplied by means of fermenting manure, but it may be obtained from other fermenting material, as tan-bark or leaves, or from heat in flues or pipes. The hotbed is used for the very early starting of plants, and when the plants have outgrown the bed,

Fig. 12. Hotbed with mortised plank frames which may be taken apart. The plants are growing in flats and boxes.

or have become too thick, they may be transplanted into cooler hotbeds or into coldframes. There are some crops, however, which may be carried to full maturity in the hotbed itself, as radishes and lettuce. The date at which the hotbed may be started with safety depends almost entirely upon the means at command of heating it and upon the skill of the operator. In the northern states, where outdoor gardening does not begin until the first or the last of May, hotbeds are sometimes started as early as January; but they are ordinarily delayed until early in March.

Heating with horse manure.—The heat for hotbeds is commonly supplied by the fermentation of horse manure. It is important that the manure be uniform in composition and texture, that it come from highly-fed horses, and is practically of the same age. The best results are generally obtained from manure from livery stables, since it can be secured in large quantities in a short space of time. As much as one-third or one-half of the whole material may be of litter or straw which has been used in the bedding. If the manure is very dense, it will not heat well, and it should have bedding, litter or well decayed leaves mixed with it.

The manure is piled in a long and shallow square-topped pile, not more than four or five feet high as a rule, and is then allowed to ferment. Better results are generally attained if the manure is piled under cover. The manure should be moist, but not wet. If it is dry when piled, moisten it throughout. If it is very wet, it will usually remain cold until it begins to dry out. Sometimes the addition of a little hen manure to one part of the pile will start the heating. If the weather is cold and fermentation does not begin, wetting a part of the pile with hot water may start it.

The first fermentation is nearly always irregular; that is, it begins unequally in several places in the pile. In order to make the fermentation uniform, the pile may be turned occasionally, taking care to break up all hard lumps and to distribute the hot manure throughout the mass. It is sometimes necessary to turn the pile five or six times before it is finally used, although half this number of turnings is ordinarily sufficient. When the pile is steaming uniformly throughout, it is fit to be placed in the hotbed. From the first piling of the manure until it is fit to put in the bed will be a period, ordinarily, of two weeks.

There are some cases in which the material will not need to be turned to induce fermentation, particularly when the manure is from grain-fed horses, as in many parts of the country. Sometimes the manure heats so quickly and so violently that it has to be wet in order to prevent it from burning, although the admixture of straw or litter with the manure will remedy the trouble. Each case is a law unto itself.

Making the manure bed.—Hotbed frames are sometimes set on top of the pile of fermenting manure, as shown in Fig. 13. The manure should extend for some distance beyond the edges of the frame; otherwise the frame will become too cold about the outside, and the plants will suffer. It is preferable, however, to have a pit beneath the frame in which the manure is placed. The pit should be a foot wider upon either side than the width of the frame, and should be about two feet deep. It may be walled with stone or brick. It is very important that it have perfect drainage. Fig. 14 is a cross-section of such a hotbed pit. Upon the ground a layer of an inch or two of any coarse material is laid to keep the manure from the cold earth. Upon this, from twelve to thirty inches of manure is placed. Above the manure is a thin layer of leaf-mold or some porous material, which will serve as a distributor of the heat, and above this is four or five inches of soft garden loam, in which the plants are to be grown. In exposed places, it is always well to have the glass as near the level of the ground as possible. Figs. 9, 15.

Fig. 13. Hotbed with manure on top of the ground.

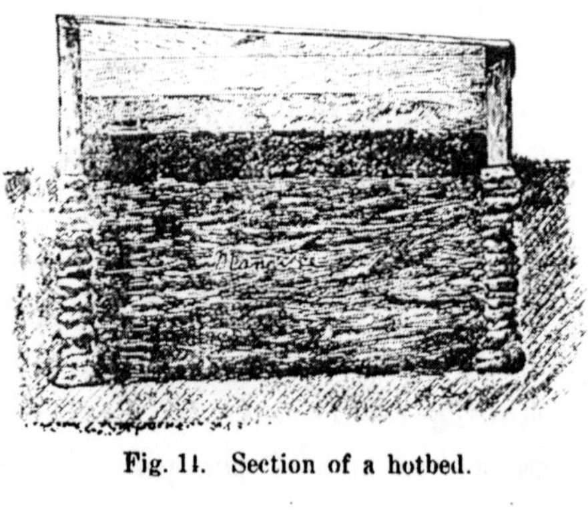

Fig. 14. Section of a hotbed.

It is advisable to place the manure in the pit in layers, each stratum to be packed or settled down before another one is put in. These layers should be

Fig. 15. Hotbeds on a Long Island market-garden, from which rhubarb is being harvested. The sash is on nearly the ground level.

from four to eight inches in thickness. By this means the mass is easily made uniform in consistency.

On the filling of hotbeds, Taft writes as follows: "The amount of heating material that will be required for a hotbed will vary with the crop, as well as with the location and season. For zero weather there should be at least eighteen inches of heating material after it has been well packed down, and twenty-four inches will be desirable in mid-winter in the northern states, while six or eight inches may answer when only a few degrees of frost are expected. For eighteen inches of manure the excavation should be made to a depth of twenty-eight inches below the level of the south side of the frame, and thirty-one inches below that of the north side. After the manure has warmed through for the second time it should be placed in the excavation, spreading it evenly and packing it down with the fork, but leaving it for a few days before tramping it. Care should be taken to have the corners well filled, that an even settling may be secured. After the manure has again warmed up, it should be thoroughly tramped. The bed is then ready for the soil, which should be quite rich and contain a large amount of sand and humus, a compost of decomposed pasture sods with one-third their bulk of rotten manure being excellent for the purpose. The thickness of the soil should vary from five to seven inches, the greater depth being desirable for radishes and other root crops. When boxes of plants are to be placed in the beds the depth of soil need not be more than three inches."

Only by experience can one learn what is the proper

consistency or texture of good hotbed manure. That which has too much straw, and which will therefore soon part with its heat, will spring up quickly when the pressure of the feet is removed. Manure which has too little straw, and which therefore will not heat well or will spend its heat quickly, will pack down into a soggy mass underneath the feet. When the manure has sufficient litter, it will give a springy feeling to the feet as a person walks over it, but will not fluff up when the pressure is removed.

The amount of manure which is to be used will depend (1) upon its quality, (2) the season in which the hotbed is made, (3) the kind of plants to be grown, (4) the skill of the operator in managing the bed. Careless watering, by means of which the manure is kept soaked, will stop the heat in any hotbed. The earlier the bed is made, the larger should be the quantity of manure. Hotbeds which are supposed to hold for two months should have about two and one-half feet of manure, as a rule. This is the maximum. For a light hotbed to be used late in the season, six or eight inches may be sufficient.

Sowing the seeds.—Ordinarily the manure will heat very vigorously for a few days after it is placed in the bed. A soil thermometer should be thrust through the earth to the manure, and the frame kept tightly closed with sash and covers. When the temperature is passing below 90°, seeds of the warm plants, like tomatoes, may be sown, and when it passes below 80° or 70°, the seeds of cooler plants may be sown. By the time the beds are ready for planting, the weed seeds probably will have germinated. Loosen and aërate the soil before sowing. Sow in rows four to six inches apart.

Plants which do not transplant well, as melons and cucumbers, may be grown in pots, old berry boxes, or on inverted sods, rather than directly in the hotbed earth. More and more, gardeners are coming to start all plants in boxes or flats (Fig. 12), for the plants can then be carted to the field or put on the market with ease and with little loss. The flats can also be shifted from one part of the frame to another, or from bed to bed, as conditions may require.

In the summer-time, after the frames are stripped, the old beds may be used for the growing of various delicate crops, as melons or half-hardy flowers. In this position, the plants can be protected in the fall. As already suggested, the pits should be cleaned in the fall and filled with litter, to facilitate the work of making the new bed in the winter or spring.

Fig. 16. Manure-heated forcing-house.

Various modifications of the common type of hotbed will suggest themselves. If the hotbed were high enough and broad enough to allow a man to work inside, we should have a forcing-house. Such a structure is shown in Fig. 16, upon one side of which the manure and soil are already in place. From two to three feet of manure should be used. The house may be covered with hotbed sash held on a rude frame of scantlings. These manure-heated houses are often very efficient, and are a good make-shift until such time as one can afford to put in flue or pipe heat.

For starting plants in a small way, a glass-covered box in the kitchen window may answer very well. An incubator is useful for the germinating of seeds.

Pipe-heated hotbeds.—Hotbeds may be heated by means of steam or hot water. They can be piped from the heater in a dwelling-house or greenhouse. Exhaust steam from a factory can often be used with very good results. Fig. 17 shows a hotbed with two pipes, in the positions 7, 7, below the bed. The soil is shown at 4. There are doors in the end of the house, shown at 2, 2, which may be used for ventilation or for admitting air underneath the beds. The pipes should not be surrounded by earth, but should run through a free air space. A flue-heated or pipe-heated hotbed may be likened to a greenhouse bench, and the arrangement of piping for the two should be similar. From two to four steam- or water-pipes are carried underneath the bed. If, however, one has plenty of exhaust steam, which is usually under considerable pressure, it may be carried directly through the soil in ordinary drain pipes. It will rarely pay

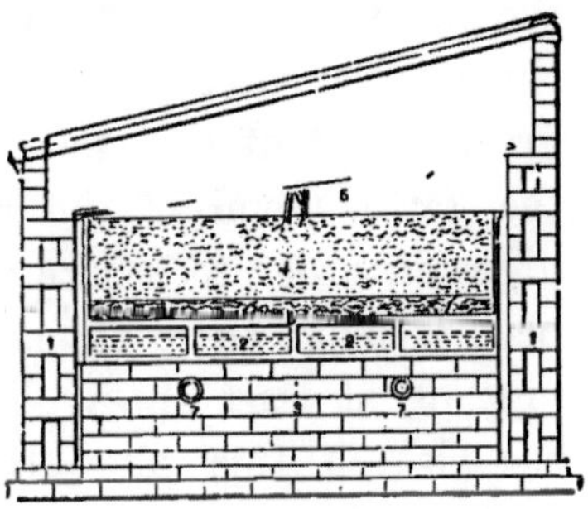

Fig. 17. Pipe-heated hotbed.

to put in a hot water or steam heater for the express purpose of heating hotbeds, for if such an expense is incurred, it will be better to make a forcing-house.

Flue-heated beds.—Hotbeds may be heated with hot air flues with very good results. A home-made brick furnace may be constructed in a pit at one end of the run and underneath a shed, and the smoke and hot air, instead of being carried directly upwards, are carried through a slightly rising horizontal pipe which runs underneath the beds. For some distance from the furnace, this flue may be made of brick or unvitrified sewer pipe, but stovepipe may be used for the greater part of the run. The chimney is ordinarily at the farther end of the run of beds. It should be high, in order to secure a good draft. If the run of beds is long, there should be a rise in the underlying pipe of at least one foot in twenty-five. The greater the rise in this pipe, the more perfect will be the draft. If the runs are not too long, the underlying pipe may return underneath the beds and enter a chimney directly over the back end of the furnace, and such a chimney, being warmed from the furnace, will ordinarily have an excellent draft. The underlying pipe should occupy a free space or pit beneath the beds, and whenever it lies near to the floor of the bed or is very hot, it should be covered with asbestos cloth.

Glazing.—The most satisfactory glass for use in hotbed and coldframe sash is double-thick, second-quality grade; and 12-inch panes are ordinarily wide enough, and suffer comparatively little in breakage.

For coldframes, however, various oiled papers and water-proof cloths* may be used, particularly for plants which are started little in advance of the opening of the season. For late work, cloth is often better than glass, because the beds do not become so hot and dry. When these materials are used, it is not necessary to have expensive sash, but rectangular frames made from strips of pine seven-eighths inch thick and 2½ inches wide, halved together at the corners and each corner reinforced by a square carriage-corner, such as is used by carriage-makers to secure the corners of buggy boxes. These corners can be bought by the pound at hardware stores. The glass is bedded in putty. No putty should be run above the panes, because it will soon be loosened by the freezing of the water which collects under it. The panes should be lapped, not butted.

Hotbed covers.—Some protection, other than the glass, must be given to early hotbeds. They need covering on every cold night, and sometimes during

*There are water-proof hotbed cloths in the market. Or one may make his own by using one of the following formulas:

1. Use a sash without bars, and stretch wires or strings across it to serve as a rest for the paper. Procure stout but thin manila wrapping-paper, and paste it firmly on the sash with fresh flour paste. Dry in a warm place and then wipe the paper with a damp sponge to cause it to stretch evenly. Dry again and then apply boiled linseed oil to both sides of the paper, and dry again in a warm place.

2. Saturate cloth or tough, thin manila paper with pure raw linseed oil.

3. Dissolve 1¾ pounds white soap in 1 quart water; in another quart dissolve 1⅙ ounces gum arabic and 5 ounces glue. Mix the two liquids, warm, and soak the paper, hanging it up to dry. Used mostly for paper.

4. Three pints pale linseed oil: 1 ounce sugar of lead; 4 ounces white rosin. Grind and mix the sugar of lead in a little oil, then add the other materials and heat in an iron kettle. Apply hot with a brush. Used for muslin.

the entire day in very severe weather. Very good material for covering the sash is matting, such as is used for carpeting floors. Old pieces of carpet may also be used. Burlaps makes excellent cover. It may be doubled; and it may have straw, shavings or wool quilted in it. Various hotbed mattings are sold by dealers in gardeners' supplies.

Gardeners often make mats of rye straw. Such mats are thick and serviceable, and if they are kept dry they will last for years. They are bulky to store and heavy to handle, however, and they are not used as much as formerly. There are various methods of making these straw mats, but Fig. 18 illustrates one of the best. A frame is made after the manner of a saw-horse, with a double top, and tarred or marline twine is used for securing the strands of straw. It is customary to use six runs of this warp. Twelve spools of string are provided, six hanging on either side. Some persons wind the cord on two twenty-penny nails, as shown in the figure, these nails being held together at one end by wire which is secured in notches filed into them. The other ends of the nails are free, and allow the string to be caught between them, thus preventing the balls from unwinding as they hang from the frame. Two wisps of straight rye straw are secured and laid upon the frame, with the butt ends outward and the heads overlapping. Two

Fig. 18. Making straw-mats.

opposite spools are then brought up and a hard knot is tied at each point. The projecting butts of the straw are then cut off with a hatchet, and the mat is allowed to drop through to receive the next pair of wisps. In making these mats, it is essential that the rye contains no ripe grain; otherwise it attracts the mice. It is best to grow rye for this especial purpose, and to cut it before the grain is in the milk, so that the straw does not need to be threshed.

In addition to these coverings of straw or matting, it is sometimes necessary to provide board shutters to protect the beds, particularly if the plants are started very early. These shutters are made of half-inch or five-eighths inch pine lumber, and are the same size as the sash — 3 x 6 feet. They are used above the matting to keep it dry and to prevent it from blowing off. In some cases they are used without matting.

4. COLDFRAMES AND FORCING-HILLS

A coldframe has no bottom heat, except that which it receives from the sun: otherwise it is like a hotbed. There are three general purposes for which a coldframe is used: (1) for the starting of plants early in spring; (2) for receiving partially hardened plants which have been started earlier in hotbeds and forcing-houses; (3) for wintering young cabbages, lettuce and other hardy plants which are sown in the fall.

Coldframes are ordinarily placed near the buildings. and the plants are transplanted into the field when settled weather comes. Sometimes, however, they are made directly in the field where the plants are to remain, and the frames, and not the plants, are removed. When used for this latter purpose, the frames are made very cheap by running two rows of parallel planks through the field at a distance of six feet apart. The plank on the north is ordinarily 10 to 12 inches wide, and that on the south 8 to 10 inches. These planks are held in place by stakes, and the

Fig. 19. A span-roof coldframe, or cold forcing-house.

sash are laid across them. Seeds of radishes, beets, lettuce, and the like, are then sown beneath the sash, and when settled weather arrives the sash and planks are removed and the plants are growing naturally in the field. Half-hardy plants, like those mentioned, may be started two or three weeks in advance of the normal season by this means.

When the heat is spent from hotbeds, they become coldframes. They can then be used, if empty, for the starting of late plants; or the plants may be hardened-off in them as they cool, thus, perhaps, obviating the necessity of transplanting to other frames.

Span-roof coldframes (Fig. 19) are very useful, as they allow of better and more uniform conditions for the growing of plants than the ordinary frame. They are covered with hotbed sash laid on a framework, and the sashes pulled down from the top for ventilation. They are essentially forcing-houses, however, and the discussion of them is foreign to the purpose of this volume.

Forcing-hills.—A forcing-hill is an arrangement by means of which a single plant or a single hill of plants may be forced where it permanently stands. It is a small coldframe. This type of forcing may be applied to perennial plants, as rhubarb and asparagus, or to annuals, as melons and cucumbers. Fig. 20 illustrates a common method of hastening the growth of rhubarb in the spring. A box made with four removable sides, two of which are shown in end section in the figure, is placed around the plant in the fall. The inside of the box is filled with straw or litter, and the outside is banked thoroughly with any refuse, to prevent the ground from freezing. When it is desired to start the plants, the covering is removed from both the inside and outside of the box, and hot manure is piled around the box to its top. If the weather is still cold, dry, light leaves

Fig. 20. Forcing of rhubarb.

or straw may be placed inside the box, or a pane or sash of glass may be placed on top of the box, to answer the purpose of a coldframe. Rhubarb, asparagus, sea-kale and similar plants may be advanced from two to four weeks by means of this method of forcing. Some gardeners use old barrels or half-barrels in place of the box. The box, however, is better and handier, and the sides can be stored for future use.

Plants which require a long season in which to mature, and which do not transplant readily, as melons and cucumbers, may be planted in forcing-hills in the field. One of these hills is shown in Fig. 21. The

Fig. 21. Forcing-hill.

frame or mold is shown at the left. This mold is a box with flaring sides and no top or bottom, and provided with a handle. This frame is placed with the small end down at the point where the seeds are to be planted, and the earth is hilled up about it and firmly packed with the feet. The mold is then withdrawn, and a pane of glass is laid on the top of the mound to concentrate the sun's rays, and to prevent the bank from washing down with the rains. A clod of earth or a stone may be placed on the pane to hold it down. This type of forcing-hill is not much used, because the bank of earth is likely to wash away, and heavy rain occurring when the glass is off will fill the hill with water and drown the plant. However, it can be used to very good advantage in cases in which the gardener can give it close attention.

A forcing-hill is sometimes made by digging a hole in the ground and planting the seeds in the bottom of it, placing the pane of glass upon a slight ridge or mound which is made on the surface of the ground. This method is less desirable than the other, because the seeds are placed in the poorest and coldest soil, and the hole is very likely to fill with water in the early days of spring.

An excellent type of forcing-hill is made by the use of the hand-box, as shown in Fig. 22. This is a rectangular box, without top or bottom, and a pane of glass is slipped into a groove at the top. The earth is banked slightly about the box, in order to hold it against winds and to prevent the water from running into it. If these boxes are made of good lumber and painted, they will last for many years. Any size of glass may be used, but a 10 x 12 pane is as good as any for general purposes.

Fig. 22. Hand-box.

After the plants are thoroughly established in these forcing-hills, and the weather is settled, the protection is wholly removed, and the plants grow normally in the open. Forcing-hills are not well adapted to large-area work, because they require too much time in the tending, being scattered over much territory. Neither do they have much advantage of protection from windbreaks, and, containing a less body of air, they do not give as early results as well-made coldframes.

5. THE MANAGEMENT OF FRAMES

Only by experience can one learn how to manage a hotbed. There are a few principles and cautions, however, which may enable one to arrive at this knowledge sooner and with less loss than by blind experience alone. The things to be sought, so far as the plants are concerned, are specimens (1) which are ready at the required season, (2) which are stocky, and (3) which have made a continuous healthy growth. The things to avoid are (1) the chilling of the plants; (2) too hot and close atmosphere, which tends to make the plants soft; (3) crowding of the plants, which tends to make them weak and spindling; (4) growing plants too far from the light, which also tends to make them soft and weak; (5) the scalding of the plants by the sun, an injury which is very likely to occur when the sun comes out after a long "spell" of dark or cold weather; (6) the wilting of the plants, due to too great heat and too little moisture.

Translated into the actual management of a hotbed, these objects may be grouped as follows: (1) maintaining the heat; (2) watering; (3) ventilating; (4) hardening-off; (5) transplanting. Above all things, the plant should be stocky when it is to be put in the field. A stocky plant is one which is comparatively short and thick, is able to stand alone, and which has a normal bright green color throughout. Plants which are not stocky are said to be "leggy" or "drawn," since their general tendency is to grow too long and weak for their bulk. A stocky plant, however, may be stunted. The ideal plant is one which is both stocky and vigorous.

The maintenance of the heat in the ordinary hotbed depends primarily on the quality and the amount of manure; but one can do something by subsequent management to maintain it. Heat will ordinarily fail sooner if the hotbed is above the ground and much exposed to winds. It may also be lessened by careless watering, particularly by soaking the manure. As already said (page 57), manure which is too heavy and concentrated may heat violently, and wetting it may tend to cool it to the point at which plants can grow; but a better way is to mix leaves or other litter with the manure, thereby preventing too rapid fermentation. Not only should the heat from the fermenting manure be maintained, but care should be taken to prevent too much of the heat from escaping. This is an important caution in very cold nights and windy weather, at which time the frame should be protected by mats or other covering. A cold and wet soil also tends to lessen the heat in the hotbed. For this reason, hotbeds should always be placed in a sandy or gravelly place, if possible; or if not, the greatest precaution should be taken to insure perfect drainage.

Watering should be done with caution. Careless

watering tends (1) to pack or to puddle the soil, (2) to chill the plants, and (3) to soak the manure and to check its fermentation. If watering is done from a hose, the danger of packing the soil is greater than when a watering pot is used, since the water is applied with greater force. Hotbed soils should be rather loose and fibrous in order to prevent the puddling. As compared with outdoor or field conditions, the amount of water applied to a hotbed is usually excessive, and the physical texture of the soil is likely to be injured unless one exercises considerable care. It is better, as a rule, not to water hotbeds towards night or when the temperature is falling, for the application of water and the subsequent evaporation tend to still further cool the bed. It is particularly inadvisable to allow the plants to go into the night with wet foliage. This caution applies with especial force to cucumbers, melons and other "warm" plants; and also to the early season, when it is necessary to keep the frame close. It is better, as a rule, to water in the morning, or at least when there is still enough sun heat left to warm the soil before nightfall. It is well also to avoid ice-cold water, for the application of water at such temperature is a decided check to plants. The water should have a temperature of 60° to 65°, if possible, particularly for warm-growing plants and early in the season. Avoid dribbling or merely wetting the surface of the soil. The soil should be wet thoroughly at each watering, and not wet again until the plants need it; but, on the other hand, one should avoid drenching the soil.

Ventilation is important, (1) to dry the air, (2) to aid in controlling the temperature. Plants which are kept close and wet tend to grow too tall and soft, and to lack in stockiness. On pleasant and sunny days, ventilation should be given by raising the sash, resting it on a notched block, (Fig. 23), or by sliding down the sash. The general tendency with beginners is to ventilate too little rather than too much. One is likely to judge the temperature by the wind and air about his face and ears, whereas the hotbed, being on the surface of the ground, is considerably warmer and more protected. Whenever the air in the bed is so moist that drops of water collect on the panes, ventilation should be given if the temperature will permit. In fact, it is the aim of good gardeners not to have the atmosphere very moist when the temperature is low and ventilation cannot be given. As the plants grow, more and more ventilation should be given until finally in sunny days the sash can be stripped from the frames. In this way the plants become accustomed to the lower temperature and to normal conditions of the atmosphere; they become "hardened." Careful attention to ventilation is one of the important means of making plants stocky.

Fig. 23. Ventilating the hotbed.

Hardening-off is also promoted by giving the plants plenty of room. As soon as they begin to crowd, some of the plants may be pulled out, or better, all the plants may be transplanted. At the transplanting, it may be well to transfer the plants to a somewhat cooler and more airy frame. With celery and some other plants, it is often allowable to shear the tops, cutting off a fourth or a fifth of the length of the plant in order to make it branch and thicken. Plants which are grown in pots, berry boxes, oyster buckets, and the like, are likely to be more stocky than those which are grown directly in the soil of the hotbed, since they have more room; and such plants may not need transplanting. If it is found that the heat is failing, it will be necessary to harden-off the plants more rapidly. Some plants, of which lettuce, cabbage and cauliflower are the common examples, can be so completely hardened-off as to be able to withstand considerable frost; and in this toughened condition they may be carried over two or three weeks of cold weather before it is safe to transplant them into the open. The general tendency is to do little transplanting in the frames because of the high price of labor, but transplanting is always advantageous to the plants, particularly if they are started very early.

In very cold weather, it is sometimes necessary to keep the mats and shutters on the hotbeds for two or three days at a time. During this time, when the plants are in comparative darkness, they are likely to become somewhat soft and tender, and great care must be exercised that they are not scalded when the covers are taken off and the sun comes out. The stockier and the tougher the plants are grown, the less is the danger of sun-scalding; but after a long period of cloudy weather, this danger is very great and the operator must watch his beds closely.

Hotbeds are more difficult to manage, as a rule, than forcing-houses, since the operator can be inside the forcing-house whatever the weather may be. In very cold and windy weather, hotbeds cannot be opened. The operator works from the outside rather than from the inside. In many of the plains regions, the strong winds make it difficult to handle the hotbed sash. In such case, the cheap forcing-house structure made of frames and heated either with fermenting manure or with pipes is more advantageous (page 62).

Beginners are likely to start a hotbed too soon. It must be remembered that the age of the plant does not count for so much as its stockiness and vigor. If, therefore, the hotbed is started so early that the plants have to be "slowed up" and stunted in order to hold them until the field is ready, very little is gained. In the northern states, it is usually thought that cabbages and cauliflower may be started with profit about six weeks before the field is expected to be ready; tomatoes, six to seven weeks; onions and beets, four to six weeks.

Wintering fall-sown plants.—It has been said (page 67) that one use of coldframes is to carry fall-sown plants over the winter and to have them ready for transplanting into the field very early in the spring. The plants are not to grow during winter: they are only protected. Having become inured to cold, they may be set in the field the minute the soil is fit. Hardy plants (lettuce, cabbage, kale, cauliflower) are used for this purpose. Seeds are sown in late fall, and when the plants have grown four or five weeks they are ready to be transplanted into the frames. It is not well that they make much growth in bulk after transplanting to the frames; but they should secure a good root-hold before freezing weather comes. Some persons sow the seeds directly in the frames, but better results are usually attained if the plants are made extra stocky by transplanting. All soft, weak and imperfect plants are likely to be destroyed by the winter. Plants which are very young and flabby usually perish. Those which are too old tend to run to seed when spring weather comes. Only by experience can one determine the proper age at which the plants should go into the winter; and this experience is likely to vary with different varieties of the same vegetables. A plant which has begun to thicken up and to show signs of a tendency to form a head will nearly always run to seed in the spring, for it seems not to have the power to resume active vegetative growth after its long check. Cabbage plants with three or four true leaves should be able to pass the winter and to give satisfactory results the following year. The novice should undertake these experiments in a small way, particularly in the North, where the practice is not common and the results are precarious.

Keep the frames uncovered until stiff freezing weather comes. Then use sash and covers. Gradually the plants and soil may freeze; but exercise care that the bright sun does not strike frozen plants and thaw them out quickly. Give freely of ventilation. Strip the frames on all fine days. If the ground is frozen, the plants may stand several days under a cover of snow on the sash; but if the ground is soft, so that some root action goes on, the plants should not be kept close and dark for more than a day or two.

In the middle states, the plants are sometimes carried over winter without frames, if they are in a protected place. As far south as Norfolk, cabbage are planted in the field in late fall. Check all winter growth, prevent sudden thawing, avoid sun-scalding.

CHAPTER III

THE SOIL AND ITS TREATMENT

MARKET, climate, soil,—these are the leading factors in determining the location of a market-garden.

A good market-gardening soil is one which is "quick." It warms up early in spring; it comes quickly into workable condition after a rain; it is easy to keep in good tilth; it responds quickly to fertilizing materials. Its physical condition is more important than its original richness in plant-food: the latter can be added. That is, in the determination of a soil for market-gardening purposes, two coördinate factors are to be considered,—the texture or physical make-up, and the content of plant-food.

Nearly all general market-gardens are on sandy loams. There are a few crops, of which onions and celery are examples, which demand particular types of soils for best results; but if one has a deep and uniform sandy soil, he can make an ideal garden of it, other things being equal. If the land is well drained, and if rainfall is sufficient, this sandy land can be made immensely productive by a combination of three things,—good tillage, the incorporation of plant-fiber or humus, the direct addition of plant-food. When thus ameliorated, it becomes a sandy loam.

The soil to avoid is hard clay. It is cold and late. Plants start slowly in it. It cannot be worked when either wet or dry; and the period in which it can be tilled is so short that much labor and equipment are required to enable one to handle it quickly and efficiently. Clay is excellent for some fruits (particularly pears and plums), and for some general farm crops; but it is not the land for vegetable-growing. However, a friable clay loam may be excellent: this loamy condition may be obtained from hard clay soil by judicious tillage, the incorporation of humus, the addition of amendments in special cases, and by underdraining. Clay loams are good lands for main-season crops of many kinds, as cabbage, pea, bean.

Reclaimed swamps usually afford excellent soil for vegetables, if the area can be thoroughly well drained, so that the land is "early," and if the vegetable matter or peat is well decomposed and comminuted. Soils which are nearly all muck have little body, and suffer from drought; these soils are mostly the deposit of peat and moss bogs. The fine loams which have accumulated in beds of shallow ponds or lakes are usually ideal vegetable-garden lands, providing the area is not too frosty.

When the object in vegetable-gardening is to grow very early crops, it is important to have quick-acting land. Such a soil contains a large amount of sand in its composition. * * * When the intention is to raise cabbages, potatoes, turnips, beets, etc., for marketing in the autumn and for crops that require but a short time to mature or that prefer a cool location, a good clayey loam is generally the best.—*S. B. Green, Vegetable-Gardening, Second Ed., 8.*

The best soils are of a friable and loamy texture; the worst, those of a very light sandy or of a stiff clayey description.—*Robert Buist, The Family Kitchen Gardener, 5.*

The soil for growing vegetables and seeds should be as near as possible a deep loam; it may be more or less sandy, but avoid clay, or anything heavier than a clay loam.—*Francis Brill, Farm-Gardening and Seed-Growing, New Ed., 11.*

Earth of a consistence that will hold water the longest without becoming hard when dry, is of all others, the best adapted for raising the generality of plants in the greatest perfection. This last described soil is called loam, and is a medium earth, between the extremes of clay and sand.—*Bridgeman, Young Gardener's Assistant, Seventh Ed., 10.*

Garden vegetables, as a rule, will thrive best, other things being equal, on a deep, sandy loam, with an open sub-soil. Almost any character of soil, with the exception of pure clay, can be brought up to a high state of fertility by adopting the proper methods.—*P. T. Quinn, Money in the Garden, 14.*

The soil should be a warm, sandy loam.—*T. Greiner, How to Make the Garden Pay, Second Ed., 30.*

Sandy loam, with a sandy or gravelly sub-soil should be selected. Such land is far better than soils resting on clay, not only because its nature is warmer, but because it is naturally well drained. A clay sub-soil, at least until deep drains have been sunk and operated a considerable time, will render any land cold, as it retains the moisture.—*W. W. Rawson, Success in Market-Gardening, 12.*

If in the selection of the land, one is confined to a single soil, he should select one consisting of a mixture of organic and inorganic matter; a light, deep, sandy loam, with plenty of humus or vegetable matter.—*A. Oemler, Truck-Farming at the South, 10.*

The soil may be anything but brick clay, theoretically a light, sandy loam is best, but here, again, astonishing results are often obtained on forbidding soils; for instance, on sticky red clays and sands, the latter seemingly no better than those of the seashore.—*Burnet Landreth, Market-Gardening and Farm Notes, 18.*

The characters already cited point clearly to what is commonly designated as a rather light soil as best for vegetable growing.—*E. J. Wickson, The California Vegetables, 43.*

The soil which is best suited for the production of vegetables is what is termed a rich loam, fully a foot in depth, with a sandy or gravelly sub-soil, through which the surplus water readily filters. —*D. W. Beadle, Canadian Fruit, Flower and Kitchen Gardener, 192.*

Quel sol convient au jardin? Je réponds que partout où il y a de la terre végétale, l'établissement d'un jardin y est possible. Il n'en est point du jardin comme de la ferme; celle-ci, en raison sourtout de son étendue, conservera toujours la qualité de son sol primitif, tandis que pour le jardin, il est toujours assez facile par des amendments, des engrais et divers procédés de culture, d'altérer ou de changer sa qualité suivant le besoin.—*Provancher, Le Verger, 169* (*Quebec.*)

Vegetable-gardening land should be rich. It should contain much plant-food material; and this material should be quickly available, for on its availability depends the earliness or "quickness" of the land, to a great extent. The plant should grow quickly and continuously. Slow-growing and intermittent-growing vegetables may not only fail to reach the market or the table at the desired time, but they are usually poor in quality. In order to secure this quick growth, the land should be very thoroughly prepared before the plants are put on it; and in most cases, an application of concentrated (or commercial) fertilizer will help.

It is usually more profitable to secure land which is already in productive condition than to take that of inferior quality and to improve it. This is true of all intensive farming; for intensive farming wants quick, positive, and large results. The closer one is to his market, the smaller his area, and the greater the variety of crops which he is to grow, the greater is the necessity of securing land in prime condition.

But if one has small capital, he may not be able to secure such land. In such case, he takes land which is either naturally inferior or which is run down. It is a favorite advice of the market-gardening writers to avoid run-down lands. It is said to be impracticable to attempt to reclaim them. This kind of advice has been over-emphasized. If run-out land lies right and is naturally well drained, it can be brought into profitable condition, in the great majority of cases, with comparatively little trouble and expense, if only the person goes at it right. It requires time and patience. The first thing to do is to till well and to add fiber (preferably by means of clover). The common notion that commercial fertilizer is the first resort in such instances is in most cases a grievous error. The fertilizer is for the purpose of adding plant-food, not of ameliorating the soil. If market-gardening is attempted on run-down land, the gardener should select the best part of the area for his more intensive efforts, giving it what manure he has and bestowing upon it his best efforts in tillage. The remainder of the place can then be slowly brought into condition by cover-cropping, rotation, and other cheaper means. Four or five years, at the outside, should usually suffice to bring the average worn-out land into good condition, without great expenditure of capital. The "run-down" character of a farm is usually more a matter of dilapidated fences and buildings, weedy fields and slovenly appearance, than of exhaustion of plant-food in the soil.

1. THE AMELIORATION OF THE LAND

Land that is "quick" is in good physical condition. It is finely pulverized, "mealy," mellow, deep. It is almost useless to apply expensive plant-food to poorly tilled and intractable land. The first efforts, therefore, must be given to drainage, tillage, the addition of fiber, rotation.

Drainage.—The best drainage is that which is provided by nature; that is, land which is naturally well drained comes into condition more quickly, as a rule, and is in more continuous good tilth than that which it is necessary to drain artificially. However, the very best results may be secured by a good system of tile-drainage. Underdraining is practiced for two purposes—to carry off the superfluous water, and to improve the physical texture of the soil. All low and boggy lands need to be drained for the first purpose. Very stiff clay lands, which are normally dry and hard, usually can be much improved in their physical texture by a good system of underdrains. The philosophy of this is simple. If water stands long in clay lands, it tends to cement or to puddle the soil. If the superfluous water is quickly taken off, however, this cementing or puddling does not take place. The soil is thereby looser or more friable. This friable condition of the soil enables it to hold more moisture than when it is hard and brick-like. It therefore results that draining to remove the superfluous water puts the soil in condition to hold more capillary moisture in its own tissues, and improves it for agricultural purposes. For vegetable-gardening purposes, particularly if quickest results are desired, it is necessary to underdrain hard clay lands, even if they are not wet. It makes them workable early in the spring after rains, and enables the plants to obtain a quicker foothold. These same lands might be used for orchards, however, without underdraining, and they might also be very productive of some general farm crops; but in such cases the crops may occupy the land for a term of years, and very quick and early results are not essential.

For temporary purposes, surface drains may be used, or the land may be ridged so that the surface water is taken off in the dead-furrows. This surface drainage, however, results only in carrying off superfluous water and does not have the effect of ameliorating the land in the way in which underdrains do.

In nearly all cases, it is better and cheaper in the end to use tile underdrains. Board drains are sometimes used, but they are not so efficient nor so permanent; and in the East they are often more expensive to begin with than the tile drains are. In stony countries, excellent drains may be made by partially filling the ditch with stones, particularly if flat stones are to be had so that a conduit can be laid in the bottom. Such drains not only give the advantages of underdrainage, but also afford a means of disposing of superfluous stone. If they have a good fall, and care is exercised not to fill the spaces between the stones with earth, they may be nearly or quite as efficient as tile drains. The deeper the drains, the deeper will be the ameliorating effect on the soil and the greater the area which they drain. As a matter of practice, however, it is found, that four feet is usually the maximum depth, and about three feet the minimum. Wet lands, or very hard clay lands, should have drains at a distance of not more than two or three rods, if the lands are to be put in the very best condition for market-gardening purposes. It may be advisable, however, to use such lands for the later, cheaper and general-purpose crops rather than for the very early ones if the gardener has other land which can be used for the crops which are desired for the early market. For detailed advice on drainage, the readers should consult special books on the subject.

Tillage.—At the present time the great emphasis in agricultural practice is placed on tillage. We have passed through that era in our development in which we have looked to recipes and special practices for the improving of the soil. The fundamental thing is to till: the later and incidental thing is to fertilize the land.

We till (1) to prepare the soil to receive the crop, and (2) to maintain the soil in good condition for the growth of the crop. To prepare the soil for the crop, the land should be loosened and pulverized as deep as ordinary roots go. To maintain the soil in ideal condition, the surface should be tilled or stirred as often as it becomes crusted or compacted. It is essential that every farmer keep in mind the differences between preparation-tillage and maintenance-tillage, for these ideas are associated with two classes of effort. Cultivating should be thought of as maintenance-tillage, not as preparation-tillage.

1. The tillage of preparation insists that the land be broken and pulverized. The depth to which this pulverization or plowing shall extend must be determined for each particular case: it depends on the character of the soil and the crop. Land which is very hard, or in which there is a high sub-soil, nearly always needs to be plowed deep; the effort must be to deepen the soil. Lands which are sandy or leachy may need to be plowed shallow and approximately the same depth every year; the effort is to compact the under soil and thereby to prevent the leaching. The root-crops demand deep soil in order that the roots may grow long and symmetrical. This is emphatically true with such long-growing roots as parsnips, late beets, carrots and horse-radish. Forty or fifty years ago it was the general advice that land be plowed deep. But neither deep plowing nor shallow plowing is the unit. The depth of plowing is a question of conditions

It is a favorite practice with the gardener to plow land in the fall. There are three objects of fall plowing: (1) To make the land earlier in the spring; (2) to be forehanded with the work; (3) to improve the physical character of the soil. Land which is plowed in the fall can nearly always be worked several days earlier than that which is plowed in the spring. It dries out sooner. Especially is this true of stiff or loamy lands. Clay lands may be very much improved in their physical texture by being plowed in the fall, so that the weather has a chance to break down and slack the lumps. It is important, however, that such land should contain more or less vegetable matter; otherwise it may run together and puddle during the winter season and be difficult to manage in the spring. If the land contains stubble of grain or grass, or if it has a covering of manure, such danger will be averted. If the land is clean and in good condition, it will not need to be plowed again in the spring, but can be worked down with heavy tools, like the spading harrows, and be got in ideal condition (Fig. 24). Whenever land is needed very early in the spring, it is advisable to plow it in the fall. This remark applies with little force to light and sandy lands, for they can ordinarily be plowed very early.

Lands may be made earlier to work if they are thrown into beds or ridges by the fall plowing, so that the dead-furrows occur every eight or ten feet. The surface water is then carried off and the ridges lie so high that they dry out quickly. This operation is sometimes spoken of as trenching, but it is more properly ridging of the land. The term "trenching" should be reserved for its legitimate use to designate the spading up or loosening up of the land deeper than the original furrow. It is only a special practice.

Fig. 24. The spring fitting of fall-plowed land. The central area is the surface left by the fall plowing. It is being broken and pulverized by the spading-harrow.

Sub-soiling is a common practice in market-gardening lands. It is nearly always advisable in lands which are hard or have a high sub-soil, and also for the long root-crops, which demand a deep soil in which to perfect their growth. Sub-soiling is not a permanent corrective of the land, for the soil very soon settles back into its original and hard condition, and the operation must be repeated. The fundamental corrective for such soils is underdraining and incorporation of humus. The growing of clover, which sends its roots deep into the soil, is also a great aid. But even with all these aids, sub-soiling may be very useful in certain cases. The sub-soil plow does not turn a furrow; it merely breaks the bottom of the original furrow. It is drawn by a separate team and follows in the furrow immediately behind the first plowman.

2. The tillage of maintenance should occur at least as frequently as once in ten days for the best market-garden conditions. Surface-tillage enables the land to drink in the water of rainfall. It also saves the water in the soil by hindering evaporation: it maintains a loose and dry layer which acts as a mulch to the moister soil beneath. A board or a forkful of manure placed on the earth keeps the soil moist because it delays evaporation. A surface-mulch of dry earth acts in much the same way. The depth of this mulch must be determined by the character of the soil, kind of crop, frequency of tillage, and character of tools; but, as a rule, from three to four inches of loosely stirred earth is sufficient. It also solves the whole difficulty of weeds. All tillage of preparation—all

fitting of the land—should be completed before the crop is put in: thereafter, only the surface-mulch is to be kept in repair. But many times the preparation-tillage is not completed in its season, and the land must be fitted after the crop is sown by means of deep and heavy cultivating; it is usually a loss of effort and efficiency when preparation-tillage and maintenance-tillage must be done at the same time.

The soil in the surface-mulch is relatively dry, and it is moved so often that roots do not secure a foot-hold in it. It is therefore out of use for the time being as a source of plant-food; but it is more useful as a conservator of moisture than as plant-food. But its food comes into use when it is turned under the following season, and it is also carried down by the rains, particularly by those of spring and fall. The gardener must bear in mind that his plants need a soil of good physical texture, one which holds moisture, and one which has much available plant-food. Deep preparation enables the soil to hold moisture, and the surface-mulch saves much of it from evaporating.

The rainfall of the growing season is often insufficient for the crop. The plants draw on the moisture which has been stored in the soil by the winter rains and snows. Therefore, it is exceedingly important to save this winter rainfall, and this is done by fitting the soil and making the surface-mulch the moment the land is dry enough to work in spring. Even if the land is not to be used until June, it should be fitted early, and lightly harrowed at frequent intervals before the crop is planted.

Addition of humus.—Land is very rapidly improved by the incorporation of fiber. This fiber is secured by plowing under any kind of vegetation, as rye, clover, manure or the refuse of the garden. When this fiber decays it becomes humus. The humus improves the physical condition of the soil by making it loose, open and mellow; by enabling it to hold moisture; by preventing the puddling or cementing of clay soils; by decreasing the heat of the surface soil in summer; and by improving the chemical condition. Humus itself contains plant-food. It also affords solvent acids which tend to unlock other plant-foods. If it is derived from leguminous plants, it also adds nitrogen. The chief reason for the almost extravagant use of stable manures by market-gardeners is the addition of humus. Lands which are thus manured year after year become quick and amenable to treatment. Fertilizers work quickly in them. The lands can be tilled at almost any time in the growing season, and when one crop is off another can be put in quickly.

One great value of the rotation of crops is that it adds fiber and humus to the soil. It is probable that there is a tendency to use stable manure in excess in garden lands; that is, the same results in the incorporation of humus can be had in many cases more cheaply by the growing of catch-crops. Particularly is this true of those areas which are some distance from the market and in which it is not necessary to practice rapid succession of market crops.

Land which receives identical treatment year by year tends to depreciate. A rotation is useful because

(1) it gives different treatments to the land, the fault of one year tending to be corrected by the management in another year; (2) no one element of plant-food is exhausted, the rotation tending to even up the demands on the soil; (3) one crop leaves the land in good physical condition for another; (4) it incorporates humus; (5) it destroys pests and weeds; (6) it economizes labor; (7) when green crops are turned under, available or digested plant-food is incorporated with the soil, and nitrogen may be supplied. The rotation of crops means, also, rotation in tillage, manuring and other treatment; and one of these may be quite as important as the other.

The philosophy of the "resting" of land is hereby explained. It is not due to any need of recuperation in the soil; but the good effects which follow are the compound results of the various benefits which are derived from tilling and rotation. Gardeners find that when soil becomes unproductive for a particular crop, a change to some other crop may result in profit. Soils which have been long kept in market-gardens may be benefited by seeding down for two or three years. Whenever possible, attempts should be made to practice some kind of a rotation in the market-garden area. Now and then, a part of the land may be laid down to clover for a year or two.

2. THE FERTILIZING OF THE LAND

When the soil has been thoroughly fitted and improved by all the foregoing means, a gardener may think of adding plant-food. This plant-food may be supplied in some concentrated fertilizer; it is also added when green-crops are plowed under or when manure or compost of garden refuse is applied. It will now be seen that the best results are usually to be expected when there is something like a rotation in the fertilizing of the land, stable manures being used alternately with concentrated or commercial fertilizers.

Fig. 25. Gardener's compost piles.—Manure on the left, sods on the right.

Composts.—In the addition of plant-fiber to the soil, much will be gained if it is thoroughly decomposed. It thereby becomes quickly incorporated with the soil, and its plant-food soon becomes available. This is the explanation of the general desire of market-gardeners to have what they call "short" or well-rotted manure, and also the very common practice of composting manures and refuse. Composting consists in piling the various materials together in long, low, flat-topped piles, which may catch and retain the rainfall, and then forking them over two or more times during the season (Fig. 25). If the materials are thoroughly disintegrated and mixed, they are in fit condition to be put on the land and they readily become an integral part of the soil. Materials like tomato vines, potato vines and even corn stalks, which are too raw and coarse to apply directly to the land, may be made into useful and valuable material when they have been composted for several months or a year; although if serious diseases infest the refuse, the material would better be burned. The addition of quick-lime hastens the decomposition of raw materials. The florist, who must have his soils in ideal condition, is familiar with methods of composting, for he usually provides his soils a year in advance.

Commercial fertilizers.— The kind and amount of fertilizers to be used are to be determined by several circumstances: (1) the earliness or quickness with which the crop is to be obtained; (2) the intensity of the operations to which the man is committed; (3) the character of the land as regards tilth and texture; (4) the character of the land as regards richness in plant-food; (5) the kind or species of crops to be raised.

There is no infallible means by which one can determine what fertilizers he shall apply. He must study his conditions and judge as best he can. A little experiment with different kinds of fertilizer on two or three of the leading crops at one side of the plantation, is the readiest means of answering the question.

The chemical analysis of the plant, while of the greatest use to the chemist in giving him suggestions, is of no practical use to the farmer in determining the kind of fertilizers or what amount shall be applied. The chemical contents of plants vary in the different seasons and in the different parts of the plant, and also with the soil in which the plant grows: the plant may take up more than it needs when some element is abundant. Even the widest variation in the amount of any one ingredient will be amply covered by the large amount of fertilizer which is ordinarily applied. Consider, for example, that the fruit of a tomato comprises .05 per cent of phosphoric acid and .27 per cent of potash. If the crop is ten tons of fruit per acre, it is probable that more than the average amount of phosphoric acid required is ten pounds and of potash fifty-four pounds. It is safe to assume that the land itself should supply at least three-fourths of these amounts. We will assume that one-fourth is to be supplied by the addition of fertilizer. We should then apply to the acre two and one-half pounds of phosphoric acid and about fourteen pounds of potash. As a matter of fact, however, the smallest amounts which are ever applied are many times in excess of these amounts. Fertilizers must always be applied in excess. It is impossible to distribute a very small quantity; roots do not occupy every part of the ground. Much is risked in the chance that some may be used.

Following are figures which show that the best advice as to the use of fertilizers does not closely follow the chemical content of the crop. The table gives the average amount of nitrogen, potash and phosphoric acid removed from an acre; then the amount of these materials recommended by Voorhees (in his book on "Fertilizers"), and others and the differences between the two:

	Yield per acre	Per cent of N. P. K.			Am't in total crop—lbs. N. P. K.			Am't taken	Am't given	Difference	
	LBS.	LBS.						LBS.	LBS.	LBS.	
Cabbage..	30,000	.38	.11	.43	114	33	129	276	333	57	excess
Carrots ..	30,000	.16	.09	.51	48	27	153	228	190	38	defic'y
Onions ...	22,800	.14	.04	.10	31.9	9.1	22.8	63.8	247	183 2	excess
Parsnips..	30,000	.22	.19	.62	66	57	186	309	190	119	defic'y
S. Potat's.	13,500	.23	.10	.50	31	13.5	67.5	112	312	200	excess
Tomatoes.	20,000	.16	.05	.27	32	10	54	96	120	24	excess

Supposing that the crop obtains none of its nitrogen, potash and phosphorus from the soil, it will be seen that the fertilizer recommended for cabbage is 57 lbs. in excess of the needs of a normal crop, and for fancy sweet potatoes 200 lbs. in excess. Yet it is probable that the recommendations are perfectly safe and economical, for the grower wants an extra rather than a good yield, he wants the crop early and quick-growing, and he wants to take no risk of failure. In parsnips and carrots, the recommended amounts are less than those required by the crop; but in these cases earliness is not a prime requisite, and the plant is supposed to draw slowly a large part of its supply from the stored food in the soil.

Another difficulty in the giving of advice for fertilizing the land is the variable character of the soil. This is particularly the case in the northern states, in which the soil is largely drift and is therefore very uneven in kind and depth. In the long stretches of sand on the Atlantic coastal plain or in the red clays of the South, and in nearly all alluvial soils, the problem of choosing a fertilizer is less complex. The sandier and more uniform the land, the more marked, as a rule, will be the effect of commercial fertilizers. The harder the clay, the less marked, in general, is the effect, although amendments (as lime) may have great effect in making such soils granular.

Again, the state of tillage has much to do with the efficiency of a fertilizer. The element which the plant needs may be afforded more cheaply by giving better tillage than by adding fertilizers; for tillage sets at work the forces which unlock plant-food. On the other hand, fertilizer is more usable by the plant on well-tilled soils: the plant can get hold of it because the material is more evenly distributed; there is more moisture to dissolve it; the plant is more comfortable and vigorous and thereby better able to appropriate it. The good gardener is the one who gets the most out of his land by means of good tillage and then adds fertilizer to get more out of it. He uses fertilizer for the purpose of securing an extra yield, not to prevent the soil from becoming exhausted. As a rule, the men who till best buy most plant-food. Fertilizer is usually a losing investment for a poor farmer.

When to apply a fertilizer depends on (1) when it is needed by the plant, (2) the kind of fertilizer, (3) the soil, (4) the kind of plant, (5) the season of normal rainfall of the district. The more soluble the fertilizer, the looser the soil, the shallower the roots, the later the fertilizer may be applied. With trees, it matters little whether fertilizer is applied in fall or spring, for it will be one or two years, as a rule, before it affects the plant. With the general run of vegetable crops and on soils in good tilth, it is usually best to apply fertilizer in the spring, sowing it on the surface and harrowing it in. On ordinary soils, very little of it will be lost by leaching. Nitrates are most likely to leach. They are soluble and pass down quickly. Therefore, nitrate of soda and sulfate of ammonia should not be applied much in advance of the planting. With annual crops, fertilizer should not be applied much, if any, in advance of the planting: the fertilizer is needed near the surface, and it should be quickly available.

There is much discussion whether fertilizer should be applied broadcast or in the hill, which proves that both methods are right. If one wants to enrich his land, or to afford sustenance to the plant throughout its growing season, apply broadcast. If one wants to use fertilizer to start the plant off and to maintain it until it gets a firm hold on the soil, apply in the hill. A most important use of commercial fertilizer in vegetable-gardening is to hasten the plant in the beginning. It is kindling-wood to start the blaze.

The only way to determine what fertilizers to use is to try. On a small plot each year the gardener should experiment with fertilizers as he does with varieties. The fertilizer question is largely a local and special problem.

The following directions given by the College of Agriculture of Cornell University, for the making of coöperative fertilizer experiments, will suggest to the farmer how he may experiment:

The field should be plowed before the plats are laid out. Then use good, substantial stakes at the corners of the plats, and mark them in such a way that the plats will not become mixed, thereby avoiding confusion. It would be well to leave a space of four feet between each two plats in order to be sure that the plants on one plat cannot feed on the other plats.

Do not lay out the plats on land that has been manured within one year. If you carried on fertilizer experiments last year, do not use the same set of plats again this season.

The following diagram [slightly modified from the original] shows the arrangement of the plats, with the spaces between. Each plat is one rod wide and eight rods long:

Plat 1—K.	15 lbs. Muriate Potash.
Plat 2—N.	20 lbs. Dried Blood.
Plat 3—P.	30 lbs. Acid Phosphate.
Plat 4—Blank.	No Fertilizer.
Plat 5—NK.	Mixed { 15 lbs. Muriate Potash. 20 lbs. Dried Blood.
Plat 6—PK.	Mixed { 15 lbs. Muriate Potash. 30 lbs. Acid Phosphate.
Plat 7—NP.	Mixed { 20 lbs. Dried Blood. 30 lbs. Acid Phosphate.
Plat 8—NPK.	Mixed { 20 lbs. Dried Blood. 15 lbs. Muriate Potash. 30 lbs. Acid Phosphate.
Plat 9—S.	Stable Manure.

Apply the fertilizers broadcast on the whole of each plat, being careful not to sow any fertilizer on the check or blank plat No. 4, and harrow into the soil as thoroughly as possible. Harrow the plats lengthwise, because particular care must be taken that none of the fertilizer for one plat is sown on or is dragged on another plat. In many cases muriate of potash injures the plant if applied just previous to putting in a crop ; so that the earlier this fertilizer is applied in the spring the less will be the danger of injury.

The blank or check plat No. 4, with no fertilizer, must not be omitted. This is the most important of any single plat, because all of the others must be compared with the blank in order to learn how much benefit the fertilizers have been to the crop.

You may grow any crop you wish on these plats. The same kind and same amount of seed is to be sown on each of the series of nine plats in the set. It must be remembered that these experiments are to be tried upon the crop planted and not upon an accidental crop of weeds. In no case will the experiments be of value if the weeds are allowed to grow on the plats. Thorough tillage is one of the most important features of the field test.

Following are some of the things to be noted in the study of the plats:

I. *Location of field.*
   - *a.* Upland.
   - *b.* Lowland. (If lowland, does the soil from the side-hills wash down upon it?)
   - *c.* Hillside, etc.

II. *Character of soil.*
   - *a.* Sandy.
   - *b.* Gravelly.
   - *c.* Clayey.
   - *d.* Loamy, etc.
   - *e.* How deep is surface soil?
   - *f.* Is there a hard-pan ; if so, how deep is it?
   - *g.* Does soil hold moisture, or dry out rapidly?

III. *Fertility of soil.*

a. Does the soil possess the required amount of plant-food, or does it "run down" quickly and need enriching?

b. Have manures or fertilizers been applied in past years? If so, how often, what kinds, and how much per acre?

IV. *History of crops previous to test.*

What crops have been grown, and with how much yield per acre, in past years? In case of cereals, consider the number of bushels of grain and tons of straw or stalks per acre.

Whilst the gardener must regulate his fertilizer practice by his own experiments and experience, he is not wholly dependent on his own resources. Scientific investigation and general agricultural experience indicate what will probably take place in a given case. The general advice, for example, is to apply a complete fertilizer,—that is, one containing nitrogen, potash and phosphoric acid in about the proportions which experience has found to be useful. This advice is particularly good when the person does not wish to experiment or to give the subject careful study. It is less useful, perhaps, when one does not wish to enrich the land as much as to give a stimulus to the young plant. It is generally considered that nitrogen promotes rapid vegetative growth. It therefore may be used most freely on plants which are desired for their foliage parts. If it promotes growth, it also delays maturity. Therefore it should be used sparingly, or only early in the season, on fruit-bearing plants which tend to mature too late, as tomatoes and eggplants. Experiments at Cornell showed that a little nitrate of soda is better than much for tomatoes; also, that a given quantity applied all at once early in the season is better than the same quantity applied at intervals, for in the latter case it promoted growth too late and the fruits did not ripen. For the person who has studied the subject and his soil, it is preferable to buy the elements in the form of high-grade chemicals and to apply each by itself. He can then apply little or much of any element to this place or to that, as he thinks best. Good commercial sources of nitrogen are nitrate of soda and sulfate of ammonia; of potash, muriate of potash and unleached wood ashes; of phosphoric acid, bone compounds and fossil phosphates (as South Carolina and Florida rocks). Of nitrate of soda, 150 to 300 pounds to the acre is a good application; of muriate of potash, from 200 to 400 pounds; of treated South Carolina rock, from 200 to 400 pounds.

Voorhees ("Fertilizers," p. 267) recommends the following "basic formula" for market-garden crops:

Nitrogen	4 per cent
Phosphoric acid	8 " "
Potash	10 " "

"For market-garden crops, a fertilizer of the above composition may be regarded as a basic mixture, which may be applied to all of the crops, leaving the specific needs of the different plants to be met by top-dressings, or applications of the other constituents. The fertilizer ingredients, nitrogen and phosphoric acid, should preferably consist of the different forms, rather than to be all of one form, though the cost of the element will naturally regulate this point to some extent. That is, a part of the nitrogen should be nitrate or ammonia, and a part organic; a part of the phosphoric acid should be soluble (from superphosphates), and a part insoluble (from ground bone, tankage or natural phosphates). The soluble portions of both nitrogen and phosphoric acid contribute to the immediate needs of the plant, and the less soluble to its continuous and steady growth, and to the potential fertility of the soil."

For asparagus, Voorhees recommends from 1,000 to 1,500 pounds per acre of fertilizer prepared on the above basic formula; for peas and beans, 500 to 600 pounds, to be supplemented, if needed, with 20 to 30 pounds phosphoric acid and 60 to 75 pounds potash; for beets and turnips, 1,000 to 1,500 pounds at time of seeding, followed by 50 to 100 pounds of nitrate of soda "once every week or ten days, for at least three or four weeks after the plants have well started." These details will illustrate the nature of the problem. The subject is taken up for the different crops in Part II.

Voorhees recommends that the market-gardener "apply a reasonable excess of all the essential fertilizer constituents to all of the crops." "Given good natural conditions in respect to soil, and a favorable season, the one thing that more than any other controls the yield and quality of market-garden products is plant-food of the right amount and kind." "In these days, it is not only the yield of a definite area that must be considered, but the edible quality of the products that are put upon the market. Quality depends upon, or is measured by, both appearance and palatability ; and palatability is determined by the succulence and sweetness of the vegetable or its freedom from bitterness, stringiness, and other undesirable characteristics which frequently exist, and which can be largely eliminated, provided the grower is thoroughly familiar with his business, assuming, of course, that varieties are the same in each case. It has been demonstrated that market-garden crops of the best quality are those which are grown under conditions which permit of a continuous and rapid development. Any delay in the growth of a radish or of lettuce is largely responsible for the sharp taste and pungent flavor of the former, and the bitterness and toughened fiber of the latter. The same principles hold true of early table beets and turnips. The beets become stringy and wiry in character, and are less palatable if during the period of normal growth there has been any delay. In a time during which there has been no progress the fibrous portion of the vegetable is toughened, and exists in too great proportion. In the case of the early turnip, if any delay in growth occurs, the quality is injured, and the peculiar, pleasant flavor, a characteristic of the perfect vegetable, is changed; it becomes unpleasant. The unfavorable conditions of growth seem to cause more or less reversion to the character of the original plant from which the improved type has been derived, mainly through selection and improved methods of cultivation."

CHAPTER IV

VEGETABLE-GARDENING TOOLS

RELATIVE to the price of land, labor is expensive in America. It must be economized. Tools and implements are a necessity.

There is a tool for every labor. Many of these tools are the products of necessity. Others satisfy the inventive fancy of the American. Foreign writers wonder at the variety of tools pictured in our rural books, but the number of tools which are in actual use far exceeds those which are described in books. To an important degree it is true that the successful American farmer is known by the number and variety of his tools. The man who has many useful implements emphasizes brain above brawn. He is tactful and resourceful. He means to be master of the situation. He is to accomplish the given result with the least expenditure of mere physical energy. He will do his work better and more expeditiously than the man who depends on his hands and his muscles. Good tools educate the man. Their use cultivates ingenuity. They teach him to think.

On the other hand, the man who is rich in agricultural implements has less intimate contact with his plants than the hand-worker has. The machine is between him and the plant. He depreciates the value of painstaking human care in the growing and the training of the plant.

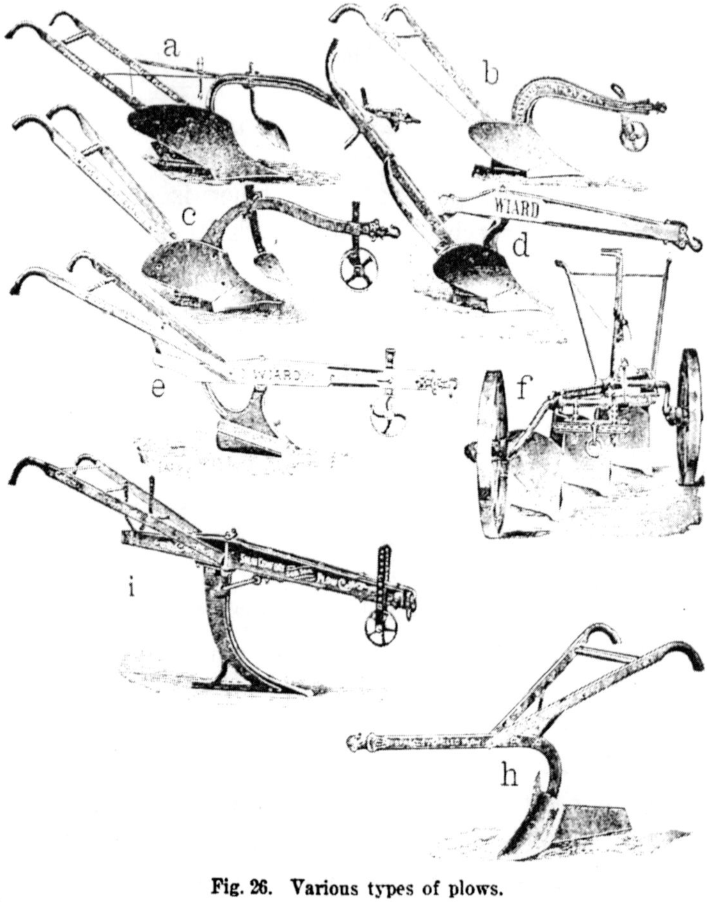

Fig. 26. Various types of plows.
f **is a gang-plow, turning three furrows at once;** ***h*** **is a winged shovel or furrowing or hilling plow;** ***e*** **and** ***i*** **are subsoil plows.**

In American conditions, however, a large equipment of tools is necessary to an abundant and cheap crop. The nicest judgment is required to make a proper

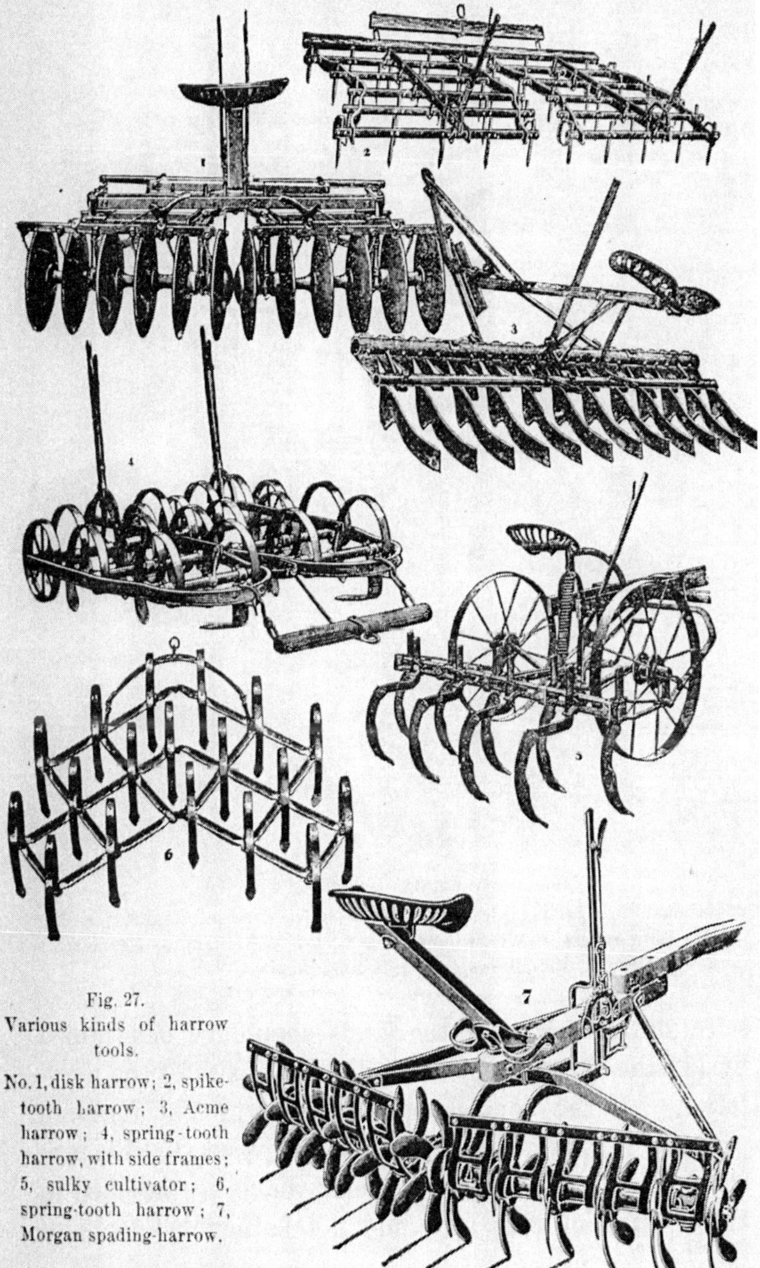

Fig. 27.
Various kinds of harrow tools.

No. 1, disk harrow; 2, spike-tooth harrow; 3, Acme harrow; 4, spring-tooth harrow, with side frames; 5, sulky cultivator; 6, spring-tooth harrow; 7, Morgan spading-harrow.

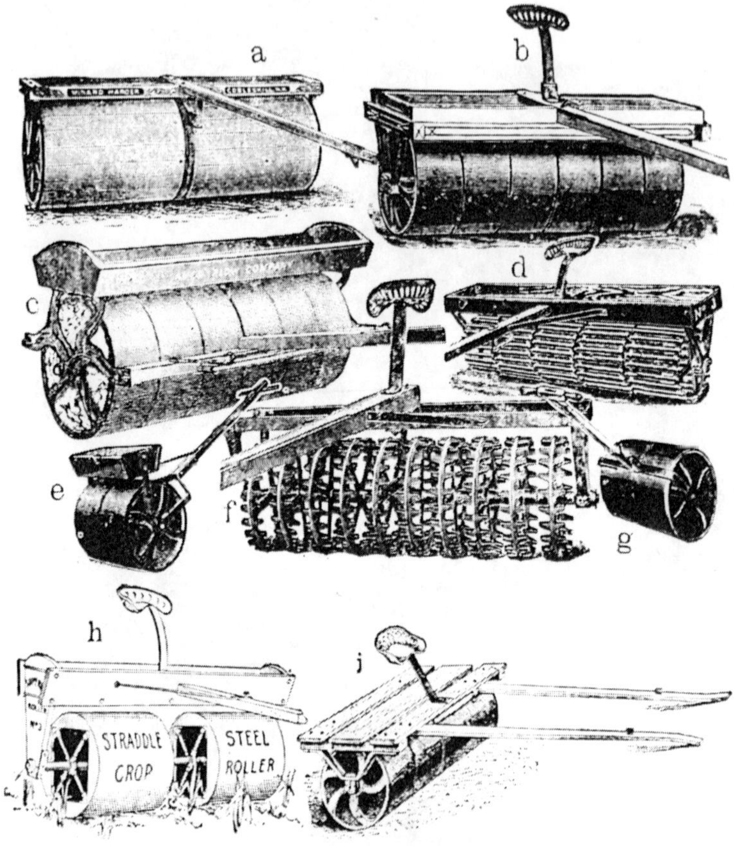

Fig. 28. Rollers.

a, National; *b*, *c*, sectional iron or steel rollers; *d*, Cyclone pulverizer; *e*, Wilder lawn roller; *f*, Wilder crusher and clod pulverizer; *g*, Henderson's lawn roller; *h*, Straddle-crop roller; *i*, 1-horse roller.

selection of tools; for the kinds should be determined by (1) the character of the soil, (2) the size of the plantation, (3) the comparative earliness of the required product, (4) the kinds of plants to be grown, (5) the personal ideals of the farmer. Tools which are adapted to the working of clay soils may not be adapted to sand.

There should be a tool for each diverse type of labor. An advantage of the variety in tools offered by American dealers is the fact that a tool may be selected for each particular purpose. Some farms are overstocked with tools. Too much capital is locked up in them. This fault is usually the result of duplication,—the various tools are too similar, they do not perform different kinds or types of labor.

It requires nearly as many tools to equip one acre of market-garden as to equip five

Fig. 29. Wheel-hoes for garden work.

acres. Consequently, it is relatively cheaper to till a fairly large area, so long as it can be tilled well.

Market-gardening tools may be roughly classified as follows:

I. *Tools for tillage.*

Tools to prepare the land for planting:
- Plows (Fig. 26),
- Harrows (Fig. 27),
- Cultivators,
- Rollers (Fig. 28),
- Hand-tools of various kinds, as spades, shovels, wheel-hoes (Figs. 29, 32).

Tools for subsequent use,—to maintain the condition of the land:
Cultivators,
Weeders (Fig. 30),
Hand-tools, as wheel-hoes, hoes, rakes, scarifiers, finger-weeders.

II. *Tools to facilitate hand-work.*
In distributing manure and fertilizer,
In marking the land,
In sowing (Fig. 37, Chap. V),
In planting,
In spraying (Chap. VI),
In harvesting,
In preparing the product for market or sale.

III. *Tools for transportation.*
Carts and barrows (Fig. 31),
Stone-boats and sledges,
Wagons.

For any market-garden which is large enough to be worked by horses, the following general-purpose tools, at the least, will be needed (see also the inventories on pp. 24–30):

1 2-horse plow,
1 1-horse plow,
1 furrowing or single shovel plow,
1 spading- or cutaway-harrow, if the land is heavy.
1 spring-tooth harrow,
1 roller or slicker,
1 smoothing harrow,

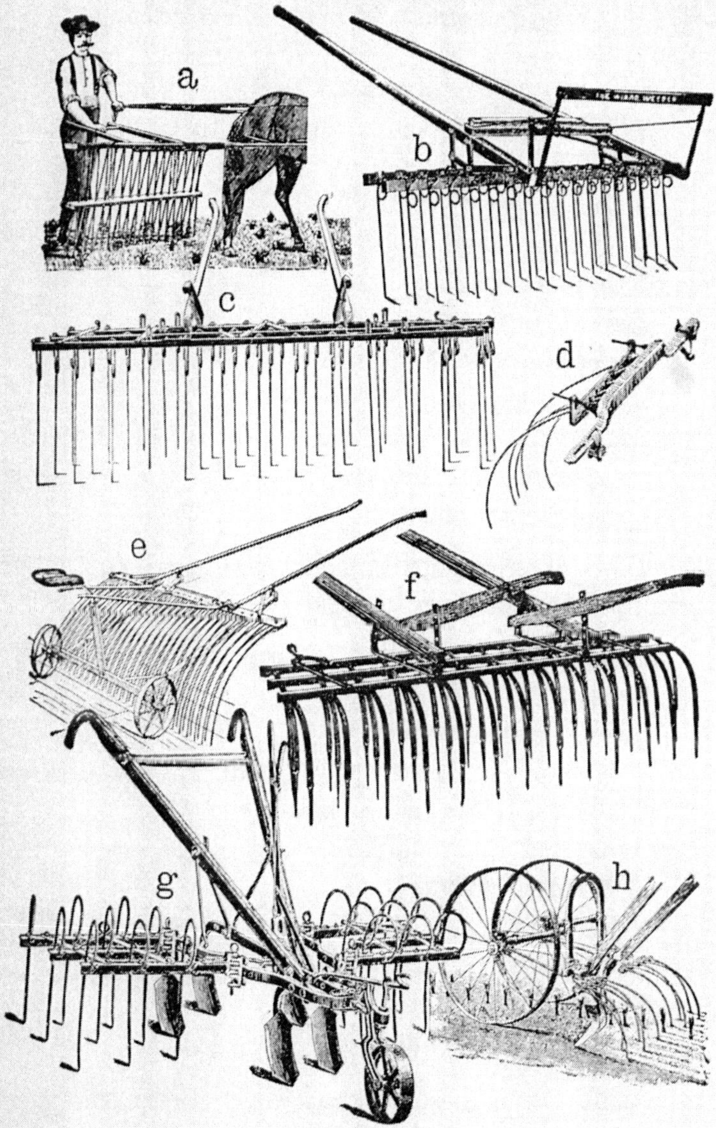

Fig. 30. Horse weeders.

a, Breed; *b*, Wiard; *c*, Eclipse; *d*, Fanning, for attachment to rear of cultivator; *e*, Aspinwall; *f*, Hallock's Success; *g*, Champion; *h*, Iron Age weeder attachment.

1 spike-tooth cultivator,
1 wide-tooth or shovel-blade cultivator,
1 marker,
1 seed-sower,
1 or more hand wheel-hoes,
1 or more wagons,
1 stone-boat,
1 wheelbarrow,
1 spraying outfit,
Spade, shovels, hoes, rakes, forks, hand-weeders, trowels and dibbers, hose, watering cans, carpenters' tools.

Tools of secondary importance, but which the well-equipped market-garden must possess, are:

Gang-plow, if the area is large,
Subsoil plow,
Swivel plow,
2 or more types of spading, cutaway, or disk harrows, if the land is heavy,
Acme and other harrows,
Wire-tooth weeder,
Various patterns of cultivators for special work,
Plant-setter,
Fertilizer distributor,
Trucks and wagons.

Aside from these various tools, there are special implements for special crops, as celery-hillers, asparagus-bunchers, potato-diggers, potato-sorters, and the like.

In selecting a tool, the buyer should know

Fig. 31. Various barrows, carts and trucks.
All of which are useful for the gardener. *f* is a good type of hand spray pump for small areas.

(*a*) what labor is to be performed, (*b*, what implement will best perform it. Many farmers buy a tool because it is perfect as a mechanism or merely because it is an improvement on what they already have. This is well; but it should be borne in mind, after all, that the tool is not the first consideration,—it is not the unit. The unit is the work to be done or the condition to be attained. A farmer may not ask, therefore, whether he shall buy a spading-harrow: he should consider his soil and what he wants to do with it, and then search for the tool which will do the work best.

The plow is the primary or fundamental farm implement. It is the general-purpose machine. Its office is to prepare the land, not to maintain it in condition. As a class, stiff and heavy soils require heavy plows and deep plowing. Sandy soils may be the better for shallow plowing, for it is often desirable to compact the subsoil rather than to loosen it. There are conditions and conditions.

Plowing has two general offices: (*a*) to break and pulverize the soil to fit it for the growth of the crop; (*b*) to begin the preparation of a seed-bed in which the plant may get a start. In the plowing of the sandy soils mentioned above, it may be the second office which is sought: only a good seed-bed is desired, for the land is loose enough without the plowing. In the clay field, both offices are sought. Not deep plowing nor shallow plowing is a principle: it is only a means of accomplishing a desired result. The unit is the condition which is to be secured in the particular soil.

The seed-bed is finished by the harrow. The soil is maintained in tilth by the harrow. The harrow, therefore, is an implement both for preparing and maintaining the soil condition. If the soil is light, loose or sandy, tillage presents few difficulties and relatively little expense. If it is clayey, tillage must be nicely managed for best results. Many people expend more time and muscle on clay lands than are required. The one important item is timeliness. When the soil is betwixt wet and dry, it breaks as it turns from the plow. Turn it up loose and open. Then let it lie for a few hours or a day. As the clods begin to dry, work roughly with a strong harrow, as a spading-harrow, spring-tooth, or Acme. Do not try to work it down fine. As the lumps begin to dry after the next rain, hit them with the boot. If they break and crumble, work the land again, this time with a lighter harrow. A few timely workings when the soil is just right will accomplish more than thrice the labor at other times. Many people make the mistake of tilling their clay lands until they become too fine. Then a rain packs and cements them, and the trouble begins all over again. Because sandy and loamy soils are best when fine and mealy, people think clays must be; but clay is not sand. The addition of humus enables one to make a clay soil mealy.

Gradually, as the texture improves, lighter tools may be used to maintain the surface mulch,—for the tillage of maintenance really has no other primary office than to keep the surface loose. When finally the wire-tooth weeder can be used, the gardener may know that his surface soil is in perfect physical condition. To most general farmers the weeder is a useless tool, but market-gardeners prize it,—which illustrates the differences in tillage between the common farm and the market-garden.

A one-horse harrow is usually known as a cultivator. But there are two types of cultivators,—those which only stir the soil and repair the surface mulch, as the spike-tooth cultivators; and those which move the soil or even invert it, as the shovel-tooth cultivators.

Fig. 32. The onion-bed condition of land. Tilling with the wheel-hoe.

Are not shovel-tooth cultivators too common and spike-tooth cultivators too rare?

In the market-garden, the wheel-hoe is important. It saves immensely of hand labor and usually leaves the soil in better condition than hand-work does. Have a number of patterns, large and small. Select a large wheel with a broad tire, that it may ride over lumps and travel on soft ground. Soil must be in good condition to be worked with wheel-hoes; therefore, they should be introduced for their educational effect. Aim at the onion-bed condition of tilth (Fig. 32).

A hand-hoe is a clumsy and inefficient tillage tool. Its one merit in this regard is the fact that it can be used between the plants, where many other tools cannot enter; but it leaves no efficient surface mulch and does not often improve soil-texture. The common hoe has two types of legitimate uses on the farm,—to aid in planting, to kill weeds. As a tillage-tool, the rake is far superior. Most persons use the hoe as they would a pick,—to chop the earth. Much hoeing usually wastes soil moisture.

Rollers have two uses: (*a*) to break clods and level the ground, (*b*) to provide moisture for seeds or newly set plants. They provide moisture by wasting it. Rolling the land establishes capillary connection with the under soil, and brings the particles into contact with the seeds. It destroys the surface mulch. The water rises and passes off into the air: in its passage, it moistens the seeds. As soon as the seedlings or transplanted plants are established, therefore, restore the surface mulch. The farmer pats his hill of corn with the hoe, thereby accomplishing the result which he secures on the wheat field with his roller. The gardener walks over his row of seeds.

If the roller is used only to break the clods, the land should be tilled again to restore the surface mulch. The roller is a poor tool in the hands of a thoughtless man. For the leveling of land, a home-made planker or slicker is a useful tool. A similar device may be attached to a cultivator frame (Fig. 33, Planet Jr. Leveler).

Fig. 33. Leveling device attached to a cultivator frame.

Spraying machinery has come to be a necessity. No one kind of pump or nozzle is best. A nozzle which throws a stream the farthest is the least useful when it is desired to apply the stream near at hand. That is, that machine is best which does the given work best; and there are many kinds of work to be done. The vegetable-gardener can use outfits running from the power of the vehicle wheels better than the orchardist can. Do not buy a sprinkler or a machine which allows the spray to fall by mere gravity. Have a pump. The liquid must be thrown with force. Use a nozzle with a small aperture, so that the material will be finely broken. A nozzle has carrying power and distributing power. As a rule, the farther it carries, the less finely it distributes the liquid. If possible, have the nozzle near its work: force the liquid through a hose rather than through the air. Have the nozzle on the end of the hose; and have the end of the hose where the bug is.

Secure a spraying outfit of large capacity. It is more efficient and more economical of labor. Be sure that the pump is strong, well made, brass-lined, and has much power. Clean it thoroughly inside before putting it away for winter. Get it out a month before it is wanted in spring; it will probably need tinkering. Year by year, spraying machinery is improving. Send to the manufacturers for catalogues. Read the papers and the bulletins.

In general, it is best to avoid combination tools which, by means of various attachments are designed to perform very unlike kinds of labor. They are likely to be less efficient than tools made directly for the given labor, and are also more liable to get out of repair. They are usually cheaper than separate tools, however, and some of them are very satisfactory.

CHAPTER V

SEEDS AND SEEDAGE

NEARLY all vegetable-gardening crops are grown directly from seeds. Therefore, the character of the seed is of vital importance to the vegetable-grower. The larger part of seed-tests and germination studies in this country are made with vegetable-gardening seeds. In fact, when seed-tests are mentioned, the vegetables or cereals are commonly the only plants which come to mind. It is important that careful attention be given to the character and quality of seeds for the vegetable-garden. The loss of a crop and of the season's labor is often the result of poor seeds.

Good seeds satisfy four general tests or demands: (1) they must be viable,* or able to grow; (2) they must be pure, or with no other kinds of seeds intermixed; (3) they must be true to name; (4) they must have the greatest possible longevity.

1. THE LONGEVITY OF SEEDS

The length of time a seed will live varies with (1) the species or variety; (2) the conditions under

*For general agricultural discussions, the word *viability* is usually preferable to *vitality*. A viable seed is one which is capable of growing; a vital seed is one which is alive, but it may not have sufficient vitality to be able to complete its germination.

which it was grown; (3) the degree of ripeness; (4) the manner in which it is stored and handled; (5) the condition as respects mechanical or insect injuries. There is a limit to the life of every seed, yet when this limit is reached there may be no evidence in the seed itself, either external or internal, to indicate the loss of vitality. The seed must be placed under circumstances most favorable to its germination, and its condition tested by its ability or inability to grow. In practice, the seeds of a given plant are tested in a greater or less quantity, the percentage of the quantity which germinates being adopted as the measure of germinative vitality. This results in a test of the species, variety, or the sample as a whole, rather than in a test of individual seeds. Hence it follows that the limit of viability in commercial tests does not represent the extreme age at which it is safe to plant, there being a constant failure of individual seeds from the first instance of loss of life until no one seed in the sample remains alive. It therefore becomes apparent that, as a rule, the fresher the seeds the better the results, independent of the figures representing extreme duration of vitality. Haberlandt shows that there is an increasing failure in seeds kept from year to year. In the tests 100 seeds were used in each case:

	1 yr. old	2 yrs.	3 yrs.	4 yrs.	6 yrs.
Wheat . . .	96 germinated.	84	60	73	4
Barley . . .	89 "	92	33	48	. .
Oats	96 "	80	32	72	48

The germinative power of seeds is sometimes tested by placing the seeds on live coals. Those which snap sharply are supposed to have been good. It is also tested by throwing the seeds into water, those which sink being regarded as viable. These practices are not to be recommended.

1. *The natural and normal limit of germinative vitality is usually a specific character, peculiar to the individual species.* Therefore no general law concerning the natural or normal limit of vitality can be enunciated. Species of very close botanical affinity often differ widely in this regard. In some instances, however, there are tolerably well-defined family traits, as, for example, in the Cucurbitaceæ (pumpkins, squashes, melons, cucumbers), of which most of the species possess a rather high longevity, and likewise in the Leguminosæ. Seeds of the Umbelliferæ, on the other hand (as parsnip, carrot, celery, parsley), have a relatively low vitality, and this trait is probably associated with the oily character of the seeds and fruits. This natural longevity is not correlated with the normal size of the seed. The minute seeds of tobacco, if perfect, grow well when seven or eight years old, but the large seeds of castor bean may fail in two years.

2. *The longevity or vitality of seeds is determined largely by the conditions under which they grew.* As a rule, the most vigorous development of plant produces the most perfect vitality of seed, although the product of such seed may not be the most satisfactory for the cultivator. Conversely, a poor season for the vegetation of any plant, or other untoward circumstance, by causing a weak plant, produces seeds of impaired vitality. Seedsmen are aware of this fact, and they

are often able to forecast the value of the seed-crop of certain plants by knowing the season and conditions under which it is grown. Seeds from poorly developed plants, if fully ripe, are seldom distinguishable by the eye from those grown under the best conditions. They often give a very high test soon after they have been harvested, but rapidly decline in value, and at planting season, the following spring, may be worthless. Consequently, tests made in autumn or early winter may be of little value to the cultivator.

What are known to the trade as "round seeds"—cabbage, turnip, radish, and the like—are very likely to be influenced in keeping qualities by the conditions which obtained during the year in which they were grown. Cabbage may germinate 70 to 80 per cent in its eighth year, and again it may fall below 40 per cent in the third year. The character of the resulting plants, as well as mere percentage of germination, may be affected. Therefore, to know the year in which the seed is grown is sometimes more important than merely to know its age. Gardeners demand fresh seeds: this is well, and yet old seeds may be better. The best seed merchants lay in an extra stock in the good years, and the discriminating buyer chooses this stock as long as it retains a fair percentage of germination.

A mechanical or other injury to the growing plant may produce the same effect on the seeds as an unpropitious season. For example, a certain fine crop of seed-cabbages was attacked late in the season by great numbers of plant-lice. The seeds produced were to appearances of good quality, and the first test gave a high percentage of germination. A test made a month later by two parties indicated a decrease of nearly 15 per cent in germination and subsequent tests indicated a constant lessening of viability. By spring the seeds were worthless.

As a rule, light-weight seeds give lower germinating percentages than heavy ones of the same variety, and the weight is often determined by the conditions of growth of the plant and its seeds. No doubt the position of the seed in the fruit has something to do with its germinative vitality, inasmuch as such position must sometimes influence its weight and other physical properties. This subject receives little definite attention, however, although the relation of the position of the seed with reference to character of its offspring, a subject with which we are not now concerned, suggests experiment. Seedsmen know that if seeds for testing are taken from the top of a bag which has been shipped in one continuous position, the percentages of germination will not often be as great as those obtained from seeds taken from the middle or bottom of the bag where the heavier seeds have settled.

A citation may be made (1st Rep. N. Y. Exp. Sta. 83) to indicate the extent to which an injury to the plant may influence the weight of seeds. One hundred seeds of each of three lots of ordinary White Globe onion seeds weighed respectively 5.91, 5.98 and 4.99 grains, or an average of 5.63 grains. One hundred grains of the same variety from a grafted plant weighed 3.97 grains, 100 from a ligatured plant weighed 4.05 grains, and 100 from a compressed stalk, 3.48 grains.

The position of the fruit on the plant or inflorescence may exercise some influence on germination. The following statement records percentages of germinations from kernels of corn and other cereals taken from the base, the middle and the tip of the ear or inflorescence, 100 kernels being tested in each case (Sturtevant, in 2d Rep. N. Y. Exp. Sta. 63):

	Base	Middle	Tip
Waushakum Flint Corn	80	72	95
White Rice Pop Corn	100	100	100
Red Rice Pop Corn	98	94	100
Minnesota Dent Corn	98	100	100
Early Dent Corn	82	24	33
Sibley's Pride of the North Corn	100	100	97
Wheat	99		100
Wheat	100	100	100
Oats	94	88	100
Oats	100	100	100
Sorghum	65	86	89

While the results of this trial are discordant, the explanations of the differences are easily suggested. It is probable that in those cases in which the germinations were higher from the tips, the kernels were not so fully matured as below, while the record states that "in the case of the dent corns, some were under-ripe and the germination imperfect," the tip kernels apparently not being ripe enough to grow. The experiment, therefore, appears to prove nothing concerning the germinating power of seeds from various parts of the inflorescence only as such position indicates comparative development and maturity. Another test made by the same experimenter in a field plot, upon Waushakum corn, gave the following results: "Of the 80 butt kernels, 56 kernels, or 70 per cent, germinated; of the 611 central kernels, 589 kernels, or 96 per cent, germinated; of the 80 tip kernels, 78 kernels, or 97.5 per cent, germinated. We may, however, conclude that in general on normal, well-selected ears, the tip and butt kernels are as likely to grow as are the central kernels." This experiment is at fault, from the fact that all the kernels of the ear were used, thereby largely obliterating any difference that might exist between the butt, the middle and tip kernels by introducing all the intermediate variations.

Abnormal seeds, being usually imperfectly formed or not fully developed, possess a low vitality as a rule. The "tassel corn" affords an illustration in point (Sturtevant):

Abnormal corn produced on the tassel

Variety	No. kernels planted	No. grew	Per cent grew
White Pop Corn	24	7	29.2
Waushakum Flint	84	19	22.6
" "	84	21	25
" "	55	16	29.1
" "	24	18	75
Blount's Prolific	24	11	45.8
" "	24	6	25

Imperfect fertilization is often the cause of low germinative vitality, or even of its absence. The seed may develop to the full size and ordinary appearance and yet entirely lack the embryo. Nägeli considers the following degrees of sterility of seeds due to imperfect fertilization: a small and imperfect fruit with empty seeds; ordinary fruit with empty seeds; ordinary or normal fruit and apparently good seeds but which have no embryo; ordinary fruit with seeds bearing a minute and imperfect embryo which cannot germinate. This absence or imperfection of the embryo is in some cases the cause of lightness of seeds, although lightness is, no doubt, oftener due to a deficiency in nutrient matter.

The color of the seed appears to exercise no influence on germination, although it is often the expression of some anatomical conformation of the seed-coats, of weight, or some other condition which may have to do with the germination of the seed. In some cases the color indicates improper handling and curing of the seeds. In itself, however, color is unimportant.

Numerous tests made with clover seeds of different colors by Beal, showed no differences in favor of one color over another. Sturtevant investigated the germinating power of light-colored and dark seeds, with the following results:

	Per cent of germination of light-colored seeds	Per cent of germination of dark-colored seeds	Weight of 100 light-colored seeds GRS.	Weight of 100 dark-colored seeds GRS.
Early Purple Cape Broccoli	79	92	4.08	4.93
Earliest Blood Red Erfurt Cabbage .	74	77	3.46	5.78
Netted Savoy Cabbage	83	98	4.23	5.09
Schweinfurt Largest White Cabbage .	96	98	3.46	5.78
Chou Mille Têtes Kale or Cabbage . .	91	100	5.86	7.40

While the results show decided advantage possessed by the dark seeds over the light-colored ones, the gains are undoubtedly due to the fuller development of the seeds rather than to their color merely, inasmuch as the dark-colored seeds are the heavier. As a light color is often indicative of less weight or less vigorous development, however, it may be looked upon, in many cases at least, as an evidence of inferior germinative vitality. The result with endive seeds, which gave figures of an opposite character, are not quoted, as the age of the seed is not designated, and as this plant usually gives anomalous results with fresh seeds.

The latitude and general climatic conditions under which seeds are grown appear to exercise an important influence on germination, although one which is commonly overlooked. Seeds grown in the North usually germinate more quickly and sometimes tend to make earlier plants than those grown in the South.*

3. *Seeds which are under-ripe tend to lose their vitality relatively early.* Seeds often may be made to germinate if gathered and dried when still very green, if only the embryo is well formed. Seeds of tomatoes which do not weigh more than two-thirds as much as fully ripe ones and which are still very green, may be made to grow when properly cured. Such seeds usually give earlier plants, although the plants are likely to be weaker; but the seeds do not long retain their viability.

Sagot (Gard. Chron. Sept., 1874, 329) succeeded in germinating green kernels of wheat which were still soft and tender, collected at a time when nutrient matters were semi-liquid. When well dried in air, these kernels weighed but half as much as ripe kernels. "All of them germinated, though slowly." Unripe peas, weighing one-half, one-fifth and even one-twelfth of ripe peas, were made to germinate by the same experimenter. The half-weight seeds germinated rapidly. Of the twelfth-weight seeds, many did not germinate, and some died soon after the commencement of their development. Half-weight seeds of beans and four-o'clock (*Mirabilis Jalapa*) also germinated.

Studies of unripe seeds as a factor in plant-breeding have been made in this country by Sturtevant, Arthur and Goff. For an epitome of the results, see Arthur in American Naturalist, 1895, pp. 806, 904.

4. *The manner of storing and handling determines the longevity of seeds to a great extent.* In fact, the most vigorous and naturally long-lived seeds may be

*See tests recorded in Bull. 7, Cornell Exp. Sta. For discussions of the philosophy of the subject, see Essay 17, in the author's "Survival of the Unlike."

spoiled in a short time by improper conditions of storing.

The failure of seeds from conditions of preservation is illustrated in a method employed by Sturtevant. The following table represents germinations of various varieties of corn, selected from a large series of experiments:

Age of seed	No. of trials	No. of seeds tried	Per cent germination
½ year	17	1,075	100
2 years	37	3,005	100
3 years	7	725	100
5 years	1	93	100

Under proper conditions, therefore, corn preserves its vitality perfectly for five years. The next table exhibits the germinations of the entire series from which the former examples were selected:

Age of seed	No. of trials	No. of seeds tried	Minimum germina'n, per cent	Maximum germina'n, per cent	Average germina'n, per cent
½ year	37	3,550	41	100	94
1 year	3	250	30	48	42
2 years	65	5,560	2	100	95
3 years	37	3,625	52	100	85
4 years	2	200	80	81	80
5 years	1	93	100	100	100

The differences between the minimum percentages and 100 per cent must be due to conditions of preservation. The average percentage of germination in each case represents an exact measure of loss. This loss amounts in the total average to 18.8 per cent.

5. *Mechanical and insect injuries usually lessen the germinative vitality of seeds.* The threshing process

often cracks seeds and thereby renders them almost valueless. Larbalétrier asserts* that the injury from the threshing machine in France, upon wheat, can always be reckoned at 15 per cent of the crop. He cut kernels with the pen-knife so as to represent the injury from the machine, and compared their germinative power with that of sound kernels, under three methods of treatment, with the following results:

Sound kernels	Cut kernels
68 per cent germinated	34 per cent germinated
74 " " "	3 " " "
99 " " "	38 " " "

Sturtevant mutilated in various ways the kernels of Waushakum Flint Corn and seeds of beans and planted them under the surface of soil:

	No. of kernels or seeds planted	No. grew
Corn, cut lengthwise to bisect germ	10	1
Corn, more or less of the albumen removed .	20	12
Corn, part of one edge removed	10	3
Corn, small portion of chit removed, the embryo not being injured	10	0
Bean, one cotyledon removed, germ uninjured .	20	13

These researches, although showing that mutilated seeds may grow, nevertheless prove that germination is feeble and that mechanically injured seeds are unreliable.

The germinative vitality of weevil-eaten or "buggy" peas is low, and the plants resulting from them are usually feeble. Beal gives† the following results with

*Le Cocq de Lautreppe, Country Gentleman, Nov. 10, 1887, 852

†Rep. Mich. Bd. Agr. 1879, 195.

the germination of "buggy" peas as contrasted with that of uninjured peas of the same variety:

Seeds	Where tested	No. of seeds planted	No. germinated
Early peas of moderate size, smooth, sound	Soaked in water	50	Nearly all
" " "buggy"	" "	50	1
" " sound	Greenhouse	25	25
" " "buggy"	"	25	4
" " sound	Soil in June	12	12
" " "buggy"	" "	25	3

These peas were tested in the spring from seeds grown the previous season. "The weevil-eaten seeds produced feeble plants." A year later the same lot of seeds was used for a second experiment. Five hundred of the weevil-eaten peas were divided into ten lots of fifty each and tested in a greenhouse. Alongside these the same number of sound peas were tested, all but four of which, or 99.2 per cent, germinated. The table gives the figures for the injured seeds:

First lot of 50	12 grew
Second lot of 50	10 "
Third lot of 50	8 "
Fourth lot of 50	12 "
Fifth lot of 50	17 "
Sixth lot of 50	11 "
Seventh lot of 50	12 "
Eighth lot of 50	18 "
Ninth lot of 50	17 "
Tenth lot of 50	13 "
	130, or 26 per cent

Trivial injury to the mere integument of the seed may hasten germination. Such injury allows of the absorption of water and the liberation of the germ. The practice of filing and notching of various hard seeds—as of cannas, moonflowers—illustrates this. The soaking and freezing of seeds have similar effects. Sturtevant (3d Rep. N. Y. Exp. Sta. 328) has experimented with mechanical injuries to the integuments. A lot of 160 Black Wax beans was divided into four lots of 40 each. Lot No. 1 was treated by slightly mutilating the seed-coat opposite the hilum. Lot No. 2 had the coat mutilated in same manner, but was afterwards greased with tallow to retard absorption of moisture. Those of Lot No. 3 were not injured. Those of Lot No. 4 were not injured but were greased with tallow. The most rapid germinations occurred in the first lot, and the next most rapid in the third lot. The slowest germinations occurred in the fourth and second lots, respectively, showing that an oily coat is a retardative of germination. Following are the figures:

Seeds	No. which had germinated in five days	No. which had germinated in seven days	No. which had germinated in eight days
Lot No. 1, mutilated	23	30	37
Lot No. 2, mutilated and greased	10	25	35
Lot No. 3, not mutilated	18	28	40
Lot No. 4, not mutilated and greased		4	29

Tables of longevity of seeds.—Perhaps the most extended and careful series of investigations yet inaugurated for the purpose of determining the vegetative duration of seeds is that undertaken by Messrs. H. E. Strickland, Daubeny, Henslow and Lindley, under the auspices of the British Association for the Advancement of Science. As many as 288 genera, in 71 orders, were subjected to test in three places, Oxford, Chiswick and Cambridge. A Seminarium was instituted at Oxford and placed in the charge of W. H. Baxter. Samples of seeds in sufficient quantity to furnish sets for testing at frequent intervals during a century or more were carefully stored. A summary of results is given in the reports for 1850, p. 160, and 1857, p. 43.

The standard figures of longevity are those contained in Vilmorin's "Vegetable Garden" ("Les Plantes Potageres"), which are easy of access, both in the original and in the "Horticulturist's Rule-Book."

The following figures are selected from a table prepared by Sturtevant, combining the tests made at the New York Experiment Station during three years. The tests were made at such widely separated intervals, upon such a number of seeds and so many varieties, that individual errors must be largely eliminated. Yet the percentages as recorded in the last column are unsatisfactory, and are proof of the assertion that any general statements of the limits of vitality are necessarily imperfect and relative. Since the report in which these results are published (4th Rep. N. Y. Exp. Sta. 58), may not be accessible to the reader, most of the figures are reprinted here:

	No. of trials	No. of varieties tested	Total No. of seeds tested	Age in years	Average per cent germinated
Artichoke (Cynara).	3	1	150	1	63
	1	1	20	2	80
	1	1	30	3	57
Asparagus	15	1	450	1	86
	3	2	150	2	65
	2	2	100	3	40
	1	1	50	9	0
Bean, *common* . .	17	13	680	0	92
	6	3	340	1	96
	6	2	240	2	69
	1	1	50	3	98
Beet	2	2	100	0	81
	22	7	1,500	1	74
	27	7	2,350	2	70
	4	2	400	3	38
	3	2	250	4	69
	1	1	50	5	88
	4	1	400	6	62

	No. of trials	No. of varieties tested	Total No. of seeds tested	Age in years	Average per cent germinated
Beet	1	1	50	7	34
	4	3	300	9	33
	2	1	200	10	14
	2	1	100	12	40
	2	1	200	13	27
	1	1	50	14	10
	4	2	400	15	18
Cabbage	8	4	800	0	91
	72	24	6,750	1	85
	70	21	5,200	2	75
	40	17	3,100	3	59
	4	3	400	4	69
	5	4	500	6	14
	6	2	600	7	9
	1	1	100	8	0
	4	3	400	10	14
	5	3	500	11	0.2
	2	2	200	16	0
	7	4	700	17	0.4
Carrot	2	2	150	0	48
	46	11	4,600	1	60
	20	9	200	2	35
	7	3	700	3	22
	3	2	300	4	7
Cauliflower	2	1	200	0	97
	44	12	4,400	1	86
	14	7	1,400	2	85
	15	10	1,500	3	62
	9	6	900	4	53
Celery	1	1	100	0	2
	11	5	1,100	1	46
	9	3	900	2	23
	1	1	100	3	0

	No. of trials	No. of varieties tested	Total No. of seeds tested	Age in years	Average per cent germinated
Cucumber	3	3	300	0	68
	23	9	1,122	1	85
	2	2	150	2	57
	4	3	108	3	95
	3	2	100	4	72
	2	1	50	5	60
	1	1	50	13	40
	1	1	50	19	14
Eggplant	8	4	700	1	50
	2	2	100	3	39
	1	1	50	4	46
	1	1	50	6	28
	2	1	200	9	15
Endive	4	1	400	1	20
	10	3	1,000	2	45
	6	3	600	3	38
	1	1	100	18	0
	2	1	200	19	0
Kale	2	1	200	0	97
	3	2	400	1	95
	2	2	200	2	93
	3	1	200	3	65
	1	1	50	4	16
	2	1	200	5	64
	2	1	100	7	58
Kohlrabi	2	1	200	0	88
	10	4	1,000	1	80
	3	2	200	2	76
	1	1	100	3	94
	4	3	400	4	51
	2	2	100	5	44
	2	1	200	17	0
	2	1	200	20	0

	No. of trials	No. of varieties tested	Total No. of seeds tested	Age in years	Average per cent germinated
Leek	14	4	1,400	1	57
	4	2	400	4	15
	4	2	400	7	5
Lettuce	45	20	4,500	0	80
	22	12	2,200	1	83
	37	17	3,694	2	78
	24	13	2,400	3	82
	17	9	1,700	4	64
	7	3	700	5	48
	8	3	800	6	36
	1	1	100	9	0
Melon, *Musk*	8	3	429	0	86
	26	10	1,120	1	88
	6	4	362	2	92
	4	1	200	3	77
	32	7	1,492	4	79
	2	2	200	6	90
	5	2	300	7	90
	4	2	200	8	92
	1	1	50	9	36
	1	1	46	10	85
	2	1	100	14	49
Melon, *Water*	39	10	968	1	58
	19	11	611	2	65
	11	4	377	3	60
	1	1	25	4	80
	1	1	25	6	80
	1	1	100	8	2
	2	1	100	9	20
	4	1	150	11	8
	4	1	150	12	10
Okra	2	1	100	1	92
	1	1	50	2	90

	No. of trials	No. of varieties tested	Total No. of seeds tested	Age in years	Average per cent germinated
Onion	12	5	1,200	0	77
	196	20	15,619	1	80
	93	20	9,200	2	56
	21	12	2,000	3	31
	7	3	650	4	5
	1	1	100	7	0
Parsley	18	6	1,800	1	57
	3	6	300	2	50
	4	1	400	3	8
	5	4	500	4	10
Parsnip	2	2	200	0	13
	7	5	650	1	28
	6	3	386	3	9
	1	1	50	4	0
	2	1	90	6	0
Pea	16	9	812	0	98
	2	1	200	1	86
	66	26	3,588	2	84
Pepper	9	9	893	0	93
	16	6	1,600	1	65
	14	7	1,150	2	58
	11	8	647	3	41
	2	1	200	4	62
	6	3	600	5	19
	1	1	50	6	4
	2	2	150	8	3
	4	2	350	9	10
	5	3	500	10	0.6
	2	1	200	13	0.5
Radish	2	2	200	0	71
	100	34	8,350	1	71
	36	17	2,500	2	57
	16	8	1,250	3	49

	No. of trials	No. of varieties tested	Total No. of seeds tested	Age in years	Average per cent germinated
Radish	6	6	350	4	54
	4	3	350	5	37
	2	1	200	6	12
	1	1	100	7	3
	2	1	200	8	14
	2	1	200	12	0
Salsify	1	1	100	0	93
	4	1	400	1	91
	4	1	150	2	73
	4	1	400	3	20
Squash	4	2	150	0	96
	20	8	542	1	73
	16	9	595	2	76
	12	8	417	3	72
	2	1	100	4	63
	1	1	30	6	10
	3	2	67	10	6
	1	1	50	14	0
Tomato	8	7	800	0	89
	19	10	1,400	1	85
	30	13	2,050	2	89
	15	10	1,400	3	89
	9	6	900	4	83
	5	2	500	5	71
	2	2	200	6	96
	5	4	400	7	74
	12	7	950	8	76
	5	3	500	9	83
	11	11	600	10	75
	2	2	150	11	63
	4	2	400	12	86
	3	2	300	13	44
	4	3	300	14	74

	No. of trials	No. of varieties tested	Total No. of seeds tested	Age in years	Average per cent germinated
Turnip	6	3	600	0	95
	77	8	4,100	1	87
	50	19	3,400	2	95
	28	12	1,900	3	94
	30	11	2,150	4	79
	6	5	600	5	67
	3	3	300	6	58
	11	6	1,000	7	56
	2	1	200	8	65
	2	2	100	12	49

2. PRESERVATION OF SEEDS

We have seen (p. 130) that the manner of storing and handling seeds has much to do with their viability. Seeds which are to be stored should be guarded against the concurrence of the chief agents which incite germination: moisture and warmth. There should also be protections from insects. Except in the case of seeds which need to be stratified, moisture is the most frequent agent of destruction of germinative vitality. All common garden, field and flower seeds should be thoroughly "cured" or "seasoned" before they are stored, by placing them in a dry and airy room.

The importance of curing is illustrated by the following tests (W. S. Devol, Rep. Ohio Exp. Sta., 1886, 236): "One kernel was taken from midway between the tips and butts of each of one hundred ears of corn that had been spread upon a floor until well dried, then stored in boxes. When tested in May, every kernel (100 per cent) germinated. A sample was taken in a similar manner at the same time, from another hundred ears of the same variety, but which had been kept in the crib in the ordinary way. When tested in May, only 77 per cent germinated." Samples were taken in like manner at another time from fifty ears which were gathered in October and properly cured. Tested in March, 100 per cent germinated. Fifty ears of the same variety, which stood in the shock until February, were selected, and kernels taken. Tested in March, only 72 per cent germinated. The same investigator made the following test: A lot of twenty-five ears of corn was selected from the bin in the middle of December, and one kernel taken from the middle of each ear and tested; 96 per cent germinated. The ears were then buried in loam, in a warm aspect. January 8 a kernel was taken from each ear and tested; 78 per cent germinated. January 21, 42 per cent germinated. March 16 and April 13, none germinated. In 317 tests, made by the same experimenter, the average percentage of germination of corn cured "by artificial heat, by hanging the ears by husks or other means, so as to admit of thorough drying, or by ricking the ears or spreading them thinly over the floor," was 87, while of corn from ordinary bins and cribs, but 69.8 per cent germinated.

The temperature which healthy seeds can endure depends very largely on the amount of moisture which they contain. Moist seeds cannot resist as high or as low temperatures as dry ones can. For this reason seed corn and many other seeds are likely to be poor after a hard winter. Dry turnip seeds may resist a temperature of 90° to 100° for five or six years. If seeds are laid on ice for a considerable length of time they usually become weak or worthless, because of the low temperature coupled with the absorption of moisture. If perfectly dry the same seeds probably would have resisted lower temperatures.

Under ordinary conditions, the vegetable-gardener will secure best results by storing his seeds in strong paper or cloth bags in a cool and dry room. Fairly tight boxes are also useful. Peas, beans and corn should be inspected frequently for injury by weevil. If the seeds are attacked, pour bisulfide of carbon into the box or bag and close it tight. The fumes will kill the pests. If the quantity of seeds is large, the bisulfide should be placed in an open dish on top of the seeds, for the fumes are heavier than air and will settle. In samples of two or three quarts or less, however, this precaution is not necessary. A teaspoonful of the liquid to one or two quarts of seeds is ample. It will not injure the seeds if it strikes them. Bisulfide of carbon is inflammable, and should not be used near a flame.

3. TESTING OF SEEDS

Seed tests are of three leading kinds: (1) tests to determine the purity of the sample as respects dirt and foreign species; (2) to determine whether the variety is true to name or kind; (3) to determine viability.

Tests to determine the content of the sample may be of more importance than those made to ascertain germinative power, yet, in practice, they are comparatively infrequent and valueless. These tests should consider two problems, (*a*) the determination of any admixture of foreign matter, as sand, stones, sticks, chaff, etc., and of seeds of other species of plants; (*b*) the determination of the purity of the sample as concerns its trueness to name and its peculiarities attained through heredity and environment. Necessarily, the latter tests are more difficult of determination, as they must be made from the product of the plants, often requiring special and expert training on the part of the investigator. They have apparently not received the attention they deserve, largely from the prevalent opinion that such matters lie beyond the control or check afforded by the tests of impartial investigators, an opinion no doubt strengthened by the so-called contract printed on seed-packets to the effect that the seller assumes no responsibility for the contents of the packet. The seed dealer certainly cannot be held responsible for failures which may be fairly associated with conditions of weather, soil or method of sowing; but the warranty clause could not shield him if he were to be negligent or remiss, or if he failed to exercise reasonable caution in the care and selection of his stock.

Testing samples to determine the foreign matter or the presence of seeds of other species is performed by carefully examining small lots of seeds under a lens. The operator should have at hand for comparison reliable samples of the seeds of weeds and other plants likely to occur in any samples.*

Tests for purity of the sample have been carefully made in Germany, extending over many years, especially at the famous "seed control" station at Tharandt, in Saxony, organized under the direction of Nobbe. This station, founded in 1869, was the first of its kind. The percentages of foreign matter found in samples, by Nobbe, vary from nothing to over 80 per cent. The

*Samples of weed seeds, put up in bottles which are mounted in a serviceable case, have been prepared by Dr. B. D. Halsted, Rutgers College, New Brunswick, New Jersey.

average percentage of foreign matters in grass seeds was 41, in the aggregate of many tests. Of the 59 per cent which was true to name only 18.3 per cent possessed germinative vitality. The adulteration of seeds in many European countries has been carried to such an extent in times past as almost to challenge belief. Seeds of various weeds, which closely resemble the seeds offered for sale, were often freely introduced, and the whole, or the adulteration, was then cooked to destroy the life of the seeds, that the growth of the plants might not expose the seller. Seeds of cabbage or cauliflower may be adulterated with mustard seed, and the whole boiled or baked. Old and worthless seeds are often scoured, rubbed, oiled or dyed to make them appear bright and healthy. It has been estimated that 20,000 bushels of old and inferior turnip seeds have been used in London in one year for purposes of adulteration. In parts of Europe it is said that a medick (*Medicago lupulina*) is grown in quantities for the adulteration of clover seed. Some years since there existed in Hamburg a factory which made counterfeit clover seed from quartz, using this material to the amount of 25 per cent or more of the total bulk of the seed sold. Nobbe found enough weed seeds in a certain sample of timothy seed to supply, if sown at the ordinary rate, twenty-four weeds to every square foot of land. Such wholesale and intentional adulteration has not been observed in this country. Grass seeds, however, have been found to be of very low quality in many cases, particularly those kinds not extensively used. Much of this is undoubtedly imported. Beal writes:* "One of the best firms in New York sent me some seeds of grass which were rotten or had been cooked. At another time the firm was about to buy what was called Bermuda grass. The material consisted of the chaff or hulls of Bermuda grass, every one of which proved to be empty or only in flower. Not one good seed was found. Results almost as remarkable were obtained in examining seeds of meadow foxtail, which were purchased of a reliable firm. The same, in one case, was true of Kentucky blue-grass, creeping bent-grass, sheep's fescue, wood meadow-grass, rough-stalked meadow-grass and reed canary-grass."

---

*Rep. Mich. Bd. Agr. 1880, 51.

In vegetable-garden seeds there need be little fear that many weeds will be introduced. Such seeds are sold in small quantities and they are most carefully cleaned. Adulterations are apparent. There is so much competition in the seed business that it rarely pays to take the risk of sending out dirty or adulterated seeds. Even if weeds were to be introduced, the thinning and tillage of a vegetable-garden would eradicate them. The greatest risk in the buying of seeds is the chance that they may not be true to name or that, if true to name, the particular strain may not be the best. If a dealer sells seeds which are true to the variety, he has satisfied the requirements of the law and perhaps of trade; but his seeds may still be inferior to his neighbor's. There are differences within varieties which may make all the difference between profit and loss. If the grower wants to be very sure of his product, it is not enough that he buy seeds of Winnigstadt cabbage: he should know what kind of Winnigstadt he is buying. There is no way of testing the seed except to raise the crop. One must, therefore, rely on his seedsman. This he can do with safety if he selects a reliable seedsman and if he is willing to pay a fair price for his seeds. The cheapest seeds may be the dearest.

The testing of seeds for viability, or for the ability to grow, is preferably made in the soil under uniform conditions. The best place for the test is in a greenhouse, but the living-room of a dwelling house may answer very well. Use a "flat" (Fig. 45) or other shallow box or earthenware pan (Fig. 34). As a rule, the best results are to be attained by planting in the soil in conditions as nearly as possible approaching the normal requirements of the particular species or variety. A light, loose loam with a good admixture of sand is the best soil for this purpose. A good method is to place two or three inches of loam in a flat, wetting it as thoroughly as possible without puddling it; then cover the soil with an inch or less of

Fig. 34. The testing of seeds in earthenware pans, known to gardeners as lily-pans.

sterilized (baked) sand, in which to sow the seeds. The loam keeps the sand supplied with moisture.

The inexperienced operator will usually apply too much water for the best results in germination. Gardeners are well aware that very conflicting results may be secured from the same lot of seed by different degrees of watering. The same remark applies to variations in temperature. Celery, for example, gives very poor tests in widely fluctuating temperatures; it is also injured by being kept at a uniformly high temperature, whereas melons and beans give the best tests in a high temperature.

The seeds should be sown carefully at uniform

depths and at equal distances apart. In order to gauge the depth, nail a cleat of the required thickness on a thin block (Fig. 35) and press this cleat or tongue into the soil to its full extent: the furrow will then be of uniform depth. The seedlings should be allowed to remain until large enough to show whether they are likely to make strong or weak plants. Not every seed that germinates is worth the planting. The following figures show that even with beans, which are strong-germinating seeds, a considerable percentage of the seedlings may be so weak as to be valueless:

Fig. 35. Planting stick for gauging the depth of planting.

Figures on eight samples of beans, germinated in soil in a greenhouse, in thirteen days after planting

Number of sample	Seeds that produced strong plants PER CENT	Seeds that sprouted, but did not produce strong plants PER CENT	Total percentage of germination
1	84	4	88
2	92	4	96
3	84	0	84
4	84	4	88
5	52	16	68
6	52	4	56
7	68	0	68
8	76	16	92

If one desires to know what percentage of any sample of seeds still retains life, he should resort to a sprouting test. This test is made in an apparatus in which all agencies are under perfect control, and the seeds are counted and discarded as soon as they have sprouted. There are various patterns of germinating apparatus. An incubator may be made to answer the requirements. Samples of seeds which give the highest sprouting tests are not necessarily the most reliable, for it is probable that the percentage of vegetation, or subsequent growth, does not always bear a direct ratio to percentage of latent vitality.

Germination is not completed until the young plant is able to support itself by its own root-hold on the ground. A seed may be able to sprout, and yet be so weak as to be worthless for planting in the soil. A seed which may even germinate in the soil in a greenhouse may still be so weak that if the plantlet were subject to the untoward conditions of the garden, it might perish. It is apparent, therefore, that any sample of seed may give very different percentages of germination, depending on the method of making test. If the test were made in a machine which, like the incubator, has a very uniform temperature, and the seeds were counted and thrown away as soon as sprouts appeared, the percentage of germination would probably be very high. If the same seeds were sown in carefully prepared soil in a gardener's flat and placed in the greenhouse, the probability is that a somewhat lower percentage would be found. If the seeds were planted in an ordinary greenhouse bed, and were to receive the ordinary watering which growing plants receive, a still smaller percentage of germination might appear. If the same seeds were planted in the open ground, the percentages would likely be still smaller.

What, now, is the fair germination test for seeds? It is apparent that the seedsman or seed-tester cannot imitate the varying conditions of a garden. He does not know what kind of a garden the buyer has; therefore, he must give all the seeds a uniform condition, and one which will show how many seeds will sprout under the most favorable conditions. What he must do is to show the greatest possibility of the sample, not what the sample may necessarily be expected to do under general garden conditions. Buyers often express disappointment that their seeds do not produce as many plants as the germination tests led them to expect. The difficulty was, no doubt, that the germination test was made under the most ideal conditions, whereas the planting was made under normal outdoor conditions. It would seem that if one desires to know what any batch of seed is capable of doing, he should make a test for himself, choosing fifty or one hundred seeds from the sample, and planting them early enough to determine the germinative vitality before it is necessary to make the regular planting. The germination tests which are made by laboratory methods are of the greatest value in showing the vitality, vigor and the possibilities of any sample of seed and in the accumulation of scientific data, but people should understand that these tests are no guarantee of what the seed will produce under actual and varying conditions. The standard set by the laboratory sprouting test is too high for actual practical conditions, and therefore is likely to mislead.

The following figures, compiled from tests made at the Pennsylvania State College (Rep. Penn. State College, 1886, 162), indicate the differences between mere sprouting and germination. The percentages of germination given in the first column were obtained from sprouting tests, while those in the second column, from the same samples of seeds, were obtained from plantings made in a hotbed. Although these figures appear to lessen the value of sprouting tests, it is nevertheless true that, in general, a high sprouting test indicates a high vegetative power; but the vegetative power is often or usually less than the sprouting power.

Plant	Per cent sprouting	Per cent of full germination in the hotbed
Early Winnigstadt Cabbage	87	73
Early Flat Dutch Cabbage	95	72
Marblehead Mammoth Cabbage	96	72
Extra Early Erfurt Cauliflower	40	30
Henderson's New Rose Celery	9	31
New York Improved Eggplant	24	12
Green-Fringed Lettuce	99	52
Yellow-seeded Butter Lettuce	99	70
Early Curled Simpson Lettuce	99	83
Early Boston Curled Lettuce	90	90
Early White Turnip Radish	72	72
Wood's Early Frame Radish	92	84
White-tipped Scarlet Radish	98	71
Livingston's Favorite Tomato	91	32
Livingston's Perfection Tomato	83	71
Cardinal Tomato	98	85
" "	88	74

The following contrasts of seeds, germinated in soil in a greenhouse and planted in good garden soil in the open, are from Cornell Bulletin No. 7. The duplicate tests were made from contents of the same seed-packet. The seeds sown in the open had every chance. Rain fell every alternate day. The soil was loose and loamy and well drained.

SAMPLES	No. of germ. in house	Per cent of germ. in house	No. of germ. in field (200 seeds sown)	Per cent of germ. in field	Per cent of difference
Endive, Green Curled, Thorburn (200 seeds).	88	44	53	26.5	17.5
Tomato, Green Gage, Thorburn (100 seeds)..	72	72	93	46.5	25.5
Turnip, Ea. Six Weeks, Dept. of Agriculture (200 seeds)	180	90	65	32.5	57.5
Pea, White Garden Marrowfat, Thorburn (60 seeds)	55	91.6	181	90.5	1.1
Celery, White Plume, Thorburn (100 seeds) .	41	41	22	11	30
Onion, Red Wethersfield, Thorburn (200 seeds.	148	74	84	42	32
Carrot, Early Forcing, Thorburn (100 seeds).	70	70	39	19.5	50 5
Carrot, Vermont Butter, Hoskins (100 seeds).	65	65	45	22.5	42.5

The average experience of careful seed-growers, seed-merchants, gardeners and experimenters should give us, in time, a set of figures representing what may be called the normal percentage of germination. These figures must be the averages of years. In some years all seeds are much better than in others. In many cases the percentages of germination are much increased by cleaning the sample, thereby eliminating the weak and light seeds. Varieties of the same species differ in germinating qualities. As a rule, the higher bred the stock, the lower is the average viability.

The following table is compiled from the actual experience of one of the largest American seed-houses. It represents what may be expected to be "good" and "fair" percentages of germination of first-class fresh, commercial seeds, one year with another. In the case of beet and sea-kale, fruits, not seeds, are sown, and each fruit contains one or more seeds: therefore the figures are above 100 per cent.

	Good	Fair
Artichoke	80	80
Asparagus	84	80
Bean	95	90
Bean, Lima	90	90
Beet	135	120 to 150 (according to variety)
Beet, Mangels and Sugar	180	200
Brussels Sprouts	90	90
Cabbage	90	90
Carrot	70	70
Cauliflower and Broccoli	90	87
Celeriac	76	75
Celery	78	75
Chicory	70	70
Collards	95	90
Corn, Pop	90	85
Corn, Sweet	86	85
Cucumber	85	85
Dandelion	65	60 to 70
Eggplant	56	50 to 60
Endive	71	70
Kale or Borecole	94	90
Kohlrabi	90	90
Leek	86	85
Lettuce	93	90
Martynia	68	60 to 70
Muskmelon	86	85
Mustard	90	90
Okra or Gumbo	76	75
Onion	85	85
Parsley	76	75
Parsnip	71	70 seeds
Pea	96	90
Pepper	66	60
Pumpkin	85	85
Radish	88	85
Rape	92	90

	Good	Fair
Rhubarb	80	80
Salsify	83	80
Sea-Kale	200	200
Spinach	79	75
Squash	80	80
Tomato	86	80
Turnip, Flat	94	90
Turnip, Rutabaga	96	90
Watermelon	81	80

	Good		Good
Barley	93	Rye	95
Broom Corn	92	Sunflower	94
Buckwheat	94	Timothy	96
Clover	90	Tobacco	78
Corn	92	Vetches	96
Grass Seeds	70	Wheat	95

Since variable results are obtained under any treatment and from the same parcel of seeds, it follows that some check must be employed in order to reach reliable results. Two kinds of checks are open to the investigator: (1) the selection of a representative sample, and (2) duplicate trials. The greater the number of seeds used in any test and the greater the number of tests, the more reliable are the results.

In choosing a sample, the contents of the whole package should be thoroughly mixed, particularly if the package has been shipped and the heavier seeds have settled. The seeds for trial should then be drawn from various parts of the package, or from its center if the package is small, and the various lots mixed and the sample for testing taken from the mixture.

4. THE SOWING OF SEEDS

Congenial temperature and a continuous supply of moisture are the two requisites of germination which the gardener has to supply. He supplies these agents by placing the seeds in some loose, moist, granular medium, as a mealy and friable soil. If this soil lies on other soil, the moisture is drawn up by capillary attraction and as it passes off into the air it moistens the seeds and promotes germination. If the soil is very loose, open or lumpy, the capillary attraction is broken and the moisture does not rise to the seeds. Or, if it does rise, the seeds are not in intimate contact with the particles of soil and do not receive much of the soil moisture; moreover, the air which is held in the large interstices tends to dry out the seed. To a large extent, a continuous and uniform supply of moisture is a regulator of temperature. It is therefore apparent why a finely divided and compact soil is the proper medium in which to sow seeds.

Whenever the soil is likely to become drier rather than moister, as it is at the germinating season, it is important to firm the earth over the seeds. In large field operations, as in the sowing of the cereal grains, the roller is ordinarily used. Under market-gardening conditions, the soil is usually compacted by a roller which is a part of the seed drill and which follows just behind the delivery spout When seeds are sown from the hand, the soil is compacted with a hoe or by walking over the row. Since this compacting of the surface establishes capillary connection with the under soil, thereby drawing up the water and passing it into the atmosphere, it is important that this condition be allowed to remain only until the seeds have germinated and are able to shift for themselves. The seeds are kept moist at the expense of soil moisture. Therefore, as soon as possible restore the surface mulch by a rake or a smoothing harrow. Seeds which are planted very deep, as peas, may have the soil compacted about them, and the surface layer may be loosened immediately thereafter, thereby preventing, to some extent, the escape of the soil moisture. The space between the rows should be kept well tilled, even before the seeds germinate, thereby saving the moisture in that area. In other words, rolling or compacting the soil over seeds is only a temporary expedient to enable them to germinate and to secure their own foothold; thereafter the surface mulch should be maintained in order to save soil moisture.

Seeds which germinate very slowly, as parsnips and celery, should be sown thick in order that the combined forces of the germinating plantlets may break the crust on the soil. This caution is always necessary on soils which tend to bake, whatever the kind of seed. It is well to sow a few strong and quick-germinating seeds with those of slow-germinating species in order to break the soil, and also to mark the row so that tillage may be begun before the main-crop seeds are up and before the weeds have taken possession of the land. Seeds of radish, cabbage or turnip may be sown in the row with celery, parsnips, carrots and the like. In some cases, a crop of radish may be obtained in this way before the main crop occupies the land, but this is only an accidental gain.

The cost of seed is ordinarily a trifling matter in comparison with the expense of the season's labor and the value of the crop. Therefore, seeds should be sown very freely in order to avoid the risk of failure. Even if five or ten times more seeds are sown than plants are required, the extra expenditure may be justified by the lessening of the risk. Another great value of thick seeding is that it allows of more extensive thinning of the plants; and thinning is a process of selection, and the best are allowed to remain. It is evident that the chances of securing the best are greater when the gardener leaves one plant out of ten rather than one plant out of three. The selection in the seed-bed or the seed-row is one of the means by which cultivated plants have been so greatly ameliorated or improved.

Nearly all the recommendations of writers as to the amount of seed for a given length of row are in excess of the number of plants actually required. It may be that some of these recommendations are higher than even the risks will warrant; but, as a general rule, it may be assumed that it is much safer to sow even the most excessive amounts than to sow just as many seeds as there are plants needed.

The following tests were made by the writer in 1888 (Bull. 40, Mich. Exp. Sta.). It will be seen that in some cases the recommendations seem to be extravagant; but in the common run of soils and conditions, and with variable seeds and seasons, they may not be excessive after all.

Quantity of Seed Required for Given Lengths of Drill.—Careful records of the quantity of seed used in those vegetables ordinarily sown in drills show that the quantity required is often much less than that recommended by seedsmen. The following figures indicate the extent to which this is true, the quantities recommended being taken from Henderson's new "Gardening for Profit:"

Peas.—One quart to 100 feet of drill recommended; 850 feet of drill used four quarts of McLean's Advancer, or one quart to every 212½ feet; 850 feet of American Wonder required three and one-half quarts, or one quart to about 245 feet of drill; 850 feet of McLean's Little Gem used three quarts, or one quart for every 283⅓ feet; 850 feet of Rural New-Yorker used three and one-fourth quarts, or one quart for over 261 feet of drill; 850 feet of Cleveland's Alaska required three quarts, or one quart for 283⅓ feet. The following figures will show that our sowings were thick enough: one pint of McLean's Advancer contains 1,600 seeds. A pint sowed a trifle over 106 feet of drill, giving something over fifteen peas for every foot of drill, or a plant every four-fifths of an inch.

Radishes.—One ounce for 100 feet of drill recommended; 1,000 feet of drill, sown thickly to Early Long Scarlet Short-top, required nine and one-half ounces of seed. In this case the recommendation is not extravagant.

Beets.—One ounce to 50 feet of drill recommended. Long Dark Blood, Eclipse and Bassano each required four ounces of seed for 334 feet of drill, or an ounce for 83½ feet, and the sowing was much too thick. An ounce of Long Dark Blood beet contains about 1,300 fruits or seed, or over fifteen and one-half fruits to each foot of drill, as we sowed them.

Parsnip.—One ounce to 200 feet of drill is recommended; 1,000 feet of drill of Hollow Crown took four ounces of seed, or an ounce to 250 feet of drill. The sowing was made in very hard ground, where a thick growth of seedlings is necessary in order to break the crust. The sowing was over twice too thick.

Carrot.—One ounce for 150 feet of drill recommended; 566 feet in hard ground used one and one-half ounces of seed, or an ounce for over 377 feet of drill, and even then the stand was much thicker than desirable.

Salsify.—One ounce is recommended for 70 feet of drill; seven and one-half ounces were used in 558 feet, or an ounce for about 74½ feet of drill. In this case the estimates were correct.

In order to determine what seeds fluctuate most in price between different dealers, a comparison was made (in 1899) of the catalogues of ten leading American seedsmen, with the following results:

Vegetables fluctuating most in price

Beans, wax,	Celery,
Beans, bush Lima,	Corn,
Beans. green pod,	Eggplant,
Beans, pole Lima,	Peas,
Broccoli,	Pepper,
Cabbage,	Tomato.
Cauliflower,	

Vegetables fluctuating least in price

Asparagus,	Parsnip,
Beet,	Parsley,
Brussels sprout,	Pumpkin,
Carrot,	Radish,
Cucumber,	Rhubarb,
Lettuce,	Salsify,
Leek,	Swiss chard beet,
Muskmelon,	Spinach,
Watermelon,	Squash,
Onion,	Turnip.

Seeds ordinarily germinate better in freshly turned or freshly worked soil than that in which has lain for some time. This is because there is more moisture in the fresh soil than in that which has been exposed to the weather. We shall find in the following chapter that gardeners expect to secure better success in transplanting when they can set plants on freshly plowed land.

If seeds are sown in land which has received heavy applications of concentrated fertilizer, care should be taken that the fertilizer does not come into direct contact with the seeds, particularly if nitrate of soda and muriate of potash are used. Ordinary quantities of these materials sown broadcast are harmless. Caution should be exercised when sowing fertilizer in the drill with seeds: germination is often hindered. For a discussion of this subject, see Hicks' "Germination of Seeds as Affected by Certain Chemical Fertilizers." Bull. 24, Div. of Botany, U. S. Dept. of Agric. (1900).

Roberts* has experimented on the influence of manure-water on the vitality of weed seeds in manure "by pumping and distributing over the entire mass, the water leached through the manure and caught in a cistern, and repeating the operation about once a week during the summer. Not a single weed seed germinated in the several samples of manure so treated, although placed under the most favorable conditions."

The depth at which seeds should be sown depends (1) on the soil, as to whether it is moist or dry, well tilled or poorly tilled; (2) on the species and size of the seed, and (3) on the season. The finer and moister the soil, the shallower the seeds may be sown. The larger the seeds, the deeper they may be sown. Seeds may be sown shallower in spring than in summer, for at the latter season the surface soil is dry. An old gardener's rule is to cover the seeds to a depth

*Annual Rep. President Cornell Univ. 1886-7, 73.

equal to twice their diameter. This applies well to greenhouse conditions, in which the soil is very finely prepared and kept continuously moist; but in the open ground, the seeds are usually planted deeper than this.

Horticultural plants are ordinarily divided into three classes in respect to their hardiness: (1) hardy, or those able to withstand the vicissitudes of climate in a given place; (2) half-hardy, or able to withstand some frosts or other uncongenial conditions; (3) tender, or wholly unable to withstand frost. Seeds of the hardy plants may be sown in the spring as early as the land can be made fit, or even in the fall. Examples of such seeds are sweet pea, onion, leek. In the northern states, however, very few seeds are sown in the fall; but the land is often prepared in the fall, and the seeds are sown as soon as the soil is dry enough in the spring. The seeds of half-hardy plants, as beets and lettuce, may be sown two or three weeks before settled weather is expected to come— that is, when it is still expected that there will be hard frosts. Tender seeds, as beans, tomatoes, egg-plants, cucumbers, melons, are sown only after the last frost has occurred and when the ground is thoroughly settled and warm.

Of plants which are normally transplanted, it is better to start the seeds in a seed-bed. These beds may be in the forcing-house, hotbed or coldframe; or, if it is not desired to force the plants beyond the normal season, it may be made in the open. There are three chief advantages in sowing seeds in a seed-bed, rather than where the plants are to grow: (1) It insures better germination, since the conditions are more uniform and congenial; (2) it saves time and labor; (3) it enables the gardener to guard against insects, fungi and accidents, since plants which are in a compact body can be sprayed, fumigated or otherwise treated to advantage. In forcing-houses and frames, it is now a common practice to start seeds in flats or boxes (see page 62 and Fig. 12).

The seed-bed should be a small area on land which is in the best of tilth. It should be near the buildings and the water supply. If the season is hot and dry, it may be well to shade the bed until the seedlings appear. The best shading ordinarily is a lath screen (Fig. 36) laid on a frame which stands two to three feet above the soil. Such a screen gives a partial shade and also allows of a free circulation of air; and the screens may be removed and the bed weeded at any time. A covering of brush is sometimes used, but it is less handy than the lath screen. If it is laid directly on beds, as is sometimes the case, the bed cannot be weeded and it is likely to become foul. Sometimes boards, matting or other dense covers are laid directly on the soil. This may do very well for a few days, until the

Fig. 36. Lath screen.
The spaces and laths are equal in width.

seeds have begun to break the ground, but thereafter this covering should be removed, else the young seedlings will be injured. The seedlings should always be given sufficient head room and light and air to enable them to develop to their normal condition. If the seed-bed is kept too wet and the seedlings are too soft, the damping-off fungi are likely to work havoc. Sometimes the seed-bed is made underneath a tree, but this is rarely advisable, since the earth usually requires too much watering and the shade may be too dense.

If it is desired to secure a quick germination of seeds in a summer seed-bed, it is well to prepare the bed the fall before, or at least very early in the spring, and to keep it covered with several inches or a foot of well-rotted manure until needed. When the bed is needed, the manure is removed; the soil is then full of moisture and the seeds germinate quickly. The fertility which has leached from the manure also enables the plantlets to secure an early foothold. This method is practiced in some of the market-gardening centers, particularly those in which late cabbages and cauliflower are grown.

When sowing seeds in the open field, the use of a seed-drill should be encouraged (see Fig. 37), not only because it saves time and labor, but also because it enforces good preparation of the land. A drill cannot be worked in soil which is hard, dense and lumpy. Seed-drills, wheel-hoes and smoothing harrows make better gardeners. If a seed-drill is not used, the seed-furrows for ordinary use may be made by drawing the

Fig. 37. Types of seed-drills and planters.

a, Model or Iron Age; *b*, Planet Jr. hill and drill seeder; *c*, Planet Jr. drill seeder; *d*, Planet Jr. fertilizer drill, and pea and bean seeder; *e*, Billings; *f*, one-row corn-planter; *g*, Henderson corn and fertilizer drill; *h*, Spangler corn-planter, with fertilizer attachment; *i*, True's potato-planter; *j*, Gem.

end of a hoe handle or rake handle forcibly through the soil. A garden line should be used to keep the rows straight. Land which is planted to potatoes, or to other deep-planted crops, should ordinarily be tilled once or twice with a smoothing harrow before the plants are up. This maintains the surface mulch, saves the moisture, and prevents the weeds from growing.

When sowing in the open, wait until the ground and the season are ready. Rarely is anything gained by sowing before this time. The seeds rot, or the seedlings are weak. The soil must be fitted after the plants are up. Have every thing ready, then make the plants grow.*

5. THE GROWING OF SEEDS

"It is certainly a reflection upon a farmer to have his seeds to buy." "It is shameful for gardeners and farmers to be buying seeds that their own soil and climate will produce, after being once furnished."

The above sentences were written by Washington to the foreman of his estate at Mount Vernon in the years 1794 and 1795. Within a century, times have changed. The growing of seeds has come to be a business by itself, requiring expert knowledge of soils and climate, and of methods of handling every kind of crop. The demand for seeds is very large. Competition is great. The quality constantly improves. Plant-breeding has come to be an important factor.

*For advice on seed sowing for greenhouses and general garden conditions, see Chap. 1 of "The Nursery-Book."

Under the present-day conditions, it is only the exception that a man can afford to grow his own seeds. With the development of intensive market-gardening interests, seed-buyers are becoming more cautions and discriminating; and probably one-fourth of all vegetable-garden seeds are now sold to persons who grow the product for market.

It is costly business to grow good seeds. It requires experience and the exercise of a man's undivided attention. No longer is it sufficient merely that seeds are sown and that the crop is harvested. The seed-grower must have an ideal and must work to it. His plantations must be "rogued." That is, all those plants which do not meet the breeder's ideal are pulled up and discarded, and the true or typical stock is left to produce the seed. The truer and higher the man's ideal, the better his stock should be. It requires years of experience to enable one to make for himself a true and practicable ideal of any variety of plant. He must know what the market wants. He must know what his customers want. He must know what will be good and useful under the greatest number of conditions. He must know what will be likely to be most stable and invariable. The ideal once apprehended, the seed-breeder must thereafter discard every plant which does not closely approach it; his stock must be uniform (Fig. 38). As soon as the "roguing" or selection is neglected, or when new ideals are introduced, the varietal characteristics tend to disappear or to change.

Experience has demonstrated that certain soils and

climates produce the best seeds of certain species. No longer are all kinds of seeds grown indiscriminately in one place. The price of labor is an important factor

Fig. 38. The seed-breeders' ideal.

A pile of Osage Orange muskmelons from which seeds have been saved, showing the uniformity in the stock.

also. Seeds which require much care and trouble in the growing are raised, if possible, where labor is most abundant and cheapest. It is no accident that radish seeds are grown in France, and Lima beans in California.

Only when a man is making a specialty of some vegetable, and lives in the place in which the seeds can be produced most advantageously, can he afford to grow his own seeds; and even then it is a question whether it would not be better and cheaper for him to delegate the business. The man who desires to secure the very best results in the growing of some specialty should know where his seeds are grown, particularly if his business success depends on the crop in question. He should not buy his seed indiscriminately in the general market. There are particular strains of all leading varieties of vegetables which are better for certain markets and conditions. These strains are likely to be most useful in the geographical area in which they are bred. Seeds of these strains are often sold as "market-gardeners' private stock." Under general conditions and in other geographical regions, these private stocks may be of no advantage, but in special places and for particular purposes they may make all the difference between success and failure; and yet the differences in the resulting crop might be of such a character that they could not be definitely described in a seed catalogue or in an experiment station bulletin. When a man is making a specialty of any crop, one of the first things to be done is to exercise the greatest care in the purchase of his seeds and to be willing to pay an extra price for a strain which will satisfy his own conditions. In the old time it was considered to be sufficient if one saved his seeds; in the present time the mere saving is of little avail: he must breed his seeds.

The gardener should buy his seeds in bulk, if possible, particularly if he is growing large areas and for a critical market. He can then demand the best. He will also secure the seeds at a cheaper rate. He should buy his seeds early. It may even be well to engage them of the seed dealer a season in advance, to be sure that he has the kind and quantity which he desires. Since seeds are poor in some seasons, it is well for him to keep at least a partial stock on hand from year to year, particularly of those kinds which retain their vitality for several years. He is then relatively independent. The gardener who grows largely for a special market of such important crops as beet, carrot, cabbage, cauliflower, cucumber, melon, lettuce, radish and tomato, will do well to purchase double the quantity of seed which he requires for the one season, in order that he may preserve stock of the strains which prove to be particularly desirable. The capital which is thus locked up in seeds is small, as compared with the risk of being unable to secure a desirable strain. Buy direct of a reliable seed dealer and not from the grocery stores.

Special care should be exercised in the selection of seeds of celery, onion, cauliflower, cabbage and squashes, for these are likely to deteriorate or to lose their varietal characteristics under poor culture and indifferent selection. Particularly is this advice imperative in the case of cauliflower. There are few areas in which good cauliflower seed can be grown, and great skill is necessary to grow it well. A sample which sells for a dollar an ounce may be much dearer than one which sells for four or five times that amount. Very cheap seeds should awaken suspicion.

More and more are vegetable seeds grown in America. Below are given the regions and countries in which the larger part of the best seeds which are sold in North America are now grown:

Asparagus—New Jersey, New York and Michigan.
Bean, bush—New York, Michigan and Canada.
Bean, Lima—New Jersey and California.
Beet—California, New York and France.
Brussels sprouts—Long Island (New York), and France.
Cabbage—Connecticut, Long Island, Germany and France.
Carrot—California, Connecticut and France.
Cauliflower—Holland and Denmark. The Danish grown is by far the best and the most expensive.
Celery—California and France.
Corn, sweet—Connecticut, New York, Michigan, Ohio and Nebraska.
Cucumber—New York and Nebraska, and also Michigan.
Eggplant—New Jersey.
Kale—Connecticut and Long Island.
Kohlrabi—France and Germany.
Lettuce—California.
Muskmelon—New Jersey and Nebraska, and also Michigan.
Onion—Connecticut, New York, Michigan and California.
Parsley—England and France.
Parsnip—Connecticut and France.
Pea—New York, Michigan, Wisconsin and Ontario, (Canada).
Pepper—New Jersey and France.
Pumpkin and Squash—Principally Nebraska.
Radish—Principally France.
Spinach—Holland and France.
Tomato—New Jersey and Michigan, and also Iowa.
Turnip—Connecticut, New York and France.
Watermelon—Georgia and Nebraska.

The yields of seeds (in lbs.) which may be expected from an acre, under good conditions, are given below:

	When crop is as near maximum as 20 bus. of wheat would be, or average of *good crop*	A maximum crop corresponding to 50 bushels wheat	Yield seedsmen would figure on in making contracts for large quantities
Bean	600	1,500	500
Cabbage	250 (two years)	800	200
Cucumber	150	700	100
Muskmelon	125	600	100
Pea	900	2,500	800
Squash, Winter	100	400	100
Squash, Summer	100	700	100
Sweet corn	1,000 to 2,500 (according to var.)	2,500 to 4,000	800 to 2,000
Tomato	100	400	100
Watermelon	150	1,000	100

NOTE.—There is no American work devoted to seeds and seed-growing. Brill's "Farm-Gardening and Seed-Growing" (Orange Judd Co.) contains brief "suggestions to seed-growers." Because of the scanty literature, the foregoing chapter has been made more extended than the nature of the book otherwise would have allowed. The standard work on seeds is in German, Nobbe's "Die Samenkunde." The seed-breeder will need the information contained in Jäger's "Erziehung der Pflanzen aus Samen."

CHAPTER VI

SUBSEQUENT MANAGEMENT OF THE VEGETABLE-GARDEN

TILLAGE is the most important item in the subsequent care of the vegetable-garden. If the land has been well fitted before the crop is put on it, subsequent tillage need be employed only for the purpose of maintaining the surface mulch in order that moisture may be saved and chemical and vital activities promoted. This tillage may be light, rapid and easy. This light tillage will keep down the weeds. Most farmers, however, are obliged to fit their land throughout the season, because it was not thoroughly prepared in the beginning.

How frequently one shall till must be determined by season, soil, crop, and amount of help. As soon as the soil becomes "baked" or encrusted, loosen it, in order to prevent the loss of moisture. As soon as the ground is fit after a rain, till it. If the soil becomes very hard and dry, it is well to till it just before a rain, that it may better hold the rainfall. Till shallow. If you are skeptical as to the value of tillage to save moisture, try an experiment. Till one part of the field thoroughly and neglect another part. The differences naturally will be most marked in a dry season.

In the cool and ambitious days of spring, put the effort and the muscle into the land: work it into condition. In the long and hot days of summer, merely keep it in condition.

1. IRRIGATION

In many parts of the country, the crop is determined by the amount of rainfall rather than by the plant-food in the soil. In many cases, the crop requires more water than is supplied by the normal rainfall of the growing season. Tillage can save much of the water which fell in the early rains and the winter snows, but there may still be insufficient moisture for a good crop. Irrigation may be necessary to supply the deficiency.

In the arid parts of the country, irrigation is a necessity. It is a general practice. In the humid parts of the country—east of the plains—irrigation is often helpful and it reduces the risk of a poor crop. It is an exceptional or special practice.

Evidently, in all regions in which crops will yield abundantly without irrigation, as in the East, the main reliance is to be placed on good tillage. Irrigation is an economic question. If, by irrigation, one can produce enough better crop to more than pay the cost, the practice is to be advised. Too often the farmer thinks of irrigation as he thinks of fertilizer—as a means of giving him crops when he does not work for them. As a matter of fact, however, it is only the well-tilled and well-handled lands that pay for either irrigating or fertilizing. The intenser the cropping, the more the capital invested, the better the market, the more likely is irrigation to pay. Ordinary crops will not pay the cost and risk of irrigation in the East. The feasibility of it will depend, also, on the lay of the land, the availability of water, the price and supply of labor, the character of the given climate.

Most vegetable-gardeners in the East do not find it profitable to irrigate. Now and then a man who has push and the ability to handle a fine crop to advantage, finds it a very profitable undertaking. It is all a local and special problem in the humid climates. If one contemplates putting in an irrigating plant, he should visit a garden in which one is in operation, if possible. He should buy a special book on the subject.

In general garden operations, the water is applied on the surface, in the furrows between the rows. The main conduits—which may be ordinary wrought-iron water pipes—are carried along the highest land. At intervals, hose-bibs are provided, so that a rubber hose can be attached and the water conveyed into the furrows. When box sluices are provided, there may be openings or water-gates opposite the furrows. If iron pipes are used, faucets must be provided at the lowest point of the run and in the sags for the purpose of emptying the pipe of water in the fall. The water supply must be ample, for when irrigation is most needed, the air is dry and hot and evaporation is rapid. The aim should be to convey the water in narrow streams or furrows close to the plants, rather than to cover the entire space between the rows.

The following notes on irrigation for the market-garden are by Frederic Cranefield ("The Market Garden," April, 1896). The experiences are drawn from experiments made at the Wisconsin Experiment Station. For full information on subjects connected with irrigation, consult King's "Irrigation and Drainage." The book discusses garden irrigation.

"It has been proved that irrigation may also be profitable even during seasons of normal rainfall. It is seldom we get a sufficient amount of rain at the time when it is most needed. Rain falls alike on the just and the unjust, and does not discriminate between gardener A, who desires a heavy shower for late cabbage just set, and gardener B, who would like to have dry weather for a few days. Rainy summers are not unmixed blessings, for they are usually cool and cloudy ones as well. The bright, continuous sunshiny days of Colorado and California, with the mineral-laden waters of the mountain streams, produce crops that cannot be equaled in the East or South. The small fruit grower is even more dependent upon an abundant water supply at the right season than the gardener. Abundant rains during April will not insure a full crop of strawberries in June. Moisture, and lots of it, is needed just at fruiting time. One acre of corn, abundantly watered just at the time the ears are setting, would yield as much as five acres not watered.

"Not every farmer, fruit-grower or gardener, may irrigate profitably. On the other hand, millions of barrels of water run to waste every summer, which at slight expense could be directed to the adjoining parched fields. The enormous outflow of dozens, if not hundreds, of artesian wells in the Dakotas was allowed to find its way to some underground lake or river for years before even the slightest effort was made to utilize it. In almost every section of our country innumerable inches of rainfall glide by our fields in brooks unchecked, that could be used for irrigation purposes at trifling expense.

"The first point to be considered is, naturally, the water supply. If that is abundant and reasonably accessible, other obstacles may be overcome. The ground level is of less importance. The profits to be derived from the work depend mainly upon the height to which the water must be lifted and the distance carried before it is applied. The question that is most often asked of those who are possessed of information on this subject, is: 'Can I depend upon a well and wind-power for irrigation?' The answer is ever the same. 'It all depends upon the well.' Professor Taft, of Michigan Agricultural College, has demonstrated that in some cases, at least, it is practicable. In 'American Gardening,' Vol. 49, pages 148–9, he describes wind-pumps that have been successfully used for irrigation purposes.

"The gardener considering irrigation should first look about for a stream of water so situated with reference to his land that it may be conducted thither and distributed by gravity. Even if a considerable distance away, arrangements might be made with the owner of the water-right and neighbors to coöperate in the construction of ditches, etc. Such locations, it is true, are rare. The next best location is in close proximity to a lake or pond, from which water may be lifted by steam or other power. The most expensive, but still often practicable means to obtain a water supply, is by lifting from a well or wells. If wind power is used in any case a storage tank is almost a necessity,—not only that the wind is quite sure to fail when most needed, but if more than an acre is to be watered a more abundant supply of water is needed than an ordinary well can supply. One important point in the distribution of water is to have a sufficient supply to cover the ground as quickly as possible.

"At the Wisconsin Station irrigated fields are adjacent to and several feet above Lake Mendota. The rude plat here given (Fig. 39) shows the plats irrigated in the horticultural department. Other fields on the farm were irrigated, but only the garden part is considered here. The letter *p* in the diagram denotes the location of a rotary pump connected with the water of the lake by a suction pipe. The pump was operated by a threshing engine. The double lines denote the cast-iron pipe used to convey the water to the fields. The heavier lines are 6-inch pipes, the others 4-inch. At each point marked *v* is a valve and riser. The water was delivered from the risers into distributing troughs. These are an important part of the outfit. They are V troughs, made of rough lumber, 12 feet long. For the larger troughs a 12-inch and a 10-inch board are used and nailed together at right angles, and cleats nailed across the top every 4 feet. As the water decreases in its onward flow smaller troughs may be used, made of an 8- and a 10-inch board. The end of one trough sets inside that of the next, and is supported

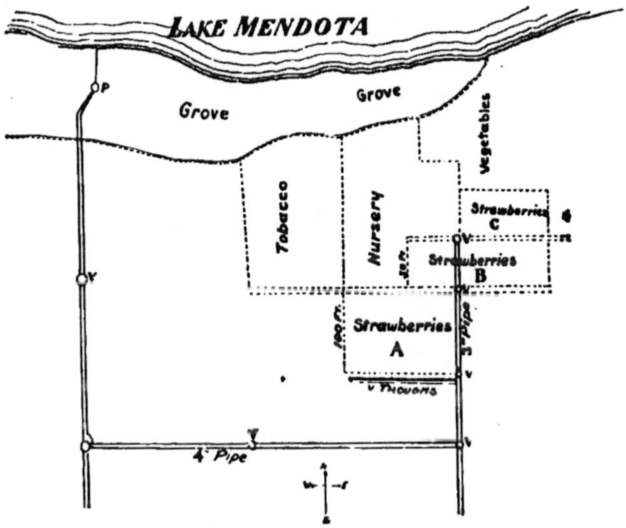

Fig. 39. Method of distributing water.

by stakes driven slanting into the ground and across each other. An iron pin placed in auger holes, bored in the stakes, serves to fasten them together. A cross-tie should be placed across the bottom to prevent the stakes from settling as the ground becomes wet. The water flows from the trough through auger holes on one side, over each of which is attached a device for regulating the flow of water. It is made of galvanized iron and consists of two pieces. There is a hole in one piece corresponding in size to the auger hole in the trough. A slide is held in place by the side edges of the first piece, which are bent over,

By the aid of these slides the flow of water may be regulated at will. If a row is receiving too much water the gate may be partially closed. Before the water is turned on, the ground between the rows should be thoroughly cultivated and small furrows run out on both sides of the rows, plowing away from the row. A hand garden plow is used, and only a very slight furrow plowed. The plan is to run small streams of water alongside the rows for several hours until the ground about the roots of the plants is thoroughly soaked. By this means the ground is all thoroughly wet and *not puddled*. Persons without experience in distributing water, are inclined in the beginning to spread the water over the whole surface of the ground between the rows. This is not the best plan. The whole surface will bake and the soil will be puddled to the depth of several inches by the attendants walking over it in distributing the water. By the plan given above it is possible for the attendants to walk on dry ground at all times."

In a more recent article (Amer. Florist, Sept. 9, 1899) Cranefield makes the following suggestion for the modification of the board trough: "Bore one-inch augur holes every few inches in one side and near the bottom. Directly above each hole attach a wooden button, slightly over an inch wide and three or four inches long, by means of a screw; this to be used as a gate or valve to control the supply of water. Place these troughs across the head of the field on a slight incline and admit the water at the upper end. By aid of these one man can attend to the watering of a very large field."

He continues: "Irrigated fields should be given thorough shallow cultivation as soon as possible, to form a mulch and conserve the water. By reference to the plat (Fig. 39) it will be noticed that two plats of strawberries were irrigated in addition to other grounds. The ground slopes gently towards the lake. By placing a row of troughs across the south and higher end of the south plat, water was carried alongside of the rows running north and south and the surplus water was run across the alley to the lower plat and the nursery. After the troughs were set up one man with a hoe was usually able to attend to all the work.

The south plat is one-half acre in extent. Eight to ten hours pumping was necessary to thoroughly wet the ground. The pump has a capacity of 55 gallons per minute, at 100 revolutions. The water was delivered through a $2\frac{1}{2}$-inch pipe, under pressure. Only those who have had experience can realize what an immense quantity of water is necessary to soak even one-half an acre.

"Not only is it necessary to have an adequate water supply, but it must be rapidly delivered, both for economy of labor and in order to do the work well. Attempts have been made to water garden plats by using a garden hose, allowing the water to spread over the ground. As a result, the ground becomes soaked and mortar-like to a depth of two or three feet for a short distance from the end next the water supply and the water does not move forward. In case the rows were of any considerable length, it would require several days for the water to reach the farther end. If water were delivered at the rate of 75 or 100 gallons per minute, a much larger area could be wet to a depth of several inches in a few hours. The slope of the ground is a matter to be considered before irrigation work is taken up. It probably would not be possible to irrigate a very steep hillside by this method, although by planting with reference to watering, fields with considerable slope may be irrigated.

"If a field slopes from north to south, with a slight incline to east or west, plant east and west and run the water across. The question is often asked: 'How can I irrigate a perfectly level field?' Such fields are very rare. Although a field may appear perfectly flat, if water were turned on it would generally be found that slope enough existed to carry the water across the field. Thorough preparation of the ground is necessary before the crops are planted. It is necessary to make the surface as nearly level as possible. It is the small dips, ravines, 'dead' furrows and hollows that need looking after. Shave off the surface of adjoining elevations to fill these, so that when the water is turned on, it will have a fair chance to do its work.

"The season of 1895 was one of the driest in the history of Wisconsin. From May 1 to October 1 the rainfall at Madison was 7.43 inches. The rows of strawberries in plat B, as indicated in the diagram, are fifty feet in length. This plat, except sixteen rows at the extreme right end, was irrigated three times in 1894, after the crop was harvested. During 1895 the plat, with the exception of the sixteen rows, was irrigated May 25, June 10 and June 22. The crop harvested from the three series is as follows:

"Twelve rows Warfield, four rows Wilson, well irrigated throughout 1894 and 1895, yielded 561.3 boxes.

"Twelve rows Warfield, four rows Wilson, well irrigated throughout 1894 but not in 1895, yielded 111.6 boxes.

"Twelve rows Warfield, four rows Wilson, never irrigated, yielded 66.2 boxes.

"Sixty rows of Fottler's Drumhead cabbage and forty rows of Henderson's Early Snowball cauliflower were planted June 22 in plats of twenty rows. The rows were 4 rods long. The ground was very dry at the time of setting, so a very shallow furrow was run along each row and a stream of water for each row was allowed to flow across the field for several hours. After the ground had become sufficiently dry, the plants were set 3 x 3 feet; thorough cultivation was given and the field thoroughly irrigated as often as needed, with the following results:

	No. of plants	No. of salable plants	Per cent of plants headed	Weight per 100 heads LBS.
Cabbage—				
20 rows irrigated . .	421	383	90.9	899
20 rows not irrigated .	442	347	78.5	590
Cauliflower—				
20 rows irrigated . . .	435	347	79.7	492
20 rows not irrigated .	361	235	65.09	306

"Although irrigation was decidedly beneficial, there was not as much difference as in other crops. Cabbage and cauliflower are strong-rooted plants, and are able to draw water from greater depths than many other plants. It is also possible that the unirrigated plats received some benefit from seepage from the irrigated plats, although separated by an alley of considerable width."

2. DOUBLE-CROPPING

Whenever land and equipment are very expensive, it is necessary that the vegetable-gardening be intensive. Capital and land should be kept at work. One of the means of doing this is to practice what market-gardeners know as double-cropping, which is the raising of more than one crop on the land in one season.

Double-cropping is of two species: (1) succession-cropping, or the growing of one crop after another on the same land; (2) companion-cropping, or the growing of two or more crops together.

Succession-cropping is a kind of short rotation. In selecting crops for succession-cropping, the following principles must be borne in mind: (1) each crop in the succession should be able to mature in less time than the whole season; (2) the tillage demanded by the first crop in the series should be such that it will leave the land in proper condition for the succeeding crop; (3) the crops should be so much unlike each other that they will not tend to exhaust the soil by demanding similar elements of plant-food, and will not carry diseases and insects from one crop to another.

It is usually preferable to use crops of different botanical families, for by this means the fertility of the soil is not so likely to be impaired, and diseases and insects are starved in the rotation. It is well to follow the root-crops with fibrous-rooted surface-feeding crops. In some cases the succession may extend over parts of two years, as when strawberries are followed by late potatoes or cabbages. In this case the strawberries are set the year before the succession-crop is grown. A crop of rhubarb or asparagus may be followed, when the crop is finally turned under, by a short-season crop, thereby allowing the cutting of the asparagus or rhubarb during its last season. It is usually best to follow a perennial crop with an annual one. When the succession-cropping extends into general farm operations, one or two entire seasons may be covered by each crop in the series. In this case we have a true rotation of crops, as that term is understood by most agricultural writers. The value of rotation in the vegetable-garden, by means of which lands are rested in clover or other sod crops, has already been discussed (Chapter III).

Following are examples of succession-crops:

Strawberries, followed by main-crop cabbage or late potatoes.
Peas, followed by cabbage, beans, tomatoes or celery.
Onions, beans, early beets, summer squash by kale, turnip, kohlrabi, winter radish.
Spring spinach, by beans and tomatoes.
Radish and bunch onions by early cabbage or celery.
Lettuce, by beans and tomatoes.
Early carrots, by autumn spinach, kale, turnip, winter radish.
Early potatoes, followed by fall cauliflower or turnips.
Cucumber, by spinach, kale, turnip, winter radish.
Early sugar corn, by second crop of same or autumn spinach, beans, tomatoes, celery.
Early cabbage, followed by late beans (for canning), or by horse-radish.
Dandelions by potatoes.
Fall-sown spinach by strawberries.
Kale, followed by potatoes or other main-season crop.

The following crops can be worked into succession-cropping schemes:

Early, or incidental crop

Beans, snap,	Mustard,
Beet,	Onion (from bulbs),
Cabbage,	Parsley,
Carrot,	Pea,
Cauliflower,	Potato,
Cress,	Radish,
Kohlrabi,	Spinach,
Lettuce,	Turnip.

Late, or main-crop

Beans, shell and Lima,	Muskmelon,
Beet (mostly a farm crop),	Okra,
Brussels sprouts,	Onion (from seed),
Cabbage,	Parsnip,
Carrot (farm crop),	Pepper,
Cauliflower,	Potato,
Celery,	Pumpkin,
Corn,	Salsify,
Cucumber,	Spinach (fall crop),
Eggplant,	Squash,
Horse-radish,	Sweet potato,
Kale (fall and winter crop),	Tomato,
Kohlrabi (fall crop),	Turnip and Rutabaga,
Leek,	Watermelon.

In *companion-cropping*, or the growing of two kinds of plants on the land simultaneously, the following principles are to be considered: (1) the crops should be such as will mature at widely different seasons; (2) one crop should be of distinctly less importance than the other, or be a "catch crop;" (3) the crops should be such as will profit by the same methods of tillage and fertilizing; (4) so far as possible, they should be of different botanical families or kinds in order that they may not tend to leave the soil unbalanced or to breed the same kinds of insects and fungi.

It will be seen that in companion-cropping there is a main crop and a secondary crop. Ordinarily, the main crop occupies the middle part, or middle and later part, of the season. The secondary crop matures early in the season, leaving the ground free for the main crop. In some cases, the same species is used for both crops, as when late celery is planted between the rows of early celery.

Following are examples of some companion-crops:

Radishes with beets or carrots. The radishes can be sold before the beets need the room.
Corn with squashes, citron, pumpkin or beans in hills.
Early onions and cauliflower or cabbage.
Horse-radish with early cabbage.
Lettuce with early cabbage.

"I have some methods of growing vegetables in this garden that I will describe. With some vegetables I have managed to grow two crops on the same ground in one year. Early sweet corn and winter squashes make a profitable combination. The small varieties of corn that do not shade the ground too much, and will be ready for market in July and August, should be planted. Plant the corn in rows 3 feet apart and 3 feet apart in the rows, and make the hills for the squashes between each alternate hill of corn, placing compost or well-rotted manure in the hills where the squashes are planted.

"Another combination is early peas and sweet corn. I plant the peas as soon as the ground can be worked with a one-horse corn-planter, cultivate the peas until the last of May, then plant the corn between the rows of peas with the corn-planter. The peas can be marketed the last of June, and the ground given to the corn. The combination can be varied by planting cabbages or celery for the late crop. A few years ago I grew a large field of peas and corn in this way, and did nearly all the work with the horse planter and cultivator.

"Early bunch onions and celery make another profitable combination of crops to grow on the same ground in one year. The onion sets should be planted very early in the spring, and when the onions are large enough for bunching, they should be marketed and the ground planted to celery. With this intensive system of culture the ground should be made very rich."—*W. H. Jenkins, Amer. Gard. XX. 350.*

Following are remarks on double-cropping by Professor Thomas Shaw, in "The Market Garden," July 1895:

A. *Three-crop system.*—"1. Onion sets may be planted early in the season and onion seeds may then be sown. In the former, between the rows and suitably spaced, cauliflowers may be planted, and later, between the cauliflowers, in the center of the squares, two or three cucumber seeds may be dropped. The onion sets may be used by taking those out first which grow around the cauliflowers, and these in turn may be removed in time to let the cucumbers develop. Midway between the rows of onions grown from seeds, plant radishes, lettuce, peppergrass, spinach or some other early relish, which will have ample time to grow and to be consumed before harm can come to the onions from the shade of any one of these crops. Then when the onions are well grown, turnips can be sown midway between the rows.

"2. When sweet corn is to be grown, the spaces for the rows can be marked out and left vacant until the time of the planting of the corn. Between these spaces and early in the season at least two rows of dwarf peas may be sown. These will be matured before the corn will harm them or before they will harm the corn. Then such seeds as squashes, pumpkins or citrons may be put in between the hills of corn. These will cover the ground occupied previously by the peas, and a bean or two may be dropped near each corn hill. The corn stalks make supports for the beans as they climb.

"3. Some kind of relish may be grown. It may be followed by early cabbages or cauliflowers, and these in turn by late cabbages or turnips, or any other kind of vegetable that may be grown late. These are instances wherein three crops may be obtained in succession the same season.

AA. *Two-crop system.*—"1. Peas of the dwarf varieties may be grown in rows. Tomatoes suitably spaced may be planted between these, and before the shade of the tomatoes injures the peas, the latter will have been used in allaying the appetites of hungry people.

"2. Early potatoes may be grown, followed by cabbages, turnips or winter radishes, and, if desired, some early relish may be grown between the rows of early potatoes.

"3. Some early crop may be grown midway between the rows of beets and carrots. As to the distance between the rows, much will depend on the character of the soil. The richer the soil, the wider apart should be the rows. About 15 inches between the rows of onions, carrots and dwarf peas may be considered average distances. By planting these in succession, two and three crops in a season may be obtained, and without irrigation, on the same piece of land. These crops will grow side by side like brothers without injuring one another, as men often do. If the later crop should grow a little too fast for the one previously sown, just nip off some of the outer leaves that protrude too far, and both crops will manifest their thanks by making a good growth.

AAA. *Two-crop and three-crop system with horse tillage.*—"Some instances may now be given of growing two crops in market-gardens where much of the labor is done by horses, and where, in consequence, the crops should not be crowded as to distance.

"1. Any kind of an early crop, as radishes, may be grown, to be followed by late potatoes, cabbages or turnips.

"2. Field peas can be sown early, to be followed by cabbages or celery or some other suitable crop. Early corn or potatoes may be removed, to be followed by cabbages or turnips, and between the rows of the corn these crops may be planted before the former has completed its maturity. Three crops may be obtained in a favorable season, as, for instance, a crop of radishes, followed by early cabbages, and these in turn by field roots, such as turnips. But in market-gardens it is usually more economical to remove the one crop before the crop which is to succeed it has been sown. The preparing of the land by horse labor is thus more easily done. Other successions of crops will occur to those engaged in the work as being more or less suitable to the conditions which they have to face."

3. TRANSPLANTING

The first consideration in successful transplanting is to have good plants. They should be well grown. Plants which are thin, slender and soft will nearly always collapse or suffer when they are exposed to field conditions. If they come from hotbeds or forcing-houses, they should have been hardened-off either in the hotbed itself or by transference to cold-frames. If the plants have been transplanted two or three times in the seed-bed, they will suffer less when they are put in the open field. Consult pp. 72–79.

The second consideration is to have the land in prime condition. It should be in fine tilth and thoroughly and deeply worked. Plants live better when they are transplanted into newly turned land. Such land is moist. The plants quickly secure a foothold.

Transplanting is more successful and is employed to a larger extent in the humid climates east of the great lakes than in the West. In fact, in the more arid parts of the country it is usually discouraged, and it is recommended that seeds be sown where the plants are to stand.

The ideal time to transplant is just before a rain. Just after a rain is also a good time, particularly if the weather comes off cloudy. Cool and cloudy days should be chosen if possible. When it is necessary to transplant in hot and dry weather, the late afternoon or evening should be chosen, if possible, in order that the plants may have time to straighten up during the night. When, however, the land is thoroughly prepared and the plants are well grown and not too large, there will be little difficulty in transplanting throughout the day. If the season is very dry, the plants may be watered. It is a common practice to have a boy follow with a pail and put a dipperful of water about each plant. Or, in larger operations, a tank on wheels is drawn through the fields. After the water soaks away, the dry loose earth should be drawn about the plant to afford a surface mulch and to prevent the soil from baking. Transplanting machines drawn by horses are now becoming popular for large-area practices, and these are supplied with a watering device. In small gardens, it is practicable to shade the plants for a day or two by setting a shingle on the south side of them, letting it slant over the plant.

When transplanting, the plants must be kept away from the sun when they are out of the ground, and they should also be kept wet. It is nearly as essential to wet the tops as the roots. The roots are wet to prevent them from dying. The tops are wet to prevent transpiration or evaporation of moisture. Puddling, or dipping the roots in mud, is sometimes advised as a protection, but it is less useful with small plants than with trees, because the fine roots are matted together by the operation. When transplanting by hand, it is customary to have a boy carry the plants in a covered basket or box, and to drop them just ahead of the planters. One boy ordinarily will drop for two rows of planters. The boy should not drop faster than the plants are required by the workmen.

Fig. 40. Dibbers.

Set the plants deep. Gardeners usually prefer to set them to the seed-leaf, even though they were an inch or two higher than this in the original seed-bed. This deep planting holds the plants in position and places the roots in the moist and cool earth. Press the earth firmly about the roots and the crown: this is very important. The best tool for opening the land is a dibber (Fig. 40), which makes a hole, but does not remove the earth. In the working hand hold the dibber; in the other hand, hold the plant; the plant is lowered into the hole made by the dibber, and both hands are then pressed tightly about the plant as the earth is closed against it. Sometimes the dibber is thrust alongside the plant and the hole filled by pressing the earth against it (Fig. 41). If the plants are rather large, and par-

Fig. 41. The dibber and how to use it.

ticularly if they have not been transplanted before, it is well to cut off a part of the foliage in order to hinder evaporation. One-half or one-third of the top may be twisted or cut off with very good results (Fig. 42).

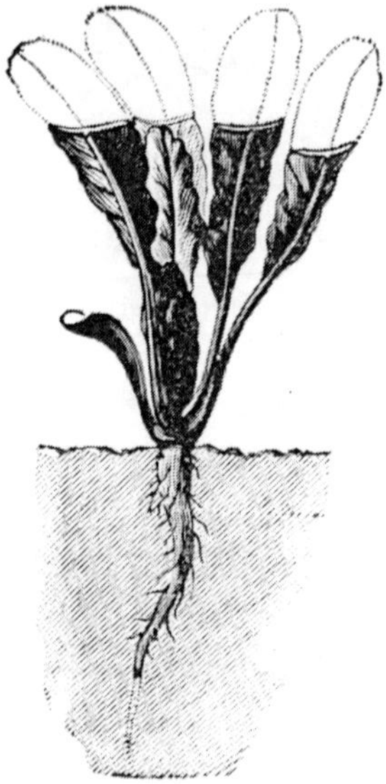

Fig. 42. Showing how much of the top may be removed in transplanting.

Of late years, transplanting machines drawn by horses have become popular for the planting of cabbages, tomatoes and other large-area crops (Fig. 43). If the plants are well grown and of the right size, these machines work very satisfactorily. They not only expedite and lessen labor, but the plants are more likely to live than when transplanted in the ordinary way. There are also various kinds of hand-transplanting devices which remove a large body of earth with the plant and drop it into a hole of similar size. These tools are useful for small areas or for amateur work, but they are not adapted to general field operations. They require too much labor and time. They are not expeditious. Lately, however, machines for aiding transplanting by hand have come into use, and are often very satisfactory.

Some kinds of plants, of which melons and cucumbers are examples, do not transplant readily. It is customary to start these in boxes, pots or on the bottoms of hard sods. The plants can then be taken to the field with the earth intact, and they will not suffer in the removal. There are various kinds of transplanting boxes in the market. Some melon growers use the ordinary splint pint or quart berry baskets, which can be bought very cheap. Others use paper oyster buckets. A common device in at least one of the melon-growing regions is shown in Fig. 44. It is a mere band or strip of basket-splint which is tacked together at the ends and has neither top nor bottom. The material is cut at a basket-factory,

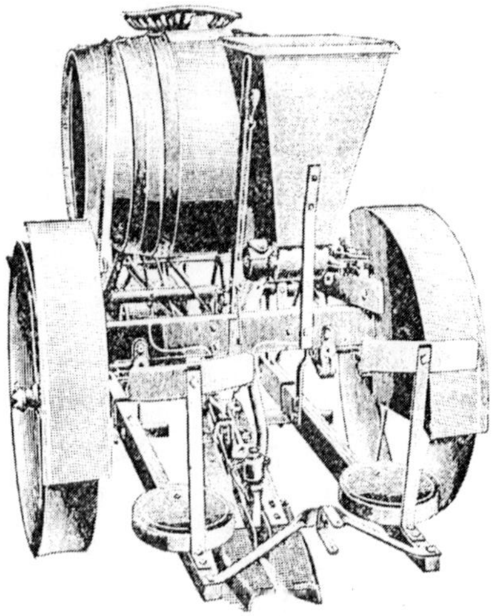

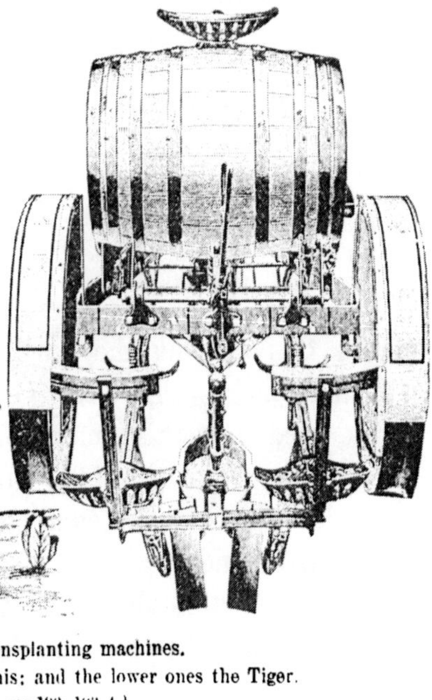

Fig. 43. Transplanting machines.
The upper one is the Bemis; and the lower ones the Tiger.
(See pages 190, 193-4.)

at an expense, in the flat, of about 85 cents per thousand. These forms are nested in the hotbed or coldframe, filled with earth, and four or five seeds planted in each. They are readily moved by running a spade, flat trowel or shingle under them. A box will make a hill of plants. If one has a greenhouse equipment, he may use 2-inch or 3-inch pots (Fig. 45); but unless he has the pots on hand for other uses, it would not pay to buy for this particular purpose. One of the best ways to handle cucumbers and melons is to plant them on sods, which are laid bottom up in the hotbed. They are cut into squares of about four inches. A little fine earth is sifted over and between them, in which the seeds are planted. With the heat and moisture of the bed, these sods decay and the plants thrive; but they will hold their shape for a month or more (Fig. 45). Old tin fruit-cans are sometimes used for this purpose. The cans are thrown into a fire, when the tops and bottoms melt off, and the sides are then fastened together with a tack or a bit of wire and are used as forms in which to grow plants. One difficulty with them is that they are too large and take up too much room. They are rela-

Fig. 44. Form in which to start melons. The flat is 14 inches long, and 3¾ inches wide, making a form or box 3 inches square and 3¾ inches deep.

tively too deep. It is usually best to use some cheap splint device, as shown in Fig. 44.

It is now customary to handle plants in flats (Fig. 45). These are shallow boxes about 3 inches deep, and of any convenient size. A box 15 x 20, or 18 x 24 inches is easily handled. These boxes may be made to order; but many gardeners make them from soap boxes, by sawing each box up into several flats

Fig. 45. Melon plants on a sod; gardener's flat; plants in 2-inch and 3½-inch pots.

or sections and adding bottoms. Such a box will hold 100 plants if they are not transplanted, or one-third or one-half that number of transplanted plants. From flats a quick man can transplant from 5,000 to 6,000 plants in a day if the soil is light and in good condition. With a horse transplanting machine several times this number can be set. Ten acres of cabbage plants sometimes may be set in a day by means of a horse machine. From 20,000 to 40,000 plants have been be set in one day. The machines are also used for transplanting nursery stock.

The transplanting machine can be used when the ground is too dry and too hard to allow of transplanting by hand, and the plants are more likely to live. The machine itself does not handle the plants. A man drives. A plow opens a deep, narrow furrow, and water is dropped into the furrow. Shoes or rollers follow and close the furrow, packing the earth. On the rear of the machine sit two boys, with the plants. It is their business to drop plants in the furrow between the opening plow and the shoes. By practice the boys can regulate the distance, and also learn just how to drop the plant so that it will be caught by the sides of the closing furrow and not fall over. A mechanical device guides the hand. By quick work, plants can be set as close as 1 foot apart. When conditions of soil and weather are just right, two men with dibbers and a boy to drop might set nearly as many plants as a transplanting machine, but they would not do the work so well. In a dry time and in hard ground, the machine shows its advantage at the best.

4. CHOOSING THE VARIETIES

One of the most engrossing incidents connected with the running of a market-garden or fruit-farm is the selection of varieties. There are the greatest differences of opinion respecting the merits and demerits of any variety. This proves that the value of a given variety is not a question of principle, but of local adaptation. It is apparent that every gardener who has had experience with a variety is able to judge of its merits for his particular conditions. His experience is a law unto him, although it may be only a suggestion to his neighbor. Choice of varieties is a local matter. Varieties must be tested for every purpose and condition. They are tested by actually growing them under the given condition and for the given purpose.

In selecting varieties, it is well to bear in mind the following points:

(1) Have an ideal, or classify your own ideas; know what kind of a variety is wanted and what it is wanted for, and then select that variety which seems best to satisfy the ideal.

(2) The older the variety, as a rule, the more reliable it is for general-purpose conditions. The very fact that it is old indicates that it has had sufficient value to enable it to persist. It may not be the best, however, for some special-purpose condition, for then a variety of peculiar or particular attributes is desired. The shorter the description in the catalogue. the greater is the probability that the variety is generally useful. It is only after varieties have been proved and have become staple that descriptions become short and tame: they do not need extravagant advertising.

(3) Prove the novelties. New varieties are to be tested, not to be grown wholesale and for the general crop. The novelties are attractively advertised: such advertising is necessary if they are to

be sold, for their merits are yet unknown. The advertising attracts the beginner and the person who desires to experiment. The novice selects the novelties.

Every gardener should have a small area in the personal part of his grounds which he devotes to the testing of new varieties. He should buy a packet of every new variety of those vegetables in which he is particularly interested. He will not have sufficient capital at stake to be disappointed if half of them fail to prove worthy under his conditions and for his ideals. The mental quest is one of the chief delights in the making of experiments. If a novelty fails, the quest is nevertheless as keen and the fun is as great. An experimental plat without failures is not worth the having. The experiment station test will be useful in suggestions, but it cannot tell what varieties will be best for your conditions, markets and ideals.

Now and then one of the novelties will prove to be useful to the man who tries it. He will then enlarge his area of it and test it on a commercial scale. In a year or two it may supplant some of the older varieties. In this way the gardener keeps abreast of the time and ahead of his competitor. Novelties are essential, for we depend on them for progress.

5. WEEDS

Weeds are mere incidents in good farming. They are the constants in poor farming. This is not because the good farmer spends more time killing weeds, but because he tills better and manages his land more skilfully. It is in neglected areas that weeds are most prevalent,—along the roadside, in the run-out meadow or pasture, in the barnyard or front yard, in the poorly tilled vegetable garden. Many farmers seem to think that good farming consists in killing weeds and bugs; but the best farming consists in not having them. Of course the farmer can not expect ever to be rid of these things, but he should think more of prevention than of eradication. A weed is only a plant that is not wanted. Horse-radish may be a weed in a potato field, and potatoes may be a weed in a horse-radish field. Potatoes are weeds in potato fields when potatoes are planted too thick.

There is no royal road to weedless farming. Following are some of the means of keeping weeds in check :

1. Practice rotation; keep ahead of the weeds. Certain weeds follow certain crops : when these weeds become serious, change the crop.

2. Change the method of tillage. If a weed persists, try deeper or shallower plowing, or a different kind of harrow or cultivator, or till at different times and seasons.

3. Harrow the land frequently when it is in fallow or is waiting for a crop. Harrow it, if possible, after seeding and before the plants are high enough to be broken by the implement. Potatoes, corn and other things can be harrowed after they are several inches high ; and sometimes the land may be harrowed before the plants are up.

4. Practice frequent tillage with light surface-working tools, throughout the season. This is hard on weeds and does the crop good.

5. Pull or hoe out stray weeds which escape the wheel tools.

6. Clean the land as soon as the crop is harvested: and if the land lies open in the fall, till it occasionally. Many persons keep their premises scrupulously clean in the early season but let them run wild in the fall, and thus is the land seeded for the following year.

7. Use clean seed, particularly of crops which are sown broadcast, and which, therefore, do not admit of tillage.

8. Do not let the weeds go to seed on the manure piles, in the fence corners, and along the highway.

9. Avoid coarse and raw stable manure, particularly if it is suspected of harboring bad company. Commercial fertilizers may be used for a time on foul land.

10. Sheep and pigs sometimes can be employed to clean the weeds from foul and fallow land. Land infested with Jerusalem artichokes is readily cleaned if hogs are turned in.

11. Induce your neighbor to keep his land as clean as you keep yours.

Rank pigweeds and their ilk are a compliment to a man's soil. Land that will not grow weeds will not grow crops,—for crops are only those particular kinds of weeds which a man wants to raise. Weeds have taught us the lesson of good tillage. There is no indication that they intend to remit their efforts in our behalf.

6. INSECTS AND FUNGI

The vegetable-gardener may expect to be troubled with insects and plant diseases. Many of these troubles are very serious and are beyond the direct control of the cultivator. The gardener must circumvent them rather than combat them. He must avoid them by means of strategy rather than kill them directly. Insects which feed openly on the tops of plants are nearly always amenable to direct treatment with poisons or other sprays. Of this class are potato-bugs and plant-lice. Those troubles which appear in the inner parts of plants or in their roots are not open to direct treatment, and in such cases the general management of the place must be relied on to keep the enemies in check. Insects and diseases are incidental or secondary facts in every garden plantation. The primary thing is to make the plants grow; the secondary thing is to keep the bugs off.

Following are some of the means by which the vegetable-gardener may hope to lessen or avert the losses from insects and diseases:

1. By means of rotation in crops and in methods of tillage. The shorter the rotation, the less is the liability to serious insect attacks. It is rare that insects and diseases appear suddenly in great numbers. They increase year by year, and in some favorable season prove very destructive. If the kinds of crops have been various, the probability is that they will not have gained a serious foothold, and that they will be held in comparative subjection. It is essen-

tial that the crops of a rotation be of such different kinds that the same kinds of insects or fungi will not thrive on them. Wireworms are starved out by a short and quick rotation. If the land is infested with them, the best thing to do, therefore, is to put the land into other crops and other uses, not to try to kill them by poison baits. They are usually most serious in those lands which have been laid down to grass for some time. The same thing may be said of the white grubs, which appear in grass lands. They are rarely troublesome when short and thorough rotations are used.

2. If the land becomes seriously infested with any one pest, it is best in general to discontinue, for two or three years, the growing of the crop on which they live. This ordinarily is cheaper and quicker than to endeavor to destroy the pest by direct means. This is well illustrated in the case of the club-root of cabbage and cauliflower. This disease may be lessened somewhat by thoroughly dressing the land with lime; but it is usually cheaper, and always more effective, to cease the growing of cabbage, cauliflower and turnips for a time, and to grow other kinds of crops on the land. It will usually be cheaper for a man to buy his home supply of cabbages than to attempt to grow them on land which is badly infested with either the club-root fungus or the cabbage maggot.

In 1894, soil from a cabbage field which was seriously infected with club-root, was sown in the hills of a cabbage field at Cornell University. The soil was clay. The plants were ruined by the disease. In 1895 cabbages and turnips were grown on the area. Five-sixths of the cabbages were ruined. About 10 per cent of the turnips were affected, but not seriously. In 1896 the area was fallow, with good tillage, until late summer, when turnips were sown. Again the turnips showed a little disease. In 1897 and 1898 the area was occupied by general vegetable crops other than cabbages, cauliflower and turnip. In 1899 cabbage and cauliflower were again grown on the area, and they were free from the disease. The region from which the soil was imported still suffers from club-root; but here it was starved out in two or three years.

3. Make every effort to secure strong, stocky, continuous-growing plants. Such plants are less liable to the attacks of many kinds of insects and fungi. Even if they are attacked, they have a better chance of coming through alive. Weak and soft plants are poor for any purpose, but they are particularly unsatisfactory when they must withstand the attacks of insects and fungi.

4. Destroy plants which are seriously affected, particularly those which are attacked by fungi. If the vines are thrown on the manure pile, the probability is that the disease will be distributed the next year in the manure. If the manure is very thoroughly rotted and composted, much of the danger will be averted; but even in that case it is wise not to take the risk with such serious diseases as club-root, potato blight and rot, and the blight of melons, cucumbers and tomatoes. In the fall, all diseased plants and products should be collected and burned.

5. In infected seed-beds, use new or sterilized soil. Do not add to the seed-bed soil from a field in which diseased crops of the given kind have grown.

This is good advice when one is filling the hotbed or the greenhouse benches. The soil in permanent seed-beds—as in hotbeds and houses—can be sterilized by heating it. W. W. Rawson gives his method of sterilizing soil in which greenhouse or winter lettuce is to be grown: "Have two large boxes that will hold a cart-load each—5 feet long, 4 feet wide and 3 feet high. Place in the bottom pipes laid 6 inches apart with holes 3 inches apart on both sides, and open at the ends. Connect these with the steam pipe from the boiler. Fill the box with soil and let on steam, with a pressure of 50 lbs., to one box at a time. When the temperature of the soil has reached 200°, shut off and let in to other box. Let each box stand for an hour, so as to thoroughly cook, then take out and put where desired to be used. Bring back soil to take place of this, and by that time the other box will be ready and the steam can be again let into the first box; then empty the other box. In this way two men will be kept busy with a horse and cart all day, if needed, and will sterilize 20 cart-loads."

6. Insects and fungi can be killed. Nowadays, spraying is the economical means. The gardener should know what insects and diseases are likely to appear on any crop and then be prepared to fight them. The time to make this preparation is before the crops are planted. In the winter season he should secure his pumps and nozzles, buy the materials for the various mixtures, and inform himself as to what difficulties will be likely to confront him. He is then forehanded and knows immediately what to do when the trouble

arises. He should know when the pests are likely to appear. He should learn something of their habits, that he may know the vulnerable points. Every gardener should buy a good book on insects and perhaps another on fungous diseases, and then keep up-to-date by reading the agricultural papers and the experiment station bulletins.

An essential point in the application of any spray is timeliness. The minute the trouble appears, the spray should be applied. The pest may be dispatched more readily at this time, and also with less expense of material and effort; and the plants will not have suffered seriously. Another important item in the spraying of plants is thoroughness. A bug will not go where poison is: the poison must be put where the bug is. The bug is likely to avoid the poison: therefore, the only safe way is to put the poison on every part of the plant. One thorough spraying, which completely covers the plant, is worth more than a half dozen sprayings when the operator merely sprinkles the tops of the leaves. Be sure that the spray is of the right kind and well made: then do not be afraid to apply it. Paris green and other insecticides, and even some fungicides, may be applied dry by means of a bellows device; but this is scarcely practicable in windy weather. Most persons prefer to apply both insecticides and fungicides in a water spray. Keep posted on spraying devices by sending for the catalogues of manufacturers and by reading the bulletins and papers.

Some of the requisites for a good pump have been

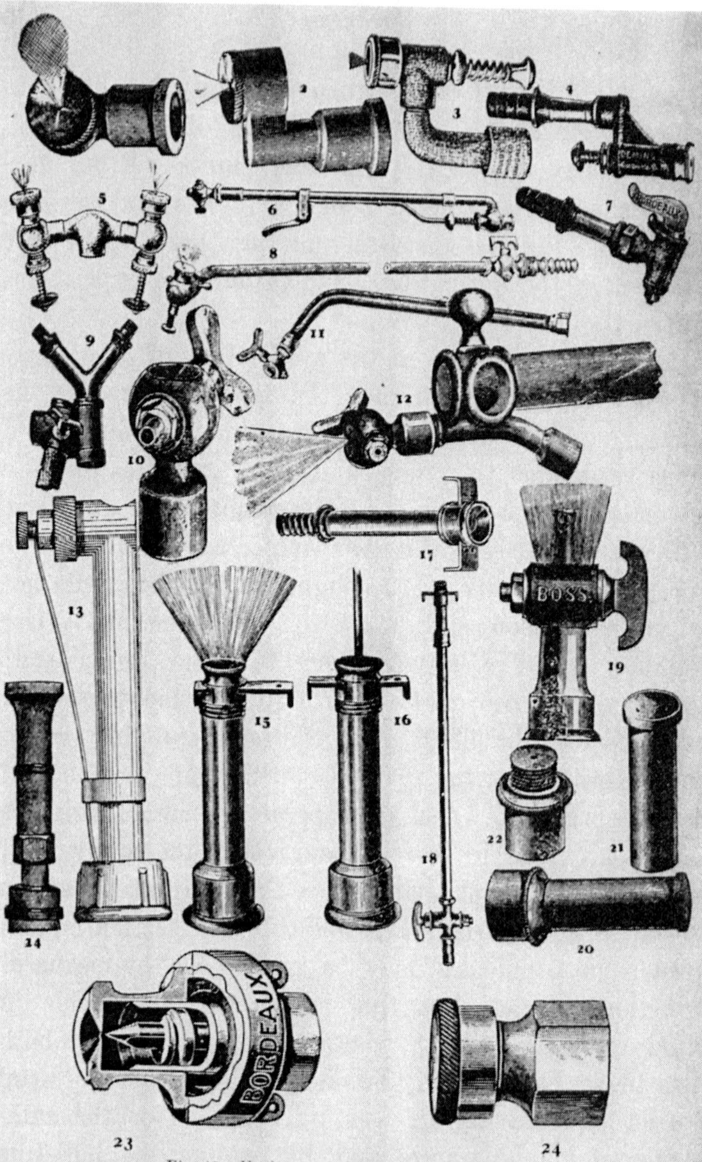

Fig. 46. Various types of spraying nozzles.

1, 2, Cyclone nozzles; 3, 4. Vermorel nozzles; 5, double Vermorel; 6, longshank Vermorel; 7, bordeaux nozzle; 8, undersprayer (Boekel); 9, Y for two nozzles· 10, carnation nozzle (Gould); 12, same, with pole attachment; 11, Masson nozzle (Gould); 13 McGowen; 14, graduated spray; 15, 16, lilly (Rumsey); 18, same with long tube; 17, calla (Gould); 19, Boss (Field Force Pump Co.); 20, 21, 22, Nixon nozzles: 23, Winkle nozzle for Bordeaux; 24, Winkle, for Paris green.

discussed on page 120. It is important that the apparatus have power. It should break up the spray and should drive it into every nook and crevice of the plant. On a pair of old wagon wheels an ingenious man can construct a good platform for the mounting of a spraying rig. See Figs. 46, 47, 48.

Fig. 47. A good rig for potatoes.

For plant diseases, the staple fungicide is Bordeaux mixture. This is a preparation of sulfate of copper and lime, diluted with water. It is probable that the lime has some slight fungicidal value, but its chief merit is to make the material adhere to the foliage and to neutralize the caustic effects of the sulfate of copper. Bordeaux mixture may be applied with advantage even before the disease appears, for it adheres closely to the foliage and prevents the germination—or, at least, the growth—of the spores of the fungi. If Bordeaux mixture is well made and well applied, it will adhere to the foliage for some weeks, particularly if it has time to set before rain falls. In case of serious attacks, however, it is well to spray every few days, because new shoots and new foliage are constantly appearing; and it is practically impossible in any one spraying to cover every part of the plant. Bordeaux mixture is a blue whitewash; it discolors the plants. If it is desired to have the foliage and

Fig. 48. Types of power and tank outfits.

1, Victor outfit (Field Force Pump Co.); 2, Caswell sled sprayer; 3, Caswell geared sprayer; 4, wagon outfit (Morrill & Morley): 5. mounted barrel sprayer, 6, Eureka tank outfit (Morrill & Morley).

fruits free from discoloration, it may be advisable to use the ammoniacal carbonate of copper solution. This material is ordinarily somewhat cheaper than the Bordeaux mixture, but it does not adhere so long, and its practical fungicidal value is generally not considered to be so great.

It is not every kind of plant disease which is destroyed or averted by means of Bordeaux mixture or other sprays. Whenever the whole plant wilts or seems to be affected internally, it is probable that there is some injury at the root or in some part of the main stem. The trouble in this case may be due to root insects, borers or to some bacterial or other internal trouble which cannot be reached by external applications. In these cases the man has no recourse except to destroy the affected plants, and then by means of strategy to avoid the recurrence of the trouble.

For insects, arsenic and kerosene (coal-oil) are the leading remedies. Of insects which feed on the external parts of the plant, there are two general kinds, so far as their manner of eating is concerned,—the chewing or biting insects, as the beetles and larvæ (worms), and the sucking insects, as the various scales, plant-lice and squash-bug. Insects of the former type are dispatched by poisoning their food. This is usually done by spraying the plants with Paris green or some other arsenical poison. Insects of the second type comprise those which suck the juices of the plant and must be destroyed by some material which kills them by contact. Of these materials, the chief are the various kerosene preparations and whale-oil soap.

Insecticides

Paris green.—The standard insecticide for all chewing or biting insects is Paris green. This material varies considerably in composition, and its price fluctuates; therefore many substitutes are in the market. Perhaps the best of the home-made substitutes is the arsenite of soda and lime, which is described below. Since Paris green may contain more or less soluble arsenic, which is caustic to foliage, it is now the practice to add lime to it, no matter on what plants it is used. Lime also makes it adhere better. The ordinary strength is one pound of the Paris green to 200 to 300 gallons of water. On potatoes and some other plants, however, it may be used as strong as one pound to 100 gallons, particularly if lime is added. If the amount of lime is one-half or one-third as much as the Paris green, it will be sufficient to satisfy the chemical reactions; but it is ordinarily advisable to add as much lime as there is Paris green, in order to increase the adhesive properties. Paris green mixes better with water if it is made into a paste (by stirring it in a little water) before it is thrown into the barrel. If it is put into the barrel dry, much of it floats and does not readily incorporate itself with the water. For potato bugs, it is sometimes sufficient to sprinkle the Paris-green water on the plants; but the best results are to be secured only when it is applied with a pump and fine nozzle, so that the liquid is broken and driven to all parts of the plant.

It is now customary to use Paris green in the Bordeaux mixture, and thereby to combat both insects and fungi at one spraying. The Paris green is added to the Bordeaux mixture as if the Bordeaux were so much water. That is, if one desires to use Paris green at the rate of one pound to 200 gallons, he adds his pound of poison to 200 gallons of Bordeaux mixture. In this case, of course, it will not be necessary to add lime to the Paris green, since the lime of the Bordeaux mixture will answer all requirements. Paris green is sometimes added to Bordeaux at the rate of eight ounces to 50 gallons.

London purple is often used instead of Paris green. It is used in the same strengths and may also be added to the Bordeaux mixture. It is generally a more variable commodity than the Paris green and is not used so much as formerly.

Arsenite of soda. — White arsenic, 2 lbs.; carbonate of soda (sal soda, washing soda), 8 lbs.; water, 2 gals.

Put all the materials into an iron kettle, which should not be used for any other purpose, and boil for fifteen minutes, or until the arsenic dissolves. Add water to replace that escaped by evaporation, making two gallons of the stock solution. This may be prepared at any time, and will keep indefinitely if put in a tightly corked bottle. Be sure to put the bottle in a safe place and label it "Poison."

To make fifty gallons of the spraying mixture but one pint of this stock solution is needed; hence the formula given is sufficient for sixteen barrels (of 50 gals. each). Two to four pounds of stone lime are slaked and added to each barrel. If the arsenite of lime is used in Bordeaux, like Paris green, it will not be necessary to use lime in addition to that already in the Bordeaux.

Kerosene and soap emulsion.—For insects which suck their food, as scales, plant-lice, and the true bugs (like the squash-bug), the kerosene compounds are the most popular insecticides. Kerosene and soap emulsion is the standard. There are several ways of making this, but the following is one of the best: Into boiling soft water (one gallon), place one-half pound of hard soap; when the soap is dissolved, add two gallons of kerosene (or coal-oil). In order to thoroughly emulsify the ingredients, run them through a pump vigorously for fifteen or twenty minutes, at the end of which time the material should be so thoroughly emulsified that the liquid has a milk-like constituency. This material may then be diluted with water ten to fifteen times when using. If the emulsion is to be used on dormant trees in the winter it is not necessary to dilute it so much. The kerosene emulsion is sure death to all plant-lice and to scale insects when they are in their young or feeding stage. When treating plant-lice, however, it is very essential that the application be made before the leaves have curled up and afforded them protection.

Kerosene and water emulsion.— A mechanical emulsion of kerosene and water is a very efficient insecticide, and has been known to be so for many years. It has not come into general use, however, because there has not been any device which would thoroughly and accurately emulsify them. Within the last two or three years, however, pumps have been invented which mix and emulsify the kerosene and water in different proportions. Some of these pumps are now sufficiently perfected to be recommended with confidence. It is probable that within the next few years these machines will be still further perfected, and the kerosene and soap emulsion will then pass away. The kerosene and water emulsion is cleaner, much more easily applied, and more easy to make than the kerosene and soap emulsion. It has been found that when the water and oil are thoroughly emulsified the foliage will endure without injury an emulsion which contains one-fourth or one-fifth of kerosene; and this strength is fatal even to the San José scale. It is always best, however, when applying the kerosene and water emulsions, to make the application on a sunny day, so that the kerosene quickly evaporates. Some plants are not injured by pure kerosene applied when the sun is shining. Recent experiments and practice have shown that an emulsion of water and crude petroleum makes a very efficient insecticide; but the grades of crude petroleum vary so much that it seems to be difficult to give general advice. The grower should secure the latest bulletins on the subject, as it is expected that considerable progress will be made in this direction within the next few years.

Whale-oil soap.—An old-time remedy for scale insects and plant-lice is whale-oil soap. This is a very disagreeable compound to dissolve and handle, however, and it is gradually giving way to the kerosene emulsion, although it is a very efficient insecticide. It is customary to dissolve one pound of whale-oil soap in four or five gallons of water. One should experiment on a few plants, if he is using a denser strength, before he applies it on very large areas. Some tender plants are injured by the formula given above.

Tobacco dust is a standard insecticide and repellent for some insects. The striped cucumber and melon beetle is usually driven away if the plants are thoroughly dusted with tobacco dust. The flea-beetle, which is an invidious enemy to many crops, may also be repelled to a certain extent with the same treatment. These insects are also driven away to a great extent when the plants are thoroughly covered with Bordeaux mixture.

White hellebore is poisonous to insect life, but is much less injurious to human beings than the arsenic compounds. It is sometimes used on cabbages and other plants late in the season, when it is considered to be unsafe to use Paris green or other arsenites. It may be applied either dry or in water. When applied in a water spray, one ounce of poison is mixed with three gallons of water. In the dry state it may be applied full strength or diluted half with flour.

Fungicides

Bordeaux mixture.—To make 1 bbl. (50 gals.): Copper sulfate (blue vitriol), 4 lbs.; stone lime, 4 lbs.

If there is any hurry, the vitriol may be quickly dissolved in a pail of hot water, but it is usually better to put it in a piece of burlap and suspend this over night in four to six gallons of cold water. If only the bottom of the burlap rests in the water, the vitriol will dissolve quicker than if it is completely immersed. Always use a wooden pail for dissolving vitriol; it will corrode tin.

It is better, but not essential, to slake the lime some time before it is needed for making Bordeaux, in order that it may become cool. If warm milk of lime is used for making Bordeaux there is likely to be more trouble with clogging of the nozzles. Only good stone lime should be used ; even a little air-slaked lime in Bordeaux is likely to give a mixture which will burn the foliage, clog the nozzles, and wash from the trees more easily. When slaking a small amount of lime do not cover it with water but add water gradually, pint by pint, as fast as the lime takes it up. If lime is "drowned" it will often take half an hour to slake, when it would take but five minutes if skilfully handled. If an ordinary oil barrel is sawed in two the halves make very handy tubs in which to slake lime and dissolve vitriol.

When ready to begin spraying, pour the vitriol solution into the spray barrel and then fill the latter about half full of water.

If not done after slaking, the lime should now be diluted to make ten to fifteen gallons of "milk of lime." This is poured into the spray barrel and unites with the vitriol solution to make Bordeaux. It should preferably be poured into the barrel through a screen of some sort to take out the unslaked lumps, which would clog the nozzle. A piece of wire fly screen or a double thickness of coarse potato burlap is excellent. Fertilizer sacking is too fine meshed for this purpose. It is not wise to mix the vitriol solution and the milk of lime when less dilute than this; otherwise the Bordeaux is more likely to burn the foliage and is lumpy. Fill the barrel with water to make fifty gallons, and stir the mixture thoroughly for a few minutes. If there is no automatic agitator attached to the pump, the mixture should be thoroughly stirred with a paddle while spraying at least every five minutes.

Bordeaux itself should always be made fresh for each spraying, as it deteriorates on standing; but the vitriol solution and slaked lime may be kept on hand ready for mixing. When much spraying is to be done it generally saves time to make a stock solution of the vitriol and slake a quantity of lime before hand. Thus forty pounds of vitriol may be dissolved in forty gallons of water. Each gallon will then contain one pound of vitriol, and four gallons will be needed to make fifty gallons of Bordeaux. The stock solution of vitriol must be kept tightly covered to prevent evaporation. A good plan is to sink the barrel containing it in the ground.

Likewise forty pounds of lime may be slaked in forty gallons of water and used like the vitriol; or it may be slaked to the consistency of putty, spread evenly over the bottom of a narrow trough, and covered with water to exclude air. Knowing the number of pounds of lime in the trough, a certain fraction of its area will contain the four pounds needed for a barrel, and this is separated off at one end when needed.

Instead of measuring the lime it is often more convenient to use the ferro-cyanide test when large amounts are slaked beforehand. An ounce of potassium ferro-cyanide may be bought in any drug store, and will be sufficient for a season.

Dissolve it in a pint of water, and label the bottle "Poison." The needed amount of lime for making Bordeaux is then estimated, instead of calculated, when taken from the stock, and enough is added to satisfy the ferro-cyanide test. This test is made by taking out a little of the Bordeaux in a small dish and adding to it a drop of the ferro-cyanide solution. If a reddish brown color appears more lime is needed, and it should be added until no change in color takes place. It is even wise to use more lime than is needed to satisfy the test. An excess of lime is not injurious and probably is beneficial.

Carbonate of copper.—A good fungicide can be made by dissolving copper and ammonia and then diluting the solution with water. This material has the great advantage over Bordeaux mixture of not discoloring the foliage or fruit. It is therefore a useful fungicide when it is needed to apply late in the season when the fruit is nearly grown, or when it is desired to spray plants that are used for ornamental effects. The material does not adhere to the foliage as long as Bordeaux mixture, however, and for that reason it does not retain its efficiency and is not so much used. The standard fungicide is Bordeaux mixture; the incidental one is carbonate of copper.

The carbonate of copper may be dissolved at the rate of an ounce in one pint to one quart of ammonia. The amount of ammonia required will depend upon its strength. It is well to use only enough ammonia to dissolve the copper, for the free ammonia is likely to injure foliage. If the very strong ammonia can be secured (that which is known as 26° Beaumé), the solution should be diluted with seven or eight times its volume of water. This stock solution may be kept indefinitely in a tightly corked bottle. When wanted for use, it should be diluted with water at the rate of one ounce of carbonate of copper to eight to twenty gallons of water. This makes a clear, bluish liquid, which is as easily applied as the water itself. The addition of lime to make the material adhere has not been very successful. The carbonate of copper may be made at home by treating sulfate of copper with sal soda; but unless one wants it in large quantity, it is better to buy.

CHAPTER VII

MARKETING AND STORING

FULLY half the profits in vegetable-gardening depend on the marketing. Where there are ten men who can grow a product to advantage there may be only one who can sell it to advantage. Horticulturists have not yet learned the art of advertising. They are afraid to spend money for natty packages, attractive labels, and advertisements in local papers. The bases of all good marketing are five: (1) a good and seasonable product; (2) uniform grades in the marketed product; (3) good packing; (4) attractive packages; (5) honesty on the part of both grower and seller. Given these qualifications, the gardener need not hesitate to push his product and to ask the buyer to pay him an extra price.

Other things being equal, the local market is the most to be desired. The grower is known, and he has an opportunity to establish a reputation. He can hold his customers year by year. All the business may be within his own observation. He knows what is being done with his products. There is a brisk demand for good vegetables and fruits at good prices. In any city of 10,000 and upwards a special trade can be established, particularly if the city is mature. This is often denied, but it is nevertheless true. If the grower sells his products in attractive packages, with neat labels if need be, and properly sorted and arranged, and places them in the hands of an enterprising grocer who caters to the best trade, he will not need to peddle his wares. The grower for the home market must be sure to have his vegetables in season; and he will do well, also, to provide a continuous and varied supply, for thereby he can hold his customers. He must set a standard and live up to it. These remarks may not apply to those who grow things on a large scale, but such persons usually find special means and outlets for disposing of their products: because they have found such outlets is the reason for the growth of their business.

1. PACKING

Conditions have changed within a generation. This is the day of small and special packages. Every pair of shoes is in a special box. Formerly prices for vegetables were high, and the gardens were near the markets. Now the prices are low, and gardens are often a thousand miles from the consumer. Then, barrels and miscellaneous boxes could be used; now attractive packages are often necessary to advertise the products, and strong ones are essential in order to provide safe transportation. The following extracts from Alfred Henderson* indicate how times have changed:

"For thirty years prior to 1875 market-gardening

*Chapter on horticulture in Depew's "One Hundred Years of American Commerce," 1895.

was a most profitable business in and around New York. Thirty years ago the New Jersey market-gardeners, mainly located in Hudson county, grew better vegetables than the Long Island men, but their limited area of land becoming less and less annually, in consequence of the inroads made for building purposes, the Long Islanders forged ahead. The Long Island men, however, have not had it all their own way, for of late years a formidable competitor has been met by them in the large truck-gardens of the South. While this competitive factor has certainly lessened their profits, even at the lower prices that prevail to-day there is still a fair profit in the business for them, certainly more than in ordinary farm crops." Such changes in conditions are reasons enough for a change in business methods of disposing of the crop.

Packing and sorting of a crop should begin in the field. The better the crop is grown, the fewer will be the culls and the less the labor of sorting and grading. In crops which are not to be carefully sorted into sizes and packed by hand, as potatoes and many of the root crops, the vegetables may be placed directly in the package in which the product is to be taken to the market. Nothing is better for the handling of heavy products than a bushel box (Fig. 49). Formerly baskets of various sizes were used for this purpose, but the bushel box is much better because it is cheaper, more durable and it stows better on the wagon or in the storehouse. One tier of boxes may be piled on another, but this is impossible with baskets unless one resorts to expensive staging.

The value of the bushel box as a receptacle for the handling of vegetables is well set forth by Professor Green* as follows: "In these days of close competition it is very important for the seller to use great care in the selection of a favorable package in which to display his goods. In the markets of St. Paul and Minneapolis the most common package for the display of vegetables is the bushel basket, and this is probably one of the poorest kinds in which to show off goods to advantage. Far better and more economical for the same purpose is the bushel box. The disadvantages of the bushel basket may be briefly summed up as follows: (1) A wagon load of full baskets is not nearly so solid nor so easily built up as a load of the same material in boxes; (2) a bushel basket costs about 50 per cent more than a well-made box holding the same amount; (3) it seldom lasts more than one-third as long; (4) the goods do not appear to such advantage in it as in a box. On the other hand, bushel boxes (1) may be made so as to fit readily into a wagon, and by the use of deck boards a very large and solid load may readily be put on that binds well together; (2) a box lasts indefinitely and is easily repaired, while a basket is of short duration and is not easily repaired; (3) a box capable of holding a bushel can be made much cheaper than a basket of

Fig. 49. Bushel box.

This is the style used extensively in the Boston markets. Its standard value is 10 cents. It is 16 inches square, and 8 inches deep.

---

*The Market Garden, November, 1894, p. 3.

the same size; (4) the box is far better for showing off goods. Perhaps the most desirable form for a bushel box for general use is sixteen inches square and eight inches deep, inside dimensions. The end pieces should be one inch thick, with a handle hole in each end. The sides and bottom should be one-half inch thick. This is the style of box commonly used in the markets of Boston and vicinity. Such a box is there sold for about ten cents. A wagon for carrying such boxes to best advantage should be wide enough to allow of placing in the body of it two rows of boxes abreast and two deep. In building a load of boxes, when ventilation is needed for those in the lower tier, a short piece of wood, one-half an inch thick, may be laid across the upper corners of the corner boxes so that the second tier will rest upon them. The deck boards may carry several tiers of boxes, which will bind well together and make a solid load."

In handling the products in the field and in the storehouse, it is important that they be kept dry and cool. Over-ripeness and decay are then prevented. They should be put on the market or in storage quickly, before they have been subjected to unfavorable conditions of weather or to accidents. Some vegetables, as onions, are not injured by being left in the sun for a few hours or even days; but, as a rule, it is better to keep the vegetables in partial shade, particularly such as remain green or soft in their marketable stage. If one has any quantity of vegetables to handle, it is well to have a packing-house or shed. In this shed there should be tables or counters on which the sorting or grading can be done. If possible, this house should have a pit or cellar at one end in which vegetables can be kept temporarily or even stored for the winter.

In the packing of vegetables, it is well to bear in mind the following essentials: (1) *Pack snug.* This is particularly important if the vegetables are to be shipped any considerable distance. A large part of the vegetables in our city markets is handled from ten to fifteen times from the field to the consumer. Vegetables that are packed snug not only bear transportation better, but they keep longer and present a more attractive appearance. In the better kinds of vegetables this snug packing is secured by placing each specimen by hand. (2) *Pack in grades.* This contributes not only to the appearance of the vegetable, but also to the snugness of packing. Vegetables like melons, tomatoes and others that are used as table delicacies and accessories, are usually sold by the smallest specimens in the package rather than by the large ones. If the specimens are sorted into two grades, the smaller ones will usually sell as well as the mixed lot, and the larger ones will sell much better. Since the grading of vegetables is a matter of mental ideals, the grade varies with every packer, and it is therefore often difficult to secure sufficient uniformity to enable one to sell his products under a trade-mark. However, if one has uniform packages and gives close attention to the details of the business, he should be able to establish a series of grades that will be associated with his name in the market. (3) In the finer or dessert vegetables it is well to pack in some

distinctive package or to use a *trade-mark or label* which will distinguish one's products from others. This is essential if one is to establish an individual reputation and to hold customers from year to year. With such heavy and staple products as potatoes, beets, or cabbages, it is usually inadvisable to attempt this kind of marketing; but even with them it can sometimes be done. It is common to associate a special package with fruits, but not with vegetables; but this condition of affairs is wrong. (4) *Pack the vegetables cool.* They should go into the packages with a low temperature, rather than warm. They keep longer and hold their quality better under such conditions. This is particularly true of dessert and perishable products. (5) Pack in relatively ***small packages***, with all the better kinds of vegetables. Aim, so far as possible, at special and dessert trade. The warmer the season, the smaller the quantity should be. If one is shipping green stuff, as cabbage, spinach and kale, the package should be well ventilated in order to prevent heating, particularly if the packages are as large as barrels. It is well to use open or ventilated packages for all green vegetables in warm weather, at least for those that are to be shipped a long distance.

Of all the packages in use at the present time, barrels are least desirable except for a staple product that is shipped a long distance and thrown on the general market. A barrel does not appeal to the individual consumer. Barrels also are relatively expensive. For the finer kinds of vegetables, new or gift packages may be used, particularly if one is aiming at the special trade. This is emphatically true with those vegetables that need careful handling in order to deliver them in good condition to the consumer. Among such vegetables are tomatoes, cucumbers, egg-

Fig. 50. Some of the packages in which long-distance shipments of vegetables are made.

plants and muskmelons. Common commercial styles of packages for vegetables are shown in Fig. 50.

The shipper should mark the packages with his name, and, in case the goods are sorted, with the trade-mark or the name of the product. The dealer is likely to receive consignments from many persons in one day, and unless the name of the shipper is on the package

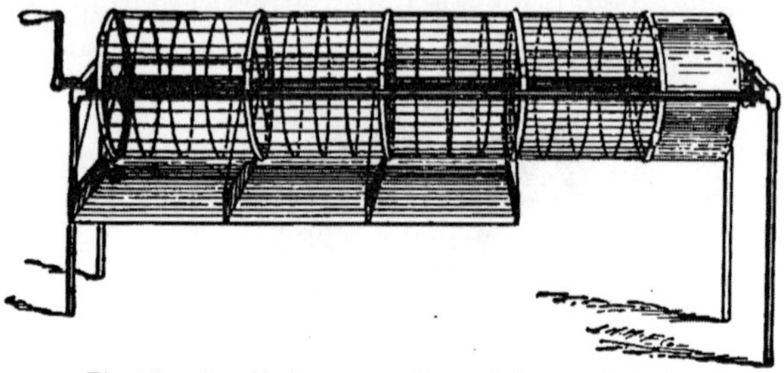

Fig. 51. A cylinder-sorter for potatoes and fruits.

confusion may result. When an important shipment is made, it is well to notify the dealer in advance, either by wire or by letter.

Although the sorting and grading of vegetables entail extra labor and expense, they nearly always pay if one desires to reach a personal customer. With certain kinds of vegetables, however, sorting machines may be used, particularly with potatoes. Some of these machines work on the principle of a revolving sieve or screen through which the crop is run (Fig. 51). The products then drop through the mesh according to size. Another type of sorting machine is an inclined box or rack with slat bottom over which the products are rolled (Fig. 52). The small specimens drop between the slats, and the large ones roll on to the end of the box and are caught in a barrel or other receptacle. Compare Figs. 82 and 83.

Usually the careful gardener will need a special kind of wagon. For use in the field he needs something in the nature of a truck with wide tires, and small wheels that will turn under the platform. On these platform wagons the boxes may be stored in two or three tiers if

Fig. 52. A slat-sorter for potatoes and fruits.

necessary. In nearly every great trucking center there is a special kind of market wagon. One of the most distinct of these is the kind used on the western end of Long Island, one of which is shown in Fig. 53. On the macadam roads of that section these wagons are often hauled twenty and thirty miles to the market. The teams are started in the evening or night and arrive in the New York City market by about two o'clock in the morning, ready for the opening of the market at daybreak (Fig. 54). One of these wagons weighs about eighteen hundred pounds. It is provided with a large canvas cover, which can be tied over the load. The wagon, with cover, and top to shield the driver, all complete, costs about three hundred and fifty dollars. One of these rigs can carry three tons of produce. In some parts of Long Island these wagons are loaded on flat cars at the railway stations and are taken into the markets by that means.

In order to do the best with one's products, the grower must keep track of the market. If possible, he should visit the market. He should consult the trade papers. He should ask his dealer about the new ideas in packages and packing. Ordinarily he will be able to secure better information if he deals continuously with one reliable firm. In every way endeavor to keep up with the times in the selling of the produce as well as in the growing of it.

2. STORING

It is impossible to enunciate principles that will apply to storing all kinds of vegetables, for these products include fruits, roots and leaves. Some of them must be kept warm and some cool. Others, as onions and squashes, must be dry; still others, as cabbages and roots, must be kept moist. Each vegetable, therefore, is a law unto itself. With the exception of root and tuber crops, most vegetables are uncertain in storage unless they are kept in an establishment that is cooled by artificial means, and which, therefore, maintains uniformity of moisture and temperature. In general, it is better to sell in the fall, even at a somewhat reduced price, than to go to the expense and risk

Fig. 53. Long Island market wagon. The canvas cover is rolled on the pole at the rear.

of storing. When, however, the fall market is so low as to prevent any profit, storing is a necessary recourse. Persons who have become expert in the handling of any one vegetable may store it with relative safety. If one has had no experience in the storing of those vegetables that are difficult to keep, it is

Fig. 54. Daylight view of Wallabout market. Brooklyn.
The covered market is in the rear, and the open-air market in the foreground. In the very front of the picture is a dilapidated stone wall and a discarded market wagon: these are not parts of the market.

generally better to put them in the hands of some one who makes a business of cold storage and pay him for his labor and experience.

In general, a low temperature is essential to the keeping of the product. It prevents over-ripening and delays the work of fungi and other disorganizing agents. Usually it is well to keep the temperature relatively near the freezing point; but there are some vegetables, as squashes and sweet potatoes, which are injured by a low temperature. Products which are either over-ripe or markedly under-ripe usually do not keep well. It is essential to any success in the storing of vegetables that the specimens be perfectly sound when put in storage, and in the proper state of maturity. No doubt some of the loss in the storing of cabbages, for example, is due to the infection of the plants with the rot fungus before the heads are put in storage. Onions that have been seriously attacked by the smut or rust may not be expected to keep well, however good the storage.

The following essentials apply to the storing of most vegetables: (1) Protect from frost. (2) Keep them cool in order to prevent decay. (3) Keep them relatively moist in order to prevent excessive evaporation and wilting. (4) Avoid a wet and stagnant atmosphere, as this is likely to engender rot, particularly when the temperature is too high. (5) Protect from heating, for heating is the natural result of the accumulation of much fresh vegetable matter.

For home use, it is well to store roots and tubers in moist sand or in sphagnum moss (such as nurserymen and florists use). Beets, carrots, parsnips, and potatoes stored in this way will keep plump and fresh for a twelvemonth or more, if the temperature is kept low enough to prevent sprouting. The reason for this good result is that the sand or moss prevents evaporation and maintains uniformity of conditions.

The house cellar is likely to be one of the poorest places in which to store vegetables, particularly if it contains a heater for the residence. In such case it is likely to be too warm and too dry. The vegetables shrivel and tend to start into growth, or to decay quickly. Cellars that contain much vegetable matter are likely to make the house unhealthy unless there is ample ventilation and pains is taken to pick over the vegetables from time to time and remove all unsound specimens. If the house cellar is used for the storing of vegetables, it is well to have a special vent or chimney. This may be a cheap board affair extending up the back side of the house as high as the roof. This flue carries off the foul and warm air, and thereby keeps the cellar pure and at a relatively low temperature. In some cases an extra flue may be provided in the house chimney when the house is built, and the warmth of the chimney will cause a strong draft.

The old-fashioned "outside cellar" usually gives better conditions for the storing of vegetables than the house cellar. It is likely to be quite as uniform in temperature, and more uniform in the moisture conditions. The "outside cellar," with various modifications, is used largely by market-gardeners for the storing of roots, leek, celery and other products that do not require a dry air. This cellar is little more than a pit sunk to the level of the ground with a gable roof covered with soil and sod so that frost cannot enter; or if the ground is likely to be moist, the pit is built partially above the ground. If an outside cellar is to be permanent, the walls may be laid of stone or brick.

If the masonry wall is lined with hollow or "lining brick," more uniform conditions will be secured. It is very important that provision be made for ample

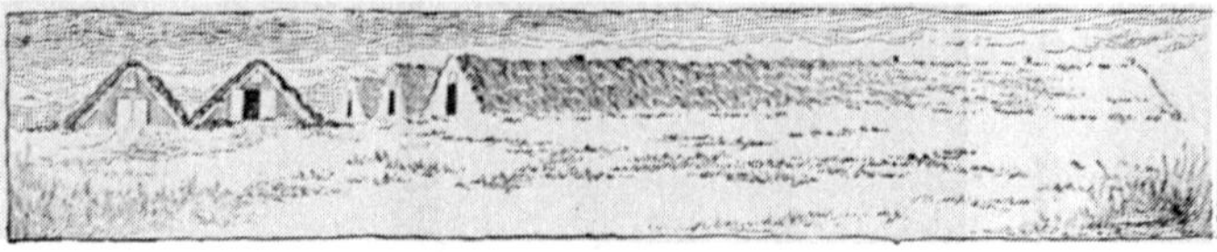

Fig. 55. Old-time "outside cellars" or pits.

drainage, and also for ventilation without opening the main doors. This ventilation is usually secured by a little cupola or shaft near the center of the structure or by windows in the gables. A vestibule entrance is desirable if the climate is severe. It is preferable that the cellar have a natural earth bottom, providing the drainage, either natural or artificial, is complete.

Fig. 56. A good outside cellar for storing green vegetables.

A great difficulty with a permanent field or outside cellar is the danger of its holding so much moisture and being so "close" as to encourage the growth of fungi and thus engender decay. An investigation by Duggar* into the causes of the rotting of celery in storage showed that the disease is associated largely with poor and damp houses. His remarks on this phase of the subject will apply to field cellars in general, and they are therefore copied here.

After describing the old-fashioned, sod-covered, post-supported house, as shown in Fig. 55, Duggar proceeds: "The greatest difficulty with these houses is that they rot down rapidly, and they may give some trouble with moisture. They are inexpensive, however. It may be suggested that in constructing root houses or storage houses of any kind the fundamental principles involved relative to the purpose of the structure should be constantly considered. To continue its vitality, succulence and crispness, celery must continue in the storage house a very slow growth—a growth sufficient to establish the roots in the soil and to complete the development of the inner leaves. Thorough freezing is fatal, but the lowest temperature at which freezing will not take place is most desirable. Not only does this temperature hold the plant in the desired condition of greatly suspended activities, but it renders next to impossible the growth of injurious fungi, which would speedily wilt and rot it. In order, then, to approach the temperature sought, the house should be so snugly constructed as to provide against freezing. Again, it should be so provided with ventilating appliances that at any time advantage might be taken of any cold intervals to rapidly and effectually chill the house, after which it might be securely closed for a warmer period; and with

Fig. 57. Interior of a model storage pit.

---

* Bull. 132, Cornell Exp. Sta.

this enclosed lower temperature remain for a time at a point more nearly that desired.

"In Figs. 56 and 57 is shown one of the most improved root houses which I have seen in operation, and the photograph here

Fig. 58.
Details of construction of a good storage house.

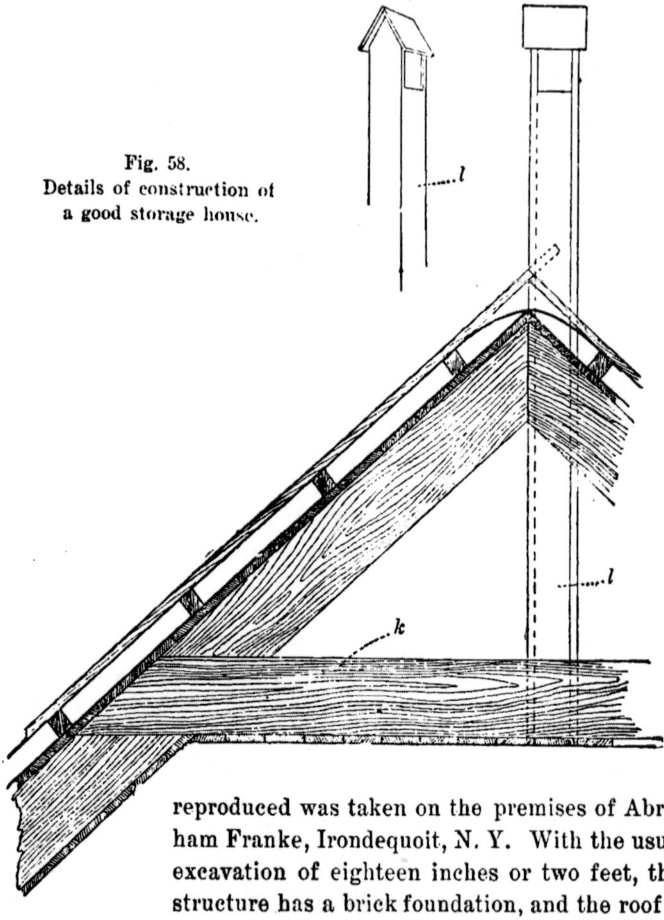

reproduced was taken on the premises of Abraham Franke, Irondequoit, N. Y. With the usual excavation of eighteen inches or two feet, this structure has a brick foundation, and the roof is well provided with air-chambers and paper linings, affording the best protection against cold. The additional large air-chamber above the collar-beams, with its separate windows, seems also desirable. There are large double doors at each end, and the space between each outer and inner door is large, and the connections well arranged for the exclusion of cold air. It will be seen that Fig. 58 shows the construction of the peak and collar-beam (*k*) of the house, and also of the ventilator (*l*, *l*). Fig. 59 shows the detail of the roof construction. The plate (*h*) is held firmly to the wall by a tongue (*i*) let into the brickwork. The rafter is *b*. On this is a thickness of sheathing upon either side (*a*, *c*), with an air-space at *e*, and outer sheathing at *g*, and

Fig. 59.
Details of a storage house.

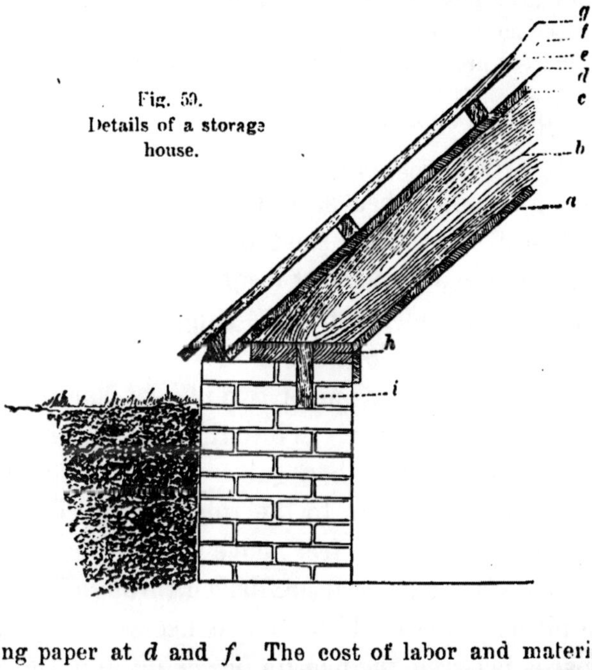

building paper at *d* and *f*. The cost of labor and materials is about $500. An interior view of this house is shown in Fig. 57. It was stocked with celery at the time this picture was made, and in spite of having been harvested early, the plants were faring well.

"I have seen a cheaper and modified form of the above structure, provided with a single air-chamber outside of the rafters and first boarding, with tarred paper covering the final layer of boards. The odor of tar in the house has caused comment; but if the house is well aired and sunned before celery is admitted, there seems to be no need to fear even local censure.

"The improved form of storage house which has been described above may be suggestive to market-gardeners who have other vegetable products to store for the winter markets, for in the storage of almost any vegetable product the same three essential features are to be borne in mind, viz: (1) protection against freezing; (2) a temperature so low that the activities of the plant may not be incited and that the growth of fungi may be discouraged; and (3) proper protection against excessive moisture."

Usually the vegetable cellar or pit is a temporary structure. A style that is much used in parts of the northern states may be described as follows: On warm and well-drained soil (preferably sand or gravel) an excavation is made from one to two feet deep, usually from fourteen to eighteen feet wide, and of the length required in order to hold the crop that one has to store. The sides of the excavation are held by one or two planks placed on edge and secured by stakes driven into the ground. The whole pit is then covered with a gable roof made by laying boards from the margin to the ridge-pole. The ridge-pole stands three to five feet above the bottom of the pit and is held on stakes that are driven through the center of the pit lengthwise. Usually it is necessary to support the boards between the margin of the pit and the ridge, and this is done by another run or plate held on stakes driven midway between the side and the ridge. Boards about twelve feet long are now laid from the ground to the ridge-pole, making a continuous roof. Ordinarily these boards are lapped, and the upper run is nailed lightly in order to hold the roof in place. The boards are not nailed very securely, however, for it may be necessary to use the boards the following year, and the subsequent covering will hold them in place. At intervals of ten or twelve feet two or three boards are left without nailing to allow of an entrance, and the place is marked by a stake driven into the ground. These pits are made late in the fall, and until severe freezing weather comes the protection of boards is sufficient; but as winter approaches, straw, grass or other litter is thrown over the roof, and subsequently manure or earth is added. In pits of this character, which contain a large body of air, very uniform conditions are secured. In them celery, leek and Brussels sprouts, and even cabbage, may be set compactly in rows. The plants often will make a root-hold in the soil, and therefore will not shrivel and are not so likely to rot as those that are thrown in loose. Pits of this character are very useful for the storing of late or winter celery. In them the celery will grow somewhat, and it will blanch by spring. If, however, it is desired to keep celery only a short time, and particularly if the crop has been blanched in the field, another kind of house is usually more desirable. In that case, a house which has a little artificial heat is usually better; and houses of this kind are used in the Kalamazoo celery region. These will be discussed when the subject of celery is considered.

Nearly all root crops, as beets, carrots, potatoes, are kept over winter with ease by burying them in the field. It is well to choose a warm and well-drained soil. It is important that the pit be covered very lightly at first, and more covering added as the cold weather comes on. If the full amount of covering is applied at first, the products are likely to heat and decay will set in. Be sure that the beets and potatoes are not attacked by fungous diseases before they are put in the pit. It is customary to make a small circular or rectangular excavation from six inches to a foot deep and from six to eight feet across. In this the roots are piled in a tall cone. Straw or salt hay or other dry litter is then thrown over the pile to protect from the early frosts. As the season advances, an inch or two of earth is thrown over the straw and finally, when winter threatens to close in, the pile is covered deep enough to give full protection. Usually ten to twelve inches of earth over the straw will be sufficient, the straw itself being four to six inches thick after it is well matted down. In severe climates the earth may then be covered with a foot or two of horse manure. Apples can be buried in this way with very good results, particularly the long-keeping varieties, as Russets.

If a great quantity of roots is to be stored, the pit may be elongated to any length required. It is well not to make it much wider than six or eight feet, else the vegetables will be likely to heat and there may be too great pressure on the lowermost tubers. An excellent modification of the long pit is the compartment-pit (Fig. 60). This has narrow partitions of earth every four or five feet, thus preventing the heating of the vegetables and also allowing one compartment to be emptied during the winter without

Fig. 60. A compartment-pit, after each compartment is covered.

exposing another. Usually these compartment-pits are sunk two or three feet in the earth and a partition of soil six to twelve inches wide is left between the excavations. Each pit is then filled until it is "rounded full" and is covered as above described. It is often difficult to make these partitions hold their shape, however, particularly in loose and sandy soil. In such cases the vegetables may be heaped in several piles in a long pit and earth tramped in between the piles.

Whatever the style of pit, it is essential that the soil be naturally well drained, and a furrow or ditch should be opened around the pit to carry off surface water.

NOTE.—If the reader desires literature on the making of a farm cold-storage building, he may consult Prof. F. Wm. Rane, Proc. 18th Annual Meeting Soc. Prom. Agric. Sci. (Detroit, 1897), and press bulletin N. H. Exp. Sta., 1900. Also Bull. 84, Kan. Exp. Sta. (April, 1899).

PART II
VEGETABLE-GARDENING CROPS

CHAPTER VIII

INTRODUCTORY DISCUSSION

In considering the culture of the various crops, it is essential that one be able to distinguish principles from mere details of practice. Gardening books and essays are replete with rules and advice; but after one has read them he may still be ignorant of the essential things that the given crop needs. The demands which are essential or peculiar to the crop should be presented at the outset; thereafter the details of practice — to show how these essentials are secured — may be considered. From the mass of detail and of special and local practice, one must pick the kernel,— the little grain of truth that applies everywhere and always.

A principle is a universal truth. Under similar natural conditions it applies everywhere. It expounds the reason why. It explains. Merely telling how to do a thing may be of little avail in a book, for if a book is good for anything it is read in many places and must apply to different conditions. One can never understand a thing until he knows the reason why. Knowing this, he can work out his method; or if he cannot work out a method, he is necessarily the servant of some one who can. Most men do not rise above details.

The main or bold facts which one needs first to know about a vegetable he would cultivate are these: (1) whether root crop, leaf crop, fruit crop; (2) demands as to season or climate,—cold-weather crop or warm-weather crop; (3) duration of its growth,—early or quick crop, full-season crop, catch-crop, companion-crop; (4) whether to be transplanted or not; (5) to be grown in hills or drills; (6) the special demands as to soil and plant-food. Knowing these things, he next inquires what peculiar treatments the crop demands in tillage and other special care, what are its enemies, and what are the means of harvesting and marketing. In the following pages an effort is made to give the comprehensive view when treating the different crops; details of practice are considered to be of secondary importance to the object which the author now has in view and he has not treated them in full, although success in the cultivation of any crop is impossible without close attention to these details.

1. CLASSIFICATION OF CROPS

The first essential in an analysis of the methods of cultivating the crops is a classification of the crops themselves. A mere alphabetical arrangement is the best for easy reference and for those who are looking chiefly for rules, but it does not contribute to an understanding of principles. Related plants demand similar care: and these plants should be thrown together in groups.

It is important that the intending cultivator classify the plant with reference to climate or season. Some vegetables are essentially hot-season or semi-tropical plants: of such are corn, tomato, cucumber, all melons, squashes and pumpkins, beans, okra, eggplant, red pepper or capsicum, sweet potato. These plants are injured or killed by light frost. They are commonly classed as "tender." They should not be set in the open until danger of frost is past. Other vegetables are cool-season or mid-temperate plants: of such are all root crops, potato, all onion-like plants, pea, spinach, all cole crops, lettuce, celery, cress, asparagus, rhubarb. They are classed as "hardy," since, when properly grown and handled, they will withstand considerable frost.

There are three general methods or schemes of classifying kitchen-garden vegetables: (1) A classification based primarily on the uses to which the crops are put. The most perfect illustration of this classification is Loudon's (*Cyclopædia of Gardening*), of which he remarks: "Though no such arrangement can be absolutely perfect, from the circumstance of some of the plants being used for different purposes, yet, by bringing together such as present most points of union something better than a mere alphabetical catalogue is formed." * This scheme, somewhat modified, is used by Burr in his "Field and Garden Vegetables of America," the only American work which has classified the subject. (2)

---

* Loudon's classification, with minor modifications, is printed on p. 258 of the fourth edition of "The Horticulturist's Rule-Book."

A classification based on botanical kinships or on natural families. This gives the most perfect scheme, so far as mere classification is concerned, but it does not elucidate principles of cultivation. (3) A classification based on essential methods of culture. Such a scheme, although necessarily arbitrary in some places I now propose. In many parts it closely parallels Loudon's.

CLASS I. ANNUAL VEGETABLES.

Sub-Class I. Crops grown for subterranean parts.

Group 1. ROOT CROPS.

Beet, *Beta vulgaris.*
Carrot, *Daucus Carota.*
Parsnip, *Pastinaca sativa.*
Radish, *Raphanus sativus.*
Salsify, *Tragopogon porrifolius.*
Scorzonera, *Scorzonera Hispanica.*
Turnip and Rutabaga, *Brassica.*
Horse-radish,* *Cochlearia Armoracia.*

Group 2. TUBER CROPS.

Potato, *Solanum tuberosum.*
Sweet Potato, *Ipomœa Batatas.*

Group 3. BULB CROPS.

Onion, *Allium Cepa, A. fistulosum.*
Leek, *A. Porrum.*
Garlic, *A. sativum.*
Shallot, *A. Ascalonicum.*
Cive, *A. Schœnoprasum.*

---

* Horse-radish and dandelion are perennials; but as now grown they do not occupy the ground more than a year.

Sub-Class II. Crops grown for foliage parts.

Group 4. Cole Crops.

Kale and Borecole, *Brassica oleracea.*
Brussels Sprouts, *B. oleracea.*
Cabbage, *B. oleracea.*
Cauliflower and Broccoli, *B. oleracea.*
Kohlrabi, *B. oleracea.*

Group 5. Pot-herb Crops (used for "greens").

Spinach, *Spinacea oleracea.*
Chard and Beet, *Beta vulgaris.*
Orach, *Atriplex hortensis.*
Purslane, *Portulaca oleracea.*
Dandelion, *Taraxacum officinale.*
Mustard, *Brassica* species.

Group 6. Salad Crops.

Lettuce, *Lactuca sativa.*
Endive, *Cichorium Endivia.*
Celery, *Apium graveolens.*
Parsley, *Carum Petroselinum.*
Cress, *Lepidium sativum.*
Upland or Winter Cress, *Barbarea vulgaris.*
Water Cress, *Nasturtium officinale.*

Sub-Class III. Crops grown for fruit or seed parts.

Group 7. Pulse Crops.

Bean, *Phaseolus, Dolichos, Vicia.*
Pea, *Pisum sativum.*

Group 8. Solanaceous Crops.

Tomato, *Lycopersicum esculentum.*
Eggplant, *Solanum Melongena.*
Pepper, *Capsicum annuum.*
Physalis or Husk Tomato, *Physalis.*

Group 9. Cucurbitous or Vine Crops.

Cucumber, *Cucumis sativus.*
Melon, *C. Melo.*

Gherkin, *C. Anguria.*
Watermelon, *Citrullus vulgaris.*
Luffa, *Luffa Ægyptiaca* and *L. acutangula.*
Zit-Kwa, or Wax Gourd, *Benincasa cerifera*
Pumpkin, *Cucurbita.*
Squash, *Cucurbita.*

Group 10. CORN. OKRA. MARTYNIA.

Sweet Corn, *Zea Mays.*
Okra, *Hibiscus esculentus.*
Martynia, *Martynia proboscidia.*

Group 11. CONDIMENTAL AND SWEET HERBS.

Group 12. MUSHROOM. (Culturally and otherwise the mushroom is so unlike other garden vegetables that it demands special and separate treatment. Therefore, it is not discussed in this book. It is not a vegetable-gardening subject, although usually so classed.)

CLASS II. PERENNIAL VEGETABLES.

Asparagus, *Asparagus officinalis.*
Rhubarb, *Rheum Rhaponticum.*
Docks, *Rumex.*
Sorrel, *Rumex.*
Artichoke, Globe, *Cynara Scolymus.*
Artichoke, Jerusalem, *Helianthus tuberosus.*
Sea Kale, *Crambe maritima.*

2. BOOKS

The person who expects to secure the best results in crops and in the pleasure of growing them should be a reader. Books, periodicals, and bulletins are suggestive of new ideas, and a new idea is worth the having for the mere novelty of it. Every book has some value. Even if its advice is all wrong, it challenges experiment and controversy, and thereby has some excuse for its being. But no book is all wrong. More often the reader is wrong, in desiring to follow its details to the letter rather than to catch its spirit and to arouse himself to a new point of view.

The following list gives a general view of the history of vegetable-gardening in America. Study the titles chronologically from 1799 to 1900, and note the ways of looking at the subject. Most of the books here mentioned are now valuable only as histories. Some of them are invaluable as practical manuals. It is not expected that the reader will buy any considerable number of them, but the list will aid him to make a selection. In those which are now out of date and out of print he may have little interest, but it should be some satisfaction, at the least, to know what has been written and who has written it. Even if one cannot use this knowledge in direct practice, he should consider that the consciousness of knowing constitutes half the pleasure of living.

Every person who would grow vegetables should have two or three books which treat the general subject, as Greiner, Landreth, Henderson, Green, Rawson. If he specializes with any crop he should procure a treatise on that particular subject. If he lives in a peculiar geographical region, he will need a book written particularly for that area, as Rolfs' for the Atlantic South and Wickson's for California. If one desires an authoritative cyclopedic work on vegetables, he should by all means own "The Vegetable Garden" (London), an English version of Vilmorin's "Les Plantes Potagères." For odd and little-known vegetables the student may consult Paillieux and Bois' "Le Potager d'un Curieux," which, unhappily, is not rendered into English. A book that discusses vegetables with particular reference to methods of displaying them at shows is Edwin Beckett's "Vegetables for Exhibition and Home Consumption" (London, 1899). Persons who are interested in growing plants for exhibition will also find help in Williamson and Dunn's "The Horticultural Exhibitors' Handbook" (London, 1892), although the English ideals in exhibition are often unlike the American. On methods of exhibiting, the reader should also consult Bull. 69, new series, of the New York State Experiment Station, (1894), on "Vegetables Grown for Exhibition."

For descriptions of varieties one must rely on the seed catalogues and experiment station bulletins. One notable American book was devoted to this subject: Burr's "Field and Garden Vegetables of America" (Boston, 1863). It is an illustrated work of 674 pages. Three years later an abridgment of this work was made under the name of "Garden Vegetables."

Finally it may be said that the student of American vegetable-gardening literature will be struck with the lack of any sustained effort to expound principles.

American Books on Vegetable-Gardening

The following inventory of books in the author's library is a practically complete list of American book writings on vegetable-gardening subjects. It comprises not only those which are wholly devoted to vegetable-gardening matters, but also books of general gardening that give any important part of their space to discussions of vegetables. The list does not include books on the forcing of vegetables.

ALLEN, C. L.

CABBAGE, CAULIFLOWER AND ALLIED VEGETABLES, FROM SEED TO HARVEST. Illustrated. New York. 1901. [c. 1901.*] Orange Judd Co. pp. xvi+127. 7½ x 5.†

ANDERSON, JAMES.

See Marshall, Charles. "An Introduction to the Knowledge and Practice of Gardening."

ARLIE, C. H.

See Greiner, T., and Arlie, C. H. "How to Grow Onions."

BAILEY, L. H.

GARDEN-MAKING. Suggestions for the utilizing of home grounds. Aided by L. R. Taft, F. A. Waugh, Ernest Walker. New York and London. 1898. [c. 1898.] The Macmillan Company. pp. vii+417. 6¾ x 4¾. [The Garden-Craft Series.] Vegetables by Waugh.

—Same. Reprinted 1898. pp. vii+417.

—Same, 3d ed., revised. pp. vii+417.

—Same, 4th ed., 1901. pp. vii+417.

THE HORTICULTURIST'S RULE-BOOK; a compendium of useful information for fruit-growers, truck-gardeners, florists and others. Completed to the close of the year 1889. New York. 1889. [c. 1889.] Garden Publishing Company. pp. 236. 6¾ x 4¾.

—Same, 2d ed., revised. Completed to the beginning of the year 1892. [c. 1892.] The Rural Publishing Company. pp. 221. 6¾ x 4¾.

—Same, 3d ed., revised and extended. New York and London. 1895. [c. 1895.] Macmillan & Co. pp. ix+302. 6¾ x 4¾.

—Same, 4th ed., 1896. [c. 1895.] pp. ix+312. 6¾ x 4¾. B. [The Garden-Craft Series.]

---

*Signifies date of copyright.
† " size of Book in inches, as measured on the cover.
[n. c.]=No record of copyright. [n. d.]=No date.

BARNARD, CHARLES.

My Handkerchief Garden; size, 25 x 60 feet. Results: A garden, fresh vegetables, exercise, health and $20.49. New York. n. d. [n. c.] E. H. Libby. pp. 69. 7¼ x 5. [1st ed]
—Same, 2d ed. Illustrated. 1893. [c. 1893.] The Rural Publishing Company. pp. 75. 7½ x 5. [The Rural Library, Vol. I, No. 17, April.]

BEADLE, D. W.

Canadian Fruit, Flower, and Kitchen Gardener; a guide in all matters relating to the cultivation of fruits, flowers and vegetables, and their value for cultivation in this climate Illustrated. Colored plates. Toronto. 1872. [c. 1872.] James Campbell & Son. pp. xvi + 391. 9 x 6.

BOCHOVE, G. VAN and BROTHER.

Kalamazoo Celery; its cultivation and secret of success. Kalamazoo, Mich. 1893. [c. 1886.]. Kalamazoo Publishing Co. pp. 29. 6¾ x 4¼.

BOSSON, CHARLES P.

Observations on the Potato, and Remedy for the Potato Plague. In two parts; containing a history of the potato, its cultivation and uses; also a treatise on the potato malady, its origin and appearances in different countries, a view of various theories concerning it, with the remedies proposed, and an inquiry into the causes producing the disease, with directions for staying its further progress. Boston. 1846. [c. 1846.] Published by E. L. Pratt. pp. ii + 118. 8¼ x 5.

BRIDGEMAN, THOMAS.

The American Gardener's Assistant. In three parts, containing complete directions for the cultivation of vegetables, flowers, fruit trees, and grape-vines. New edition; revised, enlarged and illustrated by S. Edward Todd. Part I. Kitchen-Gardening, pp. 152; Part II. Fruit-Gardening, pp. 211; Part III. Flower-Gardening, pp. 166. [The work is a revision of "The Young Gardener's Assistant."]

The Kitchen Gardener's Instructor; containing a catalogue of garden and herb seed, with practical directions under each head for the cultivation of culinary vegetables and herbs.

With a calendar, showing the work necessary to be done in a kitchen garden every month throughout the season. Also, directions for forcing or forwarding vegetables out of the ordinary season. The whole adapted to the climate of the United States. A new and improved edition. New York. 1860. [c. 1847.] C. M. Saxton, Barker & Co. pp. xii+164. 7¾ x 5.

THE YOUNG GARDENER'S ASSISTANT; containing a catalogue of garden and flower seeds, with practical directions under each head, for the cultivation of culinary vegetables and flowers. Also, directions for cultivating fruit trees, the grape vines, etc.; to which is added a calendar, showing the work necessary to be done in the various departments of gardening in every month of the year. Seventh edition, improved. New York. 1837. [c. 1837.] Mitchell & Turner. pp. vi + 360. 8¼ x 5.

—Same, 8th edition, improved. 1840. [c. 1840.] pp. vi + 408. 8¼ x 5¼.

—Same, the whole adapted to the climate of the United States. New edition, with an appendix, containing remarks on the all-eyed disease of the potato, etc. Part I. Vegetable department. New York. 1865. [1847.] William Wood & Co. pp. vi + 164. 7½ x 5. [The three parts were also published separately as "Kitchen Gardener's Instructor," "Fruit-Cultivator's Manual," and "Florist's Guide."]

BRILL, FRANCIS.

CAULIFLOWERS AND HOW TO GROW THEM; with plain practical and explicit directions in minute detail for the cultivation and management of this crop, from the sowing of the seed to the marketing of the product. Riverhead, New York. 1886. [n. c.] Published by the author. pp. 16. 9 x 5¾.

FARM-GARDENING AND SEED-GROWING. New and enlarged edition. With suggestions to seed-growers. By George Thurber. New York. 1897. [1883.] Orange Judd Co. pp. 166. 7½ x 5.

BUIST, ROBERT.

THE FAMILY KITCHEN GARDENER; containing plain and accurate descriptions of all the different species and varieties of culinary vegetables; with their botanical, English, French, and German names, alphabetically arranged, and the best mode of cultivating them, in the garden or under glass; with a description of implements and medicinal herbs in general use. Also, descriptions and characters of the most select fruits, their management, propagation, etc. Illustrated with twenty-five engravings. New York. 1852. [c. 1847.] C. M. Saxton. pp. 216. 7¾x5.

—Same, New York. 1867. [c. 1847.] Orange Judd Co. pp. 216. 7¾x5.

BURPEE, W. ATLEE & CO.

VEGETABLES FOR THE HOME GARDEN. Third ed. Illustrated. Philadelphia. 1898. [c. 1896.] pp. 127. 7½x5.

BURPEE, W. ATLEE.

ROOT CROPS FOR STOCK FEEDING AND HOW TO GROW THEM. Compiled from the prize essays and practical experience. Illustr. Philadelphia. 1888. [c. 1888]. W. Atlee Burpee & Co. pp. viii. + 72. 7½ x 5.

HOW TO GROW MELONS FOR MARKET. Illustrated. Philadelphia. 1888. [c. 1888.] W. Atlee Burpee & Co. pp. x + 81. 7¼x5.

See Pedersen, J., and Howard, G. H. "How to Grow Cabbages and Cauliflower Most Profitably."

See Darlington, E. D., and Moll, L. M. "How and What to Grow in a Kitchen Garden of One Acre."

See Greiner, T., and Arlie, C. H. "How to Grow Onions."

BURR, FEARING, JR.

THE FIELD AND GARDEN VEGETABLES OF AMERICA; containing full descriptions of nearly eleven hundred species and varieties, with directions for propagation, culture and use. Illustrated. Boston. 1863. [c. 1863.] Crosby & Nichols. pp. xv + 674. 9x6.

GARDEN VEGETABLES, AND HOW TO CULTIVATE THEM. Illustrated. Boston. 1866. [c. 1866.] J. E. Tilton & Co. pp. 12 + 355. 7¾x5. [Abridgment of the above].

CARMAN, ELBERT S.

THE NEW POTATO CULTURE; as developed by the trench system, by the judicious use of chemical fertilizers, and by the experiments carried on at the rural grounds during the past fifteen years. New York. 1891. [c. 1891.] The Rural Publishing Co. pp. 165. 8¼ x 5¾.

COBBETT, WILLIAM.

THE AMERICAN GARDENER; a treatise on the situation, soil, fencing and laying-out of gardens; on the making and managing of hotbeds and greenhouses, and on the propagation and cultivation of the several sorts of vegetables, herbs, fruits and flowers. Baltimore and Frederick, Md. 1823. [pref. 1819.] J. Robinson, and J. Robinson & Co. pp. ix + 252. 5½ x 3½.

—Same. New York. 1856. [preface 1819.] C. M. Saxton & Co. pp. 230. 8 x 4¾.

—Same. New York. n. d. [preface 1819.] Orange Judd & Co. pp. 230. 6½ x 4.

—Same. American stereotype edition. Concord, N. H. 1842. [c. 1842.] L. Hamilton, Boston. Saxton & Pierce, New York. Saxton & Miles. pp. x + 271. 6¾ x 4½. B.

—Same. Paper cover.

COMPLETE GARDENER AND FLORIST, THE; containing an account of every vegetable production cultivated for the table, with directions for planting and raising flowers. 9th ed. New York. 1849. [n. c.] Dewitt & Davenport. pp. iv + 92. 7½ x 4½. [Bound with the "Flower Gardener."]

CRIDER, MRS. H. M.

HOW TO GROW FINE CELERY. A New Method. York, Pa. 1884. [c. 1884.] H. M. Crider, publisher. pp. 14. 8½ x 5½.

CROZIER, A. A.

THE CAULIFLOWER. 1 plate. Ann Arbor, Mich. 1891. [c. 1891.] Register Publishing Co. pp. 230. 7½ x 5¼.

HOW TO COOK CAULIFLOWER. Ann Arbor, Mich. n. d. [c. 1891.] The Register Publishing Co. pp. 28. 7½ x 5.

CUMMINS, D.

See Day, J. W. "Tomato Culture."

DARLINGTON, E. D., and MOLL, L. M.

HOW AND WHAT TO GROW IN A KITCHEN GARDEN OF ONE ACRE. Edited by W. Atlee Burpee. Illustrated. Philadelphia. 1888. [c. 1888.] Published by W. Atlee Burpee. pp. vii+193. $7\frac{1}{2}$ x 5.

—Same, 6th ed., 1893. [c. 1888.] pp. vii+198. $7\frac{1}{2}$ x 5.

DAY, J. W.

TREATISE ON TOMATO CULTURE. Crystal Springs, Miss. 1891. [n. c.] pp. 25. $8\frac{3}{4}$ x $5\frac{1}{2}$.

DAY, J. W., CUMMINS, D., and ROOT, A. I.

TOMATO CULTURE; in three parts. Part I. Tomato culture in the south. Part II. Tomato culture especially for canning factories. Part III. Plant-growing for market, and high-pressure gardening in general. A practical book for those who work under either glass or cloth as protection from frost. Illustrated. Medina, Ohio. 1892. [n. c.] A. I. Root. pp. 135. $6\frac{1}{4}$ x 5.

ELDER, WALTER.

THE COTTAGE GARDEN OF AMERICA; containing practical directions for the culture of flowers, fruits and vegetables, the natures and improvement of soils, manures, and their application, wounds, diseases and cures, monthly calendar, insects, botany, etc. Philadelphia. 1849. [c. 1848.] Moss & Brothers. pp. v + 233. $7\frac{1}{4}$ x $4\frac{1}{2}$.

—Same, 2d edition, revised and improved. 1850. [c. 1848]. pp. viii + 233.

EMERSON, G.

See Neill, Patrick. "The Practical Fruit, Flower and Vegetable Gardener's Companion."

FESSENDEN, T. G.

THE NEW AMERICAN GARDENER; containing practical directions on the culture of fruits and vegetables; including landscape and ornamental gardening, grape vines, silk, strawberries, etc. Boston. 1828. [c. 1828.] J. B. Russell. pp. 307. 7 x $4\frac{3}{4}$.

—Same, 4th ed. Boston. 1833. [1828.] Carter and Hendee. pp. 307. $7\frac{1}{4}$ x 5.

—Same, 6th ed. Boston. 1832. [c. 1828.] Carter & Hendee, and John B. Russell. pp. 312. 7 x $4\frac{1}{2}$.

—Same, 7th ed. Boston and Cincinnati. 1833. [c. 1828.] Russell, Odiorne & Co.; Carter, Hendee & Co.; H. L. and H. S. Barnum. pp. 307. 7½ x 5.

—Same, 13th ed. Boston and Philadelphia. 1839. [c. 1828.] Otis Broaders & Co.; Thomas Cowperthwaite & Co. pp. 307. 7½ x 5.

—Same, 16th ed. 1843. [c. 1828.] pp. 306. 7½ x 4½.

—Same, 19th ed. 1847. [c. 1828.] pp. 306. 7½ x 5.

—Same, 20th ed. 1850. [c. 1828.] pp. 306. 7½ x 4½.

—Same, 30th ed. 1857. [c. 1828.] pp. 306. 8 x 5½. (Bound with "The Complete Farmer."]

THE AMERICAN KITCHEN GARDEN; containing practical directions for the culture of vegetables. Also garden fruits, strawberry, raspberry, gooseberry, currants, melons, etc., etc Revised from the 35th ed., and adapted to the use of families, by a practical gardener. New York. 1856. [c. 1852.] C. M. Saxton & Co. pp. viii + 120. 8 x 5½. B. [Bound fifth in Saxton's "Rural Hand-Books." 2d series.]

—Same, separate. 1852.

FISKE, G. BURNAP, Compiler.

PRIZE GARDENING: How to derive profit, pleasure, and health from the garden. Actual experience of the successful prize-winners in the American Agriculturist Garden Contest. Fully illustrated from original photographs and drawings. New York. 1901. [c. 1901.] Orange Judd Co. pp. xiv+307. 7½ x 5.

—See Morse, J. E., "The New Rhubarb Culture."

FITCH, JOHN M.

PRACTICAL SUGGESTIONS ON VEGETABLE CULTURE. For the market-gardener, the farmer, and any one interested in good things to eat. Written expressly for F. Barteldes & Co. Lawrence, Kansas. 1898. Journal Publishing Co. pp. 32. 8¾ x 5¾.

FITZ, JAMES.

SWEET POTATO CULTURE; giving full instructions from starting the plants to harvesting and storing the crop, with a chapter on the Chinese yam. New and enlarged edition. New York.

1886. [c. 1886.] Orange Judd Co., David W. Judd, president. pp. 86. 7½ x 5.

GARDEN, THE; a pocket manual of practical horticulture: or how to cultivate vegetables, fruits and flowers, embracing an exposition of the nature and action of soils and manures, and the structure and growth of plants; directions for the forming of a garden; description of implements and fixtures; instructions for sowing, transplanting, budding, grafting, and cultivating vegetables, fruits and flowers, with a chapter on ornamental trees and shrubs by the author of "How to Write," "How to Behave," etc. No. I. Illustrated. New York. 1858 [c. 1858.] Fowler and Wells. pp. xi + 166. 7 x 4.

—Same, No. 3 7½ x 5.

GARDINER, JOHN, and HEPBURN, DAVID.

THE AMERICAN GARDENER; containing ample directions for working a kitchen garden, every month in the year; and copious instructions for the cultivation of flower gardens, vineyards, nurseries, hop-yards, greenhouses and hothouses. Washington. 1804. [c. 1804.] Samuel H. Smith. pp. 204. 7 x 4½.

GREEN, SAMUEL B.

VEGETABLE GARDENING; a manual on the growing of vegetables for home use and marketing. Prepared especially for the classes of the school of agriculture of the University of Minnesota. With 115 illustrations. St. Paul. 1896. [c. 1896.] Author. Webb Publishing Co., agents. pp. 224. 7 x 5.

—Same, 2d edition, revised. With 122 illustrations. 1899. [c. 1899.] pp. 240. 7 x 5.

GREGORY, JAMES J. H.

CABBAGES: How to grow them. A practical treatise on cabbage culture, giving full details on every point, including keeping and marketing the crop. Marblehead, Mass. 1881. [c. 1870.] Messenger Steam Printing House. pp. 72. 7¼ x 5.

CARROTS, MANGOLD-WURTZELS AND SUGAR BEETS: How to raise them, how to keep them, and how to feed them. Marblehead, Mass. 1882. [c. 1877.] Messenger Steam Printing House. pp. 61. 7¼ x 5.

ONION RAISING: What kinds to raise, and the way to raise them. 7th edition (revised). Illustrated. Marblehead, Mass. 1881. [c. 1864.] Messenger Steam Printing House. pp. 42. 7¼ x 5.

SQUASHES: How to grow them. A practical treatise on squash culture. Giving full details on every point, including keeping and marketing the crop. New revised and enlarged edition. Illustrated. New York. 1889. [c. 1883.] Orange Judd Co. pp. 83. 7¼ x 5.

GREINER, T.

CELERY FOR PROFIT; an exposé of modern methods in celery growing. Illustrated. Philadelphia. Spring. 1893. [c. 1893.] W. Atlee Burpee & Co. pp. viii + 85. 7½ x 5.

HOW TO MAKE THE GARDEN PAY. Illustrated. Philadelphia. 1890. [c. 1890.] Wm. Henry Maule. pp. 272. 9 x 6.

—Same, 2d, revised and enlarged edition. 1894. [c. 1890.] pp. 319. 9 x 6.

ONIONS FOR PROFIT; an exposé of modern methods in onion growing. Illustrated. Philadelphia. 1893. [c. 1893.] W. Atlee Burpee & Co. pp. vi + 104. 7½ x 5.

THE NEW ONION CULTURE; a story for young and old, which tells how to grow 2,000 bushels of fine bulbs on one acre. The new system fully explained. Illustrated. [La Salle, New York.] 1891. [c. 1891.] pp. vi + 62. 7¾ x 5¼.

THE YOUNG MARKET-GARDENER; beginner's guide. Part I. A little pit well built. Part II. A little plat well tilled. Part III. A little purse well filled. Illustrated. [La Salle, New York.] Spring, 1896. [c. 1895.] pp. iv + 119. 7¾ x 5¼. [T. Greiner's garden series. No. 2.]

THE GARDEN BOOK FOR FARMERS. Illustrated. Philadelphia. April, 1901. [c. 1901.] The Farmer Company. pp. 190. 8½ x 5¾. B. [No. 2, vol. 3, of "The Farmer's Library." Paper.]

GREINER, T., and ARLIE, C. H.

HOW TO GROW ONIONS; with notes on varieties. Edited by W. Atlee Burpee. Philadelphia. 1888. [c. 1887.] W. Atlee Burpee & Co. pp. viii+71. 7½ x 5.

HARRIS, JOSEPH.

GARDENING FOR YOUNG AND OLD. The cultivation of garden vegetables in the farm garden. Illustrated. New York. 1897. [c. 1882.] Orange Judd Co. pp. 191. 7½ x 5.

HENDERSON, PETER.

GARDENING FOR PLEASURE; a guide to the amateur in the fruit, vegetable and flower garden, with full directions for the greenhouse, conservatory and window garden. New, enlarged edition. Illustrated. New York. 1882. [c. 1875.] Orange Judd Co. pp. v + 250. 7½ x 5.

—Same. 1888. [c. 1887.] Orange Judd Co. pp. vi + 404. 7½ x 5.

GARDENING FOR PROFIT; a guide to the successful cultivation of the market and family garden. Illustrated. New York. n. d. [c. 1867.] Orange Judd Co. pp. viii + 243. 7½ x 5.

—Same, new and enlarged edition. 1885. [c. 1874.] pp. vi + 276.

—Same, entirely new and greatly enlarged. Illustrated with numerous new engravings. 1887. [c. 1886.] pp. xii + 376.

HEPBURN, DAVID.

See Gardiner, John. "The American Gardener."

HEXAMER, F. M.

ASPARAGUS: Its culture for home use and for market. A practical treatise on the planting, cultivation, harvesting, and preserving of asparagus, with notes on its history and botany. Illustrated. New York. 1901. [c. 1901.] Orange Judd Co. pp. viii + 168. 7½ x 5.

HOGG, JAMES.

THE VEGETABLE GARDEN: A complete guide to the cultivation of vegetables; containing thorough instructions for sowing, planting, and cultivating all kinds of vegetables; with plain directions for preparing, manuring and tilling the soil to suit each plant; including, also, a summary of the work to be done in a vegetable garden during each month of the year. New York. n. d. [c. 1877.] Dick and Fitzgerald. pp. 137. 7 x 4½. B. [Cover has the legend, "Dick's Garden Hand-Books. The Vegetable Garden."]

HOLLISTER, E. J.

LIVINGSTON'S CELERY BOOK. Conclusions at the close of twenty years' extensive experience by the author on best methods of preparation of soil, cultivating and marketing the crop. Illustrated. Columbus, Ohio. n. d. [c. 1898.] A. W. Livingston's Sons. pp. 96. 7¼ x 5¼.

HOLMES, FRANCIS S.

THE SOUTHERN FARMER AND MARKET-GARDENER; being a compilation of useful articles on these subjects, from the most approved writers. Developing the principles and pointing out the method of their application to the farming and gardening of the South, and particularly of the low country. New improved and enlarged edition. Charleston, S. C. n. d. [c. 1852.] Wm. R. Babcock. pp. viii + 249. 7½ x 4½.

HOW TO GROW FRUIT, FLOWERS AND VEGETABLES; and the language of flowers. New York. Norman L. Munro. No date. Paper. pp. 68. 6½ x 4.

HOWARD, G. H.

See Pedersen, J., and Howard, G. H. "How to Grow Cabbages and Cauliflowers Most Profitably."

HUNN, C. E., and BAILEY, L. H.

THE AMATEUR'S PRACTICAL GARDEN-BOOK: Containing the simplest directions for the growing of the commonest things about the house and garden. Illustrated. New York. 1900. [c. 1900.] The Macmillan Company. pp. vi+250. 6¾ x 4¾. [The Garden-Craft Series.]

—Same, 2d ed., 1901. pp. vi+250.

JACQUES, D. H.

THE GARDEN; a manual of practical horticulture; or how to cultivate vegetables, fruits and flowers; embracing an exposition of the nature and action of soils and manures and the structure and growth of plants; directions for the forming of a garden; description of implements and fixtures; instructions for sowing, transplanting, budding, grafting, and cultivating vegetables, fruits, and flowers; with a chapter on ornamental trees and shrubs. Revised edition. Illustrated. New York. [c. 1866.] Geo. E. and F. W. Woodward. pp. xii+166. 7½ x 5.

KITCHEN AND FRUIT GARDENER, THE; a select manual of kitchen gardening and culture of fruits, containing familiar directions for the most approved practice in each department, descriptions of many valuable fruits, and a calendar of work to be performed each month in the year. The whole adapted to the climate of the United States. Philadelphia. 1844. [c. 1844.] Lea & Blanchard. pp. xii + 118. 7¾ x 4¾. [An American edition of an English work. Bound with the "Complete Florist."]

LANDRETH, BURNET.

MARKET-GARDENING AND FARM NOTES; experiences and observations in the garden and field, of interest to the amateur gardener, trucker and farmer. New York. 1893. [c. 1892.] Orange Judd Co. pp. iv + 215. 7½ x 5.

999 QUERIES, WITH ANSWERS UPON AGRICULTURAL AND HORTICULTURAL SUBJECTS. Published by David Landreth & Sons. Philadelphia. 1784. [c. 1895.] Press of Maccalla & Co. pp. 200. 9¼ x 6.

LELIEVRE, J. F.

NOUVEAU JARDINIER DE LA LOUISIANE; contenant les instructions necessaires aux personnes qui s'occupent de jardinage. Nouvelle-Orleans. 1838. [n. c.] J. F. Lelievre. pp. viii + 200. 6½ x 4¾.

LIVINGSTON, A. W.

LIVINGSTON AND THE TOMATO; being a history of experiences in discovering the choice varieties introduced by him, with practical instructions for growers. Illustrated. Columbus, Ohio. n. d. [c. 1893.] Published by A. W. Livingston's Sons, Seedmen. pp. 176. 7½ x 5¾.

LIVINGSTON'S CELERY BOOK. See Hollister, E. J.

LUPTON, J. M.

CABBAGE AND CAULIFLOWER FOR PROFIT. With fifty-three illustrations. Philadelphia. 1898. [c. 1894.] W. Atlee Burpee & Co. pp. vii + 122. 7½ x 5.

MARKET GARDEN, THE; a journal for the market-gardener. Monthly. Illustrated. Minneapolis. Jan., 1894–Sept., 1898. The Market Garden Co. 12 x 9. The first number was issued in Jan., 1894, although it bears date of Jan. 1, 1893. It is a 4-page issue. The second number appeared in July, 1894. It was not given general circulation, but was sent out for the purpose of securing opinions as to the advisability of establishing such a journal. The regular issue of the periodical began with October, 1894. This was the only attempt in North America, so far as the author is aware, to publish a journal devoted solely to vegetable-gardening interests.

MARSHALL, CHARLES.

AN INTRODUCTION TO THE KNOWLEDGE AND PRACTICE OF GARDENING; first American from the second London edition, considerably enlarged and improved. To which is added an essay on quick-lime, by James Anderson. Vol. I. Boston. 1799. [n. c.] Samuel Etheridge. pp. ii + 276 7 x 4¼.

McNEIL, J. W.

FRUITS AND VEGETABLES. Hazlehurst, Miss. 1888. [n. c.] Copiah Signal Print. pp. 21. 9 x 5¾.

MELL, P. H.

See White, "Gardening for the South."

M'MAHON, BERNARD.

THE AMERICAN GARDENER'S CALENDAR; adapted to the climates and seasons of the United States. Containing a complete account of all the work necessary to be done in the kitchen-garden, fruit-garden, orchard, vineyard, nursery, pleasure-grounds, flower-garden, greenhouse, hothouse, and forcing-frames, for every month in the year; with ample practical directions for performing the same. Also, general as well as minute instructions for laying out, or erecting, each and every of the above departments, according to modern taste and the most approved plans; the ornamental planting of pleasure-grounds, in the ancient and modern style; the cultivation of thorn-quicks and other plants suitable for live hedges, with the best methods of making them, etc. To which are annexed extensive catalogues of the different kinds of plants which may be cultivated either for use or ornament in the several departments, or in rural economy; divided into eighteen separate alphabetical classes, according to their habits, duration, and modes of culture; with explanatory introductions, marginal marks, and their true Linnæan or botanical, as well as English names; together with a copious index to the body of the work. Philadelphia. 1806. [c. 30th year of the independence of the U. S.] B. Graves. pp. v+666. 8½ x 5½.

THE AMERICAN GARDENER'S CALENDAR; adapted to the climates and seasons of the United States. Containing a complete account of all the work necessary to be done in the kitchen-garden, fruit-garden, orchard, vineyard, nursery, pleasure-grounds, flower-garden, greenhouse, hothouse, and forcing-frames, for every month in the year; with ample practical directions for performing the same. Also, general as well as minute instructions for laying out, or erecting, each and every of the above departments, according to modern taste and the most approved plans; the ornamental planting of pleasure-grounds, in the ancient and modern style; the cultivation of thorn-quicks and other plants suitable for live hedges, with the best methods of making them, etc. To which are annexed catalogues of kitchen-garden plants and herbs; aromatic, pot and sweet herbs; medicinal plants; and the most important grasses, etc., used in rural economy, with the soil best adapted to their cultivation; together with a copious index to the body of the work. Fourth edition, improved. Philadelphia. 1820. [c. 1819.] T. P. M'Mahon. pp. 618. 8½ x 5½.

THE AMERICAN GARDENER'S CALENDAR; adapted to the climates and seasons of the United States. Containing a complete account of all the work necessary to be done in the kitchen-garden, fruit-garden, flower-garden, orchard, pleasure-grounds, vineyard, nursery, greenhouse, hothouse, and forcing-frames, for every month in the year; with practical directions and copious index. Eleventh edition, with a memoir of the author, revised and illustrated under the supervision of J. Jay Smith. Philadelphia. 1857. [c. 1857.] J. B. Lippincott & Co. pp ix + 637. 9½ x 6.

MITCHELL, S. H.

TOMATO-GROWING FOR PROFIT; being a practical treatise showing in detail how to grow tomatoes by new methods; from the sowing of the seed to the marketing of the crop, so as to leave when sold the largest amount of profit to the producer; the whole being the result of over thirty years' extensive practical experience by the author. Toronto. 1895. [n. c.] Dudley & Burns. pp. 24. 9½ x 6½.

MORSE, J. E.

THE NEW RHUBARB CULTURE: A complete guide to dark forcing and field culture. How to prepare and use rhubarb. Fully illustrated with original photographs taken expressly for this work. Part II. Additional chapters on other methods. By G. Burnap Fiske. New York. 1901. [c. 1901.]. Orange Judd Co. pp. x+130. 7½ x 5.

MUNRO, NORMAN L., Publisher.

See "How to Grow Fruit, Flowers and Vegetables."

NEILL, PATRICK.

THE FRUIT, FLOWER, AND KITCHEN GARDEN. Adapted to the United States, from the fourth edition, revised and improved by the author. Illustrated. Philadelphia. 1851. [c. 1851.] Henry Carey Baird. pp. ix + 427. 7¾ x 4¾.

THE PRACTICAL FRUIT, FLOWER AND VEGETABLE GARDENER'S COMPANION, with a calendar; adapted to the United States from the fourth edition, revised and improved by the author. Edited by G. Emerson. With notes and additions by R. G. Pardee. With elegant illustrations. New York. 1858. [c. 1855.] A. O. Moore. pp. xiv + 408. 7½ x 5¼.

NIVEN, ROBERT, and Others.

THE NEW CELERY CULTURE; no banking up required. The practice of practical men. Illustrated. New York. 1892. [c. 1892.] The Rural Publishing Co. pp. 29. 7½ x 5. [The Rural Library, Vol. I, No. 7. May.]

OEMLER, A.

TRUCK-FARMING AT THE SOUTH; a guide to the raising of vegetables for northern markets. Illustrated. New York. 1884. [c. 1883.] Orange Judd Co. pp. 270. 7½ x 5¼.

OLCOTT, HENRY S., Editor.

See Roessle, Theophilus. "How to Cultivate and Preserve Celery"

ONION BOOK, THE. A practical Guide to the Profitable Culture of the Crop. By some twenty experienced growers. Illustr. New and greatly enlarged edition. New York. n. d. [c. 1887]. Orange Judd Co. pp. 36. 10 x 6¾.

PEDERSEN, J., (BJERGAARD) and HOWARD, G. H.

HOW TO GROW CABBAGES AND CAULIFLOWERS MOST PROFITABLY. Illustrated. Edited by W. Atlee Burpee, Philadelphia. 1888. [c. 1888.] W. Atlee Burpee & Co. pp. v + 85. 7½ x 5.

PRACTICAL AMERICAN GARDENER, THE; exhibiting the time for every kind of work in the kitchen-garden, fruit-garden, orchard, nursery, shrubbery, pleasure-ground, flower-garden, hop-yard, greenhouse, hothouse and grape vines for every month in the year. By an old Gardener. Baltimore. 1822. [c. 43d year of the independence of the U. S.] Fielding Lucas, Jr. pp. xii + 424. 5½ x 3½.

PRICE, R. H.

SWEET POTATO CULTURE FOR PROFIT; a full account of the origin, history and botanical characteristics of the sweet potato. Illustrated. Full and complete instructions from how to grow the plants to harvesting and storing the crop for both southern and northern latitudes. Complete discussion of the diseases and insects which injure the crop. A description of 47 varieties, with a new system of classifying them. The Chinese yam and the vineless variety are discussed. Latest improved machinery discussed, etc. Dallas, Texas. n. d. [c. 1896.] Texas Farm and Ranch Publishing Co. pp. 110. 8½ x 5½.

PROVANCHER, L'ABBE L.

LE VERGER; Le potager et le partorre dans la Province de Quebec, ou culture raisonnée des fruits, légumes et fleurs qui peuvent péussir sous le climat de Quebec. Ouvrage orné de nombreuses gravures sur bois. Quebec. C. Darveau. 1881. [Preface dated 1874.] pp. 332. 6¾ x 4½.

QUINN, P. T.

MONEY IN THE GARDEN; A vegetable manual prepared with a view to economy and profit. Illustr. New York. 1871. [c. 1871]. Tribune Assoc. pp. x + 268. 7½ x 5. [Later pub. by Orange Judd Co.]

RAWSON, W. W.

CELERY AND ITS CULTIVATION. Revised edition. Illustr. Boston. 1900. [c. 1891. 1900]. W. W. Rawson. pp. 24. 7¼ x 5.

SUCCESS IN MARKET-GARDENING; AND VEGETABLE GROWERS' MANUAL. Illustrated. Boston. 1887. [c. 1887.] Published by the author. pp. iv + 208. 7½ x 5.

—Same, 7th ed., revised and enlarged, with new matter and illustrations. Boston. 1892. [c. 1892.] Published by the author. pp. vi+240. 7½ x 5.

ROE, E. P.

PLAY AND PROFIT IN MY GARDEN. [New ed.] New York. 1893. [c. 1886.] Orange Judd Co. pp. 349. 7½ x 5.

ROESSLE THEOPHILUS.

HOW TO CULTIVATE AND PRESERVE CELERY. Edited, with a preface, by Henry S. Olcott. Colored plates. Albany. 1860. [c. 1860.] Theophilus Roessle, Delavan House. New York; C. M. Saxton, Barker & Co. pp. xxvi + 102. 9½ x 6.

ROLFS, P. H.

VEGETABLE-GROWING IN THE SOUTH FOR NORTHERN MARKETS; being concise directions for the preparation of the soil, use and amounts of fertilizers, and the planting of vegetable crops to obtain the earliest vegetables; also the best methods of packing for shipping, the raising of seed for market, and preserving it for home use. Illustrated. Richmond. 1896. [c. 1896.] The Southern Planter Publishing Co. pp. xi + 255. 7¾ x 5.

ROOT, A. I.

See Day, J. W. "Tomato Culture."

SCHENCK, PETER ADAM.

THE GARDENER'S TEXT-BOOK; containing practical directions upon the formation and management of the kitchen-garden, and for the culture and domestic use of its vegetables, fruits and medicinal herbs. Illustrated. New York. 1860. [c. 1851.] C. M. Saxton, Barker & Co. pp. 306. 6 x 4.

SHINN, CHAS. H.

PACIFIC RURAL HAND-BOOK; containing a series of brief and practical essays and notes on the culture of trees, vegetables and flowers, adapted to the Pacific coast. Also hints on home and farm improvements. San Francisco. n. d. [c. 1879.] Dewey & Co. Pacific Rural Press. pp. 122. 7½ x 4¾.

STEWART, HENRY.

IRRIGATION FOR THE FARM, GARDEN AND ORCHARD. With numerous illustrations. New York. 1883. [c. 1877.] Orange Judd Co. pp. 264. 7½ x 5.

STEWART, HOMER L.

CELERY GROWING AND MARKETING A SUCCESS. With portrait of the author; also illustrated with 13 plates, showing new tools and appliances in celery culture and the care of the crop. This is the only book ever written which covers the whole period of growing, marketing and caring for the crop, with explicit directions. Tecumseh, Mich. 1891. [c. 1891.] The Blade Printing and Paper Co. pp. 151. 7½ x 5¼.

TERRY, T. B.

THE A B C OF POTATO CULTURE. How to grow them in the largest quantity, and of the finest quality, with the least expenditure of time and labor. Carefully considering all the latest improvements in this branch of agriculture up to the present date. Illustrated by twenty engravings. Medina, Ohio. 1885. A. I. Root. pp. 42 + 8. 10 x 6½.

THOMPSON, FRED. S.

RHUBARB OR PIE-PLANT CULTURE. Illustrated. The best varieties. Essential points in growing good rhubarb. How rhubarb pays, compared with certain crops. The first and only edition on this subject. Milwaukee, Wis. 1894. [c. 1894.] J. N. Yewdale & Sons Co. pp. 76. 7½ x 5.

THORBURN, GRANT.

THE GENTLEMAN AND GARDENER'S KALENDAR; containing ample directions for the cultivation of the kitchen and flower garden, greenhouse, nursery, orchard, etc., for the United States of America, 3d ed., corrected and improved. Price, 50 cents. Ving. t. p. New York. 1821. [c. in the 36th year of the independence of U. S. A.] B. Young. pp. 132. 7 x 4½.

TILLINGHAST, ISAAC F.

A MANUAL OF VEGETABLE PLANTS; containing the experiences of the author in starting all those kinds of vegetables which are most difficult for a novice to produce from seeds, with the best methods known for combating and repelling noxious insects, and preventing the diseases to which garden vegetables are subject. Factoryville, Pa. 1878. [c. 1877.] Tillinghast Brothers. pp. 102. 6¾ x 4½.

TILLINGHAST'S PLANT MANUAL. A guide to the successful propagation of cabbage and celery plants. Illustrated. La Plume, Pa. January, 1888. Published by the author. pp. 32. 9 x 6.

TODD, S. EDWARDS.

See Bridgeman, "American Gardener's Assistant."

VAUGHAN'S CELERY MANUAL. Illustrated. Chicago. 1889. [c. 1889.] Vaughan's seed store. pp. 39. 7½ x 5¼.

VICK, JAMES.

VICK'S FLOWER AND VEGETABLE GARDEN. Illustrated. Rochester, N. Y. n. d. Published by James Vick. pp. 166. 9½ x 6½.

WARNER, ANNA.

MISS TILLER'S VEGETABLE GARDEN AND THE MONEY SHE MADE BY IT. New York. n. d. [c. 1875.] Anson D. F. Randolph & Co. pp. 140. 6¾ x 4½.

WATSON, ALEXANDER.

THE AMERICAN HOME GARDEN; being principles and rules for the culture of vegetables, fruits, flowers, and shrubbery. To which are added brief notes on farm crops, with a table of their average product and chemical constituents. Illustrated. New York. 1859. [c. 1859.] Harper & Brothers. pp. ix + 531. 8 x 5½.

WAUGH, F. A.

See Bailey, "Garden-Making."

WHITE, WILLIAM N.

GARDENING FOR THE SOUTH; or the kitchen and fruit garden; with the best methods for their cultivation, together with hints upon landscape and flower-gardening. Containing modes of culture and descriptions of the species and varieties of the culinary vegetables, fruit trees and fruits, and a select list of ornamental trees and plants found by trial adapted to the states of the Union south of Pennsylvania; with gardening calendars for the same. Illustrated. New York. 1856. [c. 1856.] C. M. Saxton & Co. Athens, Ga. Wm. N. White. pp. vi + 402. 7¾ x 5½.

GARDENING FOR THE SOUTH; or how to grow vegetables and fruits. With additions by Mr. J. Van Buren and Dr. James Camak. Illustrated. New York. n. d. [c 1868.] Orange Judd Co. pp. 444. 7½ x 5. [Second edition of above.]

GARDENING FOR THE SOUTH; or how to grow vegetables and fruits. Third edition, revised and enlarged. By P. H. Mell, With many illustrations. Richmond, Va. 1901. [c. 1901.] B. F. Johnson Publishing Company. pp. 683. 8¾ x 6¼.

WHITNER, J. N.

GARDENING IN FLORIDA; a treatise on the vegetables and tropical products of Florida. Illustrated. Jacksonville, Florida. 1885. [n. c.] C. W. DaCosta. pp. xv + 246. 7½ x 5¼.

WICKSON, EDWARD J.

THE CALIFORNIA VEGETABLES IN GARDEN AND FIELD; a manual of practice, with and without irrigation, for semi-tropical countries. Illustrated. San Francisco. 1897. [c. 1897.] Pacific Rural Press. pp. viii + 336. 9 x 6.

YEAR BOOK, THE, OF THE FARM AND GARDEN; a reliable guide to all important rural occupations, embracing concise directions for the improvement of the soil by draining, subsoil plowing, and trenching; implements of culture—their history, cost, and relative value; rural architecture, with directions for the embellishment of the mansion by ornamental gardening;

laying out and cropping the esculent garden, fruit culture, with directions for planting; lists of fruits, seeds, plants; insects injurious to farm and garden; bee culture, and other valuable miscellaneous matters. With new and beautiful illustrations. Philadelphia. 1860. [c. 1860.] A. M. Spangler. pp. 108. 7¼ x 4.

Recent Experiment Station Publications Relating to Vegetable-Gardening

The following list is designed to include the leading bulletins relating to vegetable-growing from January, 1897, to December, 1899. The publications previous to 1897 are often out of print. If the reader desires a complete index to experiment station literature, and also abstracts of the leading articles, he should consult the Experiment Station Record, published by the United States Department of Agriculture.

ALABAMA.

- No. 77. Some insect pests.
- No. 79. Some horticultural suggestions.
- No. 84. Turnips.
- No. 86. Insecticides, etc.
- No. 108. Tomatoes.

ARKANSAS.

- No. 44. Vegetable-gardening.
- No. 50. Some Irish potato experiments.
- No. 56. Tomatoes, cabbage and onions.

ARIZONA.

- No. 32. Some insect pests of Salt River valley, and the remedies for them.
- No. 35. Vegetable-growing in southern Arizona.

COLORADO.

- No. 41. Blight and other plant diseases.
- No. 47. Colorado's worst insect pests and their remedies.

CONNECTICUT (State).

- No. 125. Preparation and application of fungicides.
- No. 126. Insecticides, their preparation and use; annual reports; various articles.

DELAWARE.

No. 34. Treatment of plant diseases in 1896.

No. 41. Pea canning in Delaware.

FLORIDA.

No. 45. Three injurious insects: Bean leaf-roller, corn delphax, canna leaf-roller.

No. 46. Strawberry thrips and onion thrips.

No. 47. Diseases of the tomato.

No. 48. Insect enemies of the tobacco.

GEORGIA.

No. 38. Watermelons.

No. 45. Some important insect enemies of cucurbits.

IDAHO.

No. 17. Construction and management of hotbeds.

INDIANA.

No. 65. Formalin for prevention of potato scab.

No. 66. Indoor lettuce culture.

No. 69. Insects, fungicides and spraying.

IOWA.

No. 34. Home propagation.

No. 36. Seed-testing.

No. 42. Potato scab.

KANSAS.

No. 70. Vegetable-growing.

No. 82. Potato-stalk weevil.

No. 86. (Press bulletins 1-34.) Celery, seed-breeding, potato-stalk weevil, potato scab.

KENTUCKY.

No. 72. Potatoes.

No. 81. A method of avoiding lettuce rot. Potato scab experiments.

LOUISIANA.

No. 48. Report of entomologist.

No. 52. Report of horticultural department for 1896 and 1897.

MAINE.

No. 36. Testing seeds (Maine law, etc.).

No. 40. Celery.

No. 52. The spraying of plants.

See also articles in annual reports.

MARYLAND.

No. 46. Corn and potato experiments.
No. 48. Some common injurious plant lice, etc.
No. 50. Rust and leopard spot of asparagus.
No. 54. Tomatoes.
No. 59. Sweet potato insects.
No. 60. Some diseases of the sweet potato.
No. 62. Experiments with wheat, corn and potatoes.

MASSACHUSETTS (Hatch).

No. 43. Electro-germination.
No. 44. Tests of vegetable seeds.
No. 55. Nematode worms.
No. 60. Insecticides, fungicides, spraying calendar.
No. 61. Asparagus rust in Massachusetts.
See also articles in annual reports.

MICHIGAN.

No. 144. Vegetables—old and new.
No. 153. Vegetable tests—1897.
No. 160. Some insects of the year 1897.
No. 170. Vegetable tests for 1898.
No. 175. Some insects of the year 1898.
Special bulletin 12. Spraying calendar.

MINNESOTA.

No. 52. Potatoes—variety test in 1896 and implements
No. 55. Grasshoppers, locusts, crickets, etc., of Minnesota.
No. 64. Migratory locusts or grasshoppers.

MISSISSIPPI.

No. 41. Colorado potato beetle in Mississippi.
No. 54. Irish potato culture.

MISSOURI.

No. 43. Asparagus culture in Missouri. Winter forcing of asparagus in the open field.
No. 47. Tarnished plant bug.

NEW HAMPSHIRE.

No. 41. Potatoes.
No. 42. Tomatoes and tomato breeding.
No. 45. (Potato scab) Fruit and potato diseases.
No. 51. Sweet corn for New Hampshire.
No. 52. Muskmelons.
No. 60. Green corn under glass.
No. 62. Forcing pole beans under glass
No. 63. Third potato report.

NEBRASKA.

No. 49. Suggestions for chicory culture.

NEVADA.

No. 36. Some common injurious insects of western Nevada.

NEW JERSEY.

No. 120. Field experiments with potatoes for 1896.

No. 121. Harlequin cabbage bug and melon plant louse.

No. 129. Asparagus rust.

19th Ann. Rept. Peas, beans, tomatoes, Lima beans, etc. In botanical section, fungous diseases.

No. 138. Crude petroleum as an insecticide. Annual reports, various articles.

NEW MEXICO.

No. 20. Seeds.

NEW YORK (Geneva).

No. 119. Downy mildew of cucumber.

No. 120. Fighting cutworms in onion fields.

No. 121. Spray pumps and spraying.

No. 123. Spraying potatoes on Long Island, season of 1896.

No. 130. A bacterial disease of sweet corn.

No. 137. Commercial fertilizers for potatoes.

No. 138. Experiments and observations on some diseases of plants.

No. 139. Plant lice.

No. 143. Green arsenite.

No. 144. A spraying mixture for cauliflower and cabbage worms.

No. 146. Some experiments in forcing head lettuce.

No. 154. Commercial fertilizers for potatoes.

No. 156. Spraying cucumbers in the season of 1898.

No. 158. Combating the striped beetle on cucumbers.

No. 121. Appendix—spray pumps and spraying. Annual reports, various articles.

NEW YORK (Cornell).

No. 130. Potato culture.

No. 132. Notes upon celery.

No. 140. Second report on potato culture.

No. 144. Notes on spraying.

No. 149. Some spraying mixtures.

No. 156. Third report on potato culture.

NORTH CAROLINA.

No. 147. A study of lettuces.

No. 159. Horticultural experiments at Southern Pines, 1896.

NORTH DAKOTA.

No. 30. Preliminary report upon the selection of potatoes for planting.

No. 36. A study of the root systems of corn and potatoes.

No. 37. Prevention of potato scab.

OHIO.

No. 76. Potatoes.

No. 77. Chinch bug, etc.

No. 89. Prevalent diseases of cucumbers, melons and tomatoes.

No. 96. Army worm and other insects.

No. 102. Seed and soil treatment and spray calendar.

No. 105. Further studies of cucumber, melon and tomato diseases, with experiments.

No. 106. Experiments with insecticides.

OREGON.

No. 48. Spraying.

No. 49. Paris green.

PENNSYLVANIA.

No. 39. Potatoes. Annual reports—various articles.

RHODE ISLAND.

No. 43. Additional tests of garden seeds.

No. 44. Celery.

No. 52. Suggestions as to spraying.

No. 55. Forcing rhubarb.

1897. Report—Garden lettuce and its cultivation; classification and description of varieties of garden lettuce; asparagus rust.

SOUTH CAROLINA.

No. 28. The sweet potato as a starch producer.

No. 36. Diseases of plants.

No. 38. Asparagus rust in South Carolina.

SOUTH DAKOTA.

No. 57. Injurious insects.

No. 59. Forage and garden crops in the James river valley.

No. 61. Forage and garden crops in the James river valley.

TENNESSEE.

Vol. X, No. 2. Pot culture of lettuce.

TEXAS.

No. 42. The Irish potato.

UTAH.

No. 49. Spraying.

VERMONT.

No. 60. Insects of the year. Clubroot and black rot of cabbage and turnip.

No. 72. Certain potato diseases and their remedies.

VIRGINIA.

No. 92. The influence of commercial fertilizers upon the quality of the Irish potato.

WASHINGTON.

No. 27. A few facts about insects.

No. 35. Miscellaneous injurious insects.

WEST VIRGINIA.

No. 49. Vegetables.
Folio spray calendar 1898.

WISCONSIN.

No. 65. A bacterial rot of cabbage and allied plants. Annual reports—various articles.

WYOMING.

No. 32. Potatoes.

UNITED STATES DEPARTMENT OF AGRICULTURE.

Farmers' Bulletins.

No. 61. Asparagus culture.
No. 62. Marketing farm produce.
No. 68. Black rot of cabbage.
No. 73. Experiment Station Work IV. Seed selection.
No. 76. Tomato-growing.
No. 84. Experiment Station Work VII. Forcing asparagus.
No. 91. Potato diseases and their treatment.
No. 92. Experiment Station Work IX. Culture of potato.
No. 94. The vegetable garden.
No. 105. Experiment Station Work XII. Fertilizers, etc.
No. 107. Experiment Station Work XIII. Forcing rhubarb.

Office of Experiment Station Bulletins.

No. 57. Varieties of corn. (E. L. Sturtevant.)
No. 68. A description of some Chinese vegetable food materials.

Division of Entomology.

No. 23. New series. Some insects injurious to garden crops (1900).

CHAPTER IX

ROOT CROPS

Radish,	Parsnip,
Beet,	Salsify,
Carrot,	Scorzonera,
Chervil,	Scolymus,
Turnip,	Horse-radish.
Rutabaga,	

Root crops require a cool season and deep soil. They are grown in drills, and usually are not transplanted. They are used both as main-season and secondary crops. All are hardy. No special skill is required in growing them.

The necessity of deep soil is apparent when one considers that the value of a root depends to a large extent on its straightness or symmetry. In hard and shallow soils roots are short and they tend to be branched and irregular. Fine tilth does much to insure quick growth, and quick growth improves the quality. Tile-draining and subsoiling greatly improve land that is to be used for root crops. The use of clover as a green manure is also desirable, as it loosens and ameliorates the soil to a greater depth than most other green-manure crops.

Most root crops succeed best in cool soil. They thrive in the North, or in the cool season in the South. Those that do not require the entire season in which to complete their growth usually thrive best in spring and fall.

Root crops are of two general classes as respects the purposes for which they are grown—fodder crops and vegetable-gardening crops. The former are not intended here; neither are sugar beets. Most of the vegetable-gardening root crops are able to secure their food from relatively unavailable combinations, and they generally use rather freely of potash, although they are also heavy nitrogen and phosphorus feeders. In order to start them quickly, a light dressing of some available nitrogen compound is useful, particularly if the roots are needed for a particular season. Voorhees writes* that these crops, as a class, are much more exhaustive of the plant-food elements than the cereals and legumes.

Probably the most laborious part of the growing of root crops is the harvesting, particularly of the long late kinds. This labor is much lessened by plowing out the roots. Even if the roots are too deep for the plow, two or three furrows may be thrown from either side of the row, and the pulling is made easier. Usually, however, hand-pulling is unnecessary. As soon as the roots are out the tops should be cut off about an inch above the crown, if the crop is to be stored or sold in bulk. The roots should lie in the sun until the soil is dry enough to shake from them, when they may be stored in the pit or cellar or sent to the market. They are easy to keep.

The market value of a root depends largely on its looks. All strong side roots should be cut off, and

* Fertilizers, p. 257.

branchy specimens should be discarded. Early in the season, such roots as beet, carrot, radish, and turnip are sold in bunches of 6 to 12; but as the season advances and prices fall, they are sold in bulk. When sold in bunches, care should be taken to have all the specimens in the bunch of uniform size and shape. The leaves are allowed to remain, and the bunches are tied neatly by a cord passed around the leaf-stalks. The bunches should be kept well sprinkled and away from the sun, for wilted leaves give them a stale and unattractive appearance.

Special literature: Gregory, "Carrots, Mangold Wurtzels and Sugar Beets," Burpee, "Root Crops for Stock Feeding and How to Grow Them."

RADISH

Quick and continuous growth, rather cool weather, protection from the root maggot—these are prime considerations in the growing of radishes. *The radish is a partial season crop.* It is easy to grow.

In America the radish is known mostly as a spring crop, although it is sometimes grown in the fall. In the Old World, however, it is known also as a summer crop, but the varieties grown in the hot weather are usually unlike those raised in the spring and fall. There are three general types of radishes: the ordinary small spring or fall radish, usually light red or clear white; the large turnip radishes, useful for summer cultivation, and which are white, gray or black; the winter radishes, which make a long, hard, woody root that is red, white or black in color. The winter radishes are relatively little grown here. They are said to be popular in China and Japan. They are usually sown late in the season, as late turnips are, and the roots may be kept over winter as other roots are kept.

Radishes are usually treated as a companion-crop when grown in the open field. They may be sown in drills between the rows of cabbages, peas or other later-maturing vegetables. Sometimes they are sown

Fig. 61. Seedlings of radish. Nearly natural size.

directly in the drill with the other vegetables. The seeds are quick to germinate and thereby break the crust and mark the row and thus facilitate tillage, and the roots may be harvested before the other crops need the space. For family use, radishes are often grown in beds by themselves. In clean, friable land they are sometimes sown broadcast. If the soil is loose and rich, radishes should come to edible maturity in four to six weeks. The roots are of better quality when they are relatively small and crisp. When growth ceases the roots become stringy, bitter and often hollow. Sow at frequent intervals for a succession. Radishes are easily grown in hotbeds.

If radishes are to be grown during the hot weather, the soil should be as cool as possible and supplied with an abundance of moisture in order to keep them growing continuously. Radishes do not come to their full perfection in soil that is hard and dry. The roots are so small and short that the plants are essentially surface feeders. Radishes are marketed in bunches (Fig. 62).

Fig. 62. Early spring radishes.

The seeds of radishes are large and germinate quickly. Better roots and a more uniform crop are secured by sowing only the large seeds. The small ones may be sifted out by means of a hand screen.

The root maggot can be destroyed by injecting bisulfide of carbon into the ground about the plants (see *Cabbage*); but this operation is so expensive and troublesome in comparison with the value of the plants that it is not to be advised. The best alternative is to grow the plants on land in which the maggot has not been breeding. If the whole garden is infested with the root maggot, it is advisable to cease growing radishes and related crops until the maggots have been starved out. There are no other very serious pests.

Radishes are usually sown as early in spring as the ground is fit, even before frosts are past. Sow in rows 6 to 12 inches apart, or farther apart if a wheel hoe is to be used. Cover ½ inch. Thin to 2 or 3 inches apart. For family use, sow at intervals of 7 to 10 days. As the season advances, select a cooler site, as a northern exposure. Usually the sowings are discontinued from the last of June until late August. One ounce of seed sows 100 feet or more of drill; 8 to 10 lbs. is required for an acre.

The most popular variety is French Breakfast. Other good kinds are Olive-shaped, Scarlet Short-top, Chartier, Wood Early Frame, White Box. For summer, good varieties are White Naples, White Vienna, Strasburg, Stuttgart. For winter, Scarlet Chinese, Black Spanish, White Spanish may be mentioned.

The radish is an annual; or the roots may be kept over winter and planted out in the spring, when they will quickly run to seed. Spring and summer radishes run to seed the same season if left in the ground, but the best seed is produced from plants that are transplanted when young. Little radish seed is grown in North America, probably largely because of the high price of hand labor.

The radish, *Raphanus sativus*, is one of the Cruciferæ or Mustard family. It is unknown in a wild state. It is probably a development of the wild Charlock, *Raphanus Raphanistrum*, which is an annual weed of the Old World and is now naturalized in parts of the eastern states. (Consult Carrière's experiments as reported in his pamphlet "Origine des Plantes Domestiques demontrée par la Culture du Radis Sauvage," Paris, 1869.) The garden radish occasionally runs wild, when it loses its thick root. For a history of the radish, see Sturtevant, American Naturalist, April, 1890, pp. 320-326. For description and classification of varieties of radish, see Goff, 6th Rep. N. Y. State Exp. Sta. (for the year 1887), pp. 146-168. The classification is based on form and color of root:

A. Root oblate, spherical or top-shaped.
- White.
- Yellow, light brown or grayish.
- Red.
- Purple.
- Black.

AA. Root oval.

(Color as above.)

AAA. Root conical or cylindri-conical.

(Color as above.)

The varieties were reduced to 43 by Goff. In 1889 (Annals Hort.) 81 varieties were offered by American seedsmen.

For experiments on value of different sizes of radish seed, see Galloway, Agric. Science, 1894, p. 557.

For recent discussions of insects and diseases see:

Cabbage maggot, Cornell Bull. No. 78: Advises tarred paper or bisulfide carbon.

Club root. See cabbage.

White rust, N. J. Rept. 1890, p. 350.

BEET

A loose deep rich fresh relatively cool soil and a continuous growth are the requisites in the cultivation of garden beet. *It is usually a companion- or succession-crop in the vegetable-garden.* The crop is hardy and easy to raise. There are no special difficulties. The round varieties are relatively surface feeders and early in their growth. The land should be kept well tilled in order to conserve the moisture and to keep down weeds, particularly during the early part of the season.

There are two general types of beets grown for vegetable-gardening purposes: the short-season turnip varieties, and the main-season long-rooted varieties. The long-rooted varieties are less popular than a few years ago, for the turnip varieties may be grown in the fall for winter use, and fresh beets are to be had from the South during the winter season. Formerly the long blood beet was used for stock-feeding to some extent, but in recent years the mangel-wurzel has largely taken its place.

Vegetable-gardeners now chiefly know the early turnip-rooted varieties. These varieties may be grown either as a spring or fall crop. They mature in two to three months, and roots large enough for bunching of some of the earliest varieties may be had in six weeks to two months. For fall use these turnip-rooted beets may be sown in July and August, or, in some places, even as late as the first of September. When sown late in the season, however, it is very important that the land should have been well tilled previous to sowing, in order that it may not be too dry. The seeds require considerable moisture in order to germinate. This is largely because the "seeds" are really fruits with hard shells, each fruit containing from two to five small seeds. The husks or walls of the fruit are relatively impervious to water. For the reason that the fruits rather than the seeds are sown, beets are likely to come up in little clumps, and careful thinning is therefore essential if the best results are to be secured. The long or blood beets are usually sown in early May in the northern states, and they occupy the ground the whole season. The early turnip varieties may be sown as soon as the land can be worked in spring if one wishes to secure an early crop. They may be followed by some later crop, as celery, late potatoes, cabbage or cauliflower. In some cases, they are grown as a companion-crop in the rows with some main-season crop, as cabbage. For very early results, it is well to sow the early varieties in hotbeds or coldframes. They may be allowed to mature in the frames, or in special cases they may be transplanted into beds, although transplanting is rarely done, as it does not pay. For home use, two or three rows fifty feet long, the seeds being sown at intervals extending over a month, should give a sufficient supply for the spring and early summer. Similar sowings may be made late in the summer or early in the fall for autumn and early winter use. The

Fig. 60. Seedlings of beet. Natural size

firmest and best roots may be stored for winter in pits or in the cellar in boxes of earth or moss.

Young beets are much used for greens. They are rarely grown especially for this purpose, but the seed is sown thick and the thinnings are sold in bunches or in small packages. The whole plant, root and top, is thus used as a pot-herb. There are certain kinds of beets that produce thick leaves rather than roots, but these are essentially leaf crops and are discussed under that head. See *Chard*.

Early beets are usually sold in bunches of about six,

but the later crop is sold in baskets or barrels. The price depends much on the earliness and freshness of the product.

Sow in drills as soon as the ground is ready, and thin to 6–8 inches apart, using the thinnings for greens. The drills should be far enough apart to admit of wheel-hoe tillage,—12–18 inches. Field beets should be far enough apart for horse tillage. Five to eight pounds of seed is required for an acre; 1 ounce sows 75 to 100 feet of drill. Average crop is 300-400 bushels per acre.

Good early and mid-season beets are Egyptian, Bassano, Eclipse, Bastian, Columbia, Edmand. A standard winter variety is Long Blood. There are many other good varieties.

The beet has descended from *Beta vulgaris*, one of the Chenopodiaceæ, and which is a perennial herb of the seacoasts of Europe. It has been cultivated for more than 2,000 years. The thick root is the result of domestication. The beet is grown both for its foliage and root. The thick-rooted form which we know as beet is called beet-root in England. Of foliage beets there are two types: chard, used for greens; ornamental beets, used in flower gardens and lawns for their bright and colored foliage. Of root beets there are three types: garden beets; mangel-wurzels, or stock beets; sugar beets. The cultivated beet has very little resemblance to its wild prototype. For an accessible horticultural history of the beet, see Sturtevant, Amer. Nat., 1887, pp. 433–436.

In 1889 (Annals Hort.), 42 varieties of garden beet and 31 of mangels were offered by American seedsmen. In 1887, Goff reduced the garden beets to 23 varieties (6th Rep. N. Y. State Exp. Sta., pp. 120–132). The classification was based on shape and color:

A. Root oblate or top-shaped.
  B. Color red.
  BB. Color yellow.
AA. Root oval.
  (Color as above.)
AAA. Root half-long.
  (Color as above.)
AAAA. Root long-conical.
  (Color divisions.)

Three diseases of beets are sometimes serious, particularly on sugar beets: root-rot, for which apply lime to the soil; leaf-spot, kept in check by spray of Bordeaux mixture; scab, prevented by not growing beets on the infested land. See Duggar, Bull. 163, Cornell Exp. Sta.

CARROT

Very clean and mellow soil, particularly one that will not "bake" over the seeds, and close attention to surface tillage, are the prime requisites for the culture of carrots. The crop is easy to grow after the plants are well established.

Carrots are of two leading types: those grown for spring or early summer use, and those grown as a main crop and used in the winter. Carrots are stored like beets and other root crops. The main-season carrots are not cultivated very extensively as a vegetable-gardening crop, although they are used to a considerable extent for stock-feeding. Young, fresh carrots may be shipped from the southern states so cheaply that there is relatively little need of storing the roots for market. Aside from this, the American people eat relatively few carrots, and the trade in them is small.

The seeds of carrots are small and germinate slowly. Unless the soil is in good condition and free of weeds the young plants are likely to suffer. It is well to sow seeds of radishes, turnips or other quick-germinating things with the carrots in order to mark the row and to break the crust.

The carrot is a hardy plant, and the early varieties may be sown as soon as the land is fit in the spring.

The late varieties may be sown as late as the middle of June in the northern states. Carrots mature rather slowly, and even the early varieties require from 2 to $2\frac{1}{2}$ months to bring them to edible size, unless they are aided in their growth by a covering of sash. On land

Fig. 64. Seedlings of carrot. Natural size.

that is to be used for late carrots, it is well to sow some early stuff in the spring, as radishes, and to keep the ground clean until it is needed for the carrots. The early weeds will then be killed, and the young carrot plants will have an opportunity to grow. In their early stages, carrot plants are shallow-rooted and delicate, and the tillage should be very carefully done.

Carrots are sown in drills from 10 to 18 inches apart, depending largely on the variety and the method to be employed in tilling. The early crop is thinned to 4 or 5 inches apart in the row, and the late, large varieties to 7 or 8 inches. If it is not desired to plant the late varieties for fall use, one may use the early varieties for that purpose, sowing the seed late in July or even the first of August. Unless the soil is in very fine tilth and moist, however, it is difficult to secure a stand as late in the season as this. Carrot seed should always be sown thickly in order to allow for any failure in germination. For an acre, 2 lbs. of seed is required; for 300 feet of drill, 1 oz., if the seed is fresh.

The stump-rooted or half-long varieties are now chiefly grown. These are early or mid-season varieties fit for using either early in the season or late in summer. The Early Forcing is one of the best for growing in hotbeds or coldframes, or for growing in the fall for home use. The Half-long Danvers is one of the reliable mid-season varieties. For late or main-season crop, the Long Scarlet is excellent; and for stock-feeding the Long Orange and Long White are used. These latter varieties are also good for home use, although when they are allowed to reach their full size they are likely to be somewhat coarse in texture. A good crop of carrots is 200–300 bushels per acre.

The carrot is an annual or sometimes a biennial. The early varieties will send up flower-stalks the same year if left in the ground; but the roots of the late varieties must be stored during the winter, and set out the following spring, when they will quickly run to seed. The carrot has run wild extensively in the eastern part of the country, where it is a bad weed in meadows and along the roadsides. It loses the fleshy character of root and is a partial biennial or an annual. It inhabits dry and poor fields. Giving attention to securing more grass is the best remedy. It is rarely troublesome in cultivated fields.

For accounts of plant-breeding with carrots, consult Lévêque de Vilmorin, "Notice sur l'Amélioration de la Carotte Sauvage," Trans. London Hort. Soc., Ser. 2, vol. 2, p. 348; republished in Paris in a new edition in 1886. See, also, Carrière, Gardeners' Chronicle, 1865, p. 1154.

The carrot is one of the Parsley family, Umbelliferæ. It is known to botanists as *Daucus Carota*. It has been in cultivation for more than 2,000 years. Its native country is probably Europe and western Asia. See Sturtevant, Amer. Naturalist, 1887, pp. 527–532, for history.

In 1887, Goff (6th Rep. N. Y. State Exp. Sta., p. 133–146) made a classification of the varieties of carrots based on shape, size and color of root, as follows:

A. Root distinctly pointed.
B. Root long,—the length exceeding 4 times the diameter.
c. White.
cc. Yellow.
ccc. Orange or red.
cccc. Purple.
BB. Root half-long, length not exceeding 4 times the diameter.
(Color divisions.)
AA. Root distinctly premorse, or blunt at the lower end.
(Root and color divisions.)

He reduced the varieties to 28. In 1889, American seedsmen offered 33 varieties.

There are no serious insects or diseases.

TURNIP-ROOTED CHERVIL

This is a small-rooted plant, something like carrot, except that the roots are gray or nearly black and of different flavor. The seed does not germinate well if kept dry over winter. It is, therefore, sown in August or September, although it usually does not germinate until spring. Otherwise the culture is like that for carrot. The root is used as carrot is. It matures in early summer, but improves by remaining in the ground. It is little known in America.

Tuberous or Turnip-rooted Chervil is *Chærophyllum bulbosum*, a native of southern Europe, and one of the Umbelliferæ. Salad Chervil is a different plant (see Chap. 14).

TURNIP

Cool, short season and a moist soil are the requisites for best turnips. The seed germinates quickly. Hardy.

The true turnips usually have flat or very oblate roots, soft white flesh, and green, rough-hairy leaves. Fig. 66. They do not require the full season in which to mature, and are therefore grown as a spring or fall crop. The herbage is very hardy, withstanding

Fig. 65. Seedlings of turnip. Two-thirds natural size.

considerable frost without injury. For early use turnips are sown as soon as the land can be prepared in the spring. They should give roots large enough for the table in six to ten weeks. For the fall crop, seeds may be sown in the northern states as late as the last week in July, and in the middle states as late as the middle of August. The plants will grow until heavy freezing weather, at which time they may be pulled and stored as other roots are. Unlike parsnips and salsify, the roots will not stand hard freezing.

The value of the turnip as an article of food lies

very largely in its tenderness and succulence. If the plant grows slowly, it is woody, stringy and bitter. In order to secure a quick growth, the land should be rich and moist, and in fine tilth.

The turnip is one of the easiest of all plants to grow, except that it is very seriously attacked by the root maggot. This pest can be kept in check by injecting bisulfide of carbon into the ground about the plants, but this labor is usually more than the turnips are worth. It is better, therefore, to grow turnips on land that has not been infested; or, if there is no such land on the premises, it is advisable not to grow turnips until the insects are starved out.

For garden use, particularly for the early season, turnips are sown in drills 10 to 18 inches apart. In drills, use 1 ounce of seed for every 200–300 feet, or 1 pound to the acre; broadcast, use 2–3 pounds to the acre. The plants should be thinned until they stand at first 3 inches apart; and then, as some of the young roots are removed for eating, until the main crop allows a foot of space for the development of each full-sized tuber. The late or fall crop is often sown broadcast, particularly if it is to be used for stock-feeding. Better results are secured, however, if the plants are grown in rows. For general field purposes, the rows are placed from 18–30 inches apart, so as to allow of wheel-hoe or even horse-hoe tillage. If the plants are grown from broadcast seeding, the land should be in excellent condition and free from weeds, as no subsequent tillage is possible. It is an adage in many parts of the northern states that

On the 25th of July
Sow turnips, wet or dry.

Staple kinds are Milan, Purple-Top Munich, Teltow (excellent for home use). 600–1,000 bushels may be grown to the acre.

The turnip is one of the Cruciferæ or mustard family. It is known as *Brassica Rapa*. It is an annual plant if the seeds are sown in the spring. The plant is ordinarily regarded as biennial. The turnip sometimes runs wild as a weed and then loses its fleshy root and is annual. Native to Eur-Asia. It has been cultivated from earliest times. See history by Sturtevant in Amer.

Fig. 66. Turnip.

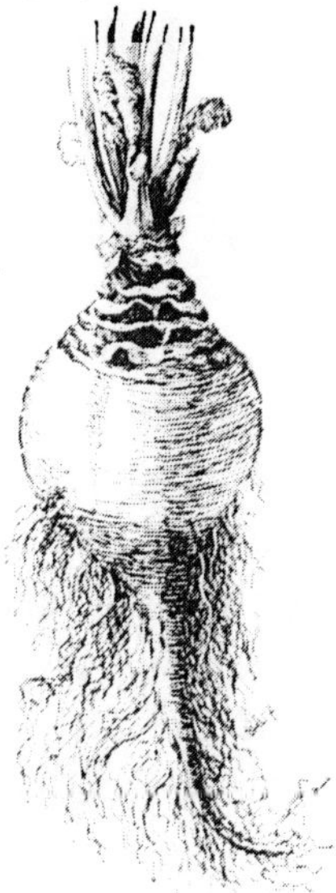

Fig. 67. Rutabaga.

Nat., Sept., 1891, pp. 803-806. For discussion of the botany of turnips and allies, see Bailey, "Garden and Forest," 1897, pp. 321, 322.

Goff makes 41 varieties of turnips (6th Rep. N. Y. State Exp. Sta., pp. 168–190), including rutabagas. In 1889, American seed dealers sold 50 varieties classed as turnips, and 31 classed as rutabagas. Goff's classification was based on form and color:

A. Root distinctly conical, or cylindri-conical.
B. White.
BB. Yellow.
BBB. Grayish, brown or black.
AA. Root oval.
(Color divisions.)
AAA. Root spherical or top-shaped.
(Color divisions.)
AAAA. Root distinctly flattened.
(Color divisions.)

RUTABAGA

The requirements for the growing of rutabagas are the same as for the growing of turnips, except that the plants require a month to six weeks' longer time in which to mature.

Rutabaga differs from the turnip in having a denser and mostly yellow-fleshed root, which is rounded or elongated and not distinctly flat, the leaves glaucous-blue and not hairy, the crown long and leafy, the roots arising from the under side of the tuber as well as from the tap-root. Compare Figs. 66 and 67. It is a richer vegetable than the turnip. It is grown either as a spring or a fall crop and is used also for stock-feeding. As in the case of the turnip, the product that is grown for stock is raised from summer-sown seeds. For the main crop, the seeds are usually sown as early as the first of July or the latter part of June.

The rutabaga, known in England also as Swedish turnip and turnip-rooted cabbage and in French as chou-navet, is *Brassica campestris*, native of Eur-Asia.

PARSNIP

A cool, very deep rich soil and one that does not "bake" over the seeds, and a full length season, are the requisites for parsnip-growing.

The parsnip occupies the land during the whole season. The seeds are sown in the spring as early as the ground is fit. The roots may be harvested in the fall and stored in the cellar or in pits, or they may be left in the ground until spring. The hard freezing of winter does not injure them. In fact, many people believe that the quality of the roots is improved by freezing. This notion, however, is unfounded, for if the roots are not allowed to shrivel during the winter, their quality is as good as when allowed to remain in the ground. If one is growing parsnips for the market, it is important that at least a large part of the crop be stored for the winter,

Fig. 68. Parsnip seedlings. Two-thirds natural size.

for the highest prices are usually secured before the roots can be dug from the field in the spring.

The parsnip makes a long-cylindrical, tapering root: therefore the ground should be deep. Much of the value of the parsnip as a market crop is destroyed when the roots are branchy and forking. Land that is shallow and lumpy tends to make such roots. Good parsnip roots should be 1 foot long, and straight, clean and comely.

The seeds of parsnips germinate rather slowly, and retain their vitality only a year or two; therefore they should be sown thick. It is well to plant with them some quick-germinating seeds in order to break the ground and to mark the row. Seeds are usually sown in drills far enough apart to allow of wheel-hoe or horse tillage, and the young plants are thinned to stand about 6 to 8 inches apart in the row. Subsequent treatment consists only in keeping the land well tilled and free from weeds. There are no serious pests. One ounce of fresh seed is used to 200–250 feet of drill; 4–6 lbs. is generally used to the acre. A good crop is 500–600 bushels to the acre, but more than this is secured under the best conditions.

The parsnip (*Pastinaca sativa*) is one of the Umbelliferæ family, and is allied to carrot, celery and parsley. It is a native of the Old World. It is biennial. The flower-stalks arise from the roots that were produced the year before. In some cases, when the season is dry and long, roots may send up flower-stalks the very year in which they grow. The parsnip has run wild as a weed in old fields. It is then a biennial. It is not a serious weed in well tilled lands, and this fact suggests the proper treatment if it should become a nuisance. The strong flower-stalks of the parsnip are said to be slightly poisonous by contact to some persons.

Goff (2d Rept. N. Y. State Exp. Sta., p. 180, and 4th Rept., p. 139), reduced the varieties of parsnips to 3. In 1889 (Annals Hort.) American dealers offered 15 named varieties. The Hollow Crown and Student parsnips are the standard varieties. For an account of the experimental origin of the Student parsnip, see Buckman, Gardeners' Chronicle, 1862, p. 721. For a history of the parsnip, consult Sturtevant, Amer. Nat., Jan., 1890, pp. 46-48.

"In the parsnip the tap-root is very long, and tapers very slowly after the first few inches in depth. In a plant of the Long Hollow Crown variety, examined September 17, we traced the tap-root downward a distance of 30 inches, beyond which it was too delicate to follow. Branches leave the tap-root throughout its length, many starting out below the clay line. One of these, at a depth of 2 feet, we followed a distance of 7 inches through very stiff clay. The fibrous roots in the upper layers of the soil are numerous, but short, the longest ones appearing to extend but about 14 inches from the main root. Considering the proportion of the roots that lie deep in the soil, the parsnip is a deep-rooting plant."—*Goff, 3d Rept. N. Y. State Exp. Sta., p. 311.*

SALSIFY

Deep, rich cool soil and the full-length season are required for the production of good salsify.

The salsify plant is grown for cooking only, not for stock. The seed is sown in drills as soon as the ground is ready in spring and the young plants thinned to 4 or

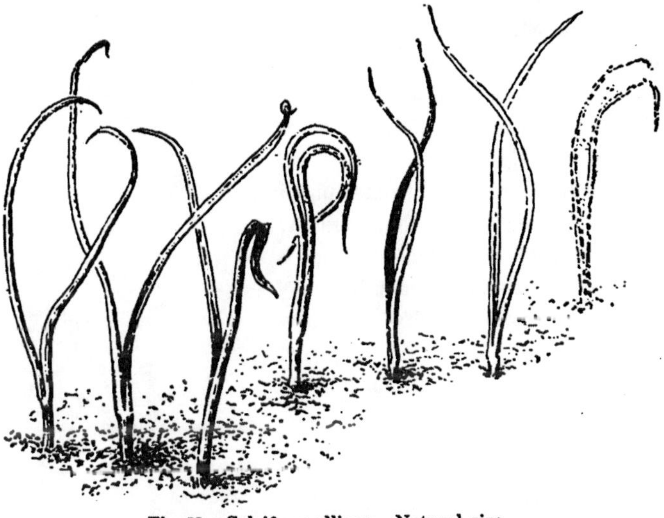

Fig. 69. Salsify seedlings, Natural size.

5 inches apart. The plant is perfectly hardy and the roots may be left in the ground over winter, as they are not injured by frost. If one desires to use the plant during winter, however, or wishes to find the best markets, a large part of the roots should be stored in the cellar or in pits. There are no serious pests of the salsify plant, and the seeds germinate readily. These seeds are really fruits, and they are long and stick-like, and are rather difficult to sow with the seed drill.

Salsify is one of the few members of the Compositæ family which produces edible parts. It is *Tragopogon porrifolius* of the botanists. It is biennial. It has been comparatively little improved by domestication. There is a relatively large-rooted form known as the Mammoth Sandwich Island, and another called the Improved French. Even of the largest varieties, the roots are small, rarely more than 2 or 3 inches in diameter at the crown. Because of its flavor of oysters, it is commonly known as the oyster plant or vegetable oyster. For history, see Sturtevant, Amer. Nat., July, 1890, pp. 635, 636. Salsify sometimes runs wild, and then loses the fleshy character of the root. It makes a straight stalk 2-3 feet tall, and bears large handsome purple flowers, which close about midday. It is native to southern Europe. There are no serious enemies.

An ounce of salsify seed sows about 70 feet of drill; 8-10 pounds sow an acre: 200-300 bushels per acre is a good crop.

Fig. 70. Spanish salsify. Scolymus Hispanicus.

SCORZONERA, OR BLACK SALSIFY

The cultivation of this plant is in all ways like that of salsify. It is perennial, however, and the roots continue to enlarge without becoming inedible if left in the ground for more than one year.

Scorzonera Hispanica (Compositæ) has a long black root, yellow flowers, light-colored seeds, and broader leaves than salsify. It is used in the same way as salsify. It is little known in this country, but it is a good addition to the home garden. History by Sturtevant in Amer. Nat., July, 1890, p. 643.

SCOLYMUS, OR SPANISH SALSIFY

Cultivated like salsify, and the roots used for the same purposes. Fig. 70.

"A vegetable that promises to be of considerable value in this country, if once generally introduced, is the so-called Spanish salsify, a native of southern Europe. I have grown this for two years. It makes a root much like salsify, except that it is much lighter colored and considerably longer. Its flavor is less pronounced than that of the salsify, but when carefully cooked it possesses a very agreeable quality which is somewhat intermediate between that of the salsify and parsnip. It is adapted to all the methods of cooking employed for those vegetables. The particular value of the vegetable, aside from affording a variety in the kitchen garden, is its large size and productiveness as compared with the salsify. We raise almost twice the crop upon a given area than we can secure from salsify, and no doubt it could be sold for that vegetable in the general market. The seeds are much easier to handle and sow than those of the salsify. It is sown and cultivated in exactly the same manner as that vegetable, and can be dug either in the fall or spring. Fig. 70 shows a good root. Perhaps the greatest disadvantage of the plant is the very prickly leaves, which may make it unpleasant to handle. But on the whole, it is worth introduction into American gardens. Seeds are offered by some American seedsmen.

"Spanish salsify (*Scolymus Hispanicus*) is closely allied to the cardoon and artichoke, and its young leaves are sometimes bleached and eaten like cardoons."—*Bailey, in Bull. 37, Cornell Exp. Sta. (1891)*.

HORSE-RADISH

A very deep, cool, rich soil and late-season growth are the essentials for success in the raising of horse-radish. It is perfectly hardy. Propagated by root cuttings.

Horse-radish is grown for its root, which has a pungent quality that makes it prized as a relish. It is perennial, the roots enlarging and becoming woody for several years. As a commercial crop, however, it is grown wholly as an annual, being propagated from cuttings of the small side roots. These cuttings are made from the trimmings when the roots are dressed for market. A good cutting should be from the size of a lead pencil up to that of one's little finger. It is usually made from 4 to 7 inches long, and the lower end is cut slanting in order to designate the right end up. These cuttings or sets are tied in bundles and stored in the cellar or pit, as the roots are. They may be planted at the first opening of spring, but since the plant makes the larger part of its growth late in the season, it is customary to hold them rather late and to plant them with some other crop They are often planted in the rows of early cabbages or beets. When the cabbages are off, the horse-radish takes the land. The sets are dropped right end up in furrows or holes, which are made with a strong-pointed stick or crowbar. They are usually placed in a somewhat slanting position, although the upright position is probably as good. The top of the cutting usually stands 3 to 5 inches below the top of the soil. This deep planting delays the appearing of the plants and thus prevents interference with the combination-crop. The rows are far enough apart to allow of horse tillage, and the plants should stand from 12 to 18 inches apart in the row. The horse-radish plant will stand much abuse. If it grows so rapidly as to interfere with the cabbages or other

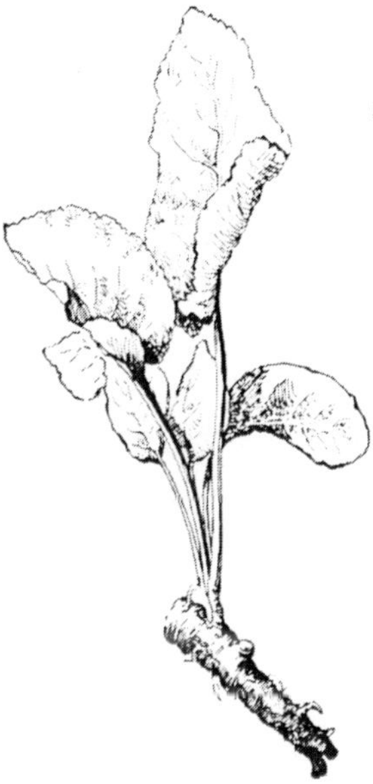

Fig. 71. Set planted slanting. A.

Fig. 72. Set planted wrong end up. D.

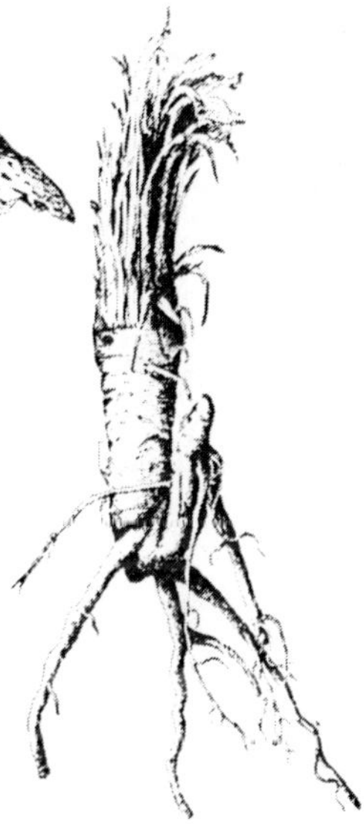

Fig. 73. Result of plant set wrong end up. D.

plants with which it is planted, the tops may be cut off two or three times early in the season. After the other crop is removed, the land is given merely good surface tillage. Sometimes horse-radish is made the main crop, and other crops are grown incidentally. In this case, it is planted in rows 3 to 4 feet apart on ridges, and spinach, early beets or lettuce are grown on the sides of the ridges.

The horse-radish will grow until freezing weather.

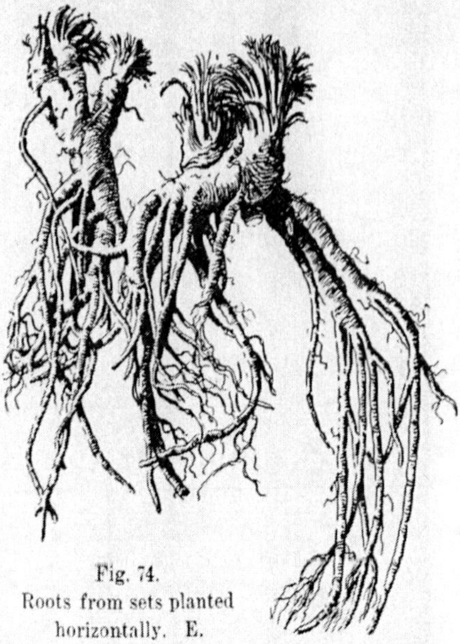

Fig. 74.
Roots from sets planted horizontally. E.

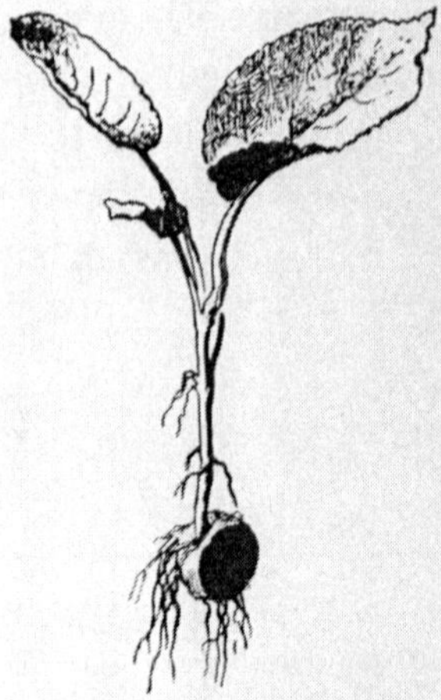

Fig. 75.
One-fourth-inch piece. F.

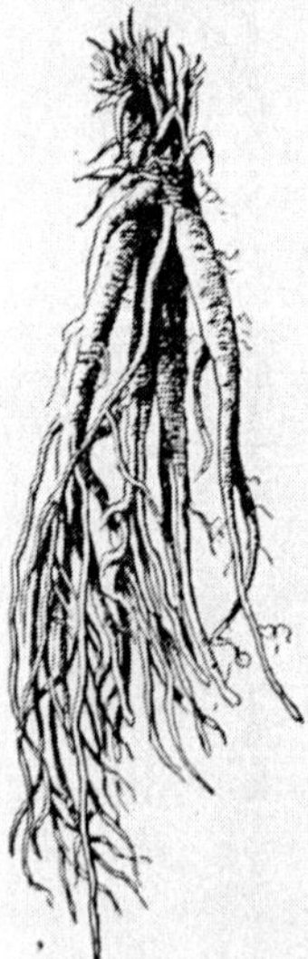

Fig. 76. Roots from one-fourth-inch piece. F.

Fig. 77. One-inch set. G.

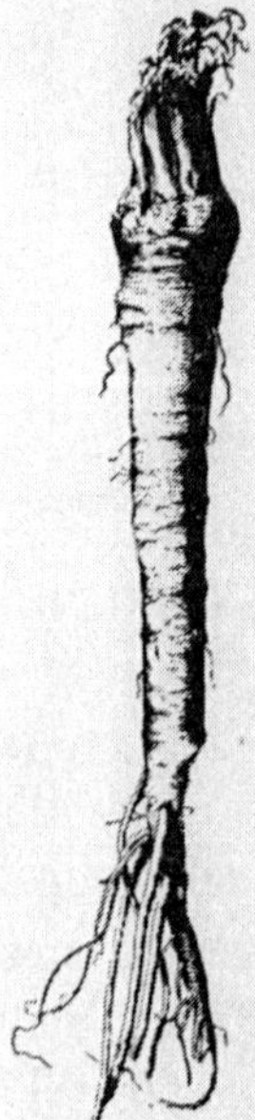

Fig. 78. Product of one-inch set. G.

It is best to plow out the roots in the fall and to store or sell them. As the horse-radish is likely to become a bad weed, it is necessary that all the small roots be taken out of the land. When the crop is harvested, therefore, all the loose roots are picked from the furrow and destroyed. If these furrows are left open until spring many more of the roots will be exposed, and they may then be removed. Subsequent plowing and dragging will often expose still others. It is usually impossible to get all the roots out of the land, but if the ground is occupied with other crops and is kept in good tillage, the horse-radish should not become a nuisance.

The roots are washed and trimmed before they are sent to market. For special trade, the roots may be tied in bunches of 6 or 8, but the crop is generally marketed in barrels or in bulk.

Fig. 79. Horse-radish graters.

In some parts of the country the growing of horse-radish is coming to be an important industry. Since the roots must be grated before they are used, it is necessary that they be long, symmetrical, uniform and as large as possible in order to fit the grating machines. Fig. 79. In fact, small and branchy horse-radish can scarcely be sold at any price. Although it grows in old gardens with no care whatever, the plant must have deep, rich soil and good care if a marketable crop is produced. The price per ton varies from ten to fifty dollars, and from two to four tons should be raised on an acre, the latter quantity when the ground is deep and rich and when the plants do not suffer for moisture.

Horse-radish, *Cochlearia Armoracia*, is one of the Cruciferæ or Mustard family. It has been cultivated for a thousand years and more, probably having been spread from eastern Europe. It is now a common weed about old homesteads. The early leaves are pinnatisect, but the later ones are broad and only toothed. The plant blooms profusely, bearing many small white flowers in a large cluster which stands 1–2 feet above the ground. Seed-pods are frequently formed, but good seed is practically unknown. The plant is always grown from pieces of the roots. For domestic use it is grated and placed in vinegar. The grated product should be kept in a tight vessel, for it loses its strength on exposure. There are no horticultural varieties. For history, see Sturtevant, Amer. Nat., May, 1888, pp. 431–32.

Horse-radish will grow from a very small root-cutting (even if ¼ inch or less long), but the resulting plants are usually small. General experience has designated the 6-inch cutting as the best under usual conditions, although experiments are needed in respect to the best kind of cutting for particular soils and circumstances. In old home grounds, horse-radish is allowed to remain year after year. This is well enough for the small home supply, but it does not pay commercially nor does it give a product of the best quality. It is customary to plant the old crowns, but sprawling, crooked roots are the result.

At Cornell University the following experiments have been made (never published) with horse-radish cuttings (1890-91):

EXPERIMENT I

(Soil a clay loam)

1. *The cuttings*—

A. Cuttings 1–2 inches long, made from scraggly and much-divided roots, planted slanting.

B. Cuttings 1-2 inches long, made from straight roots.

C. Commercial sets, 6-8 inches long, planted top end up.

D. Commercial sets, 6–8 inches long, planted bottom end up.

E. Commercial sets, 6–8 inches long, planted horizontally.

F. Cuttings ¼ inch long, from side roots.

G. Cuttings 1 inch long, from side roots.

2. *The results*—

A. Crop very poor, the roots being long, small and prongy. The crop came up well, and the plants were vigorous. Fig. 71 shows a plant six weeks old.

B. Roots small, but fairly straight. Decidedly better crop than A.

C. Crooked, irregular, rather short, but better than D and E.

D. Few good roots, but better than E. The roots show clearly that the horse-radish cutting knows when it stands on its head. On July 4, the plants looked as in Fig. 72, the shoots coming from the lower (top) end of the cutting. Fig. 73 shows the final product. The plants came up quickly, and the rows were indistinguishable, when growing, from C.

E. Very branchy and worthless, with scarcely a marketable root. Fig. 74. The plants made the best stand of any in the whole experiment.

F. Roots long and finger-like, worthless for market. Fig. 75 shows one of the young plants six weeks after planting, and Fig. 76 is a full-grown root. The plants came up slowly and made a poor stand.

G. A good straight lot, better than any other. The plants came up rather slowly and the stand was not the best. Fig. 77 shows a young plant, and Fig. 78 a mature root.

Experiment II

(Clay loam)

1. *The cuttings* —

J. Commercial sets, 6–8 inches long, as large as the end of one's little finger. Set slanting, with top of cutting near the surface.

K. Commercial sets, slanting, with top of cutting 3 inches deep.

L. Commercial sets cut in two,—3–4 inches long. Set slanting, 3 inches deep.

M. Commercial sets cut in two, slanting, 6 inches deep.

N. Commercial sets cut into 1-inch lengths, and dropped in furrow 3 inches deep.

O. Commercial sets, 4–9 inches long. Set vertical, with top of cutting at surface of ground.

P. Commercial sets, vertical, 3 inches deep.

Q. Commercial sets, slanting, 7 inches deep.

R. Commercial sets, vertical, 3 inches deep, bottom end up.

S. Sets 4-8 inches long, made of prongs of roots and about ¾ inch thick. Set vertical, 3-4 inches deep.

T. Sets as in S, but cut in ½-inch lengths and sown in furrow 3 inches deep.

U. Old roots, 4-8 inches long, 1-2 inches thick at top, made from roots 2 or 3 years old.

V. Crowns from roots 8 or more years old.

2. *The results*—

J., K. } The two crops not distinguishable, both good.

L., M. } More branching and prongy than J and K. Very few plants of M came up.

N. A very straight lot, but roots rather small. Perhaps a richer soil would have made up the size.

O., P., Q., R. } Very little difference between these four lots. All good.

S. A good lot, hardly distinguishable from J and K.

T. Roots not so straight and even as N.

U., V. } Very prongy and misshapen; valueless for commercial purposes.

CHAPTER X

TUBER CROPS

Potato, Sweet Potato.

The tuber crops, as the term is understood in this writing, are two, the common or Irish potato, and the sweet potato. The former is staple in the North and the latter in the South. The two are so unlike that it is not expedient to endeavor to state principles that shall apply to both.

POTATO

Deeply pulverized cool soil holding much capillary moisture and rich in potash, deep and early planting, level culture, frequent surface tillage to conserve moisture, spraying to insure healthy foliage: these are requisites of the best potato culture. The potato is propagated by means of tubers. It thrives best in a relatively cool climate: in the South, it is successful only as a spring and fall crop, for the midsummer season is too continuously hot.

In most cases a heavy yield of potatoes is largely a question of moisture. If planted late, the crop loses the benefit of much of the winter precipitation, since the moisture passes from the soil early in the season unless the land receives frequent surface tillage. Planting on ridges or hills wastes the soil moisture in most cases. "Hilling up" is often necessary, however, because the land is not deep enough to allow the tubers to grow well below the surface. The ground should be such as to allow the tubers to be planted at least four inches beneath the level. If the potatoes are dropped in a deep furrow, the earth is plowed over them, and the surface may be harrowed two or three times before the plants

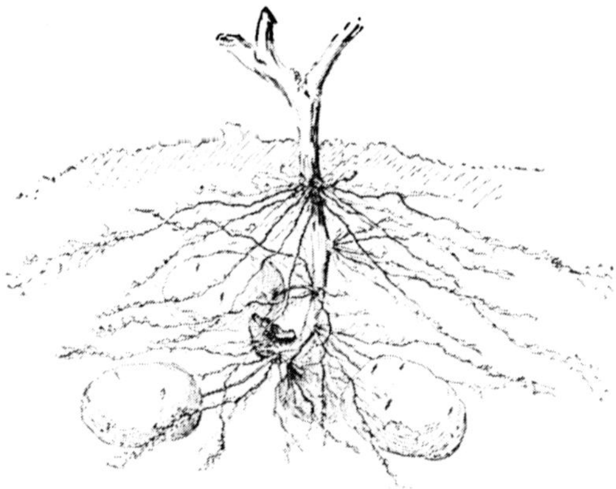

Fig. 80. A potato plant in deep soil. The old seed-piece is seen near the bottom.

are up, thus conserving moisture and destroying weeds. Land should have been well prepared before the planting in order to render plant-food available and to make it retentive of moisture. Figs. 80 and 81 (both directly from nature) show the habit of the potato plant.

From five to eight light surface tillings are required during the season in order to save the moisture. Even after the vines have begun to spread and to cover the ground, tillage may be necessary in a dry year.

The early crop, for market-gardening use, is secured

by (1) selecting "early" soil and site; (2) by preparing the land the fall before, either by means of special plowing or by growing a late-tilled crop; (3) by using quickly available concentrated fertilizers; (4) by choosing early varieties; (5) by sprouting the potatoes in a

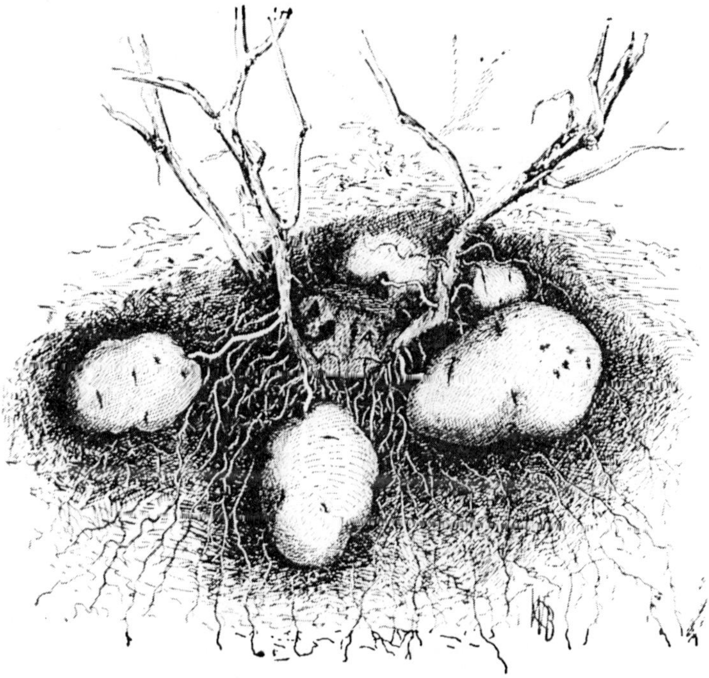

Fig. 81. A hill of potatoes in stiff clay soil. The tubers are toc near the surface. The old seed-piece is at A.

warm place before planting (before the tubers are cut), allowing the sprouts to become 3–6 inches long.

In the southern states, the common or Irish potato (also called "round potato" and "white potato") is a minor crop in general farm operations. The crop must be grown either early or late in the season in order to avoid the long, hot summer. It is then difficult to keep the potatoes from the spring crop until the next spring, or even until it is time to plant the second crop in August (in the Gulf states). "Seed" is commonly secured from the North, and only a spring crop is grown for the northern market.

The potato is inveterately attacked by the potato-bug, flea-beetle, and various blights. Arsenic, as in Paris green, is a specific for the bug, and Bordeaux mixture for the true blight or rot. For the flea-beetle there is no sure remedy, but it may be kept away to a great extent by heavy spraying with Bordeaux mixture. Much of the so-called blight is chargeable to this insect. There is no vegetable-gardening crop for which spraying is so imperative as for the potato. For scab, grow the crop on uninfected land and use clean seed; or if the seed is suspected, soak it after cutting in corrosive sublimate solution or formalin.

Nowadays potatoes are planted in drills or continuous furrows, which are 3-3½ feet apart. Single pieces of tubers are dropped at intervals of 12–18 inches. If the pieces are cut to one strong eye and dropped at above distances, from 8–10 bushels will be required to plant an acre. Many people use too little seed. The yield of potatoes averages about 75 bushels per acre, but with forethought and good tillage and some fertilizer, the yield should run from 200–300 bushels, and occasional yields will much exceed the latter figure. In large-area operations potatoes are planted and harvested by machinery, or by specially made plows. Fig. 82. There are various devices for sorting them, one of which is shown in Fig. 82, *i* and another in Fig. 83.

The size in which pieces of the seed tuber should be cut has been the subject of much controversy, but the question is easy of solution if careful and comparable experiments are made. Arthur

Fig. 82. Potato implements and machinery.

a, Aspinwall potato cutter; *b*, Scofield Jr. planter; *c*, Aspinwall planter; *d*. Goslee tobacco rigger and potato coverer; *e*, Hitchcock potato digger; *f*, Planet Jr. digger; *g*, Planet Jr. sweet potato digger; *h*, Scofield Jr. digger; *i*, Aspinwall sorter; *j*, Hoover potato digger.

T

has shown (Proc. Soc. Prom. Agr. Sci., 1891, p. 11; Bull. 42, Purdue Univ.) that the unit in such tests should not be the number of eyes to the piece, but the size of the piece. The piece

Fig. 83. A potato sorter.

contains food. The more food the stronger the initial growth of the plant; and the stronger the initial growth, the better the crop, other things being equal. But if the piece is too large it contains so many eyes that there will be too many stalks to appropriate the food and to struggle with each other. The pieces on the tip or "seed end" may contain several eyes, but those from the other parts of the tuber usually should contain only one or two eyes. See Fig. 84. Seed should not be cut any considerable time in advance of planting unless it is rolled in plaster.

The varieties of potatoes are numerous and poorly defined, and it is not worth the while to enumerate any of them here. In the year 1889 the seed merchants of the United States are known to have offered at least 889 varieties (Annals Hort.). Because of variation and inattention to selection, varieties of potatoes soon run out (see "Survival of the Unlike").

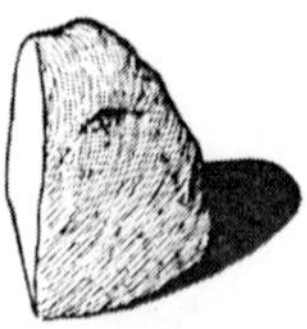

Fig. 84.
A good cutting or seed-piece.

One of the most interesting chapters in the history of pestilential diseases of plants is afforded by the virulent spread of potato blight. It caused the famine in Ireland in 1846. It overran this country. Periodically it is serious at the present day, although it cannot withstand Bordeaux mixture when the material is applied early and with a purpose. For an early American inquiry into this disease, see Charles P. Bosson, "Observations on the Potato, and a Remedy for the Potato Plague," Boston, 1846.

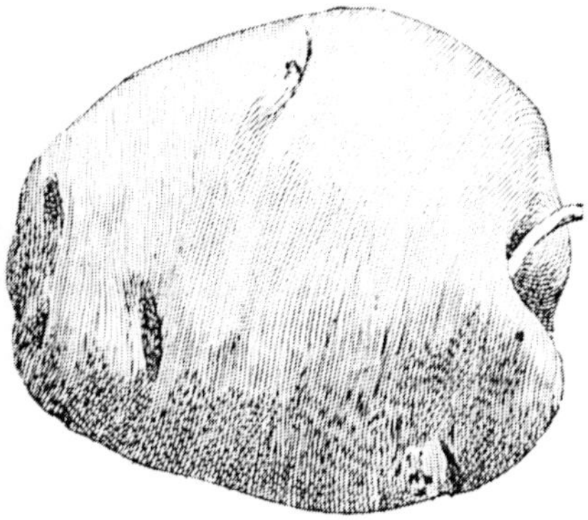

Fig. 85. A potato tuber is a stem with eyes or buds.

On keeping potatoes in the South from the spring crop to the fall crop, McKay makes the following discussion (in Bull. 54, Miss. Exp. Station): "If exposed to the hot sun a few hours Irish potatoes will become blistered. To prevent this, dig on cloudy days or else arrange to remove to a shady place or cover in some way shortly after they are dug. Several methods of keeping potatoes during the hot summer months are practiced, and with varying success. Upon examination it will be found that, as a rule, those left in the field, scattered through the soil, keep better than those that are carefully housed. Taking this lesson from nature, we have tried the method of bedding the potatoes in the field, somewhat after the usual plan of bedding sweet potatoes for growing slips, and with good success. We are careful to see that the potatoes are covered to the depth of 6 or 7 inches with dirt, and that the bed is well drained. We have practiced the same method of bedding the potatoes in the shade of spreading trees, and on the cellar floor. A cool, shady situation is better than the open field. We have had much better success with pota-

Fig. 86. A potato placed in a jar of water will throw out shoots. The food is in the potato.

toes covered with soil than with those spread out in open air in the cellar, or under trees where we covered with leaves. In no event should the potatoes be piled or heaped together, so long as warm weather continues. If potatoes intended for the table are exposed to the light for any considerable length of time they will turn greenish in color and become unwholesome for food. If not spread in a dark place they should be covered with leaves, straw or dirt."

The potato (*Solanum tuberosum*) is native to temperate parts of Chile and northward to southern Colorado. The northern form differs little from main type. It is known as var. *boreale*. It was

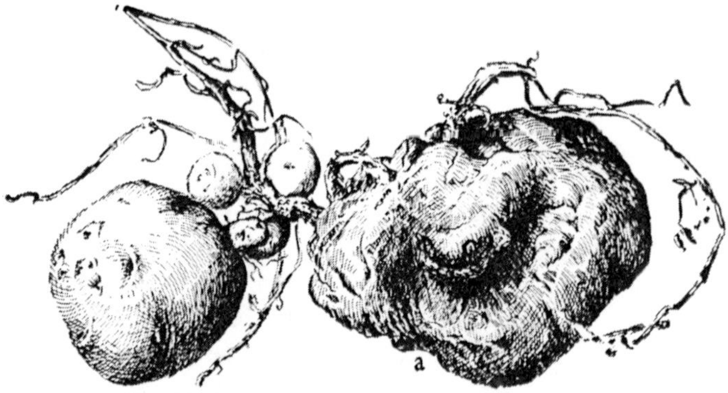

Fig. 87. New potatoes growing from an old one.

probably first taken from the Andean region. It was in cultivation by aborigines on the discovery of America. For history, see DeCandolle's "Origin of Cultivated Plants;" Sturtevant, in Amer. Nat., April, 1890, pp. 315–318; Gardeners' Chronicle, Oct. 30 and Dec. 4, 1886 (being a report of the potato tercentenary; also see The Garden, vol. 30, pp. 530, 535). Rev. Chauncey E. Goodrich, of Utica, N. Y., made an effort, in the middle of the century, to breed blight-proof varieties from newly imported native stock from S. Amer. Trans. N. Y. Agric. Soc. 1852; Pat. Off. Rep., 1852–3.

For a botanical account of the species allied to the potato, see J. G. Baker, "A Review of the Tuber-bearing Species of Solanum," Journ. Linn. Soc. xx : 489. For a sketch of the Mexican wild potato (*Solanum tuberosum*), see Bull. 49, Cornell Exp. Sta. For an account of grafting potatoes on tomatoes, and vice versa, see Bull. 61, Cornell Exp. Sta.

The potato tuber is a thickened stem, with eyes or buds (usually more than one bud in each eye). Fig. 85. The tuber is a storehouse of food, largely starch. The sprouts feed on this food for a time. Fig. 86. In the bin late in spring a potato may throw out a root-like stem and produce new tubers from its own substance. Fig. 87. In some cases a tuber grows inside the old one.

The literature of the potato is voluminous, although there is no single commanding book. Consult "The $100 Prize Essay on the Cultivation of the Potato" (Wylie and Compton), pub. by Orange Judd Co.; T. B. Terry, "A B C of Potato Culture;" and E. S. Carman, "New Potato Culture." The "new potato culture" of Carman is the trench or furrow system as distinguished from the hilling system; this system, adapted to farm conditions, has recently been urged by Roberts and his colleagues in Bulls. 130, 140, 156, Cornell Exp. Sta.

For some of the recent literature on insects and diseases, see:

Stalk weevil, N. J. Bull. No. 109; Kansas No. 82. Remove all dead vines; stimulate plant growth if larvæ appear.

Flea-beetle, N. Y. Bull. No. 113; Cornell No. 113. Use Bordeaux mixture.

Rot, Dept. Agric. Rept. 1888, p. 337; N. H. No. 22; Cornell No. 113; Farmers' Bull. No. 91; N. Y. No. 123. Bordeaux begun before appearance.

Early blight, Vt. Rept. 1892, pp. 66–70; Cornell No. 113, colored illus.; N. Y. No. 123; Farmers' Bull. No. 91. Use Bordeaux.

Scab, Ct. Rept. 1890, pp. 81–95, 1891, pp. 153–160; Cornell No. 113; Farmers' Bull. No. 91. Corrosive sublimate (2.5 ounces in 2 gallons hot water; after 12 hours dilute to 15 gallons; immerse 1½ hours and dry. Formalin (better—not poisonous) 8 fl. ounces formalin (40 per cent formic aldehyde) with 15 gallons water. Soak 2 hours.

Diseases in general, Vt. No. 72. Very good résumé of ten years' work.

Insects, Me. No. 68.

SWEET POTATO

A warm sunny climate, long season, loose warm soil, liberal supply of moisture in the growing season and a less supply when the tubers are maturing — these are some of the requirements of a good sweet potato crop. The plant is tender to frost. It is propagated by means of its tubers, usually from the slips or cuttings which arise when the tubers are planted in beds or frames.

The sweet potato is one of the leading crops of the South, and it is extensively grown as far north as the sandy lands of New Jersey. In the northern states it is often grown in a small way on ridges in the garden.

It is the custom to grow all varieties from "slips" or "draws," although the Spanish variety may be cut and planted like the Irish potato. The slips are grown in beds and transplanted to the field. Many growers prefer to plant only a small part of the field with the slips and the remainder with the prunings from the growth of these slips. Propagation is usually accomplished by means of slips and cuttings. (1) Slips are the sprouts which arise from tubers when they are planted or buried. Tubers of medium size are laid on a mild hot-bed and covered two inches deep with loose soil or leaf-mold. In the extreme south the tubers are sometimes "bedded" in loose, warm earth, without bottom heat, but unless the weather is settled the tubers are likely to rot and the vegetation is slow. When the shoots are 3–5 inches high they are broken off next the tuber and set in the field. Roots will have formed while they were still attached to the tuber. Two to four crops of "slips" or "draws" may be taken from one tuber. The tuber is usually planted whole; but large and sound tubers may be cut in two lengthwise and the cut side laid downwards, although this treatment invites decay. (2) Cuttings are made from the ends of vines. They are taken from the earliest-planted or most vigorous vines; sometimes a few vines are set very early for the particular purpose of securing plants for the remainder of the field. The cutting is usually 10–12 inches long. The leaves are removed, except at the tip, and the cutting is buried directly in the soil where it is to grow permanently, being laid in a nearly horizontal position, with only an inch or so of the tip projecting.

The sweet potato requires a deep, well-drained, sandy loam. The soil should be liberally supplied with well-rotted manure. Wood ashes is often found to be a most excellent fertilizer. The soil should be well prepared before the slips are set, so as to avoid the necessity of cultivating close to the roots. Clean tillage should be practiced until the ground is too thickly covered by the vines. After this large weeds should be removed with hand tools. The slips are set in rows about 3 feet apart, and the slips themselves are 18 inches apart.

The purpose for which the crop is grown will determine very largely the variety, and the variety will determine the care necessary; e. g., the Red Bermuda will grow in almost any soil and under very adverse conditions of climate and moisture, but the quality cannot be compared to that of the so-called yams.

Immediately after the first frost the potatoes should

be gathered. A very common method is to clear away the vines and then to plow up the potatoes with a "hill sweep" (2-winged furrowing plow). They are gathered into small piles, where they remain until removed from the field. The common method of storing is to bank them in a cone-shaped pile. This pile is then covered with hay, and this is thatched with cornstalks, or covered shingle-like with pine bark. It should be kept dry and should be on a slightly elevated place.

Fig. 88. Vineless sweet potato.

One bushel of ordinary sweet potatoes will give from 3,000 to 5,000 plants, if the sprouts are taken off twice. The plants are usually set in drills, which are 2½–3 feet apart. The plants stand 12–18 inches apart in the drill. At 18 x 36 inches, 9,680 plants are required for an acre. These should be produced by 2 3 bushels of "seed" tubers. An average good yield of sweet potatoes is 200–400 bushels per acre. Yields twice as high as these are sometimes secured.

The sweet potato is one of the Morning-glory and Moonflower tribe, *Ipomœa Batatas*. It has been cultivated from very remote times by the aborigines. It is probably native to tropical America, although it is widely distributed in tropical countries. The top is a trailing vine, which roots at the joints and bears variable but mostly halberd-form leaves. Some varieties have longer vines or tops than others, and some have short not-running tops, as the "Vineless Yam," now popular in the South (Fig. 88). The sweet potato blooms only rarely, and even then it may not produce seeds.

Sweet potatoes are grown very extensively in the United States, and they are shipped to all parts of the country, being one of the common foods in all northern cities. They are little known to the people of central Europe. Nearly 50,000,000 bushels is produced annually in the United States. The largest quantities are grown in the Carolinas, Georgia, Texas, Alabama, Mississippi, Virginia, New Jersey. As with other crops, every state produces the best quality, depending on where one lives. Certain varieties of sweet potatoes are called yams in the southern states, but the word "yam" properly belongs to a very different kind of plants, the Dioscoreas.

In the South a soft, sugary sweet potato is desired. In the North a firm, dry tuber is wanted. Spanish, Sugar, Barbadoes, and Hyman are popular far south. Nansemond and Jersey are prized for the North. The vineless (Fig. 88), a variety with short tops or vines ("vineless" meaning "not running," or "bushy"), is now a very popular kind. Price gives the alternative of two schemes for classification of varieties of sweet potatoes:

A. Leaves entire (not lobed).
AA. Leaves shouldered (lobed or halberd-shape at base).
AAA. Leaves deeply cut or lobed.

The second classification is based on the tuber:

A. Tubers white-skinned.
AA. Tubers dull straw color.
AAA. Tubers light red.
AAAA. Tubers purple.

There are several serious fungous diseases of sweet potato (see bulletins N. J. Exp. Sta.). The leaf-blight may be held in check by spraying with Bordeaux mixture, but the tuber diseases are treated to best advantage by rotation of crops and using only healthy tubers for seed.

There are two special books on sweet potatoes, by Fitz and Price. See list, pp. 251, 259. For history, see Sturtevant, Amer. Nat., August, 1891, pp. 698, 699.

CHAPTER XI

BULB CROPS

Onion,
Ciboule or Welsh Onion,
Shallot,
Leek,
Garlic,
Cive.

All the bulb crops are hardy, require a cool season and moist, rich soil with a loose surface. Usually they are not seed-bed crops. They are used both as main-season and secondary crops. They are propagated by both seeds and bulbs. These crops are grown chiefly for the underground bulbs; but the leaves are often used in stews and seasonings.

The onion is the only commercially important plant in the above group in this country. Garlic, leek and the others are known chiefly to citizens of foreign birth or to those who grow products for the large cities.

The leek is the most important of these minor bulb crops, and it should be better known. Its flavor is usually milder than that of onions. The soft bulb and thick leaves are used in cookery, mostly as a seasoning. It is grown from seeds (Fig. 89) sown early in the spring. It usually requires the entire season. It is stored green, after the manner of celery, being set in the ground in the pit or cool cellar.

Garlic is a plant of very strong flavor. It is propagated by "cloves," which are parts or bulbels of compound bulbs. The clove is comparable to one of the cores of the multiplier onion. The cloves are planted in early spring, and the bulbs should mature by midsummer or fall.

Shallot is very like garlic in manner of growth, but the cloves are separate at maturity, whereas they are inclosed in a common skin in the garlic. They are mild in flavor. Cultivation as for garlic.

Ciboule, or Welsh onion, is like a common onion without the bulb. It is grown for its leaves, which are used in seasoning. It is mild in flavor. Propagated from seeds as onions are.

Fig. 89. Leek seedlings. Natural size.

Cive is a small perennial plant growing in dense tufts and not producing bulbs. The leaves are used for seasoning. It is perfectly hardy. It is a neat and interesting plant for a permanent edging along the garden walk. It is propagated by division of the clumps.

The onion-like plants may be contrasted as follows :

A. *Plant truly perennial*—

Cive, *Allium Schœnoprasum*. Lvs. slender, hollow. Native to N. Europe and the northern parts of N. America.

AA. *Plant practically annual or biennial —*

B. *Leaves cylindrical, hollow—*

Welsh onion, *Allium fistulosum.* Not producing large or evident bulbs. Siberia.

Shallot, *Allium Ascalonicum.* Producing pointed oblong bulbs in clusters; leaves small. Syria.

Onion, *Allium Cepa.* Producing bulbs of many sizes, shapes and colors. Native to southwestern Asia. Top onion, var. *bulbellifera.* Multiplier onion, var. *multiplicans.*

BB. *Leaves flattish, not hollow —*

Leek, *Allium Porrum.* Strong-growing, with a single bulb which is little thicker than the neck. Native to Europe.

Garlic, *Allium sativum.* Bulbs small, dividing into bulbels or cloves. Native to Europe.

ONION

Cool, rather moist and level land, soil with the best possible surface tilth and containing much quickly available plant-food, careful attention to the selection of seed, the most perfect surface tillage, are some of the essentials in the growing of a good crop of onions.

Onion crops are of two general kinds: the main- or late-season crop, and the early spring crop. In the main-season crop, the onions are sold in their dry state and are a staple product in market quotations. In the early-season crop, the onions are sold in their immature or green state and mostly tied in bunches.

The main-season onion crop is grown from seeds, and these are sown directly in the field where the crop is to grow. (Fig. 90.) The early spring crop is grown from either seeds or bulbs, usually from bulbs. These bulbs are of three kinds: "top onions," or bulblets that are produced on the top of the flower stalk, in the place of flowers; "sets" (Fig. 91), which are small onions, arrested in their growth; "potato onions," or "multi-

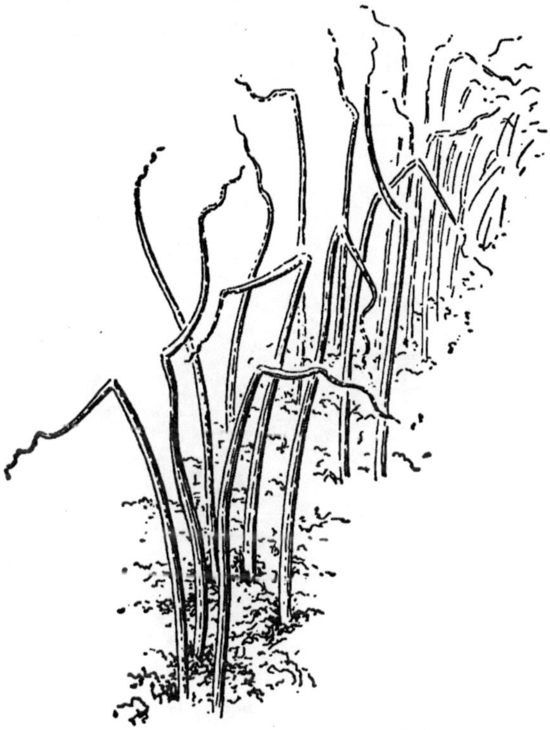

Fig. 90. Onion seedlings. Natural size.

pliers," which are compound bulbs, each component part forming a new bulb. The top onions (sometimes called "tree onions") and the multipliers are distinct races or types of onions, but sets are only the partially grown bulbs of any common onion which it is desired to propagate in this way. To raise sets, seeds are sown very thickly on a rather light and dry piece of ground. The plants soon crowd, and by midsummer the tops begin to die for lack of food, moisture and room. The bulbs should not be more than one-half or three-fourths inch in diameter. They are cured and stored as ordinary onions are. The following spring, when planted, they

Fig. 91. Commercial onion sets.

resume growth, and in a very short time give edible onions. Fig. 92 shows a multiplier onion. A cross-section (Fig. 93) shows that it has three "hearts" or "cores." As these cores grow, each gives rise to a separate bulb (Fig. 94). If allowed to remain in the ground, each part develops two or more cores; and so the multiplication continues. The top onion also starts into growth quickly in spring and soon makes an edible bulb. If the bulb is planted out the following year, it sends up a stalk and produces a new crop of "tops."

Very recently, early onions have been grown to a considerable extent from transplanted seedlings. This method is known as "the new onion culture." The plants are started January, February or March in hotbeds or the forcing-house, and are transplanted to the open when the season will permit. The large quick-growing southern types of onions, as Gibraltar and Prizetaker, may be grown to perfection in the North by this method, whereas the season may not be long enough for plants started in the open.

Fig. 92.
A multiplier onion.
About ½ natural size.

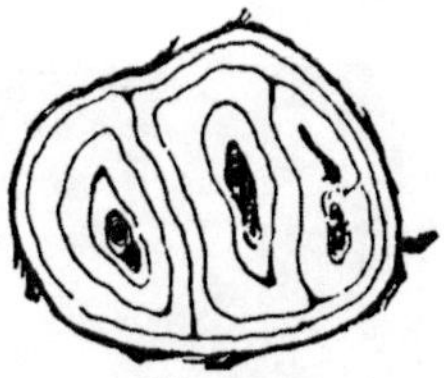

Fig. 93.
Cross-section of a multiplier onion.

In the growing of the main season crop, earliness is not particularly desired, and there is less necessity, therefore, of making heavy applications of fertilizers which are quickly available. All onion lands need to be well fertilized, however, particularly with the materials rather rich in potash. Onions are relatively surface feeders, therefore the top of the soil should be very finely prepared, and the fertilizer should not be plowed under. Every attention should be given to preventing the soil from baking and to keeping the surface in uniformly good tilth. Soils that become dry and hard produce a poor crop of onions. The best soils are those that are naturally loose and moist, therefore lowland areas are nearly always selected for the growing of onions.

Reclaimed marshes, from which the roots and peat have been removed, are excellent. It is also of great advantage to have level land, as it facilitates the use of the hand tools and the finger work which are so essential in the growing of a good crop of onions.

Fig. 94. Multiplier onion beginning to separate into its parts. Each part will produce an onion.

It is customary to prepare onion land the previous fall. This not only insures earliness but it also allows the surface to become weathered and comminuted so that it is in perfect condition for the seeds as soon as the season opens. All clods and stones should be removed by a garden rake, horse weeder, or other fine-toothed tool. The land should have been in good cultivation for some years previous, if possible, in order that it may not contain seeds of weeds; for weeds are very difficult to eradicate in an onion bed. Raw and coarse stable manures are rarely used on onion lands because they make the land rough and keep it too open, and they usually bring in seeds of weeds. Lowlands usually have sufficient humus, but if they have not, it may be supplied by top-dressings of old and fine manure. Commercial fertilizers are usually to be advised in preference to fresh stable manures. It is customary to apply wood ashes as a surface dressing either in the fall or spring. This is likely to improve the texture of the soil and it adds an available supply of potash and phosphoric acid Lands that contain relatively little vegetable matter and which are rather dry in spring may receive an application of some soluble nitrogenous fertilizer. Onion seed germinates rather slowly and the plantlets are delicate and slender-rooted. The plants must take hold at once if they are to make a good growth. The onion-bed condition of tilth is considered by gardeners to be the measure of good treatment of land. There is no vegetable-garden crop raised on a large scale which demands such careful treatment of the surface soil as the onion.

Onion seed should be sown as early in the spring as possible. This is because the onion delights in a cool season, and also because the plants should become established before the dry, hot weather of summer. In garden practice, the seed should be sown thick, for there is likely to be failure of the seeds to germinate; and if the first sowing does not give a good stand it is rarely advisable to make a second sowing because of the lateness of the season. In field culture, thinning is expensive, and one must take great care to secure good and viable seed. The seed is sown with various kinds of hand seed-drills, one of which is shown in Fig. 95.

The character of the onion crop depends very largely on the seed stock. The onion is a plant that quickly runs down or deteriorates if the seed stock is not carefully selected and grown Cheap onion seed is always to be avoided. Those who make a business of growing onions prefer to buy seed from parties whom they know, even though it costs twice as much as the ordinary seed of the markets. Poor seed may mean mixed varieties, lack of uniformity in the crop, the production of scullions or onions that do not make large bulbs.

It is very important that onion rows be perfectly

Fig 95. A four-row onion seeder.

straight, as this facilitates tillage. Fig. 32, p. 118. Usually the rows are placed about 14 inches apart, and the tillage is done by means of hand wheel-hoes. If the land is rough, hard and uneven, these hoes cannot be worked to the best advantage. The land should be so finely pulverized that the lumps and clods will not roll on the young plants. Usually the onion patch will need to be weeded by hand once or twice early in the season; although in land which is very clean and free of weeds this expense may not be necessary. The better the preparation of the land the year before, the less will be the trouble and expense of growing the onion crop.

On some soils onions tend to run too much to top, particularly on those which have been newly turned over from sod, or which are wet, or those which have received too great an application of rough stable manures. Dry soils and dry seasons tend to produce small top growth and a relatively large bulb, although the plants may mature so early in the season that the bulbs do not reach the actual size that they attain on moister land. If the tops are still rank and green late in August, or early in September, and show little tendency of ripening naturally, it is well to break them down in order to check the growth. A common way of doing this is to roll a barrel lengthwise the rows. The best onion crops, however, are those that ripen naturally. Late growth is sometimes due to the seed. If the seed has been grown for a number of seasons in a long season and moist climate, as in England, the plants will tend to grow very late in the season.

The onion is a somewhat difficult crop to handle and to store unless the fall season is warm and one has good facilities for handling the bulbs. The onions are usually allowed to dry or cure for a day or two before they are put into storage. If they cannot be handled in the field, they should be cured under cover, for the bulbs should be dry and free from dirt when they are sent to market or put into winter storage. Curing under cover is more expensive than curing in the field, but it usually gives brighter-colored bulbs and is to be advised when one caters to a special market. The tops must be removed. It is customary to pull the onions before the topping is done. Three or four rows of onions are thrown into one, making a small windrow. After they have

Fig. 96. A New York onion field at harvest.

cured for two or three days, the tops are removed with strong shears, or usually with a shoe knife. Fig. 96. The tops are cut about one-half inch above the bulb. If they are cut shorter than this the bulb is likely to rot or shrivel, and if they are cut much longer the bulb has an untidy appearance. The top should be cut off clean, leaving no ragged ends, and care should be taken not to tear the covering of the bulb itself. Some growers cut the tops from the bulbs before the crop is harvested.

This may be done if the tops have died naturally. It is usually rather more expeditious than the other way.

If the crop is uneven, as will usually be the case, it is advisable to grade the bulbs if the best prices are to be secured. All small, inferior, misshapen bulbs are removed, and also those that are of unusual color.

Fig. 97. Sorting onions in the field.

A good means of grading onion bulbs is to run them over a rack with slat bottom, shown in Fig. 97, the slats being at such distance apart as to allow the large bulbs to pass over, but to catch all the small ones and to drop them through the spaces. The large bulbs are worked over the end of the table into baskets or barrels.

Mature onions ordinarily will not stand freezing and thawing. Therefore, if they are stored for the winter, they must be put in a frost-proof place. They must be kept dry. Winter storehouses in the North are often provided with fire heat. Onions may be frozen with safety, however, provided they do not thaw out until spring and the thawing is then gradual. They may be stored in the loft on the north side of a building, where the sun does not strike the roof, and covered several feet thick with straw or loose hay. In the spring the straw is gradually removed and they are allowed to thaw slowly. When the winter temperature is very uniform, this method of keeping onions may be safe; but in regions in which there are great fluctuations in winter temperature it is not to be recommended. In fact, it is always hazardous.

Most onion-growers prefer to sell the crop in the fall. Usually it is put in temporary storage in open sheds, much as corn is stored in the crib. One of these sheds is shown in Fig. 98. There are wide spaces in the outside boarding of the shed, and the floor is raised a few inches above the ground and cracks are left in it. The eaves should project enough to carry all water clear of the sides. If the onions are dry and clean when put into storage and the tops have been carefully removed, the onions may be stored several feet deep in narrow bins or cribs of this kind.

Sow onion seed as early in the spring as the ground can be made ready. In mild climates, seed is sometimes sown in the fall. Sets, tops, and multipliers may be planted at intervals until steady warm spring weather comes.

One ounce of seed is sown in about 150 feet of drill, and 3½ to 5 pounds to the acre. A good crop of onions is 300–400 bushels to the acre, but 600–800 are secured under the very best conditions.

The two old-time standard varieties are Yellow Danvers and Red Wethersfield. At the present time, however, a true globe-shaped onion is the most popular in the large markets. The White, Red, and Yellow Globe are now the great commercial varieties. Southport Globe is another name for these varieties. The handsome color secured on the bulbs at Southport, Conn., is secured by curing under cover away from the sun. Other popular onions for the North are Michigan Globe, Queen, Portugal, Pearl, Barletta,

Fig. 98. An onion shed. The onions are stored in bins along the sides, like corn.

Bermuda; various small Italian sorts are popular for home use. For large late varieties, some of the giant Italian sorts are desirable, and the flavor is mild.

"Growing onions from seedlings started in the seed bed and transplanted to the field has within the last few years gained considerable popularity at the East under the name of 'the new onion culture.' The procedure by transplanting is probably new as claimed in this country east of the Rocky Mountains; but, as is shown by Wickson in his book on 'California Vegetables,' it is more than a quarter of a century old in California, and was brought to this state by growers from the south of Europe, where it is probably a time-honored practice. Transplanting of autumn-grown seedlings is much more popular in California than growing from 'sets,' and is largely relied upon for the early crop. The practice could often be more widely followed with profit, as this spring's experience shows. Very profitable rates could have been gained for a month or more back for early maturing onions, grown on light soils in parts of the state with a warm winter and moderate rains."—*Pacific Rural Press, May 5, 1900.* See Huntley, Bull. 22, Idaho Exp. Sta., for recent experiments on the transplanting of onions.

In 1889 (Annals Hort.) 78 varieties of "seed" onions were offered by American dealers, and also about twenty kinds of multipliers, potato onions and sets. For purposes of careful scientific study, the varieties may be classified into geographical races, but for purposes of description they may be assembled into groups characterized by such arbitrary features as form and color of bulb. Goff (6th Rept. N. Y. State Exp. Sta., for the year 1887, pp. 190–214) classifies first by shape of bulb and then by color. He makes four primary groups: bulb oblate, spherical, top-shape, oval or pear-shape. Each of these groups is divided into three sections: color white, yellow or brownish, red or reddish. Another classification (Bailey, Bull. 31, Mich. Agric. College, 1887) makes three primary sections on methods of propagation: propagated by division (multipliers), by bulblets or "tops," by seeds (or sets). The last section (seed onions) is divided into bulbs silvery white and bulbs colored, and these groups are divided on shape of bulb.

The maggot is a serious onion pest. It burrows in the root. There is no practical means of combating it except to use infested lands for other crops. The rust and smut diseases may be held in check to some extent by Bordeaux mixture spray. Rotation is the best remedy for smut. Following are references to recent experiment station literature on onion troubles:

Onion Thrip, N. Y. Bull. 83, p. 680, with illus.; Iowa Bull. 27, p. 139: Fla. Bull. 46: Kerosene emulsion, 1 to 10.

Downy mildew, Wis. Rept. 1, pp. 38-44, desc. and illus.; Conn. Rept. 13, pp. 155, 156; Vt. Rept. 10, pp. 61, 62.

Remove all blighted vegetable matter. Weak Bordeaux.

Smut, Conn. Rept. 13, pp. 119–148, desc. and illus.; Conn. Rept. 19, pp. 176–182: Transplant seedlings or use sets.

The onion has been cultivated from the earliest times. For history, see Sturtevant, Amer. Naturalist, Jan., 1890, pp. 36–40.

Special treatises on onion-growing in North America are: Greiner's "Onions for Profit," and "The New Onion Culture;" Greiner and Arlie's "How to Grow Onions;" Orange Judd Company's "Onion Book"

CHAPTER XII

COLE CROPS

Cabbage,	**Cauliflower and broccoli,**
Kale, borecole and collards,	**Kohlrabi.**
Brussels sprouts,	

All cole crops are hardy and demand a cool season and soil, and abundance of moisture at the root. Except the kales and kohlrabi, all are seed-bed crops, and even kales are often started in beds. Each plant requires considerable space in order to develop well. Cole crops are grown for the vegetative aërial parts rather than for fruits or roots.

CABBAGE

Cool soil which is deep and has power to hold much moisture, continuous growth from start to finish, frequent and thorough surface tillage, extra care in the selection of seed, avoiding the root maggot, club root, and rot by means of rotation, destroying the cabbage-worm as soon as it appears,—these are essentials in cabbage growing. Cabbage is grown for the dense rosette or head of leaves.

Young cabbage plants will stand frost if properly grown. For the early crop, the plants are raised under glass. For the main-season or late crop they may be started in seed-beds in the open. Seeds for late cabbages are sometimes planted directly in the field where the crop is to stand, but this is unwise, for the young plants cannot receive proper care and the bugs get them. See that the young plants are stocky. It is customary to set the plants in the ground up to the first true leaves, and gardeners think that such setting gives better heads, but this belief was not verified in three years' tests at Cornell (summary in Bull. 37). It is important that the young plants make continuous growth, for if stunted they do not give as good crops. The seeds germinate quickly. Fig. 99.

Make the land rich and keep the cultivator moving. Use every means to save the soil moisture. If the nearly mature heads cease growing and are then started into growth again by means of tillage or rains, they are likely to crack.

In storing cabbages, it is imperative that they are not infested with the black-rot fungus. Keep the water from the middle of the head, and then keep the heads as cool as possible, without actually freezing hard, and always prevent drying out.

The treatment of all cole crops may be compared to that of cabbage. The story of growing a crop of cabbages is well told in the following sketch by the late J. M. Smith, Green Bay, Wisconsin, who was one of the most expert market-gardeners of his region. The article was written for the author some time ago, and has never been published. "The longer I live," wrote Mr. Smith at the time, then in the midst of a serious drought, "the more firmly am I convinced that plenty of manure and then the most complete system of cultivation make an almost complete protection against droughts of an ordinary character." Mr. Smith's article now follows:

Importance of the Crop.—There is probably no article in the entire vegetable list of which the consumption has increased so rapidly within the last ten years as that of the cabbage. A few years ago the consumption of sauer-kraut was confined principally to Germans and other foreign-born citizens. Its use has not only increased among them, but our native Americans are now using it largely. Tens of thousands of barrels are manufactured yearly, where a few hundred barrels would have supplied the demand twenty years ago. A very large amount of food can be grown per acre with cabbage, and when grown it is valuable either for man or beast. For instance, if an acre were set with

Fig. 99. Cabbage seedlings. Two-thirds natural size.

some of the compact, close-growing varieties requiring 10,000 plants, the land being well enriched and then thoroughly cultivated, it would not be unreasonable to expect the plants to average five pounds each, including the outside leaves. Here are twenty-five tons of food per acre if used for cattle, and about half or two-thirds of that amount if used for man. If some of the large-leaved varieties, like the Premium Flat Dutch, are grown, a much greater amount of food for stock may be raised per acre. Even when it is grown for market, the large quantities of waste leaves are well worth saving for stock food.

Soil.—I prefer a sandy loam, rather heavy than light, and rather damp than dry, but it must be thoroughly drained. Cabbage is a gross feeder, and hence plenty of manure is a necessity. Forty good two-horse loads per acre is not too much if one expects large crops, and there is no danger of making the land too rich. I prefer to put about half of the manure on the land and plow under, then spread on as much more and harrow in thoroughly, unless the manure is coarse, in which case I would plow all under.

Raising the Plants and Setting Them.—We commence setting about as soon as we get the ground in good condition in the spring. Sometimes we have a hard frost after our first plants are set, which will of course put them back a few days, but will not seriously damage the crop if the plants have been properly hardened in the hotbeds. This hardening is done by removing the sash every day for a week or ten days before taking out the plants, at least part of the day, and if the nights are not too cool leaving them off during the night, thus accustoming the plants to the open air. We continue setting plants from the early spring until about the 15th of July. For the last date we need the quick-growing varieties, to mature before the cold weather comes. If the Premium Flat Dutch is used, it should be set not later than July 1. In fact, June 26 would be preferable in this latitude. This variety should be set at least thirty inches apart each way.

It may be asked, Why not set the entire crop early in the season, or as soon as the weather becomes warm and settled? One reason is that if plants are set too early the heads become ripe and burst, and are very soon worthless. The other reason is that we wish to double-crop our ground as far as possible. For instance, our strawberries are generally gone by the 10th of July, and we can get a good crop of cabbage on the ground by setting a quick-growing sort, and then taking good care of it. For all our cabbage except what we call first- and second-earlies, we sow the seed in the open ground in the garden, sowing some about as soon as the ground is fit to work, and then continuing to sow at intervals of a week or ten days until from the 1st to the 5th of June, when we sow the seed for our last setting in July.

Very few growers now attempt to grow their own seed. Seed-growing has become a business by itself, and the gardener can purchase good seed if he deals directly with reliable seedsmen. To depend upon the papers that are to be found in the windows of the grocers would be the height of folly. The safest way, if possible, is to deal direct with the growers, and then, if there is failure, we know where the blame belongs.

For early cabbage, two feet apart each way is sufficient. For marking off the ground, we use a marker similar in form to a common hand hay rake, the head being of some light kind of dry timber, usually a 2 x 4 pine scantling 12 feet long, with holes bored at different distances apart in such a manner that the teeth will slope a little back instead of forward, as with the hay rake. With this a man can mark two acres in a day, and do it well. For early cabbages, we start our seeds in a hotbed about five or six weeks before they will be needed for setting in the open ground. Some persons advocate sowing them very early, and then transplanting them into a mild hotbed or coldframe, four or five inches apart each way, so as to have them larger and more stocky than is possible in the original hotbed, before putting them in the open ground. I have tried it repeatedly and had plants large and beautiful in appearance, but when the crop was grown I have never once had it as good as when the plants were taken direct from the hotbed to the open ground. I can give no reason for this and will not attempt any. The plants from the coldframe may make heads a few days earlier, but the crop has in every case been an indifferent one, and we abandoned the plan years ago as no longer worthy of trial.

Fig. 100. Good head of summer cabbage.

When the ground is prepared and marked, let a man go ahead with a potato hook and loosen the ground where the plants are to be set, if it is hard. Then let a boy follow with a basket of plants and drop one at each crossing of the marks. The boy must be followed by the setters, but must not be allowed to get ahead of them, as a few minutes of dry and hot sunshine will seriously damage the plants. The setters go upon their knees between the rows, setting two rows as they go. They pick up the plant with the left hand, and at the same time with the right open the ground and set the plant, press the earth back, and then with the closed hands press the earth firmly about the newly set plant. This is all done very quickly. Some of my men will set 6,000 or 8,000 plants per day, and do it well. After setting, unless the ground is quite damp and the weather wet, it is best to put at least half a pint of water upon each plant. I know of no plant that will bear transplanting, even in very dry, hot weather, better than the cabbage, provided it is well watered. In the summer we often put one quart of water on the plant instead of half a pint, and even then it is sometimes necessary to repeat the operation within three or four days. You may think all this pains in setting and watering quite too much trouble, but the doing of the work well or ill, and doing it at the right time, make the difference between a paying crop and a partial, or perhaps total, failure.

Tilling.—The plants will need cultivating very often if they are to grow rapidly. It is well to go through them the first time with a hand cultivator, as the plants are so small that a horse cultivator will cover some and damage others. But when the plants are well started, we like the horse and the Planet Jr. cultivator. As the plants are but two feet apart, and the cultivator needs careful handling, we let a boy lead the horse. Nearly all the work is done with the horse and cultivator, except a very little near the plants. Although they are very strong and rapid growers, but few plants are more sensitive to neglect than the cabbage, or more favorably affected by extra good care. We had a good illustration of this last summer. The weather was very dry, and we were doing our best to protect them against the drought by extra cultivation. They had become so large that we were, as we well knew, going through them for the last time. The ground was apparently as dry as hot ashes and almost as mellow to walk upon. Few persons would have thought that any further cultivation would have been of any use, so apparently perfect was the condition, and one would hardly have been able to find weeds enough to fill his pockets from the three or four acres. Still I thought going through them again might possibly aid them in their struggle with the drought. But a shower came in the afternoon and drove the cultivator out, leaving about three-fourths of an acre undone. In the morning on going to the garden, I found my teamster at work elsewhere, and on asking him why he had not finished cultivating the cabbage, he said he had tried to do it, but found they had grown so much in the night that he thought his work there would do more harm than good, and after myself examining them I fully agreed with him, and they received no further cultivation. Now for the result: when we came to harvest the crop, we found that the portion left uncultivated was not nearly as good as the balance of the piece, although the variety was the same, the land, the manure, and cultivation were the same except the last cultivation. My son and myself estimated that the cash value of that three-fourths of an acre was at least fifty dollars less for lack of that last few hours' work. One was simply a good crop, while the other was a very large one.

Varieties.—Like other garden vegetables, the list of new varieties enlarges rapidly. It is well to test some of the more promising novelties, but do it in a small way at first, and if on trial they prove better than those you now have, adopt them. Different varieties thrive best in different sections of country. The Bergen Drumhead is one of the finest varieties in the region of New York city, but has never done equally well with me, while the Newark Flat Dutch, its near neighbor, is one of the best and most profitable varieties I have ever cultivated. In fact, if I could have but one variety, and was allowed to choose, I believe I should take this in preference to any other that I have ever tried. The Chicago Market is very good and is valuable in the gardens near that city, but with me not equal to others. Try the standard varieties first, experiment carefully, and you will soon find what you can safely rely on for a crop, if you do your work thoroughly and well.

For first early, the Charleston Wakefield stands at the head of the list. If it is planted out as early as the season will allow with us, and well cared for, we usually expect to begin to market the crop in June. The Newark Flat Dutch and Henderson Early Summer are among the best for second-early, being only about two weeks later than the Wakefield, and as they are larger are chosen in preference to the other. Hence we only set enough of the

Wakefield to last until the others are grown. Early Spring is only a few days behind the Wakefield. The great drawback with us in growing early cabbage is what we call the cabbage maggot. It is the product of a fly very similar to a small house fly. Paper pads (p. 345) are good preventives of attack. As a main-season variety the Premium Flat Dutch has been invaluable. It grows an immense mass of leaves, and if grown for feed would have extra value on that account. But it is also an excellent variety for the table. The heads are nearly round, very solid, of excellent quality, and also very good keepers. Then in case of a few cold and freezing days or nights before cabbages are gathered, this will not be damaged as much as the quick-growing varieties. This variety is now displaced by Autumn King, Succession, and others.

Marketing and Storing.—Our cabbage is mostly shipped away from our city, the best market being outside. During the summer and until late in the fall it is cut and packed in crates that will hold from 50 to 100 each. Being sold by the head, we have found that it gives better satisfaction to our customers to put in the crates neither the very largest nor the smallest heads, but to have them of good, fair size and to run as evenly as possible, leaving the very large ones and the small ones to be worked into kraut. I rarely throw them on the market, but supply retail grocers and others who sell direct to the consumers. It is always our object to keep just as near the consumer as possible. Late in the fall we often sell in bulk to those who are laying in a stock for winter. We always prefer to sell our entire crop in the fall in preference to keeping it through the winter. It is bulky to handle, requires a good deal of room and more or less care, and there is sure to be more or less loss and waste. We have sometimes kept a few hundred in the following manner:

Dig a trench about four feet wide and at least one foot deep. Pull up the cabbage without shaking the dirt from the roots and retaining all the leaves. Place the heads in the trench with the roots up, close together, and wrap the leaves closely around them. Throw a few inches of straw over them and then cover with earth,—not more than three or four inches at first. Two dangers must be guarded against: If you get them too warm they will surely rot; or if you let them freeze too hard they will just as surely be spoiled when the frost comes out in the spring. After the weather

Fig. 101. A typical Long Island cabbage field.

becomes cold, freezing somewhat, put on more earth. I think a foot will do no harm. I have had good success with cabbage kept in this manner, but have again lost the entire lot by too hard freezing. Hence, we prefer, if possible, to sell the entire crop in the fall, even if we are obliged to sell at a low rate. Cabbage is now stored on shelves in a cool dry building.

Costs and Profits.—Following were figures for the growing of a market-garden crop of cabbages 10 years ago. We need first-class land, and will assume it to be worth $200 per acre:

Interest and taxes per year	$15 00
Forty loads of manure at $1 per load	40 00
Plowing and fitting the ground	3 00
10,000 plants at $4 per thousand	40 00
Setting and watering	5 00
After-cultivation	10 00
Harvesting and marketing	50 00
Total	$163 00
If we get 8,000 heads and sell them at $3.50 per hundred	$280 00
It will give a net profit of	$117 00

I have placed the cost of growing at a fair price (I believe more than it will cost me), and a crop of 8,000 from a setting of 10,000 is only moderate. At present these figures cannot be reached. Sometimes the crop is sold at a loss.

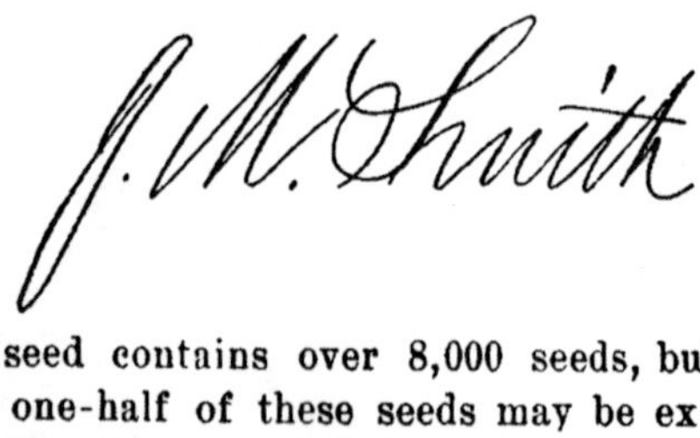

One ounce of cabbage seed contains over 8,000 seeds, but not more than one-third or one-half of these seeds may be expected to make good plants. Early varieties are set 18 x 24 inches, or 24 x 24 inches (about 10,000 plants to the acre); late varieties 2 x 3 feet (about 7,000 plants). Four to six ounces of seed is usually required for an acre.

For Chinese Cabbage or Pe-Tsai, see the next chapter.

KALE OR BORECOLE

As compared with cabbage, *kale requires less exacting care, is hardier, and the seed is usually sown where the plants are to mature. Kale is grown for its large leaves.* Kale may be likened to a cabbage plant that produces no heads. In fact, it is a form of the cabbage species that is very near the aboriginal type. The plants are extremely hardy and are therefore grown mostly for fall or spring use. Greens from kale are prized in the market only very late or early in the season when many other kinds cannot be had in quantity. In the North, kale is ordinarily sown in the spring, the seeds being placed where the plants are to stand. The rows may be far enough apart to allow of horse cultivation, and the plants may eventually stand, after the thinning process, from ten to twenty inches apart, allowing each plant an opportunity to develop to its best. The plants are not used until late fall or even winter. Often they are allowed to stand in the field all winter and are not injured by freezing, not even in the northern states. The older leaves and leaf-stalks are usually improved by being frozen. The tenderest leaves are picked from the plants at intervals, or the whole plant may be harvested at once. For early spring use the seed ordinarily is sown in late summer or early fall in the South and middle South, and the plants stand out of doors during the whole winter and are ready for use very early in the spring. In the northernmost states, however, these young plants are likely to perish unless protected under frames; therefore fall-sown kale is relatively little known in the colder parts of the country. It is grown on a very extensive scale about Norfolk, Virginia, and is shipped to the northern markets from New Year's until the opening of spring.

In the southern states a form of kale known as collards is much grown, particularly in those regions which are so warm that good cabbages cannot be raised. The plants are grown as cabbage plants are, the seed being sown very early in the spring, usually in a seed-bed under protection, in order that the plants may get a good growth before hot weather sets in. The leaves are ready for eating in the fall. Sometimes young cabbage plants are raised for greens and are known as collards.

BRUSSELS SPROUTS

The culture demanded by Brussels sprouts is essentially that required by kale, except that the plants are always grown as a fall crop and they are usually started in seed-beds. The plant is grown for the small heads along the main stalk.

Brussels sprouts is closely allied to kale, but along the straight, strong stem little buds or miniature cabbages are borne, and these are the edible parts. A good "sprout," as one of the buds is called, averages from one to two inches in diameter. When the sprouts are small and tender, they constitute one of the best and most delicately flavored vegetables of the cabbage tribe.

The treatment for Brussels sprouts is essentially that for cabbage. In the North the seeds ordinarily are sown rather late in order that the plants may not mature too early, for the sprouts are most prized in late fall and winter. A large part of the growth of the plant is made in the cool weather of fall. If seeds are sown in June, the plants may be set in the field after the manner of cabbages in late July or August. In the middle states the plants may be left out of doors during the winter as the light freezing does not injure the sprouts. In the northernmost states, however, plants are usually dug late in the fall and planted out in pits, something after the method described for celery and leeks, on page 232. A good crop of Brussels sprouts is dependent very largely on the strain of seed, as the plants tend to run down when careful selection in seed-raising is not practiced. A strong plant of the ordinary varieties of Brussels sprouts makes a stalk from two to three feet high, producing sprouts from near the base to the large canopy of leaves at the top. There are dwarf varieties, however, which grow from sixteen to eighteen inches high and which are in favor in short-season climates.

CAULIFLOWER

From cabbage, the culture of cauliflower differs chiefly as follows: *The plant is more particular as to climate, requiring a relatively cool, moist season; it demands a constant supply of soil-moisture; care must be exercised that the heads do not sunburn; it is vitally important that the very best strain of seed is used.* The plant is grown for its white tender heads formed of the shortened and thickened flower-parts.

Cauliflower is a difficult plant to grow to perfection

in the hotter and dryer parts of the country. Its requirements are similar to those of the cabbage except that it is injured by hot suns and dry weather, and it therefore needs a cool and moist atmosphere. Along the seaboard of the northeastern states, near the Great Lakes, and in the Puget Sound region, cauliflower is grown with success, as it is, also, in special locations in many parts of the country. Wherever irrigation can be practiced, it may also be grown successfully. In the American climate the effort is usually made to secure the crop early or late and thereby to avoid growing it in the heat of midsummer. When thus grown, its range of adaptability is much extended. Under this system, the early crop is usually off in June or July. This crop is secured by growing the early varieties, like the Snowball and Paris, and by starting the plants under glass. The late crop is matured late in the fall from seeds that are sown in summer in seed-beds. For this crop some of the later and larger-growing varieties may be used. There is a family of long-season and late-maturing cauliflowers, relatively little grown in this country, which is known under the general name of broccoli.

In order that the heads of cauliflower may be white and tender, care should be taken that they are not sunburned. If the heads mature in midsummer, it is well to tie the leaves together over the head or to break a few of the leaves over it in order to shade it.

Every effort should be made to conserve the moisture by deep preparation of the land in the first place and by frequent surface tillage thereafter. Low but well-drained bottom-lands are usually chosen in order that the plants may have a constant supply of moisture. On Long Island, however, where the cauliflower is very largely grown, this precaution is unnecessary, since the atmosphere is moist from proximity to the ocean and the water-table is not deep.

Probably there is no other vegetable which so quickly runs down from poor seed as the cauliflower. It is, therefore, exceedingly important that the very best strain of seed be secured if the best results are to be attained. The best cauliflower seed is expensive, running as high as three to five dollars per ounce; but the cheap seed gives a smaller percentage of heading plants and the heads are usually irregular and broken. The cauliflower has a tendency to "button" or to throw up irregular growths from the head. This is due to poor seed, dry soil and too great heat, and also to allowing the plants to become checked and then starting them into new growth by renewed tillage. Keep the plants in a uniform condition of thrift. The cauliflower seed of the market is grown in the Old World, the best of it coming from Denmark; but just now the Puget Sound country is developing as a region for the growing of cauliflower seed.

KOHLRABI

The treatment required by kohlrabi is that demanded by flat turnips. The plant is grown for the tuberous stem.

Kohlrabi produces a turnip-like tuber just above the ground. It is grown mostly as a stock food and is relatively little known in this country outside of Canada. However, the plant is a very excellent garden vegetable if used before the tubers become large and stringy. The tubers should be used when they are from two to three inches in diameter; it is essential that they should have grown quickly and continuously, otherwise they are tough and bitter. Successive sowings may be made and the plants should be thinned to six to ten inches apart in the row. White Vienna is the leading garden variety. Fig. 102.

Fig. 102. Kohlrabi.

Seed required per acre and distances apart for Brussels sprouts and cauliflower are essentially as for cabbage; kale is usually allowed to stand somewhat closer in the rows. For kohlrabi, estimate as for turnips.

In 1889 (Annals Hort.) American seedsmen offered 110 varieties of cabbage, 29 of kale, 7 of Brussels sprouts, 53 of cauliflower, 7 of kohlrabi. Goff classifies cabbages as follows (5th Annual Rept. N. Y. State Exp. Sta. for 1886, p. 185):

A. Foliage smooth.
  B. Head flattened.
  BB. Head round.
    C. Foliage green.
    CC. Foliage red or purple.
  BBB. Head egg-shaped.
  BBBB. Head elliptical.
  BBBBB. Head conical.
    C. Foliage green.
    CC. Foliage red.
AA. Foliage blistered (Savoys).
  B. Head round.
  BB. Head elliptical.
  BBB. Head conical.

The cole plants (known to the French under the generic name of *chou*) are probably derivatives of one European sea-coast species, *Brassica oleracea*. It belongs to the *Cruciferæ* or mustard family. The plant is perennial and now grows on the cliffs of southern England and other parts of Europe. The cultivated offspring are mostly biennial. The wild cabbage is very like a tall kale. See pictures in Cyclopedia Amer. Hort. under *Cabbage.* The types may be arranged as follows:

Brassica oleracea, wild or original form.
Var. *acephala.* Kale.
Var. *gemmifera.* Brussels sprouts.
Var. *capitata.* Cabbage.
Var. *botrytis.* Cauliflower.
Var. *caulo-rapa.* Kohlrabi.

In some of its forms cabbage has been cultivated from the earliest times. For history, see Sturtevant, Amer. Nat., June, 1887, pp. 520-523 for cabbage; September, 1888, pp. 805–808 for kale; May, 1887, pp. 440–442 for Brussels sprouts; August, 1887, pp. 701–703 for cauliflower.

On insects and diseases the following publications may be consulted:

Root maggot, Cornell Bull. 78. Very complete. Illustr. The really efficient means of circumventing or destroying the cabbage maggot, aside from rotation, are very few. See Slingerland, Cornell Bull. 78, who recommends tarred paper cards placed snugly about the plants; rubbing eggs from base of the young plant; injecting crude carbolic acid emulsion, or bisulfide of carbon into the ground about the plants. The injections are best made with a specially constructed syringe.

Cutworms, Cornell Bull. 104.

Worm, or Butterfly, N. Y. Bull. 83, p. 657; ill. N. Y. Bull. 144. Capture. Persistent use of Paris green on first crop. Resin-lime mixture: Pulv. resin, 5 lbs.; concentrated lye, 1 lb.; fish oil or any cheap animal oil, except tallow, 1 pt.; water, 5 gals.

Looper. Same as for worm.

Aphis, N. Y. Bull. 83, p. 673. Fla. Bull. 34, p. 270. Bisulfide of carbon; kerosene emulsion diluted with ten parts water; on lower and upper sides of leaves if possible when small. Tobacco; pyrethrum; Persian insect powder.

Harlequin Cabbage Bug, N. Y. Bull. 83, p. 683. N. J. Bull. 121. Fla. Bull. 34, p. 268. N. Y.: Hand-picking. Should not get foothold. N. J.: Clean culture and cleanliness to deprive of winter shelter.

Club root, N. J. Bull. 98. N. Y. Rept., 1895, p. 525. N. J. Bull. 108, p. 17. N. J.: Air-slaked stone lime, 75 bus. to acre. Rotation: see p. 200 of this book.

Special book literature: Gregory, "Cabbages;" Pedersen, et al., "How to Grow Cabbages and Cauliflower most Profitably;" Lupton, "Cabbage and Cauliflower for profit;" Crozier, "The Cauliflower" ("How to Cook Cauliflower" is a reprint of one chapter in this book); Brill, "Cauliflowers and How to Grow Them;" Allen's "Cabbage, Cauliflower and Allied Vegetables."

CHAPTER XIII

POT-HERB CROPS

Spinach,	Pe-tsai,
Chard or leaf-beet,	Dandelion,
Orach,	Purslane.
Mustard,	

Pot-herb crops, or "greens," are grown for their leaves: therefore they must make quick growth in order to be crisp and tender; the ground must have good surface tilth and much available plant-food; the application of soluble nitrogenous substances is usually important, particularly when the growth is nearing completion. Most pot-herb crops demand a cool season; and nearly all of them are partial-season crops, and are therefore treated as succession- or companion-crops.

SPINACH

Spinach is essentially a spring and fall crop. It delights in cool, moist weather. It is grown mostly in drills. It is usually a succession-crop.

Spinach or spinage is the standard plant for spring and fall greens. For home use it may be had during the summer by making successional sowings in rather cool and moist ground; but as a commercial crop, it is not grown in warm weather. Formerly spinach was brought to early maturity in the North under glass on a rather large scale, but of late years it is grown in such quantities about Norfolk and other parts of the South that it is seldom grown in frames in the North except for home use.

The early spring spinach is grown from seeds that are sown in the field in September. The land should be rich; also well drained, that the plants may not "heave" by frost. It is customary to plow the land into low ridges or beds 6–9 feet wide, in order to secure perfect surface drainage. Lengthwise these beds the spinach is sown in rows 12–18 inches apart, the distance depending on the means that are employed for tillage. The plants should become thoroughly established before winter, having made a spread of leaves of three or four inches at least. The crop is usually left uncovered in the North, even as far north as New York state; although if material is at hand, it may be covered lightly with straw or litter to prevent heaving and thawing. On the first opening of spring the spinach resumes growth. In fact, in mild seasons it may grow throughout most of the winter. It should be ready for use in April and May, and be off the ground early in June, even in the northern states, leaving the land for other crops. In the South it is marketed from late November to March and early April. Since spinach is prized for its crisp, tender leaves, it is a crop that profits by an application of soluble nitrogenous fertilizers. It is customary, in some parts of the country, to sprinkle the ground early in the spring with a weak solution of nitrate of soda or sulfate of ammonia, using from 50–75 pounds of the fertilizer per acre at each of two or three successive applications. These applications may be made from ten days to two weeks apart. The applications are often applied by means of a street sprinkler or similar arrangement. Sometimes the beds are top-dressed with manure in the fall, and the leachings from the manure will then start the plants quickly in the spring. Hen-manure is sometimes used.

There is always more or less loss of fall-grown plants in the northern states. For home use, and some-

Fig 103. Spinach seedlings. Two-thirds natural size.

times for market, plants are started in the spring in a warm position, the seed usually being sown where the plants are to remain. It is more easy to secure a good stand by this spring sowing, but the plants do not mature so early. Spinach is sometimes started under glass and transplanted to the open; and it is sometimes grown to edible maturity under frames. Sometimes beds of fall-grown spinach are covered with sash in February or March in order to hasten the plants.

The New Zealand spinach, which is a distinct species from the above, is sometimes used for summer greens, although it has never gained much popularity, one reason being that greens are not in great demand in hot weather.

Drills for spinach are usually 12–18 in. apart. In the drills the plants may stand 4–6 in. apart. For an acre, 10–12 lbs. of seed is used; 1 oz. sows about 150 ft. of drill.

Spinach, *Spinacia oleracea*, is one of the *Chenopodiaceæ*, or pig-weed family, allied to beet. It is probably native to southwestern Asia, and appears to have come into cultivation within the Christian era. The plant is annual, sending up its flower-stalk in summer if sown in early spring. There are two races, the prickly-seeded and round-seeded (the "seeds" are really fruits), and these are regarded as distinct species by some writers. The prickly-seeded is hardiest and is commonly used for fall sowing. Other standard kinds are Viroflay, Bloomsdale, Round-Leaved. Nineteen varieties were in the American trade in 1889. Goff (6th Rep. N. Y. State Exp. Sta., pp. 225–230) reduces the varieties to 10, dividing them into "seeds not prickly" (9 vars.) and "seeds prickly." For history, see Sturtevant, Amer. Nat., August, 1890, pp. 724–726.

For spinach troubles, see:

Leaf miner, N. Y. Bull. 99; R. I. Bull. 41. N. Y.: Clean cultivation to destroy all lamb's quarters; late fall or early spring plowing of fields.

Various fungous diseases, desc. and ill. in N. Y. Bull. No. 70. Mildew, Anthracnose, Leaf Blight, White Smut. Burn all affected parts. Rotation. Treat soil with mixture of flowers of sulfur and air-slaked lime.

New Zealand Spinach is not a spinach, but a member of the Fig Marigold family (*Mesembryanthemaceæ*). It is *Tetragonia expansa* of the botanists. It is annual. It endures hot weather and therefore may be substituted for spinach in summer. Sow at intervals, as for spinach. "This plant was first found by Sir Joseph Banks, in 1770, at Queen Charlotte's Sound, New Zealand, and its merits discovered to the sailors of Captain Cook's expedition round the world. It reached Kew Gardens in 1772."—*Sturtevant, Amer. Nat., Jan., 1890, p. 32.*

OTHER GREENS

Many kinds of plants aside from spinach are used as greens or pot-herbs. Some of the common weeds are much prized for this purpose in the rural districts, particularly the common white pigweed or lamb's quarter, pusley or purslane, dandelion and dock. The following are garden plants.

Chard, or *leaf-beet*, is one of the best of pot-herb plants. It ordinarily requires nearly a full season in which to mature, although it will give a supply of edible foliage from early summer until fall. The chard has very broad and thick leaf-blades and midribs, which are usually white or tinted rather than green. Sometimes these are blanched by tying up the bunch of foliage. Seeds are sown early in the spring as ordinary beet seeds are, and the plants are thinned as used until finally they stand 6–12 inches apart in the row. Small plants of the common beet, as explained on page 279, are often used for greens.

Orach is allied to the amaranths, or pigweeds. It is grown for the large succulent root-leaves. It is essentially a cool-season plant, the seed being sown early in the spring and the foliage used before midsummer. By midsummer, or later, the plant sends up a strong flower-stalk four or five feet high, and thereafter it is of no use as a pot-herb plant.

Mustard is much used for greens in home gardens, and it is also grown to a large extent in parts of the South, where the climate is too hot for many other pot-herb crops. Some of the improved varieties of curled-leaved mustard are amongst the best of all pot-herb plants. In midsummer the plants run to seed. The seeds are sown very early in spring, and the tender bunch of foliage is ready for use in May or June. In fact, even in the northern states, on sandy warm soil the seeds may be sown in the fall and the plants will be ready for use in early spring, although the seeds may not germinate in the fall. Care should be exercised not to let the plants seed themselves too freely, as they are likely to escape into unoccupied areas and become weedy. In the South, the Southern Giant-Curled Mustard is much used, largely taking the place of both spinach and lettuce. The Chinese Broad-Leaved is a most robust plant, and gives a large amount of herbage. The mustards represent several species of Brassica.

Chinese cabbage, or Pe-tsai, resembles a large and dense-headed lettuce plant rather than a cabbage. It is really a mustard. It is one of the best and most delicate-flavored of all the pot-herb plants. It is little known in this country, and people usually make the mistake of treating it like an ordinary cabbage. It is a cool-season succession-plant, and runs to seed without making much foliage if sown late in the season. It should be sown very early in the spring, like mustard. It may also be grown as a fall crop by sowing the seeds late in the summer, or early in the fall in the more southern parts. When well grown, the plant makes a thick, oblong head, resembling a Cos lettuce, and the broad white midribs and tender leaf-blades make it a very acceptable product.

Dandelion.—The dandelion has been much improved by the French, and is grown in Europe to a considerable extent as a garden plant. It is also grown in private gardens of this country, and in parts of the East it is an important commercial crop. Some of the varieties with large leaves and others with cut or frilled leaves are great improvements on the wild plant, and the foliage is often handsome for garnishing as well as useful for food. In cultivation the dandelion is treated as an annual crop. The seed is sown in early spring and the crop is harvested in the fall, or the plants are allowed to remain in the ground until the following spring. Although dandelion will grow anywhere, it must have deep rich soil and good tillage if it is to make large and succulent foliage. Occasionally the seed is sown in seed-beds or in frames, and the plants are transplanted to the field; but usually the seeds are sown where the plants are to stand. The young plants are thinned until they stand one foot apart in the row. The distance between the rows will depend entirely on the value of the land and the means that are employed for tilling. If the plantation is to be tilled by hand tools, the plants may be allowed to stand as close as one foot apart each way; but if horse tools are used, the rows should be two or more feet apart. Since the demand for greens is usually greatest in early spring, the plants are generally allowed to stand where they grow through the winter. They are then ready for use as soon as the early growth starts. The rosette of foliage should be dense and wide-spreading, covering a space from 12–20 inches across. The crop is harvested by cutting off the rosette of leaves just at the crown. The land is then plowed, and there is no danger that the plant will become a pest. The small and inferior plants which are not fit for sale should also be cut in order to prevent them from going to seed and becoming a nuisance. The roots of the garden-grown dandelion are sometimes taken up in the fall and removed to the hotbed or forcing-house, and greens may be had during the cold weather. Sometimes they are forced in this way in a dark place in order to give blanched leaves. Even in the field the leaves may be tied up so as to blanch the inner part of the crown, much as endive is treated.

Fig. 104. Spray of French purslane (× 1/8).

Purslane, or "pusley," has been much improved by the arts of the plant-breeder. The ordinary pusley of the field is a weak-stemmed plant trailing on the ground, whereas the improved, or French purslane, grows more or less erect, and has very thick and succulent stems and very large leaves. Fig. 104. It is easily grown in any good, quick garden soil from seeds sown in early spring where the plants are to stand. It matures quickly, and, unlike many other kinds of pot-herb plants, it is not injured by warm weather. However, the crop is usually harvested before midsummer, as greens are not in demand at that time. There seems to be little danger of the cultivated purslane self-sowing and becoming a bad weed.

Other Pot-herb Plants.—To the plants discussed in the foregoing pages, several others might be added. The strawberry blite (*Chenopodium capitatum* or *Blitum capitatum*) is a native pigweed-like annual of easy culture, which is sometimes offered by seedsmen. It seems to have no unusual merits. An allied plant is Quinoa, which is grown in all ways like orach. Kale (see Chapter XII) is really a pot-herb plant; and it would not be great violence to include cabbage in this group. Several docks and sorrels are grown as pot-herbs, but as these are perennial they are discussed in Chapter XX.

CHAPTER XIV

SALAD CROPS

Lettuce,
Endive,
Chicory,
Cress,
Corn Salad,
Parsley,
Celery,
Celeriac.

As a general statement, it may be said that salad plants require cool moist soil, and a quick continuous growth if the best results are attained. They are often benefited by a special application of quickly available fertilizers during growth, particularly of nitrogen in those species which are desired chiefly for a quick growth of leaves. The plants included in this chapter are a somewhat heterogeneous company, and it is difficult to state principles that apply to all of them. They are closely connected with the pot-herb crops. Celery and lettuce have little in common, but the above grouping seems to be as satisfactory as any. Some of the plants are used both as salads and pot-herbs, as endive; but they are placed in the group to which their most common use assigns them. A salad is eaten uncooked; a pot-herb or "greens" is boiled. Horse-radish is properly a salad plant.

On the necessity of giving extra care to the rearing of salad plants, Waugh writes* as follows: "Doubtless

*Bull. 54, Vt. Exp. Sta.

all vegetables ought to be fresh; but with salad plants the demand is imperative. A good salad cannot be made from wilted or stale plants. For this reason the best salads are practically prohibited to people who do not have their own gardens. The plants should be freshly picked within half an hour of meal time. Up to this time they should have been rapidly and vigorously grown. A rich spot of ground, plenty of water, clean and thorough culture with favorable weather, must combine for best results. Dry, tough, wilted, weed-choked plants are not worth gathering. Yet most of the true salad plants reach edible maturity so quickly that any reasonable attention should secure good returns. Here again it is not time and money that are required for success, but a little thoughtful promptness of action."

LETTUCE

Lettuce is a hardy, cool-season, short-season succession- or companion-crop, requiring mellow, moist soil, quickly available fertilizers and continuous growth from start to finish. In this country it is known in the open mostly as an early spring crop. It is very easy of culture in rich and well-prepared soil.

Lettuce is usually grown as a seed-bed crop. It is always a succession- or companion-crop. In some cases, particularly for the midseason and later crops, the seed may be sown where the plants are to stand. Lettuce is little grown in America during the hot summer months. There are certain varieties, however, which thrive in the hot weather, those of the Cos strain perhaps being the best. Lettuce may be followed by cabbages, early cauliflower, celery or various other succession-crops. Sometimes lettuce is transplanted between the plants of early cabbages or cauliflowers, since it will mature before the other plants need all the space. Such companion-cropping is shown in Fig. 106. Lettuce may be grown in the fall from seeds that are sown

Fig. 105. Lettuce seedlings. Natural size.

late in August or in September. In such case it is best to sow in a seed-bed, because the moisture conditions can be controlled better, and a field is usually too dry at that time of the year to give quick germination. It is essential that lettuce make a quick and succulent growth to be at its best. The large-heading varieties are not so much grown as the others, since they demand somewhat greater care and are more particular as to soil. Lettuce usually does best in a soil that is loose and warm, or one that the gardeners call "quick." Soils that are very heavy, and particularly those that have much clay, are ill-adapted to the crop. For the late spring and summer crops the seed is usually sown rather thickly and the thinnings are used on the table. The plants that are to attain the largest size should stand as much as a foot apart.

Fig. 106. Lettuce as a companion-crop to cabbage.

Successional sowings may be made as often as once in ten days to three weeks. The earliest spring lettuce taken from the open is usually started in frames or forcing-houses, or sometimes in boxes in the house. If one's soil is moïst, and particularly if the exposure is somewhat cool, the ordinary spring lettuce may be grown with success throughout the summer. In order to secure a quick growth, it is sometimes advisable to apply nitrate of soda soon after the plants are set. The nitrate is usually sprinkled broadcast on the surface and raked or cultivated in. An application at the rate of 200–300 pounds to the acre may be made with good results. The surface of the ground should be kept well tilled in order to conserve the moisture and to promote all those activities which result in quick growth.

Lettuce is commonly grown in rows 8–12 inches apart, and thinned eventually, as the young plants are taken out, to 6–12 inches apart in the row. For early use, start in forcing-house, frame or kitchen. Sow in succession till warm weather. Calculate on 1,000 plants for each ounce of seed. Most of the forcing varieties, started under glass, are good for early use, as Tennisball, Boston Market, Simpson. For summer use, plant varieties that withstand the heat, as Deacon, Hanson, Summer Cabbage, Cos.

Lettuce (*Lactuca sativa*) is probably native to Europe and Asia, although its wild prototype is not definitely known. By some it is supposed to have descended from *Lactuca Scariola*, a tall homely plant that has now become a weed in many parts of the country. There are four well-marked tribes or races,—head lettuce, cut- or curled-leaved, Cos, and narrow-leaved. The last is little known to gardeners. Goff (in 4th Rept. N. Y. State Exp. Sta., pp. 156–202) reduces the varieties to 87. His classification is as follows:

- A. Leaves roundish or but slightly oblong, spreading.
  - B. Borders of leaves plain or nearly so.
    - C. Foliage green.
    - CC. Foliage more or less tinged or spotted with red, brown, or purple.
  - BB. Borders of leaves ruffled.
    - (Color divisions as above.)
- AA. Leaves oblong, tending to grow upright.
  - B. Leaves oval or spatulate.
    - (Color divisions as above.)
  - BB. Leaves lanceolate.
- AAA. Leaves pinnately lobed.

Kinney (10th Rept. R. I. Exp. Sta., 1897) classifies lettuce chiefly on the shape, color and margin-characters of the leaves. He describes 99 varieties. A condensation of his scheme is as follows:

A. Leaves entire near the apex.
  B. Leaves as long as or longer than broad.
    C. Color red or blotched.
      (Minor divisions.)
    CC. Color green.
      (Minor divisions.)
  BB. Leaves not as long as broad.
AA. Leaves dentate near apex.
  (Divisions much as in A.)

American seedsmen offered 119 varieties of lettuce in 1889. For history, see Sturtevant, Amer. Nat., Nov., 1888, pp. 984-7.

Field-grown lettuce has few enemies.

ENDIVE*

Endive affords a good supplement to lettuce, since *it is essentially a summer and fall crop and thrives at a season when lettuce is somewhat difficult to grow to perfection. The culture is not unlike that of lettuce, except that the plant requires a longer time in which to mature.* Seeds sown in June may be expected to give plants fit for the table by August and September.

In respect to soil, tillage, distance apart and other treatment, the care of endive differs little from that of lettuce. The plants should stand about a foot apart each way. The green, rank leaves are likely to be bitter

---

* One desiring accessible historical sketches of some of the following vegetables may consult Sturtevant's writings in American Naturalist: Endive, Nov., 1887, p. 980; Chicory, Aug., 1887, p. 711; Cress, Oct., 1887, p. 903; Corn Salad, Sept., 1887, p. 831; Parsley, Jan., 1890, p. 42.

and tough. It is customary to blanch the interior leaves of the crown or head by gathering all the leaves into a bunch and tying them near the top. By thus excluding the light, the inner leaves are whitened. This tying is done two or three weeks before the plant is desired for

Fig. 107. Endive seedlings. Two-thirds natural size.

use. In very hot and wet weather the heads are sometimes blanched in ten days; but under ordinary conditions it requires nearly or quite twice that length of time. If heavy rains and cloudy weather follow the tying, the crowns must be examined occasionally to see that they are not decaying. After the interior leaves are well blanched, they must be used quickly or decay will set in. The later plants, taken in the fall, are sometimes blanched by being set in cellars or pits; or if the heads are packed securely in well-ventilated barrels, they may blanch in transportation.

Endive is little known to people of American parentage, although it is much prized by foreigners and there is considerable demand for it in the larger cities. It deserves to be better known.

Endive is a perennial or biennial, *Cichorium Endivia*, closely allied to chicory.

"Endive is frequently blanched like celery or Cos lettuce, by tying up the leaves, drawing the soil up to the plants, and similar means. When blanched in this way, the white varieties especially give very pretty white leaves from the inside of the head. For eating cooked, however, we prefer to take the plants quite young, and before they have had time to make heads. With ordinary outdoor culture they will lose rather than gain in tenderness between this stage and the time when satisfactory heads can be produced.

"Endive may be sown early in coldframes or in the open ground like lettuce. Sowings may also be made at any time during the summer, although plants grown in the heat of midsummer have not the best quality. Fall-grown plants may be taken up with a good supply of adhering earth and stored in a dry cellar or coldframe for winter use. From forty-five to fifty days is required to grow the crop."—*F. A. Waugh*, Bull. 54, Vt. Exp. Sta., on "Salad Plants."

CHICORY

The tender blanched leaves that arise from the crowns of chicory roots make excellent salads. The unblanched leaves are sometimes used for greens, as dandelions are. *The plants are grown as root-crops are; the leaves are gathered in their natural state, or are developed from roots that are transferred to a dark place.*

The roots are grown as parsnips or carrots are, and cuttings of leaves may be made during the season. One may also leave the roots in the ground over winter and gather the crown of leaves in the spring, or he may take them to the cellar or greenhouse and secure the leaves in winter. It is usually preferable to grow a new lot of plants each year.

For the production of blanched leaves, the strong

roots are usually taken up in the fall. The roots are buried in a sloping direction in sand in a pit or cellar, the crown projecting an inch or so above the earth. The place should be kept dark. In a month or less, the small leaves (sometimes known as barbe de capucin) are produced.

Or, the best roots may be trimmed and then planted upright under greenhouse benches, and the crowns covered two feet with manure or other loose material. The

Fig. 108. Seedlings of chicory. Two-thirds natural size.

crown of leaves forming beneath the manure will resemble small heads of lettuce. These heads are often known as witloof.

Chicory is also grown for the roots, which are eaten as carrots or beets are. The young tender roots are chosen.

The dry roots of chicory are also used as a substitute for coffee, and the plant is now coming to be grown in this country for that purpose. See Circular 29, U. S. Dept. Agric., 1900.

Chicory (*Cichorium Intybus*) is a perennial tall-growing blue-flowered plant of the Composite family.

CRESS

Cresses are grown for their piquant leaves, which are used in salads and garnishings. There are three kinds of cresses in somewhat common cultivation, belonging to three genera, although they are all members of the Cruciferæ or mustard family.

Water cress (*Nasturtium officinale*) is a prostrate perennial, with small, roundish leaves, thriving in very moist places and in running water. It is readily propagated by seeds, which may be scattered along cool brooks, or by bits of the stems planted in the mud. In order that it may reach its best development, the water should be pure, cool, and clean. When once established in a permanent place, it will persist indefinitely, taking care of itself. When a natural brook is not to be had, it may be grown in a moist, shady place in the garden where it may be watered frequently. Sometimes it is grown in the pit of an abandoned hotbed, into which water may be run with a hose. If the ground is kept moist, or even wet, the plant will thrive and it will not be necessary to have it covered with water. The plant is best grown, however, by being colonized along brooksides and about springs.

The common garden cress (*Lepidium sativum*) is a short-season annual. Fig. 109. It is a cool-weather plant. Usually the leaves are not desired in the summer. Seeds may be sown as soon as the ground is fit in the spring, for the plant is hardy or half-hardy. A rather cool and rich soil is to be chosen, for the value of the foliage will depend, to a large extent, on the vigor of its growth. Late in the season and in warm weather, the plant runs quickly to seed. For fall use, the seeds may be sown late in summer and in early fall. It is easily grown in pots or boxes in the house in winter.

Fig. 109. Curled cress seedlings. Two-thirds natural size.

Leaves fit for use may be had in six to eight weeks from the sowing of the seed, under ordinary conditions. There are a number of varieties, some of them with beautifully curled foliage. The garden cress is less popular in America than abroad.

The upland or upright cress (*Barbarea vulgaris* and *B. præcox*) is usually a biennial, the young plants becoming established from seeds dropped in summer, and sending up the flower-stalks early the following spring. In cultivation, it is treated as an annual or as a winter perennial. The seeds may be sown late in the season and the young plants are ready for use the following spring; or seeds may be sown in earliest spring. The plant is perfectly hardy and it is common in the natural state over a large part of the United States. Although a common plant, it is little known in general cultivation either in this country or abroad.

"Upland cress bears a considerable resemblance, both in form and flavor, to the better known water cress. It will be acceptable to many gardeners and cooks on that account. The leaves lie flat upon the ground, and are thereby apt to be soiled by rains. The plant does not run rapidly to seed, as does the garden cress, but during hot weather the leaves soon become tough and bitter. The summer crops are better grown in partly shaded situations. The upland cress requires a longer time from planting to picking than the garden cress. The crop sown this year July 28, was ready September 18, or fifty-two days after sowing. This term might doubtless be shortened by treatment proper to that end."—*F. A. Waugh*, Bull. 54, Vt. Exp. Sta.

CORN SALAD

Corn salad is grown as lettuce is. It is a cool-season crop. It is hardy and may be sown as soon as the ground is fit in spring. It matures in six to eight weeks, giving a bunch of leaves somewhat like small-leaved spinach. In warm weather and in dry places, the plant soon runs to seed. It may be sown in the fall and

Fig. 110. Corn salad seedlings. Two-thirds natural size.

protected in winter as advised for spinach. If sown late in summer, the plant will give edible herbage in the fall, and in a mild climate or an open winter it may be used all winter.

Corn salad or fetticus (Fig. 110) is used both as salad and pot-herb, chiefly the former. It belongs to the Valerian family, and is known to botanists as *Valerianella olitoria*. It is native to Europe. The plant is little known in America, but is prized as a fall and winter salad abroad. It is very easy of culture in any cool soil. Plants should stand about 6 in. apart in the row. An ounce of seed should give 2,000–3,000 plants.

PARSLEY

A cool moist soil is best suited to parsley. Not all the leaves should be removed from the plant at any one time. Parsley demands no special care.

Parsley is the most popular of all garnishing herbs. The leaves are used also for salads and for flavoring.

Fig. 111. Parsley seedlings. Natural size.

The plant is biennial, but the foliage is gathered the first year, and the plants are then destroyed unless seed is wanted. The seed is slow to germinate, and it is best to sow in a seed-bed unless the ground is in excellent tilth and is moist to the top. Thin or transplant to 8 to 12 inches apart each way. Make successional sowings. It usually requires three months from sowing to bring good foliage for gathering. The strongest plants may be covered with sash, and leaves may then be gathered all winter. The plants will stand considerable frost. It is a good plan to lift a few roots in late fall and set them in pots or boxes in the house: from these a winter supply may be secured.

Parsley (Fig. 111) is one of the Umbelliferæ or Parsnip family. It is more or less subject to parsnip and celery insects and diseases. It is native to S. Europe. To botanists it is known as *Carum Petroselinum*.

SALAD CHERVIL

The salad chervil is an annual plant much like parsley and very popular in Europe, but little known in this country. It is used for garnishing and seasoning, for which the curled-leaved variety is the most popular. The plant is of easy culture, giving a cutting of leaves in six to eight weeks from the seed. It does not thrive in our hot, dry summers, and therefore should be grown as a spring or fall crop, unless the particular location is cool. It is hardy, and where winters are not severe can be carried over the cold season by light cold-frames or even by protection of brush. The plant reaches a height of nearly two feet when mature, but the young foliage is most desired. The plants should stand 10 to 12 inches apart. Salad chervil is *Scandix Cerefolium*, one of the Umbelliferæ, native to southern Europe. For turnip-rooted chervil, which is another plant, see Chapter IX.

CELERY

Cool, very rich and very moist land, the best surface tillage and the most careful attention to all care of the plant, are requisites of good celery culture. Celery is always a seed-bed crop. It may be treated as a succession- or companion-crop, although it usually is the sole occupant of the land in any season. The leaf-stalks, which are the edible parts, must always be blanched. The crop must be stored from frost if kept during winter.

Celery is nearly always grown on bottom lands because it then receives a sufficient and constant supply of moisture. Usually, also, such lands are very rich. Celery of excellent quality can be grown on uplands; but ordinarily more care is required in securing deep tillage and in conserving moisture, and more expense is entailed in adding fertilizers. Successful commercial celery growing on high lands is usually possible only when much stable manure is added and when irrigation is practiced. Under those conditions, however, the celery grown on high lands may be fully as good as that raised in reclaimed marshes. For home use celery can be grown in almost any well-tilled and rich garden soil. Level black-soil marsh or bottom lands, in which the water-table does not fall below 2 or 3 feet in summer, are usually chosen for commercial celery growing. Fig. 113.

Celery is always a transplanted crop. The seeds are small and slow to germinate, and the seedlings are delicate. Fig. 112. It is only in a well-prepared seed-bed that satisfactory results can be expected in raising the plants. This seed-bed should have perfect surface tilth and should retain moisture to the top. Preferably, it should be protected from hot and dry winds. Some persons prefer to have the bed partially shaded; but if the shading is too dense, the plants are likely to be soft and tender when taken to the field, and they are killed by sun-scald. It is advisable, whenever possible, to have the seed-bed in such place that it can be watered every

Fig. 112. Celery seedlings. Natural size.

evening if necessary; but care must be exercised that the watering is not so heavy that it packs and puddles the soil. Sometimes the bed is covered with boards, brush or straw, in order to maintain the moisture until germination has taken place. This may be advisable, but if the covering is left on too long, the plants make a very weak and spindling growth and are worthless. If covering is used, it is well to remove it gradually as the plants germinate. The ideal seed-bed, however, is one that does not need a cover, but which holds the moisture of itself. In order to secure stocky plants, they should be transplanted once or twice in the seed-bed, or they may be thinned until they finally stand at 2 or 3 inches apart. The labor of transplanting is so great that most growers now prefer to secure stocky plants by the thinning process and then by shearing off the remaining plants when they become too tall. The plants may be cut back a third or a half their growth by shears or sickle, or on large beds by a scythe.

Celery is grown as a short-season crop; that is, it does not occupy the land during the whole of the growing season. The main crop is sometimes planted as a succession, early cabbages or other spring crops having been grown on the land. In the case of lowland celery fields, however, the celery crop is commonly the only one grown, since the land is usually too wet in the spring to allow of any early planting. In some celery-growing regions, two or three crops of celery are raised on the land at the same time, the later or main crop being planted between the rows of the early crop. The main or late crop, which is used for winter consumption, may be planted in the field as late as the middle or last of July in the northern states. The early crop may be set in the field as soon as the weather is settled in the spring, but there is relatively little demand for very early celery. The plants should be 4 or 5 inches high and stocky and dark green when they are planted. Plants are usually set from 6 to 12-inches apart in the rows, and the distance between the rows varies with the method of blanching.

Celery must be crisp, tender and well blanched to be fit for use. The blanching is accomplished by excluding the light. There are three common methods of

Fig. 113 Celery growing, the work of one season.

The upper field shows the original marsh. Land broken, June 1–12, 1896. Chemical fertilizers applied and plants set June 15. The lower picture shows the result, Sept. 26, 1896. Blanching with boards. New Haven Marshes, Huron Co., O. Put under cultivation by E. J. Hollister.

blanching celery in vogue at the present day: by the use of boards; banking up with earth; blanching in pits or storage.

Blanching by means of boards (see Fig. 113) is employed only for the early or summer celery, because protection from frost must be supplied to the celery which remains in the field after the first of October, and the boards usually do not afford sufficient protection. Use boards one foot wide and one inch thick, and about twelve or fourteen feet long. If the boards are much longer than this, they are awkward to handle. These boards are set on edge close against the crown of the plant, one on either side of the row, and the tops are tipped together until they are only two or three inches apart or until they rest against the plants. The boards are held in this position by cleats nailed across the top, or by wire hooks. The first "boarding" is made when the celery is only tall enough to show a few of its leaves above the boards. The plants shoot up for light, making slender, soft stalks. The foliage fills the space between the boards and excludes the light from above. In from ten to twenty days in warm "growing" weather, the celery may be blanched by this method. In any means of blanching in summer one must see that the plants do not rot at the heart, as they are likely to do if they are too wet at the core. The board method of blanching celery is one of the most economical and is now extensively used in the large celery fields. Growers usually find that it pays to obtain a good quality of lumber and to use it year after year. Some commercial growers think it best to have the lumber dressed on both sides. In the boarding system the rows may be put simply far enough apart to allow of good horse tillage, say from 2 to 3 feet.

Blanching by earth usually gives a somewhat better quality of celery; but this method of blanching is expensive and it cannot be employed so well in midsummer, since the plants are more likely to rot at the heart. Usually two or three "handlings" or bankings are given. When the plants have spread so much as to make a crown or head a foot or eighteen inches across, the celery is "handled" by gathering the leaves in the

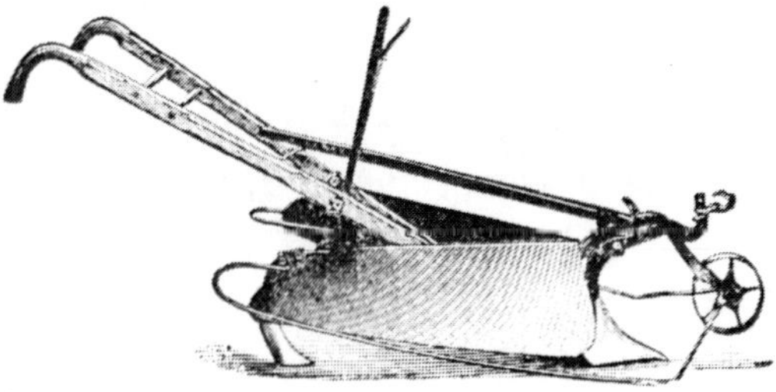

Fig. 114. Celery hiller. Planet Jr.

hand and holding them whilst earth is shoveled against the plant so as to cover it two-thirds or more of its height. In ten days or two weeks the "handling" is repeated. In late years the banking of celery, particularly in large areas, is done almost entirely by means of celery plows, which are implements with very high moldboards that throw a great quantity of earth against the plant. Fig. 114. If celery is to be blanched by the banking process, the rows are rarely less than 3½ feet apart, and if the tall-growing varieties are used, the rows are often put at 4 feet.

Late winter celery is ordinarily blanched in storage. If it is thoroughly blanched before putting in storage, it will not keep well. It is usually advisable, however, to handle the crop at least once in the field in order to induce a straight, upright growth and to begin the blanching process. Thereafter the plants are set in pits or sheds so close together that the blanching proceeds.

Still a fourth system of blanching has been advocated in the last few years in the system known as the "new celery culture." This consists in growing the plants so close that the light is excluded and the plants blanch themselves. Plants are usually grown as close as 6 or 8 inches apart either way. It will be seen that this system can be used only when the soil is very rich and when there is a large supply of moisture. Under ordinary conditions, it is not successful. Whenever the water-table is close to the surface or when one can practice irrigation, it may be considered. It is usually successful in small home gardens where one can use a hose.

There are two or three methods of storing celery. Storing in outside cellars or pits has already been described on pages 229, 232. The early winter and mid-winter celery, however, is usually stored in special celery houses, which are permanent sheds with windows at intervals along the roof, in order to supply light enough for the workmen. Wooden chimneys are provided to afford ventilation. These houses are sometimes provided with heat by means of stoves, so that the temperature does not fall much, if any, below the freezing point.

In beds in these houses the celery plants are set close together and the blanching proceeds during storage.

For market, celery is prepared by being thoroughly washed and usually scrubbed, so that all earth and sand are removed. The outside leaves are removed and usually the root is trimmed away, leaving a pointed base to the whole cluster. These plants are then shipped in open trays or boxes, the style of box and the number to be packed in each depending largely on the market in which one sells.

In celery, calculate from 20,000 to 30,000 plants per acre. There is usually much loss in seeds and young plants, and it is therefore advisable to sow the seed very thick. One ounce of seed to 200 feet of row in the seed-bed is a liberal allowance. Some gardeners estimate 2,000 good plants from each ounce of seed, but this allows for an unusual amount of loss. An ounce should give from 5,000 to 10,000 good plants, after allowing for several times that amount in loss. One pound of celery seed should give enough strong plants to set four to five acres.

Celery is planted 6 to 12 inches apart in the row. The rows vary from 2 to 4 feet apart. In the "new celery culture," or self-blanching system, the plants are set 6 to 7 inches apart each way, requiring about 150,000 to the acre.

White Plume, Golden Self-Blanching, and Kalamazoo are popular summer and fall varieties, and are also used for winter. For late winter or spring use, the product being blanched in pits, Boston Market or Arlington is a standard. There are pink-stemmed varieties; also very tall varieties, now little grown.

Thirty-seven varieties were advertised by American seedsmen in 1889 (Annals Hort.). Sturtevant has written the history of celery in Amer. Nat., July, 1886, pp. 599–606. See also brief note by the same author in Amer. Nat., Aug., 1887, p. 705. Goff has monographed the varieties in 6th Rept. N. Y. State Exp., Sta. (for 1887), pp. 217–225. He reduces the varieties to 26. The classificatory scheme is as follows:

A. Stems neither self-blanching nor tinted with red.

AA. Stems not self-blanching, but more or less washed or tinted with red.

AAA. Stems distinctly self-blanching.

Celery is *Apium graveolens* of botanists. It belongs to the Umbelliferæ, together with carrot, parsley, parsnip. It is native to Europe, Asia and Africa, and was in cultivation before the Christian era. The long, thick, blanching leaf-stalks are a result of domestication. If careful attention is not given to selection or "rogueing" in the seed-field, the varieties soon run down and become green-stemmed, slender, stringy and worthless.

On insects and diseases, consult:

Mich. Bull. No 102. Insects injurious to celery.

Leaf blight, Dept. Agric. Rept. 1886, pp. 117–120; N. J. 12th Rept. 1891, p. 250; Cornell Bull. 132, pp. 203 205; Ct. 21 Rept., pp. 167–171. Cornell: Copper carbonate. Dip young plants in weak solution, and treat young growing plants at intervals of 2 weeks. Ct.: Sulfur dusted on.

Leaf spot, N. Y Bull. 51; Cornell Bull. 132. N. Y.: Reject diseased seed. Treat with Bordeaux in seed bed; continue with Bordeaux if attack is anticipated.

Diseases in storage, Cornell Bull. 132. See p. 229 of this book.

Special celery literature: Consult the special books by Greiner, Vaughan, Van Bochove, Hollister, Rawson, Stewart, Crider. Roessle's "How to Cultivate Celery," 1860, long since out of print, was the first American Book to be devoted wholly to a special vegetable-garden crop. It is beautifully printed in large clear type, and it has a colored frontispiece of "Rose Colored Celery." Mr. Roessle had other similar handbooks in view, but none of them seems to have been published. Greiner's is a general treatise. Vaughan's gives particular attention to methods employed about Chicago; Van Bochove's to Kalamazoo methods; Hollister's to large-area work in marsh lands; Rawson's to the Boston methods; Stewart's to methods in vogue in Southern Michigan.

CELERIAC

Celeriac is a form of the celery species, in which the root is enlarged like a small tuber, and this tuber is the edible part. It is used either as a salad or as a cooked vegetable. The plant is dwarf and celery-like in appearance, but requires no blanching. It is grown as celery in so far as seed-sowing, transplanting, and tillage are concerned. Sometimes the seed is sown where the plants are to stand, but since the seeds are as slow to germinate as those of celery, this is usually not the best plan. The plants are given 6 or 8 inches space in the row, and the rows are only far enough apart to allow of convenient tillage. The roots may be kept in winter by being packed in sand or moss, as other vegetables often are.

Celeriac is much prized abroad, but it is little known to native-born Americans. It deserves to be better known. Several varieties are offered by American seedsmen; six were advertised in 1889. Goff described five types in 1887 (6th Rept. N. Y. Exp. Sta., pp. 215-217). Sturtevant writes of its history in Amer. Nat., August, 1887, pp. 703–4. It is known to botanists as *Apium graveolens* var. *rapaceum*. It is sometimes known as turnip-rooted celery. A good root should be 3–4 inches in diameter. In seeding, calculate quantity of seed as for celery.

CHAPTER XV

PULSE CROPS

Pea, Beans.

BOTANICALLY peas and beans are very closely related, but they have few points in common from the cultural point of view, since peas are hardy, cool-season plants and beans are tender and warm-season plants. Both are leguminous crops, and are therefore capable of using atmospheric nitrogen. As garden crops, however, they may need applications of nitrogen in order to secure a quick start, particularly if an early crop is desired. "It is frequently the wiser economy to apply nitrogen, particularly if they are raised upon land which has not been previously planted with these crops, and thus may not possess the specific nitrogen-gathering bacteria." *

PEA

Peas are a partial-season crop, requiring cool season and a soil not over rich; seed is sown where the plants are to stand; grown in drills; hardy.

Garden peas are of the easiest culture. They thrive best in spring rather than in summer, but they also thrive in fall from late-sown seeds. In summer they

*Voorhees' Fertilizers, 269.

are very liable to mildew. Peas and onions are the first vegetables to be sown in the open ground. Even before freezing weather is past, peas may be planted. It is customary to plant them 3–5 inches deep: the roots are then deep enough to be in cool and moist soil.

A light soil is preferable, particularly when earliness is desired. A very rich soil tends to make the plants run to vine and to delay the crop. Successional sowings should be made at intervals of six to ten days.

Fig. 115. Pea seedlings. Two-thirds natural size.

For early use, the dwarf varieties should be selected. For the main or late crop the tall or climbing sorts, which are more productive, are preferred. Pinching-in the excessive growths tends to make the tall varieties somewhat earlier. Early in August in the Northern states dwarf varieties may be sown for fall use. As a field crop, peas are now extensively grown for canning factories (see Bull. 41, Del. Exp. Sta.). For this purpose they are sown broadcast or drilled in. If broadcasted they are not tilled. Better results are secured by sowing in drills and giving two or three tillings.

Peas are usually sown in two rows that stand 6–8 inches apart. If tall varieties are grown, one row of brush or chicken-wire (the wire is better) will answer for both rows; if the dwarf kinds are grown, one row will help to support the other. Between each two pairs of rows a space should be left wide enough for convenient tillage. The plants should stand 3–4 inches apart in the row. One pint of seed of the small-seeded varieties will sow 100–125 feet of single drill. In drills, 1-2 bushels will sow an acre; broadcast, 2–3 bushels.

Peas are of two kinds: the seed wrinkled and the seed smooth. The wrinkled are the better in quality, but the seeds are more liable to decay when planted very early. There are dwarf and tall varieties of both the wrinkled and smooth types. For very early there are many popular strains, as First-of-All, Philadelphia, Daniel O'Rourke, American Wonder, McLean Little Gem, Blue Peter. For late, Marrowfat, Champion of England, Telephone, Telegraph, and Stratagem are popular names.

A race of peas with edible pods, comparable to string beans, is considerably grown abroad but is little known here. These are known as edible-podded, or sugar peas. These are of the same species as the common pea, *Pisum sativum*.

The field pea, with purple-and-white flowers and gray angular seeds, is probably only a modified form of *Pisum sativum*. It is known as *P. sativum* variety *arvense*. The pea is native to southwest Europe. It has been cultivated 2,000 years and more. For history, see Sturtevant, Amer. Nat., Feb., 1890, pp. 144–149.

In 1889 (Annals Hort.), American seedsmen catalogued 154 names of peas. Goff (in 3d Rept. N. Y. State Exp. Sta., pp. 228–283) fully describes 98 varieties. The main points of his classificatory scheme are as follows:

A. Plant exceeding 4 feet in height.
  B. Seeds cream-colored or white.
    C. Smooth peas.
      D. Pod straight.
      DD. Pod recurved.

CC. Wrinkled peas.
(Pod as in C.)
BB. Seeds green, bluish, etc.
(Divisions as in B.)
AA. Half dwarf; plant 2–4 feet high.
(Divisions as in A.)
AAA. Dwarf; plant not exceeding 2 feet.
(Divisions as in A.)

For insects and diseases, see:

Pea-weevil or bug, Farmers' Bull. No. 45; Florida No. 36. The leading pea pest. Kill the insect in the dry peas by bisulfide of carbon.

Moth, Canadian Exp. Farms Rept. 1894, p. 187; Rept. 1897, p. 194. Picking early, and rotation.

Powdery mildew, N. J. Rept. No. 14, p. 357. Fungicides in spray.

Louse, Div. Ent., U. S. Dept. Agr., Bull. 26; Del. Bull. 49. Device is used for brushing lice off, the cultivator following.

BEANS

Garden beans represent several species, but all the common kinds are very tender to frost and require a warm season and sunny exposure; seed is sown where the plants are to grow; usually grown in drills, except the tall kinds; the common bush beans are partial-season plants.

The common bean is grown in two general types: the bush bean, and the pole bean. In this country the bush bean is by far the more important since its growing obviates the labor and expense of providing support on which the plants may climb. Bush beans are grown both as a field crop and a garden crop. As a garden crop they are used mostly as "string" beans, the pods being picked when they are two-thirds grown, and the pod and beans together being eaten. There are certain strains of bush beans that are particularly adapted to this use. They are such as have thick and fleshy pods, with very little fibrous tissue on the sutures. The pods of a good string bean are those which have no "strings." The pods snap cleanly in two, and this gives rise to the common term of "snap" beans. In order that string beans may be of the best quality, they should make a

Fig. 116. Seedlings of wax bean. Two-thirds natural size.

rapid and continuous growth. The soil should be rich and in excellent tilth. Plant only after the weather has become thoroughly settled. In late summer, plant again for fall use. A succession may be had all summer. Although beans are nitrogen-gathering plants, it is nevertheless advisable to apply a little nitrogen at the start on land which is not well supplied with humus or in which beans have not been grown within a year or two.

There are other types of garden beans used as "shell" beans. The large, soft seeds are used just before they begin to harden, and the pods are not eaten. Some of the best of these shell beans are pole or running varieties, the Cranberry or so-called Horticultural Lima being amongst the most popular.

Lima beans demand a long season and continuous growth, particularly the tall or true Lima varieties. Very often the flowers are blasted by the hot, dry weather of midsummer. It is well, therefore, to get

Fig. 117. Lima bean seedlings. Two-thirds natural size.

the plants established as early as possible in order that some of the fruit may set before the hottest weather. It is important that only the earliest and quickest soil be used and that quickly-available fertilizers be applied when the seeds are planted. Soils that are light and sandy are usually preferable. In these, plant-food acts quickly and the plant secures a good and very early start. The tall varieties must have poles. When poles are scarce, it is a good plan to set rather strong stakes 10 to 12 feet apart and to run wires or heavy cord from pole to pole, one strand near the top and one within a foot or so of the ground, and then to connect these horizontal strands with perpendicular cords. Sometimes several plants or hills of Lima beans are planted in a semicircle around one strong stake, and strings are run from the top of the stake to the ground, making a cone. This is a very good plan for the home garden, since the

Fig. 118. Broad or Windsor bean seedlings. Two-thirds natural size.

vines are well exposed to the sun, but is too laborious for general market cultivation. In commercial plantations, one bare pole is ordinarily provided for each hill.

In the northern states, it is usually inadvisable to attempt to grow the large, late Lima beans unless one's soil is particularly quick and the exposure is very warm. The seasons are usually too short, and the nights are likely to be too cool. Under such conditions it is best to rely largely on the Sieva kinds, none of which are very high climbers and some of which, as Henderson and Jackson, are nearly or quite "bush" in form and in habit. These Sieva beans are very heavy croppers and mature in the short seasons of the North. Although the beans are not very large, the quality is good. The dwarf Limas are excellent for northern gardens.

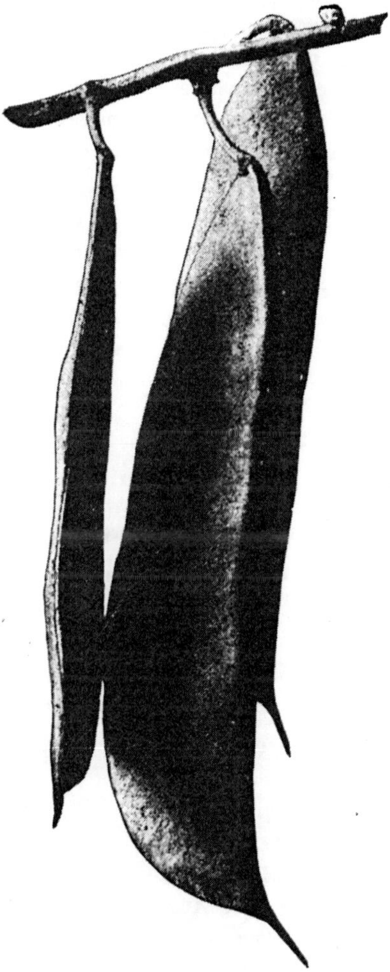

Fig. 119. Willow-leaf Sieva bean. Full size.

Bush beans are sown in drills, the rows being 18 to 30 inches apart to allow of easy tillage. The plants should stand 5 to 10 inches apart in the row. One pint will sow from 75 to 125 feet of drill, depending on the variety. In drills, 1 bushel to 5 pecks is sown to the acre. The tall or pole beans are usually grown in hills.

Lima beans are usually grown in hills 3 to 4 feet apart each way. Five or 6 plants may stand in each hill.

The White Dutch Runner bean (*Phaseolus multiflorus*) is grown as the tall forms of the common bean are. Used mostly as shell beans, but sometimes as snap beans.

The Broad, Windsor, or English Dwarf beans (*Vicia Faba*) are erect-growing plants, much raised in Europe, but littie grown in this country because of our hot climate. They are used as shell beans; also for stock. They are as hardy as peas. Sow early in a cool place in drills 2 to 3 feet apart.

In 1883, Wing described 102 varieties of beans, distributed in several species (2d Rept. N. Y. State Exp. Sta., p. 235-259). They were first classified into their species. The subdivisions were made chiefly on the shapes and colors of the seeds. In 1889, American seedsmen listed 141 names of garden beans, 4 of Windsor or Broad beans, 13 of Limas.

The garden beans are all members of the Leguminosæ. The botanical places of the commonest kinds are as follows:

Bush and ordinary pole beans, *Phaseolus vulgaris.* Fig. 116. Now believed to be a native of tropical America. See Gray and Trumbull, Amer. Journ. Sci. 26:130 (Aug. 1883); Sturtevant, Amer. Nat., May, 1885, pp. 448–452, and April, 1887, pp. 327–333; Wittmack, Berichte der Deutsch. Bot. Gesell. 6:374 (1888).

Sieva or Carolina Limas, *Phaseolus lunatus.* Tropical America. Fig. 119.

Tall or Large Limas, *Phaseolus lunatus* var. *macrocarpus.* South America. Figs. 117, 120-123.

White Dutch Runner and Scarlet Runner, *Phaseolus multiflorus.* South America.

French Yard-Long, *Dolichos sesquipedalis.* South America.

Soy., *Glycine hispida.* Japan.

Broad or Windsor, *Vicia Faba.* Asia. Fig. 118.

Velvet, *Mucuna utilis*, Asia; sometimes eaten.

For a monograph of the common bean (*Phaseolus vulgaris*) the student should consult Von Martens' "Die Gartenbohnen," 1869.

For an account of the Dwarf Limas, see Bailey, Bull. 87, Cornell Exp. Sta. (1895); of the Pole Limas, Bull. 115, Cornell Exp. Sta. (1896). For further history of Lima beans, see Sturtevant, Amer. Nat. Aug., 1899, pp. 665–67.

"The Lima beans are natives of warm countries. The large flat Limas are perennials, or at least plur-annuals, in their native countries. They therefore require a long season, and one who expects to grow them in the North should endeavor in every way to shorten the period of growth. This may be done, in the first place, by planting the earlier varieties; and, in the second place, by exercising great care in the selection of soil and in giving particular attention to cultivation. Light and so-called 'quick' soils are best. Soils which are naturally sandy and loose, but which have been enriched in previous years by the addition of manure, are excellent for Lima beans, especially if they have a warm exposure.

Fig. 120.
Leaf of Extra-Early Lima, one of the large Lima class (× ¼)

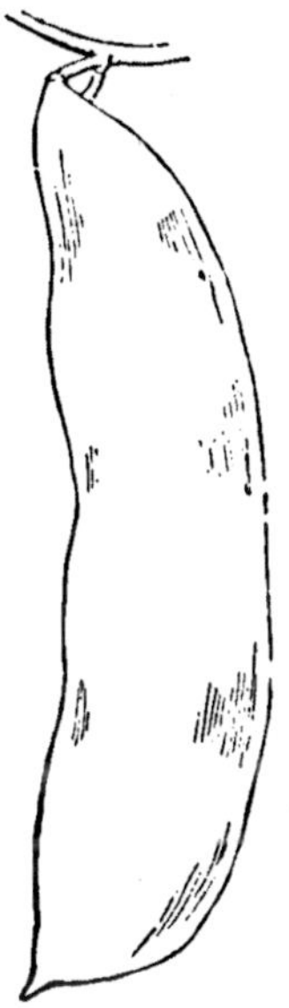

Fig. 121.
Mammoth Kidney-shaped. Half size.

The soil should also be dry. Coarse, raw manure should be avoided for Lima beans, because it tends to make too rank and too late growth. If any fertilizer is applied the year in which the beans are planted, it should be such as will become available very quickly and therefore tend to hasten the maturity of the crop. We prefer, therefore, to use some of the concentrated fertilizers, especially those which are rich in potash and phosphoric acid, and avoid those which contain very much nitrogen. If nitrogenous fertilizers are used at all, they should be applied in comparatively small amount and be of such kind that they will give up their fertility early in the season. If ordinary stable manure is used, it should be applied in the fall in order that it may become thoroughly incorporated with the soil and be ready for use at the earliest moment in the spring."—*Cornell Bull. 115.*

The Limas may be thrown into the following classes:

1. The Sieva or Carolina bean (*Phaseolus lunatus*), a small and slender grower as compared with the large Limas, early and rela-

Fig. 122. Leaf of Challenger, one of the Potato Lima class (× 1/6).

Fig. 123. Challenger. Half size.

tively hardy, truly annual, with thin, short and mostly broad (ovate-pointed) leaflets, numerous small papery pods which are much curved on the back and provided with a long upward point or tip and which split open and twist when ripe, discharging the seeds; beans small and flat, white, brown, or variously marked with red. Fig. 119.

2. The true Lima bean (*P. lunatus* var. *macrocarpus*), distinguished from the Sieva by its tall growth, lateness, greater susceptibility to cold, perennial in tropical climates, large, thick, often ovate-lanceolate leaflets, and fewer thick, fleshy, straightish (or sometimes latterly curved) pods with a less prominent point and

not readily splitting open at maturity; seeds much larger, white, red, black or speckled. Of this true or large Lima there are two types in cultivation:

(*a*) The Flat or Large-Seeded Limas, which have large, very flat and more or less lunate and veiny seeds, very broad pods with a distinct point, and broad ovate leaflets. See Figs. 120 and 121. Burpee Dwarf is a form of this.

(*b*) The Potato Limas, with smaller and tumid seeds, shorter and thicker pods with a less prominent point, and long-ovate leaflets tapering from a more or less angular base into a long apex. See Figs. 122, 123. Challenger and Kumerle are examples. There are dwarf forms.

For insects and diseases of beans, consult:

Weevil, Lintner, 7th Rept. N. Y. Entomologist, p. 255, very full, with ills.; Me. Rept. 1893, p. 171, ill. Use bisulfide of carbon, as for pea bug.

Anthracnose, N. Y. Bull. 48, very fully ill. Remove infected seedlings from field. Cover with Bordeaux mixture.

Rust, N. Y. Bull. 48.

CHAPTER XVI

SOLANACEOUS CROPS

Tomato,	Pepper,
Eggplant,	Husk Tomato.

Tomatoes, eggplants, and their kin are hot-season plants. They require nearly or quite the entire season in which to mature. Usually they grow until killed by frost, at least in the North, and the production of a heavy crop depends largely on securing an early start. They are seed-bed crops, and they need abundance of quick-acting fertilizers applied relatively early in their growth. They are grown in hills.

These plants are here called solanaceous crops because they belong to the family Solanaceæ. To this family also belongs the potato, so that these plants have not the exclusive right to the name; but the writer knows of no other single term which can be applied to them.

TOMATO

Essential points in the culture of tomato are: *long, warm season; "quick" soil with available fertility; frequent, or at least two or three transplantings to obtain stocky and continuous-growing plants, particularly in the North; early fruiting to mitigate loss from fruit-rot and to secure a heavy crop before frost; planting in hills.*

In most parts of the United States, the tomato is grown with the greatest ease. In fact, the fruit is grown more abundantly in this country, and to a greater degree of perfection, than elsewhere in the world. The plants are usually started from four to eight weeks before they

Fig. 124. Tomato seedlings. Two-thirds natural size.

are transplanted to the field. For the home garden it is well to handle the young tomato plants in pots; but in commercial operations this is scarcely practicable. The present custom is to grow them in small flats not more than ten or twelve inches square and that hold about two inches of soil. In some cases, even smaller flats are used. In these boxes the plants are displayed in the grocery stores for sale to amateur planters. In flats of various sizes, the plants can be readily handled from the frame to the field. In commercial business, the young tomato plants are now rarely transplanted. They are thinned in the flats so that they stand two or three inches apart each way, or farther than this if the plants are started very early. Sometimes the plants are sheared if they become too tall and "leggy," although this is not the best practice. In the Middle and Southern states, cloth-covered frames are often used for starting tomato and other plants. Fig. 125. The cloth is rolled up during the day. The securing of a good crop of tomatoes in the North depends very largely on having vigorous and stocky plants that are well in advance of the

Fig. 125. Cloth-covered frames.

Used in the South for tomatoes, tobacco, and other plants. The muslin is used for protection at night and in cold weather, and is rolled up, as shown, in the day. (After Earle.)

season, and a warm, quick soil. The plants should be set in the field as soon as the weather is settled. Thereafter they need no special care except to keep the land well tilled.

It is commonly said that very rich soil is not to be advised for the tomato. This is probably true as respects the heavy application of stable manure, for such manure usually gives up its fertility somewhat slowly and tends to keep the plant in vigorous growth and to delay fruiting. If, however, the soil has been made rich by previous applications of manure, or of available commercial fertilizer early in spring, the best results may be expected. Experiments at Cornell University have shown that a rather light single application of nitrate of soda about the time the plants are set, gives better results than twice that amount applied at intervals as late as the middle of August.

Tomatoes usually give earlier and better results when the vines are trained; but the expense of training precludes its use in large commercial plantations. The best mode of training for early results is to prune the plant to a single stem, tying it to a perpendicular cord. The cord is secured at top and bottom to horizontal strands which are stretched between strong stakes. When tomatoes are trained in this way, they may be set as close as 18 inches apart in the row. There are various styles of racks for supporting tomato plants. The best are those that give the plants full exposure to sun and allow all the fruits to hang toward the outside of the trellis rather than to be covered by foliage. In commercial plantations, the plants are allowed to spread as they will, although the fruit-rot disease is usually more serious under such conditions, particularly if the surface soil contains much coarse manure. Pinching-in the shoots is thought to conduce to early bearing.

When frost threatens, the largest green tomatoes may be picked and allowed to ripen in drawers or in other dry and close places. Usually they color well and develop a good quality. If the fruits have not reached their full size, the whole plant may be pulled with the fruits on and hung in a barn or other dry place and the fruits will abstract nourishment from the vine and sometimes complete their ripening.

Tomatoes are now grown on a very large scale for canning factories. They are then a field crop, and are given no greater care than corn. A rather light, warm soil is chosen. Frame-grown plants are used and they may be set with a transplanting machine. Thereafter no special treatment is given the crop except to keep the land well tilled.

Tomato plants are usually set 4–5 feet apart each way in rich garden soil. In field conditions, they are usually set 3–4 feet. On light and early lands they are sometimes planted 3 x 3 feet. From 1 ounce of seed, about 2,000 to 2,500 good plants should be obtained. At 3 x 4 feet, an acre will require 3,630 plants. A large yield is 12–16 tons to the acre; the average is much below this.

Varieties quickly run out (see Essay 24, "Survival of the Unlike"), and it is scarcely worth while to mention the particular kinds in a book like this. Even though the Trophy name is still in catalogues, it is very doubtful whether the variety as originally known is now in existence. Large round "smooth" varieties—without angles or creases—are now grown almost exclusively. Fig. 126.

"Most commercial growers [in the South] use cotton cloth for covering coldframes, as it is much cheaper than glass, and is much easier to handle in opening and closing the beds. Fig. 125. Ordinary unbleached, double-width or ten-fourths wide sheeting is used. One side is nailed fast to the back side of the bed or in double beds to the ridge-pole, and the other is nailed between two 1 x 2-inch strips, thus making a square roller on which the curtain is rolled up when it is wished to open the bed. By starting with one short and one long piece, so as to break joints, such a roller can be made any desired length. It will be necessary to provide some extra cover for each coldframe to use on very cold nights, for the single thickness of cloth will not turn more than a slight frost. The beds should always be well banked at the ends and sides with earth."—*F. S. Earle*, Bull. 108, Ala. Exp. Sta. (1900).

"*Consolidated Summary of Results of Methods of Training*

VINES, HOW TREATED.	YIELD SOUND FRUIT.	YIELD ROTTEN FRUIT.	PER CENT ROTTEN.
Untrained	157 lbs. 14 oz.	34 lbs. 7 oz.	20.
Staked	197 " 5 "	15 " 7 "	7.9
Hilled	184 " 10 "	20 " 14 "	10.8
Mulched	253 " 14 "	44 " 4 "	17.5

This summary shows that (*a*) the smallest yield was given by the untrained vines; and that (*b*) the percentage of rotten fruit on

Fig. 126. Type of the large round American tomato.

these was greater than in any other case; that (*c*) staked vines gave a larger percentage of sound fruit than untrained, and (*d*) showed the smallest percentage of decayed fruit in the experiment; (*e*) hilling did not give any striking results; (*f*) mulching greatly increased the productiveness, and (*g*) also the tendency to rot. These are the results obtained during a year of unusually large precipitation during June, and marked by light rainfall in August and September."—*John Craig*, Bull. 47, Iowa Exp. Sta. (1900).

"By pruning, commercial growers mean the pinching out of all lateral branches as soon as they appear, thus confining the growth strictly to one stem. When about three clusters of fruit are set the vines are topped, thus stopping all farther growth of vine, and turning the energies of the plant entirely to the growth and maturing of the fruits that are already set. The advocates of this system claim that it greatly increases the size of the individual fruits and that the bulk of the crop ripens several days earlier than on unpruned plants. Of course each plant produces fewer fruits than when allowed to grow unchecked, but this is partly compensated for by increased size and by the closer planting that is possible on this system, thus allowing a greater number of plants to the acre. In several of the more important tomato-growing regions this system is very widely followed."—*F. S. Earle*, Bull. 108, Ala. Exp. Sta.

"*Tomatoes in very Severe Locations.*—When there is danger of frost in August, a sufficient supply of tomatoes for family use may be grown on the south side of a house, wall or other protection, especially if the plants are covered on cold nights. Where this seems to be impracticable, a most excellent way is to grow a few plants in barrels placed in warm corners about the buildings. To do this, at planting time select a barrel as large as a coal-oil barrel, bore three or four holes in the bottom, sink the barrel about one-third its depth in the ground and pack the earth around it. Fill it about half full of fresh horse manure well tramped down and pour a bucketful of hot water on this manure. Then put on 8 inches of good soil and then a mixture of well-rotted manure and rich black loam in about equal quantities, until you reach within about 12 inches of the top of the barrel; then heap up manure around the outside. Set three plants in this and trim to two shoots each. Train one of these shoots from each plant to stakes or nearby building, but allow the other three shoots to grow naturally over the sides of the barrel. Be careful to give plenty of water daily—a gallon each day will be none too much. Three or four old barrels treated in this way and placed in sunny exposure will produce all the tomatoes needed by a family of four or five persons."—*Green*, Veg. Gard. 2d ed., p. 197.

Following are summary conclusions respecting the field cultivation of tomatoes as derived from six years' experiment (Bull. 32, Cornell Exp. Sta.):

"*Fertilizing.*—Very heavy fertilizing with stable manures or concentrated fertilizers has uniformly increased yield in our experiments, although the common opinion is to the contrary. But in order that fertilizing shall produce early fruits, the food materials must be quickly available. If stable manure is desired, only the most thoroughly disintegrated part should be used. Nitrate of soda is a good tomato fertilizer on soils containing abundance of potash and phosphoric acid, but like other incomplete fertilizers it has little value when used alone on poor soils. Nitrate of soda appears to give heaviest yields when used in two or three applications, but in this latitude it should not be applied later than the first of August, else it prolongs growth too late.

"There appear to be differences in varieties as to the readiness with which they respond to fertilizing. In our tests of 1891, unimproved or Cherry tomatoes, while showing a less increase in number of fruits than the large varieties under heavy fertilizing, suffered no loss in size of fruits and consequently gave a greater proportionate crop.

"In 1889, tests indicated that poor soil may tend to render fruits more angular. [Probably due to the dryness of the poor soil.]

"*Starting the Plants, Transplanting, etc.*—Frequent transplanting of the young plants and good tillage are necessary to best results in tomato culture in this latitude.

"Plants started under glass about ten weeks before transplanting into field gave fruits from a week to ten days earlier than those started two or three weeks later, while there was a much greater difference when the plants were started six weeks later. Productiveness is greatly increased by the early planting.

"Very early setting of stocky plants in the field, even in dark and raw weather, augmented earliness and productiveness in 1890. This year [1891] the same results were secured except that there was less gain in earliness from very early setting. The tomato can endure much more uncongenial weather when set in the field than is commonly supposed. Early setting on well prepared land therefore appears to be advisable.

"In 1891, two transplantings gave better results than one or three; but the value of transplantation depends almost entirely upon the earliness of sowing, the character of the plants and facilities for handling.

"Seedling plants are better than cuttings.

"Trimming the plants lightly in midsummer appears to increase yield and earliness. But it should not be performed in this latitude after the first half of August.

"*Training.*—Training to stakes is not desirable unless the plants are pruned. Plants tied to two or three stakes, the vines being wound about them, as often recommended, ripen their fruits unevenly and the labor of picking from the tangled mass of foliage is great.

"A platform of boards laid under the plants and supported by blocks 4 or 5 inches high and then covered with straw keeps the tomatoes clean and renders picking easy, but it appears to increase the rot.

"A cheap and rough rack which gives good results is made of narrow slats laid crosswise the row upon two parallel bents which stand on either side of the row and about 3 feet apart. These bents run lengthwise the row and are made by nailing a light board to stakes every 6 or 8 feet. The bents or sides stand about a foot high. The plants lop on the cross slats—which may be laid on loosely—and the fruits ripen uniformly and are usually more exempt from rot than those lying on the ground.

"Training to a single stem greatly increases the yield per square foot, gives earlier fruits, and decreases injury from rot. This system is advisable for home use, and in some cases for market plantations.

"Hilling the plants twice, as potatoes are hilled, has given no beneficial results.

"'Leggy'" or badly drawn plants can be made to give fairly good results by setting them deep and burying the larger part of the slender stem. But even then they are inferior to stocky plants."

For history of the tomato, see Sturtevant, 6th Rept. N. Y. State Exp. Sta., pp. 279–284, Amer. Nat., Aug. 1891, pp. 702–706, and Sept. 1891, pp. 800–803; Bailey, Bull. 19, Mich. Exp. Sta. (1886) and Essay 30, "Survival of the Unlike"; also brief note by Gray & Trumbull, Amer. Journ. Sci. 26, p. 128 (Aug. 1883). The tomato is native of Peru, and perhaps of other parts of the Andean region. It was cultivated by the aborigines and was early taken to Europe. At first, the tomato was grown as a curiosity. Its commercial cultivation is scarcely more than 75 years old. In 1889, American dealers catalogued tomatoes under 81 varietal names. In 1887, Goff (6th Rep. N. Y. State Exp. Sta.) described 65 varieties.

Following is a botanical classification of the tomato (Bailey, Bull. 32, Cornell Exp. Sta.*):

The common tomato species, *Lycopersicum esculentum*, may be divided into five primary divisions: the cherry tomatoes (var. *cerasiforme*), plum and pear tomatoes (var. *pyriforme*), the common market tomatoes (var. *vulgare*), the large-leaf kinds like Mikado (var. *grandifolium*), and the upright or tree sorts (var. *validum*). The common tomatoes (var. *vulgare*) can again be divided for purposes of classification into three subdivisions: the oblong, angular and apple-shaped tomatoes. The currant tomato is a distinct species, *Lycopersicum pimpinellifolium* or "pimpinella-leaved tomato." In tabular form, the classification of the tomato may stand, therefore, as follows:

I. *Lycopersicum pimpinellifolium.* This has not yet varied to any extent in cultivation, and the one variety is known as the Currant and German Raisin.

II. *Lycopersicum esculentum.* The parent of all commercial tomatoes.

(*a*) Var. *cerasiforme.* Cherry tomatoes, characterized by slender growth and small light-colored foliage, and small globular fruits which are normally 2-celled. Red and yellow varieties are known.

(*b*) Var. *pyriforme.* Pear and plum tomatoes, distinguished

---

* Consult also Bull. 19, Mich. Agric. College (1886), and Bull. 31 (1887).

from the preceding subdivision chiefly by the pear-shaped or oblong pendent fruit. Red and yellow varieties are known. The Nesbit's Victoria has foliage much like that of Section *d*.

(*c*) Var. *vulgare*. The common tomatoes, represented by three main groups:

1. Oblong tomatoes: Fruit as long as or longer than broad, the walls very thick and firm, the placentæ usually not meeting the inside of the wall, causing the fruit to feel as if hollow. Red and purple varieties are known. Represented by King Humbert and Criterion.

2. Angular tomatoes: Fruit medium or below in size, mostly very flat, plane on top, more or less cornered, the lobes most conspicuous on the bottom and sides. This is the type of the original Large Red, the first market tomato. The type is almost lost in many of our later improvements, and it is now too inconstant, perhaps, to be relied upon as a sectional character. The angular tomatoes are practically out of cultivation in this country. In many of the varieties the leaves are singularly curled. Only red varieties are known, but many of them are very light or orange-red, and one, the German Gestreifte, is striped with orange.

3. Apple-shaped tomatoes: Fruit various in size or shape, but in normal forms more or less rounded on top, the monstrous or overgrown specimens developing a scar-like line or ring on the top and the ends of the fruit turning downwards. These comprise by far the larger number of the tomatoes of the present time. Some of the varieties, like Green Gage, Peach, and White Apple, are much like the Cherry tomatoes (var. *cerasiforme*) and should, perhaps, be classed with them. Red varieties predominate, but purple, yellow and white varieties exist.

(*d*) Var. *grandifolium*. Large-leaf tomatoes. Habit and fruit as in section *c;* leaves very large; leaflets fewer than common (about two pairs), large (the blade three to four inches long and an inch and a half wide), entire, the lower side strongly decurrent. Leaves of very young plants entire! The terminal leaflet is often six inches long and four or more inches broad. Represented by

Mikado, Puritan, Shah, and others. The first of the well-marked *grandifolium* varieties were purple, but a yellow one is grown, and this year [1891] a red one (Red Mikado) has appeared.

(*e*) Var. *validum*. Upright tomato. Stem very thick and stout, the plants nearly sustaining themselves, two to two and a half feet high; leaves very dark green, short and dense, the leaflets wrinkled and more or less recurved. An odd plant with much the aspect of a potato plant. Represented by the French Upright or Tree, which has red fruits. The Dwarf Champion is perhaps a cross between this type and the common tomatoes. The Station tomato which is a cross between French Upright and Alpha (var. *vulgare*) has given an interesting series of variations.

Diseases, etc. The chief diseases of tomatoes are rot and blight. There is no specific for either disease. Rot is rarely very serious during the entire season. Endeavor to get the crop early, before the rot takes it. For blight, practice rotation, and burn diseased vines (do not throw them on the manure pile). Consult the following:

Tomato worm, Fla. Bull. 48, desc. and ill.; Ky. Bull. 66. Use Paris green.

Rot and fruit mold, Dept. Agric. Rept. 1888, p. 339, desc. and ill. Thorough spraying with Bordeaux mixture recommended by some. See remarks on p. 392, two last lines.

Scab, Dept. Agric. Rept. 1888, p. 347, desc. and ill.; Conn. Bull. 115. Train high and use Bordeaux mixture.

Blight. Practice rotation. See paragraph above.

For special literature on tomatoes, consult the books of Livingston, Root, Day, Mitchell.

EGGPLANT

The essentials in eggplant culture are practically the same as in tomato culture, except that *the plant requires a still longer season, and greater pains must be taken that the young plants are not checked.*

The eggplant is emphatically a hot-climate crop. It is grown in the South to a large extent as a commercial crop and even as far north as New Jersey and Long Island. In the northernmost states, it is grown only for home use, as a rule. It demands a long season, a warm, loose and fairly dry soil. It is not adapted to clay lands. The plants are started under glass, and they should be 6 or 8 inches high and thrifty and stocky when placed in the field. In the northern states the plants may be even larger than this when transplanted. It is very important, however, that the plant receives no check from the germination of the seed to the setting of the fruit. If the plants in the forcing-house or hotbed become crowded and stunted, and the stems begin to harden, the crop will be very much lessened. For home use, and sometimes for special market conditions, it is advisable to handle the young plants in two-inch or three-inch pots. They then suffer no check when taken to the field.

The exposure should be warm and sunny. The land should not be so moist as that which is best adapted to early peas, beets and other cool-season things. The ground should be rich also, but it is very important that whatever fertilizer is added should be quickly available so that the maturity of the crop may not be delayed. Take every precaution to forward the crop in order to secure it before the closing of the season, particularly in the northern states. The ground should be kept in thorough tillage from first to last.

The fruits are fit for eating from the time they are one-third grown until they are nearly or quite fully ripe. Even after the fruits have reached their full size and color, they may remain on the plant for a time without much deterioration, although a very ripe fruit is worthless. A heavier crop may be secured by taking off the fruits before they reach their full size. It is necessary, however, that they be well colored in order to find sale in the market, and usually, also, the fruits of fair or rather large size sell best. In the northernmost states the gardener is satisfied if he averages two or three good fruits to a plant of the large varieties.

Fig. 127. Black Pekin Eggplant.

Eggplants are set in rows that are far enough apart to admit of horse tillage, usually 3½–4 feet. In the rows the plants are set from 2–4 feet. The distance is determined largely by the variety. An ounce of eggplant seed should give from 2,000 to 3,000 strong plants.

The New York Improved and the Black Pekin (Fig. 127) are the leading commercial types of eggplant. Good-sized marketable fruits of these varieties are 6–9 inches in diameter. Unless started very early and given a warm place and quick soil, however, these varieties are not likely to yield much before frost in the northernmost states. In these short-season climates, some of the dwarf varieties, particularly the Early Dwarf Purple, are to be advised. The white eggplants are not popular, since the color is usually of a yellowish cast. There are varieties with striped fruits and others with long and coiling fruits, but these are known mostly as curiosities.

Eggplant has been grown from the earliest times. It is probably native to India. It is a low spreading, bushy, more or less hairy and spiny herb (or subshrub), with large blue flowers. It is known also as Aubergine and Guinea Squash.

It is the *Solanum Melongena* of botanists, but the aboriginal type is not in cultivation. An historical sketch by Sturtevant appears in Amer. Nat., Nov., 1887, pp. 975-9. Goff reduced the varieties to twelve in 1887 (6th Rept. N. Y. State Exp. Sta., pp. 273-9); fourteen names were offered by American seedsmen in 1889. He divided them into four main groups on color distinctions, and made minor divisions on shape of fruit. In 1891 the present writer described (in Bull. 26, Cornell Exp. Sta.), fifteen varieties. He made the following botanical scheme:

I. *Solanum Melongena*, var. *esculentum*. Plant stout and erect, mostly tall; leaves and branches more or less densely scurfy; leaves mostly conspicuously angled or lobed, thick; flowers large and thick, on stout peduncles; fruit various, globular or oblong, white or purple. The ordinary form of the eggplant is well shown in Fig. 127.

Var. *serpentinum*. This differs from the var. *esculentum* chiefly in the greatly elongated fruit, which is curled at the end, and perhaps it is not worth separation. It is a most singular eggplant.

Var. *depressum*. Plant low, weak and diffuse, dark colored, nearly smooth, always spineless; leaves small and comparatively thin, more entire, often scarcely angled; flowers small, mostly long-peduncled; fruit purple, pyriform.

II. *Solanum integrifolium*. This species is sold as the Chinese Scarlet and Ornamental eggplant, and it is the one that has been lately distributed as a great novelty under the name of tomato eggplant. It goes under the name of *Solanum coccineum*. Its nativity appears to be wholly unknown. Dunal says that *S. integrifolium* is a native of Mauritius, but Baker, in his flora of Mauritius, does not mention it. It is probably African. At any rate, it appears to be proper to recall the name under which it was long known in early times, and call it the Ethiopian eggplant. The Ethiopian eggplant is a coarse plant three feet high, with large lobed leaves and the stems, petioles and midribs armed with strong and very sharp spines a half inch long. The small white flowers are usually borne in clusters of two to six. The fruit is small, rarely much exceeding 2 inches in diameter, bright scarlet or yellow and conspicuously lobed after the manner of the old Early Red tomato. We have grown two types of this plant, one of strong upright growth with purple stems, petioles and midribs,

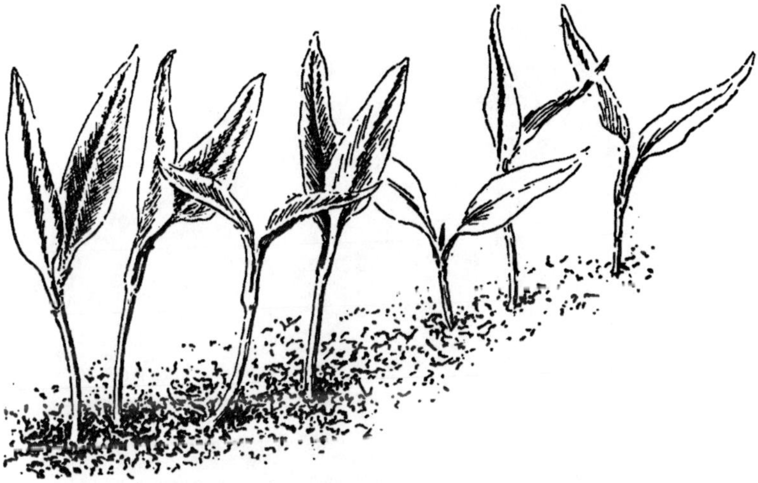

Fig. 128. Seedlings of red pepper, or capsicum. Natural size.

the other of spreading habit and lighter color. The species is only curious and ornamental, the fruits not being eaten.

Two or three obscure fungous diseases attack the eggplant in the South, for which the only treatment is to practice rotation and to destroy the affected plants. The potato bug often attacks eggplants. Use Paris green, 1 pound to 75–100 gallons of water, and plenty of lime.

For account of leaf spot, see N. J. Rept., 1890, p. 355. Use Bordeaux spray.

PEPPER

Peppers require the treatment advised for tomatoes, but *they will thrive in a rather cooler season and will endure some frost, although best results are secured in a warm climate. Some of the varieties mature in a relatively short season.*

Fig. 129. One of the Chili Red Peppers.

Peppers are not an important crop in most parts of the country, since their use in cookery is incidental.

The greatest demand is for the making of mixed pickles, and for this purpose the small Cayenne, Chili, and Cranberry varieties are grown. Fig. 129. The large "sweet peppers," of the Sweet Mountain and Ruby King type, are used for the dish known as "stuffed peppers."

The plants are started in frames, and are set eight to twelve inches apart in the row. There are no serious pests or diseases.

The pepper (often called "red pepper," although there are yellow-fruited and white-fruited varieties) is a Capsicum, the common garden forms now being referred to one species, *C. annuum* It is very distinct from the pepper of commerce, which is the fruit of *Piper nigrum*, of another family. The capsicums are native to the American tropics. For history, see Sturtevant, Amer. Nat., Feb., 1890, pp. 151-157; also Irish's monograph in 9th Rept. Mo. Bot. Gard., pp. 53-110, with many plates (1898). *Capsicum annuum* is remarkably variable, and many of the cultivated forms have been described as species at one time or another. Originally the fruit had two cells or compartments, but under the influence of domestication, the compartments have been multiplied.

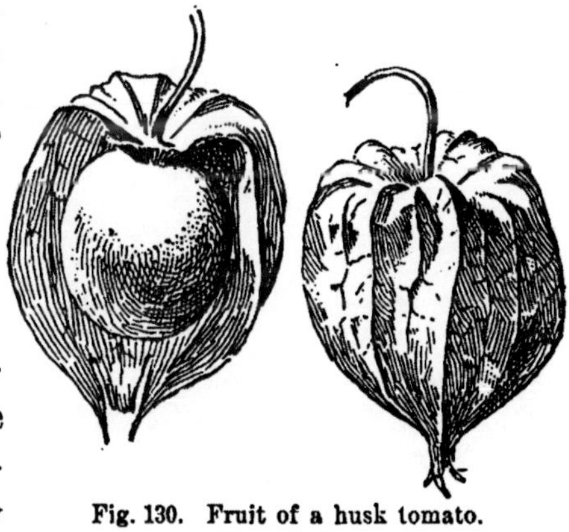

Fig. 130. Fruit of a husk tomato. Natural size.

HUSK TOMATO

Two or three species of Physalis are cultivated as husk tomato and strawberry tomato. They are very diffuse or even decumbent hairy herbs that produce a yellowish often glutinous berry inside a papery husk.

There are several native species, some of which are known as ground cherry. The soft, sweetish fruits are sometimes used for preserves and pickles, or they may be eaten raw or cooked. The plants are of the easiest cultivation. In the North it is preferable to start seeds in frames. The Cape Gooseberry is a species that rarely ripens a full crop in the northern states, but the Dwarf Cape Gooseberry produces freely as far north as Ontario. The Cape Gooseberry is *Physalis Peruviana* (Fig. 130), a tropical species; the Dwarf Cape gooseberry or common husk tomato, is *P. pubescens*, a native species. For sketch of the cultivated species, see Bull. 37, Cornell Exp. Sta.

CHAPTER XVII

CUCURBITOUS OR VINE CROPS

Cucumber,	Pumpkin,
Gherkin,	Squash,
Muskmelon,	Preserving Melon,
Watermelon,	Luffa.

Cucurbitous crops are annuals, grown for their fruits; they are tender to frost; they require a warm season and a full exposure to sun; they are long-season crops and with most of them a quick start is essential in order that they may mature the crop before fall; they are grown in hills, as a main crop; they are planted in the field or in frames, depending on the region and the period at which the crop is wanted; they transplant with difficulty, and if the plants are started in advance of the season they are grown in pots, boxes or on sods.

Cucurbitous crops are so called because they are members of the family Cucurbitaceæ. They comprise a very natural group, both botanically and culturally.

There are no fundamental differences in the cultivation of the various cucurbitous crops. They are all very tender to frost and they usually grow, at least in the North, till overtaken by frost or disease. They all demand light and very quick soil. Success lies in gaining an early start and in not allowing the plants tc suffer a check. The one place at which most people fail in growing these crops is that the young plants do not secure a quick hold on the soil. This is usually due to the fact that the soil is not thoroughly well prepared or is not warm and well drained, and there is not sufficient available fertilizer within reach of the young plant. In the North, this quick start is exceedingly important, since the season is so short that every day must be made to count. In cucumbers, the quick start is not so important as in melons and squashes, since the plants come into bearing earlier. Many fields of squashes in the North are lost because the plants do not get to work before July or August, and then the dry weather comes and the blooming is delayed so long that the young fruits are caught by frost.

All cucurbitous crops are grown in hills. Usually each hill should be specially prepared, at least in the northern states, and on land that is rather hard and coarse. A space 1 or 2 feet across is spaded up loosely, and light, loose earth or scrapings from the barnyard are mixed with it. A handful of fertilizer should be scattered in the soil. If the land is hard and late, it is well to remove the soil and to fill the space with fine earth and manure. In the warm and light melon lands of the South, where the seasons are longer, this precaution may not be necessary.

The young plants are very likely to be ruined by the attacks of the striped beetle and other enemies. It is important, therefore, that the seed be sown freely. If one-fourth or one-fifth of the plants escape their enemies, the grower may consider himself fortunate. In some cases growers plant pumpkin or squash seeds in the field very early in order to attract the striped beetle where they may be killed, and the later frame-grown melon or cucumber plants are then relatively safe.

Squashes, watermelons and cucumbers are usually planted in the field, although if early results are wanted and if the region is cold and the season short, it is well to start them in frames. Muskmelons are usually started in frames. All cucurbitous plants transplant with difficulty; therefore it is advisable to plant the seeds on inverted sods, in pots or in small boxes. These methods have been described in some detail on pages 190 to 194. It is imperative that the plants be stocky and hard when taken to the field, although they must not be stunted. If they have been grown too warm and are "soft," they will be injured by the sun and winds when transplanted, and will be later than plants that are started directly in the field.

The land should be given the best of surface tillage. Every effort should be made to get the plants so well established that the fruits begin to set before the severe weather of midsummer. The plants and the fruits are succulent and need much moisture, and if this moisture is lost in the spring through lack of proper preparation of the land and neglect of surface tillage, a good crop may be impossible, even though the subsequent tillage is perfect. The land should also contain sufficient humus or vegetable matter to hold a good supply of moisture. It is ordinarily best to have the plants so vigorous that several fruits set simultaneously. If one fruit sets two or three weeks in advance of the others, it is likely to consume so much of the energy of the vine that the subsequent fruits remain small. In fact, it may be well to pick off the first fruit if it sets much in advance of the main crop. Although the land should be rich, the fertility should be available early in the season rather than late, else the growth may be delayed too long. Lands that are very rich in nitrogenous materials may cause the plants to grow to vine at the expense of fruit. If there seems to be a tendency for the plants to go to vine, it is a good practice to pinch off the ends of the leading shoots. Usually, however, this practice is not necessary unless the season is very short.

Since the fruits of cucumbers are used when they are young, the productivity of the plants may be greatly enhanced by picking the fruits as soon as they are fit. The patch should be gone over every two or three days at least, and if the area is large, it should be picked over every day. If one fruit is allowed to ripen it may prevent the setting of other fruits on the vine. If seeds of cucumbers are desired, it is best to reserve a few hills especially for that purpose. Cucumbers for the main or pickling crop are usually grown from seeds planted directly in the fields as soon as frost is past.

CUCUMBER AND GHERKIN

Hills of cucumber are usually made about 4 x 4 or 4 x 5 feet apart; sometimes they are 4 x 6, for the large late varieties. At 4 x 4 feet, 2,722 hills are contained on an acre. Four or five plants are allowed to remain in each hill. About two pounds of seeds are calculated to plant an acre, or 1 ounce for 70–80 hills. If the striped bugs are bad, plant heavily. An average acre should yield 100 bushels for pickling. Under the best conditions, 400 and 500 bushels of pickling cucumbers are raised to the acre.

For very early, some of the small-fruited cucumbers may be planted, as Early Russian. For midseason and late, the White Spine, in various strains, is the standard. Giant Pera, Nichol Medium Green and Tailby are favorites. In 1889, 64 varieties were listed by American seedsmen.

The cucumber is *Cucumis sativus*, native to southern Asia. It has been in cultivation from remotest times. Gherkins are very

Fig 131. Seedlings of cucumber. Two-thirds natural size.

small, immature cucumbers, used for pickles. The name is also applied to the small prickly fruits of *Cucumis Anguria*, a species known as the West Indian or Bur cucumber. This is sometimes cultivated, and its fruits are used for pickles. For accessible history of cucumber, see Sturtevant, Amer. Nat., Oct., 1887, pp. 906–910. A monograph of varieties by Goff will be found in 6th Rept. N. Y. State Exp. Sta., pp. 230–242. The varieties were reduced to 26, including *Cucumis Anguria*. He divides them into two classes: young fruit green, young fruit white or greenish white. Waugh (Bailey, Cyclo. Hort.) divides the field varieties into Black Spines and White Spines, and makes subdivisions under each.

For enemies and diseases, consult the following, amongst others:

Root and stem: Squash vine borer, N. J. Bull. 94, desc. and ill.; N. Y. Bull. 75, desc. and well ill. Destroy eggs, larvæ and moths.

Leaves: Flea beetle, N. Y., Bull. 113, good ill. and desc. Thorough spraying with Bordeaux throughout season.

Striped beetle, N. J. Bull. 94; N. Y. Bull. 75, desc. and illus.; N. Y. Bull. 158, desc. of remedies; remedies; Ga. Bull. 45, insects. Plant squash as a trap crop, and poison the beetles on the squash vines. The poison is likely to injure the vines; so plant the squashes profusely and do not poison all of them at once. Poison with Paris green and lime. Spray the cucumber vines with Bordeaux mixture. The hills may be covered with mosquito netting, held above the plants by means of hoops, until the plants begin to show signs of running.

Downy mildew or blight, N. Y. Bull. 156. Ohio Bull. 105. Spray thoroughly with Bordeaux mixture.

MUSKMELON

Four by six feet is a customary distance for the hills of muskmelons, making 1,185 hills to the acre. The quantity of seed required is about the same as for cucumber. Sometimes two crops are grown on the same land, a very early and a main-season crop. The early crop is planted 4 x 5 feet, and two or three weeks later the main crop is planted between. Three or four good fruits to the plant is a good yield.

American seedsmen offered 88 varieties of muskmelon in 1889. Leading commercial varieties at present are Rocky Ford, Osage, (Fig. 38), Montreal Market, Hackensack. Commercial melon-growing is confined to light and sandy soils. New Jersey is an important melon center. There are special melon centers in many parts of the country, even as far north as Canada.

Cucumis Melo, muskmelon, is native to southern Asia. It was grown by the ancients. It is immensely variable. The most important types are the cantaloupes (var. *Cantalupensis*), with hard and warty rinds, little grown in this country, although the word cantaloupe is much used; the nutmeg or netted type (var. *reticulatus*) comprising most of the American commercial varieties;

the winter melons (var. *inodorus*) ripening late in the season and keeping well into the winter, little known in this country. Consult Sturtevant, Amer. Nat., Aug. 1889, pp. 671-4, for history. The

Fig. 132. Muskmelon seedlings. Nearly natural size.

notion that muskmelons are contaminated by cucumbers that grow near them is an error.

For melon diseases and insects, see Cucumber. For the anthracnose, consult Dept. Agric. Botanical Division, Bull. 8, p. 64; Md. 1891 Rept., p. 387.

WATERMELON

The first requisite in watermelon culture is a location with sufficient length of season to insure maturity of crop.

"Rotation is all-important. In no case should melons follow melons the next season, and at least four years should intervene before the land is again planted in this crop. By that time insect depredators, attracted by the first melon crop, will have probably become exterminated and the drain from the soil of specific plant-food (especially potash) will also have been, to a certain extent, at least, made good."—*Hugh N. Starnes*, Bull. 38, Ga. Exp. Sta., on "Watermelons."

The South Atlantic and Gulf states have occupied first place for size and quality of melons. Recently, the mid-continental states are coming to the fore. The ideal soil is light sandy loam with only a medium or small amount of nitrogen. Much nitrogen is thought to diminish the essential saccharine constituent. A point of special emphasis is that of thorough drainage. Swampy or "soggy" land will not produce favorable results. In the South the field for melons is often plowed in the fall, to expose the soil to the pulverizing action of frost. Watermelons are always planted in hills, which are usually 10 feet apart each way. The hills are made at the intersection of check-rows. This "checking" is

Fig. 133. Watermelon seedlings. One-half natural size.

usually done with shovel- or turn-plow. The hills are made by mixing several shovelfuls of well-rotted manure with soil and then covering the whole with several inches of soft earth, into which the seeds are planted directly. All danger of frosts should be over before planting. Avoid baking or crusting of the soil on the hills, especially before germination of seeds. Only hand tools should be used in the cultivation of crop after the vines have begun to run, as lifting or turning the vines will injure quality and size of fruit. At 10 x 10 feet, 435 hills are contained in an acre. About 4 pounds of seed is used to the acre.

When is a watermelon ripe?—"Unquestionably the flat, dead sound emitted by a melon when 'thumped' is the readiest indication of ripeness, and the one most universally depended on.

If the resonance is hollow, ringing or musical, it is a certain proof of immaturity.

"Frequently on turning the melon and exposing the under side, the irregular white blotch formed where the melon has rested on the ground affords an indication of maturity. When this begins to turn yellowish and becomes rough, pimply or warty, with the surface sufficiently hard to resist the finger-nail when scratched, it is usually a fair sign of ripeness.

"But there is one more test that is corroborative. After the melon 'looks' ripe and 'thumps' ripe, if, on a steady pressure of the upper side or 'top' by the palm of the hand, while the melon lies on the ground, instead of resisting solidly the interior appears to have a tendency to yield—a 'givey' sort of feeling, as it were — accompanied by a crisp crackling, half heard, half felt, as the flesh parts longitudinally in sections under the pressure, the melon may be pulled with absolute confidence. It is certainly ripe. This test should never be resorted to with melons intended for shipment, as their carrying quality is necessarily impaired thereby.

"Yet all this, as stated, comes largely by instinct to the expert, and it is rarely that one finds it necessary to 'thump,' much less to 'press,' a melon before deciding as to its maturity."—*Hugh N. Starnes*, Bull. 38, Ga. Exp. Sta.

Fifty-eight varieties of watermelons were catalogued by North American seedsmen in 1889. Only a few of these are commercial varieties, and the kinds that are popular in the South require a too long season for the North. Only in favored places are watermelons grown in the northernmost states. They are more uncertain than muskmelons, because of the short and cool seasons, and are less grown in the North. There are a number of varieties, however, that ripen without difficulty in the northern states and Ontario when a warm soil and exposure are at hand and where small boys are absent. The plants may be started under glass, as advised on p. 413.

The watermelon is *Citrullus vulgaris*, native to Africa. It has been in cultivation from a remote period. It is more popular in North America, probably, than elsewhere in the world. In fact, it is a feature of American living. The vegetable known as citron is only a kind of watermelon with hard, inedible flesh. The rind is used for preserving. The true citron of commerce is the fruit of a tree allied to orange and lemon.

For insects and diseases, see Cucumber.

PUMPKIN AND SQUASH

When grown by themselves, pumpkins and field squashes are planted in hills 8 to 10 feet apart. About 3 pounds of seed is required for an acre with the field or running varieties. Two or three mature fruits to a vine is a large crop.

The bush squashes are grown as close as 3 x 4 feet in gardens, but the hills should be 4 or 5 feet apart if possible. From 4 to 5 pounds of seed is required to the acre.

In pumpkins, as the term is understood in this country, the

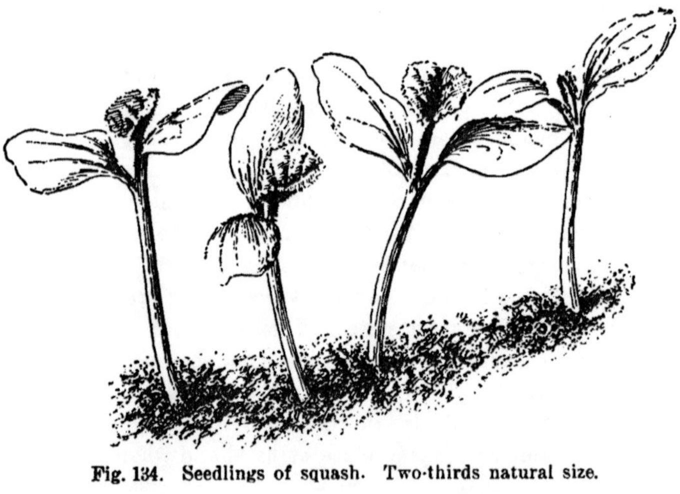

Fig. 134. Seedlings of squash. Two-thirds natural size.

standard variety is the Connecticut Field. It is a long-running plant. The large orange-colored sleek furrowed fruits are used for pies, and to feed stock; and the small boy prizes them for "jack lanterns." It is commonly grown in corn-fields. This plant is a form of *Cucurbita Pepo.* Fig. 135. The vegetable marrow, much prized in England, is a long-fruited form of this species.

Of field or winter squashes the leading types are the Hubbard, Marblehead, Boston Marrow, Essex Hybrid, Turban. These are kept for winter. They should have a dry and fairly warm place (temperature above 50°). Where they are grown extensively,

Fig. 135. A Pumpkin—Cucurbita Pepo.

special stove-heated houses are built for them and they are stored on shelves or in shallow bins. In order to keep well, the fruits must be ripe, free from bruises and internal cracks, not frosted, and have the stem on. These squashes are *Cucurbita maxima*.

The bush squashes are of many kinds. They are "summer squashes." The leading types are Crookneck, and Scallop or Patty-pan. These are forms of *Curcurbita Pepo.*

Cucurbita Pepo and *C. maxima* do not cross, although the common notion is to the contrary.

A third specific type is *Cucurbita moschata*, to which belong the Cushaws or Winter Crooknecks, Dunkard, Tennessee Sweet Potato pumpkin, and some others.

It is now believed that *Cucurbita Pepo* and *C. maxima* are natives of tropical America, although they are unknown anywhere in a truly wild state. *C. moschata* may be east-Asian. See Gray and Trumbull, Amer. Journ. Sci. 25, p. 372; Sturtevant, Amer. Nat., July, 1885, pp. 658-663, and Aug., 1890, pp. 727-744; Wittmack, Berichte der Deutschen Bot. Gesell., 6, p. 378. For descriptions of varieties, see Goff, 6th Rep. N. Y. State Exp. Sta., pp. 243-273; 55 varieties of squashes and pumpkins are described.

For insects and diseases, see:

Squash bug, N. J. Bull. 94; N. Y. Bull. 75, very good desc. and ill.; Fla. Bull. 34. Keep fields free from rubbish. Trap with bits of squash leaves, etc. Examine daily. In early spring pick old bugs.

Melon louse, N. Y. Bull. 75; N. J. Bull. 94, good, with ill.; Ky. Bull. 53; Use bisulfide carbon, or hydrocyanic acid gas: Get at winter quarters. Check first appearance.

Powdery mildew, Mass. State Rept. 1892, p. 225, with plate; Cornell Bull. 31; Cornell: ammoniacal copper carbonate.

Downy mildew, Mass. State Rept. 1890, p. 211, with plate; N. Y. Bull. 119, excellent; N. Y.: Bordeaux (1 to 8 formula) once every 8 or 10 days to frost.

OTHER CUCURBITS

Various other cucurbitous fruits are grown for eating. Of late years, *Benincasa cerifera*, the wax gourd of the Orient, has been introduced as the Chinese preserving melon. It is used for the making of preserves and sweet pickles. The fruit is the size of a watermelon, hairy, and usually having a waxy covering. Cultivation as for muskmelon. See Cornell Bull. 67.

The Dish-Cloth gourds or Vegetable Sponges, two species of Luffa, are in cultivation as curiosities and for the fibrous interior, which is used, when dried and macerated, as a sponge. The young fruit may be eaten when cooked or dried, but it is scarcely known as a kitchen-garden product in this country.

CHAPTER XVIII

SWEET CORN. OKRA. MARTYNIA

THE plants mentioned above are all *warm-weather crops; they are annuals, or grown as such, and they are cultivated for their immature fruits; they should have quick soil; usually they are not transplanted; other than good tillage, no special treatment is required.*

Corn, okra and martynia are culturally somewhat related, but they have little else in common. They are placed together here because none of them fits well into the other groups.

SWEET CORN

As a garden or horticultural crop, sweet corn or sugar corn is the only kind of corn that need be considered here. It is grown for the immature ears, which are eaten when the grains are yet soft. Although practically unknown in other parts of the world, it is a very important product in North America. Its importance has greatly increased in recent years because it is extensively canned. It is now one of the most important of horticultural field crops in many parts of the country. Sweet corn is not grown in the southern states; or if it is, the seed is renewed every year from the North. It holds its peculiar attributes only in the short, sharp seasons of the northern states and parts of Canada.

The cultivation of sweet corn is not unlike that of field corn, with the exception that greater attention is paid to earliness and to the development of each individual plant. It is therefore given, if possible, an earlier and warmer soil, with quickly available fertilizers, and it is usually grown in hills rather than in

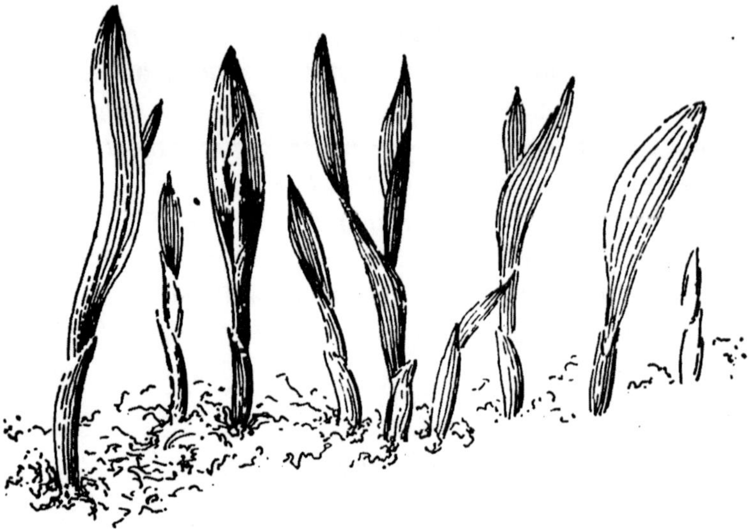

Fig. 136. Sweet corn seedlings. Nearly natural size.

continuous drills. The idea is to secure as many ears as possible, and therefore each stalk should be given an abundance of room. In field corn, on the contrary, particularly since the advent of the silo, the fodder may be quite as important as the grain. If the season is short and the soil is hard and backward, it is well to add a little commercial fertilizer to each hill in order to start the plants off quickly. Seed is planted for the early crop as soon as the ground is thoroughly warm. Since sweet corn seed is particularly liable to rot in cold and damp ground, it is well to make the first planting rather heavy. It is never transplanted. The early plantings are usually made of the extra-early varieties, as the Early Minnesota, Early Vermont and others. The main crop is usually secured from the later or main-season varieties, of which the Stowell Evergreen is the standard. Successional plantings may be made at intervals of one to two weeks, particularly for the home garden or for a continuous supply for the market-garden. In market-gardening, the value of the green-corn crop is often determined by its earliness. Two or three days in time of ripening may make a difference between the profitable and unprofitable crop, particularly when one is under strong competition with neighboring gardeners. In such cases the grower secures the early crop by means of the very earliest varieties and particularly by having quick and well-prepared land to which only quickly available fertilizers have been added. If the land is inclined to be hard and rough, it is well to turn it up loose in the fall.

Fig. 137. Plant of sweet corn.

Although corn is a hot-weather plant and thrives in the fullest exposure to sunlight, it nevertheless is not able to withstand drought as well as potatoes and many other crops. This is because it is relatively a surface feeder. Every effort should be made, therefore, to preserve the moisture in the soil. The moisture content is increased by deep preparation of the land and by the incorporation of vegetable matter. Thereafter the moisture is saved by frequent light surface tillage.

In the general market, corn is nearly always retailed by the dozen ears, the price ranging from 25 cents a dozen early in the season down to 10 and even 5 cents when the main supply comes in. As a field crop for the canning factories, the ears are ordinarily sold by the ton, 8 to 12 dollars being an average price for that quantity after all small and imperfect ears are discarded and some allowance is made for extra husks. The ears of the second setting will develop better if those of the first setting are picked just as soon as they are fit for use.

Rows of corn are made at 3–4 feet apart. In the row the hills (of 3–5 stalks each) are planted at 2½–3 feet apart, or single kernels may be dropped every ten to twelve inches. At 2½–3 feet apart, the crop may be tilled in both directions. When the corn is small, the ground may be harrowed without destroying the plants. In hills, one peck to the acre is required for planting. 8,000 to 10,000 ears should be secured from an acre.

Sweet corn is a race or variety of common Indian corn, or *Zea Mays*, one of the grass family, and a native of America, although the wild type is unknown. For a general botanical and horticultural account of corn, see "Varieties of Corn," Bull. 57, Office of Exp. Stations (U. S. Dept. Agric.), by the late E. L. Sturtevant (1899). For history of sweet corn, see Sturtevant, Amer. Nat., July 1885, pp. 664–5. In 1889, American seedsmen listed 76 varieties of sweet corn and 22 varieties of pop corn.

For insects and diseases, see, amongst others, the following:

Wire-worms, Cornell Bull. 107, desc. and ill. Fall cultivation. Short rotation, including thorough cultivation in fall.

Cut-worms, Cornell Bull. 104, desc. and ill.

Chinch-bug, Ky. Bull. 74, desc. and ill.; N. Y. Rept 15, pp. 531–33, desc.; Ohio Bull. 69, desc. and ill., very good; Ohio: Ditching, plowing, harrowing, etc. Natural checks, rain and fungi.

Cornstalk disease, Neb. Bull. 52.

OKRA OR GUMBO

Okra is a hot-weather perennial, but is cultivated as an annual, the seeds being sown each spring. It is generally grown in the southern states, where its partially matured pods are in much demand for soups and stews. These pods must be cut when still tender and pulpy, before they have developed strings or woody fiber. Pods

Fig. 138. Okra seedlings. Two-thirds natural size.

are also canned and dried for subsequent use. Okra is grown in essentially the same way as corn. The seeds are sown where the plants are to stand, as the young plants do not transplant with ease. In the Northern states, however, the plants are sometimes started in pots, boxes or on inverted sods in frames. Okra is a large-growing plant and the rows should be from 3 to 4, or even 5, feet apart for the larger varieties. In the row the plants should stand from 1 to 3 feet. In the northern states, certain dwarf and early-maturing varieties are usually grown, and these may stand as close as 1 foot apart in the row.

Hibiscus esculentus, the okra, is native to tropical Asia. It is one of the Mallow family, and is therefore allied to hollyhock and cotton. It is now widely grown in tropical countries. For history, see Sturtevant, Amer. Nat., Jan., 1890, pp. 33–35. There are no very important insects or diseases. There are few varieties, only 11 being offered in North America in 1889.

MARTYNIA

Martynia is grown for the half-matured seed-pods, which are used for pickles. The plant requires a warm soil and exposure. Give much room, for a good plant will spread over an area 3 or 4 feet across. It is a nearly prostrate plant, with very large, hairy leaves, odd showy flowers, and long-beaked hairy pods. It demands no special treatment. Seeds may be started in frames or planted in the open as soon as warm weather comes.

Two or three confused species are in cultivation, but the commonest one is *Martynia proboscidea*, native from southern Indiana to Iowa and southward. Others are tropical. They are annuals. They are members of the *Pedaliaceæ*, a small family allied to the Bignonia family. See historical note by Sturtevant, Amer. Nat., Aug., 1889, p. 670.

CHAPTER XIX

CONDIMENTAL AND SWEET HERBS

ALTHOUGH there is little desire on the part of Americans for condimental and flavoring herbs, nevertheless every complete home garden should have a small area set aside for the cultivation of at least a half dozen of the leading kinds. What are commonly known as "herbs" in the trade comprise a great variety of plants. Some of them are grown for medicinal purposes, some for flavoring, some for the decoration of culinary dishes and others for salads and minor home uses. What are commonly known as "the sweet herbs," however, are such plants as are used as an incident to cookery. Of these the most popular in America is sage.

Nearly all the sweet herbs are of the easiest cultivation. They thrive in any loose, warm and open soil. Although the growth is usually most profuse in rather heavy and moist soils, it is believed that the aromatic qualities, for which they are particularly esteemed, are more pronounced in soils in which the plants do not make an exuberant growth. The land should always be rich enough, however, to produce a full development of the plant.

The sweet herbs are of two general classes as respects the general methods of cultivation: the annuals, or those that must be resown every year; and the perennials, or those that persist for a number of years. It is well to grow all the sweet herbs together on one side of the garden, whether they are annual or perennial. It is advisable to devote a strip of land to this purpose and to grow a clump of a particular herb each year in its accustomed place. Even the perennial species, as sage and hyssop, should be resown or replanted frequently in order to keep the plants in vigorous condition, particularly if the climate is severe and if the plants are not given some winter protection. The grower may readily save his own seed by cutting off a few plants when the seeds are nearly ready to be shed and hanging the plants in a dry, cool place, as in a barn.

The strongest-growing perennial species may be propagated easily by division of the roots. When the clump begins to fail, it is well to dig it up and discard all the older parts of the roots and to replant the younger and more vigorous parts. When such species are grown from seed, they are usually not strong enough to supply a heavy product until the second year, although some of them may give a cutting the first fall if they are started early and if the soil is good. Ordinarily a space 4 feet square will contain enough of any herb to supply a family, although twice that area may be desired for such popular species as sage, caraway and spearmint. A strip 3 or 4 feet wide along one side of a garden can be made a collecting-place for these herbs; and the place will have more than a commercial or culinary interest.

Some of the sweet herbs are prized for foliage, and others for seeds or fruits. In fact, the species to which the name sweet herb should be more particularly restricted, are those that have aromatic foliage. Of such are sage, hyssop, thyme, mints, tansy, horehound. Most of these plants are members of the mint family, or Labiatæ, although some of them, as tansy and wormwood, are members of the sunflower family. Those species of which the seeds are used are mostly members of the parsley family, or Umbelliferæ. Of such are caraway, coriander and dill. The larger number of these seed-bearing plants are annual. The plants that are grown for herbage are usually cut when the plant is in full growth and before it has become woody. The stems are cut off near the ground and are then tied together in bundles and hung in a dry, còol place, as an attic. The dried herbage is then in condition for use during the winter. Continual cuttings of the young herbage may also be made during the season for current uses. It is evident that if the plants are cut severely and continuously they will be weakened, and that it may be necessary to raise a fresh stock to take their places. The species that are grown for seeds arc allowed to ripen before the product is gathered. The plants are usually cut or pulled just before the seeds are ready to fall. The plants are then dried under cover and the seeds are threshed out. Seeds of the seed-bearing herbs and dried herbage of the true sweet herbs are usually to be had at drug stores, but there is much satisfaction in growing one's own. Sometimes there is a fair market for home-grown herbs.

The following lists contain the leading species of sweet and culinary herbs cultivated in this country, arranged with reference to their duration. (Man other plants of minor importance might be included).

Annual or grown as such

anise,
sweet basil,
summer savory,
coriander,
caraway (biennial),
clary (biennial),
dill (biennial),
sweet marjoram (biennial or perennial).

Perennial

sage,
lavender,
peppermint,
spearmint,
hyssop,
thyme,
marjoram,
balm,
catnip,
pennyroyal,
rosemary,
horehound,
fennel,
lovage,
winter savory,
tansy,
wormwood,
costmary,
tarragon.

CHAPTER XX

PERENNIAL CROPS

Asparagus,	**Artichoke,**
Rhubarb,	**Sea-Kale.**
Dock,	
Sorrel,	

THE management of perennial crops differs from that of other vegetable-gardening crops, in the fact that *they are more or less permanent occupants of the ground, and therefore must be given an area to themselves where they will not interfere with the customary plowing and tilling; in the fact that the chief tillage and care are required early and late in the season; and also because the fertilizing is secured chiefly by surface dressings in spring and fall.* It seems to be advisable, therefore, for cultural reasons, to place these vegetables in a group by themselves, although otherwise they have little in common. All cultural classifications are more or less arbitrary.

ASPARAGUS

A deep, rich, fertile, moist, cool soil, a warm exposure, thorough preparation of the land, heavy manuring, thorough tillage in late fall and early spring, are general requisites of asparagus culture. The plants should be allowed to become well established before a crop is cut, and the cutting of the plants should cease in early summer in order to allow them opportunity to grow and to store up energy for the following year. The tops are mown in late fall, and the land is top-dressed with manure before winter sets in. Asparagus is grown for its young shoots, and the quality is determined by the succulence of these shoots. A good plantation should last twenty years and more, at least in the North. Propagated by seed.

Asparagus is a gross feeder. Land can scarcely be too rich. If the land is originally hard and coarse, it should be prepared a year or two in advance by the raising of some thoroughly tilled crop, as potatoes, and with this crop as much manure as possible should have been used. The asparagus plantation should be made for a lifetime. Therefore it is well to give careful attention to the selection of the soil and to the choice of a place that can be permanently set aside for the purpose. In the home garden, asparagus should be in rows at one side of the plantation, so that it will not interfere with the plowing of the garden area. It usually looks best at the farther side of the garden, where its beautiful herbage makes a background border in summer and fall. The old idea was to have asparagus "beds." The new idea is to plant asparagus in rows as one would plant rhubarb or corn, and to till it with horse tools rather than with hoes and finger weeders. For the ordinary family, one row alongside the garden, 75 to 100 feet long, may be expected to furnish a sufficient supply. As a field crop, it is ordinarily grown in the best and richest soil available. The permanency of the plantation will depend largely on the original quality of the land, the preparation of the soil, the method of planting, and particularly on the subsequent care and fertilizing of the plantation. Aim to secure large, broad crowns.

The roots of asparagus should be in moist, cool soil. They should have opportunity to forage as far as they

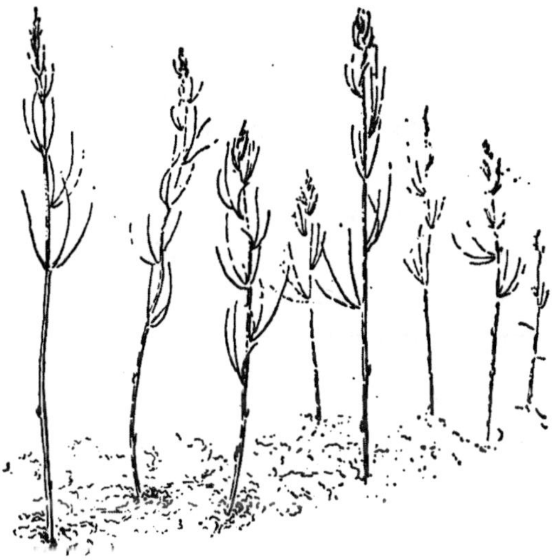

Fig. 139. Seedlings of asparagus. Natural size.

will. The roots run horizontally rather than perpendicularly. It is well, therefore, to place the rows not closer than 4 feet. The plants should be set deep. The custom is to subsoil the land, if it is hard beneath the surface, plowing in a heavy coating of well-rotted manure if necessary. The plants are then set in furrows 6 to 10 inches deep. The crown of the plant is covered with loose earth or old compost to the depth of 2 or 3 inches. As the plants grow, the trench is gradually filled. If the trench is filled at first, the young plants may not have strength enough to push through the earth. In a commercial plantation, this filling may be done by the subsequent tillage. Sometimes the furrows are partially filled by running a light harrow over the ground. The plants are usually set in spring, and by the succeeding fall the furrows should have been filled. The plants should be set about 3 feet apart in the row. They should be one-year-old seedlings. Two or three-year-old plants usually give less satisfactory results.

Since the crowns of asparagus are so far beneath the surface, it is possible to till the whole area with shallow-working tools late in fall or early in spring. It is essential that this general tillage be given in order to keep the plantation free of weeds and to maintain the physical texture of the soil. During the growing season, little tillage can be given. When the crop is being harvested, it is not practicable to till to any extent; and later in the season when the tops are allowed to grow, the whole surface is occupied. It is well to dress the plantation heavily in the fall with manure, to which one may add night soil, refuse salt or animal fertilizer, if these are available. It may be well, also, to make another dressing of more quickly available fertilizer early in the spring. It is very important that the plantation be given the best of surface tillage for the first one or two years in order to get it into ideal condition. When the bed finally comes into full bearing, the asparagus appropriates so much of the plant-food and moisture that there is less danger from pernicious weeds.

The plants should grow two full years before shoots are cut. Sometimes a few stalks may be taken the second year, but it is usually better to wait until the third year and to allow the plants to become thoroughly established. It is also easy to injure the bed by cutting it for too long a period each season. Whilst the crop is being harvested, however, every stalk should be removed, even though it is too small and poor for eating: the bed should be "cut clean." Only in rare cases should the bed be cut after the 4th of July, and it is usually better to stop before this time. Thereafter the tops are allowed to grow as they will. It should be remembered that the energy of the crown and roots is supplied from the foliage that developed in the previous summer. Without a heavy growth of top, one cannot expect a good growth of roots and a heavy crop the following year. The tops should be mown late in fall. Some persons allow these tops to lie on the ground as a winter protection. If, however, the plants produce many berries, there will be so many seedling plants as to make trouble; in that case, it is better to burn the tops. It is also well to remove and burn them in order to allow a thorough tillage to be given in the fall. The bed should then be given a dressing as already advised, both for the purpose of affording winter protection and to supply plant-food. In the spring the dressing may be cultivated under, or if it is too coarse for that purpose, the rougher parts may be forked off. After a thorough spring cultivation, it is well to again cover the bed with litter or manure in order to afford some nourishment, but particularly to conserve the moisture and to afford material for covering the tender shoots in case there is danger of frost. The value of asparagus lies in its succulence and tenderness, and these qualities are usually associated with large size of shoot. These attributes are secured by very rich soil and by thorough attention to good tillage.

It is customary to harvest asparagus by cutting off the shoots 3 or 4 inches beneath the surface by means of a long knife. There are special asparagus knives (Fig. 140), but any long butcher-knife will answer the purpose. It is important that this knife be inserted in an oblique direction so as not to injure the new shoots which are rising from the crown. A little experience in the use of the knife will enable one to cut the shoots without injury to the succeeding picking. Some of the best growers now advise the breaking of the asparagus shoots rather than cutting them. There is then no danger of injuring the crown, and the shoot will not break in the tough and stringy part and therefore the product is sure to be tender and crisp. This is no doubt the ideal method, but the formal demands of the market make it difficult to sell broken asparagus in some places, notwithstanding its better quality.

In this country asparagus is chiefly used in its green or unblanched state. There is a common notion that asparagus with white stalks is the tenderest and best, but this is an error unless the stalks are artificially blanched. When grown without blanching, the green part of the shoot is the best. Asparagus is often blanched in the field. This is done by hilling up the rows early in spring by means of the furrowing plow, much as one would hill celery. If asparagus is to be grown for blanching, it should be planted somewhat deeper than under ordinary conditions. Blanched asparagus is more popular in the Old World than here.

Asparagus is sold in bunches 4 or 5 inches in diameter. These are tied with soft cord or raffia, although some growers now use rubber bands. Usually the market requires that the butt end of the bunch be cut off square. An average bunch is 7 to 9 inches long. Asparagus "bunchers"—which are forms for holding the bunch and cord, and a knife for cutting the butts—can be had of dealers in gardeners' supplies. Fig. 140.

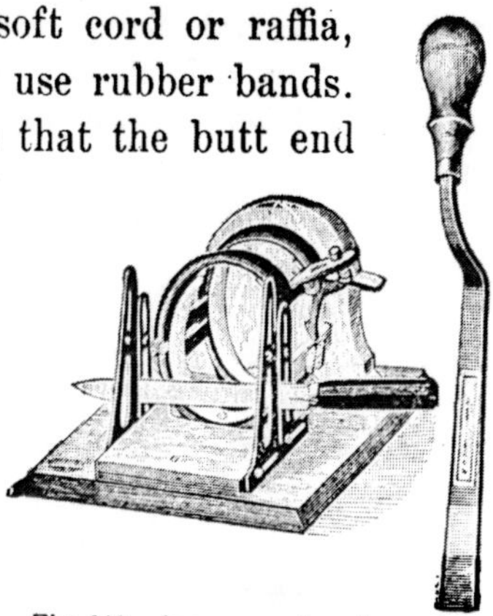

Fig. 140. Asparagus buncher; also knife or spud for cutting the plants in the field.

One can buy asparagus plants of seedsmen. It is usually better, however, to grow one's own plants, particularly if he has a rich piece of land and can give it careful attention. The seed is sown in drills from a foot to 18 inches apart and it is covered about an inch in depth. The seeds may be soaked in warm water a day before planting. The plants should be thinned to stand 3 or 4 inches apart in the row. Give frequent tillage throughout the season. The following spring these plants will be ready for setting in their permanent places. Seedlings may be expected to vary considerably.

At 3x4 feet, 3,630 plants are required for an acre. These plants should be secured from 1 pound of good seed, although 4-5 pounds is often recommended. About 400 dozen bunches is a fair yield per acre.

There are few varieties. Only nine were listed by American seedsmen in 1889. Conover Colossal is the leading kind.

Asparagus has been cultivated for 2,000 years or more. It is native to temperate Europe and Asia. It is one of the lily family, and it has several allies in cultivation in greenhouses for the graceful foliage. These greenhouse species are climbing or drooping. Asparagus is known to botanists as *Asparagus officinalis*. For an accessible history, see Sturtevant, Amer. Nat., Feb., 1887, pp. 129-131.

"If I can have a trusty hand to do the gathering, I do not allow a knife to be taken into the field. The gatherer takes two rows at a time, breaking off the shoots just beneath the ground, at the lowest point where they will snap squarely off. In the growing season the field is gone over every day. Asparagus should be sold by weight, like lettuce and pie plant; but, unfortunately, our retailers have not as yet taken this progressive step, and we have asparagus, not only of all grades of quality in the market, but bunches of all lengths and sizes. Since I have used rubber elastics instead of string or bark for tying, the process of bunching has been greatly abridged. Five dozen bunches can be put together in an hour by an expert hand and neatly squared at the ends.

"It is a custom among many of our gardeners, by the use of the knife, to give their bunches the required length by cutting far beneath the surface, lowering the quality of their product and demoralizing the market. By following my method of breaking the stems, there is no waste and the quality of the lower part of the stems is as excellent as any part of them. The doing away with the necessity of careful rules for cutting asparagus and the forms of implements best fitted for the purpose, the simplifying of the tying process, and the elimination of a large proportion of the expense in preparing the field, are decidedly important steps in progressive asparagus culture."—*Chas. W. Garfield* before Mich. Hort. Soc., July, 1889.

The leading insects and diseases are discussed in the following:

Beetle, N. Y. Bull. 75, p. 425, good plate; Dept. Agric. Yearb. 1896, p. 342, good ills.; N. J. Rept. 1898, p. 457. Destroy all volunteer asparagus. In beds being cut, leave small trap-shoots; twice a week cut these and destroy. In young beds treat with fresh air-slaked lime as soon as larvæ appear; application while yet damp; thoroughness. In hot weather brush off and insects are baked on soil. In rare cases, Paris green or London purple, 1 lb. to 50 lbs. of dry hydrated or air-slaked lime; second application a week later; be very careful with poisons on asparagus that is to be used.

Rust, N. J. Rept. 1896, p. 407; Farmers' Bull. No. 61, p. 30; Ct. 20th Rept., p. 281 and plates. Mass. Bull. 61 : Iowa Bull. 53. The cutting, careful collection and immediate burning, not only of all visibly affected stalks but of all asparagus brush, both cultivated and wild, early in the autumn. Exercise every effort to secure vigorous plants, and in very dry seasons practice irrigation if possible.

Book literature: Hexamer's "Asparagus."

RHUBARB OR PIE PLANT

Rhubarb delights in a deep rich soil. Since its value depends on the succulence and size of the leaf-stalks, every care must be given that will contribute to leaf growth. It is an early spring crop; the land, therefore, should be quick, and the plants should have made a sturdy growth the previous year in order to have energy to start quickly and vigorously. A well-prepared and well-handled rhubarb plantation should last twenty years or more. Propagated by divisions of the root or by seed.

Rhubarb is one of the most popular of all perennial vegetable-garden plants. It is prized for its large, thick, juicy acid leaf-stalks, which are used in early spring for sauces and pies. The size of the stalks depends partly on the variety, but particularly on the soil and the tillage. There are only three or four popular varieties, of which the best known are Victoria, Linnæus, and Mammoth Red; but the old-fashioned rhubarb will often produce a better leaf-stalk when given high cultivation than the best strain of Victoria will when grown under neglect. The rhubarb is not particular as to soil, but it thrives best in land that is mellow and fertile to a considerable

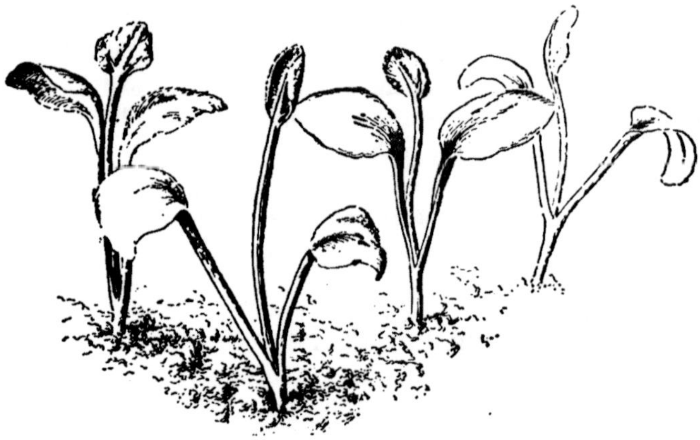

Fig. 141. Rhubarb seedlings. Two-thirds natural size.

depth. Soils that have a high subsoil or hard-pan are to be avoided. The rhubarb plantation should last for a number of years, and it is therefore important that the original preparation of the land should be of the best. Land should be heavily fertilized. There is little danger of adding too much stable manure, particularly if the soil is either very hard or very loose. If the land is not in good tilth, it is best to grow a preparatory crop, as potatoes or some root crop, and to use liberally of stable manure in that year. If the land is not naturally deep, it is well to subsoil it just before the rhubarb is planted. The rows should be far enough apart to allow of easy horse tillage,—not less than four feet for the strong-growing varieties. Fig. 142. In the row the plants may be placed from 3 to 4 feet apart. Good surface tillage, as for corn or potatoes, is all that is demanded. In the fall the bed should be given a heavy

Fig. 142. A Long Island rhubarb field in early spring, before harvest has begun.

dressing of stable manure. This dressing serves the purposes of enriching the soil, of preserving the texture of the surface, and of affording a winter mulch and protection. Lands that are heavily mulched do not freeze so deep as those that are left bare, and the plants are likely to start earlier in the spring. This surface mulch may be removed early in the spring and a thorough cultivation given to the land; or if the land is in good tilth and free from weeds, it may be forked from the crowns and allowed to lie between the rows until the crop is harvested. Some growers hill up the rows in fall by means of a plow and do not apply a fall mulch.

The commercial rhubarb season is short. It rarely extends over more than two months. The leaves are pulled, and they separate readily at their insertion. Only the largest and best leaves are harvested. Others are usually allowed to remain unless they are very numerous, in which case the larger part of them are pulled off in order to allow the strength to go to the main ones. After the market season of rhubarb is past, the plants are allowed to grow as they will except that the seed-stalks are cut off as fast as they arise in order to force the energy of the plant into the production of foliage and roots. A heavy crop of rhubarb in any year depends to a large extent on the strong leaf-growth of the year before. In order to renew rhubarb plantations, the roots are sometimes taken up and reset; but it is usually a better practice to trim the roots with the plow or the spade, breaking off the strong projecting parts.

Ordinarily, rhubarb is propagated by means of division of the roots. The root may be cut into as many pieces as there are strong eyes, and as much as possible of the root is allowed to remain with each eye. These pieces are planted 3 or 4 inches deep. The plants should grow two years before a cutting is made, and they will not give a full crop until the third year. Rhubarb is readily grown from seeds, but this requires a year's more time and the seedlings are likely to vary to some extent. The seeds may be sown early in the spring in drills 18 inches apart, or closer if the land is valuable, and the young plants are thinned to 6 to 8 inches apart in the row. The plants are set in permanent positions the year following, that is, when they are one year old. In the Northern states rhubarb is nearly always planted in the spring whether from seedlings or root-cuttings, but in milder climates it may be planted in the fall.

An acre of rhubarb requires about as much seed as an acre of asparagus. The number of seeds in an ounce is about the same as in asparagus. It is a good plan to leave alleys at intervals in a rhubarb field to allow the entrance of wagons. From 2 to 5 stalks are tied in a bunch for market, and an acre should produce 3,000 dozen bunches. In 1889, North American seedsmen offered six varieties of rhubarb. Sometimes used for wine.

Rhubarb (*Rheum Rhaponticum*) is one of the Polygonaceæ or buckwheat family. It is native to eastern Asia. For historical sketch by Sturtevant, see Amer. Nat., April, 1890, pp. 328-332.

There are no troublesome insects or diseases.

Book literature: Consult Morse and Thompson.

DOCKS AND SORRELS

"Various species of docks and sorrels have long been cultivated as pot-herbs. Some of them are very desirable additions to the garden because they yield a pleasant food in very early spring, and, once planted, they remain for years. We have grown two of the French docks for years and find them to be very good. One is the Spinage Dock (*Oseille Épinard*), the other the Large Belleville (*Oseille Large de Belleville*). The former is the better of the two, perhaps, and it has the advantage of being a week or ten days earlier. The broad crisp leaves appear early in April when there is nothing green to be had in the open garden, and they can be cut continuously for a month or more. This dock is the Herb Patience, or *Rumex Patientia* of the botanies. It has long been an inhabitant of gardens, and it has sparingly run wild in some parts of this country. It is a native of Europe. The Belleville is also a European plant, and is really a sorrel. It is *Rumex Acetosa* of botanists. It has also become spontaneous in some of the eastern parts of the country. It has thinner, lighter green and longer-stalked leaves than the spinage dock, with spear-like lobes at the base. The leaves are very sour, and will probably not prove to be so generally agreeable as those of the spinage dock; but they are later, and afford a succession. In some countries this sorrel yields oxalic acid sufficient for commercial purposes. The Round-leaved or true French sorrel (*Rumex scutatus*) would probably be preferable to most persons.

"All these docks are hardy perennials, and are very acceptable plants to those who are fond of early 'greens.' Some, at least, of the cultivated docks can be procured of American seedsmen."—*Bull. 61, Cornell Exp. Sta.*

ARTICHOKE

Two very unlike plants are known as artichoke. The one commonly known under that name in this country is the plant known abroad as Jerusalem artichoke. It is one of the sunflower tribe and is grown for its thick, potato-like, underground tubers. The other, or the true artichoke, is a plant allied to cardoon and thistles, and the edible part is the large unopened flower-head; the young shoots are also sometimes blanched and eaten as salads. It is often known as the globe or bur artichoke.

The Jerusalem artichoke is little prized in this country as a garden vegetable, although it is so exceedingly productive and thrives under such adverse conditions that it might be made to supply a considerable

Fig. 143. Globe artichoke seedlings. Two-thirds natural size.

amount of food. The tubers may be eaten raw or cooked. It has a tendency to become a weed in waste places, spreading inveterately by means of its long underground, tuber-bearing stems. In poorly cultivated lands, the plant is likely to spread rather than to diminish because the tubers are severed and transported by the cultivator. If the plant becomes a weed, it may be eradicated by thorough tillage, by means of which the tops do not have an opportunity to grow. If the field is plowed in the fall, many of the roots will be exposed and they may be picked out. In fact, this is one of the best means of harvesting the crop. Swine are very fond of the artichoke, and if they are turned into the field they will soon destroy the plant, if it becomes weedy. As a cultivated crop, the artichoke is nearly always placed in some remote or little used corner, in order that it may not encroach on the cultivated areas. When once planted, it will take care of itself; but it will produce more freely of tubers if the roots are broken and divided now and then, as they are by the customary digging of the tubers. The plant is perfectly hardy. It is native to the northern parts of the United States and parts of Canada. It was cultivated by the Indians (see Gray & Trumbull, Amer. Journ. Sci. 25, p. 244). In the Old World the plant seems to be more prized than here as a garden crop, and there are improved strains of it. In this country there are no named varieties that are generally known. The plant belongs to the sunflower genus, being known to botanists as *Helianthus tuberosus*.

The true or globe artichoke is a strong-growing, upright perennial, with large woolly divided leaves. The plants grow 4 or 5 feet high. They should be planted 3 to 5 feet apart each way. The plants are propagated either by seeds or by suckers from the root. The seeds do not reproduce the variety, however, and are therefore not to be recommended if one desires the best strains. Seeds may be sown where the plants are to stand, and the second year the plants may be expected to produce edible heads. Seedlings started early in a hotbed may give edible heads the same year, but they must be transplanted with much care. Suckers are freely produced about the crown of the plant, and these are chiefly used in the Old

World for the propagation of the variety. The suckers are usually planted directly where the plants are to mature, and in the second year the heads may be gathered. Usually the plant begins to decline after it has borne two or three heavy crops. It is therefore advisable to replant it frequently. In cold climates the crowns should be well protected in winter with straw or litter. The edible parts of the flower-head are the fleshy portion on the inside of the large outer scales and the "bottom" or receptacle of the head. The heads are gathered before the blue flowers begin to show, that is, when the head is in the bud. Fig. 144. As soon as the head begins to expand, it is too old and woody for eating. In this country the artichoke is little prized, but it is much used in parts of Europe. The plant is quite worth the growing as an ornamental subject.

Fig. 144. Globe artichokes. One-fourth natural size.

Cynara Scolymus, the artichoke, is native to the Mediterranean region. See Sturtevant, Amer. Nat., Feb.,1887, p. 125. For notes on culture and methods of cooking, see Circular 22, Division of Botany, U. S. Dept. Agric. (1899).

SEA-KALE

Sea-kale is a low, fleshy-stemmed perennial, the young leaves and shoots of which are blanched and eaten. In the kitchen, it is prepared after the manner of asparagus. The plant is little known in this country, although it is deserving of popularity. After the plants are well established, the young shoots are blanched by covering the crown to the depth of a foot or more with loose, fine earth in early spring. Sometimes the shoots are allowed to grow upward into a dark receptacle, as into a box inverted over the crown. After the early spring shoots are removed, the plant is allowed to grow as it will for the remainder of the season for, as in asparagus and rhubarb, the vigor of the young shoots of any season depend, to a large extent, on the vigor and energy of the plant in the preceding year. The soil should be deep and rich, and rather moist.

Sea-kale is propagated either by seeds or divisions of the roots. In either case, the crop is not to be harvested until the plants have grown two or three years. If the root divisions are large and the soil is strong, some shoots may be cut the following year, but it is better to allow them two seasons' growth. The plants should not be less than 3 feet apart each way, and if the land is not too valuable, they may stand as far apart as 3½ or even 4 feet. The "seeds" are really fruits. They are ordinarily sown without being shelled. Two or more plants are likely to come from each of these fruits, all but one of which should be removed. Sea-kale will retain its vigor for a number of years, but if the plants begin to show signs of decline, a new crop should be started. It is much benefited by an autumn dressing of straw or light manure.

Sea-Kale is *Crambe maritima*, one of the Cruciferæ or Mustard family. It is native to sea-coast regions of Western Europe. Sturtevant has an historical note in Amer. Nat., July, 1890, pp. 644–5.

INDEX